"Dr. Hardy's *Racial Trauma* is a long overdue and deeply important guide to an essential topic, and to the effects of racialized trauma on our individual bodyminds, our relationships, our communities, and our collective consciousness. Every—and I mean every—clinician needs to read, reflect on, and make use of this book."

—**Resmaa Menakem**, MSW, LICSW, SEP, author of *My Grandmother's Hands*, *The Quaking of America*, and *Monsters in Love*

"Dr. Kenneth Hardy presents a potent analysis of the impact of racial socialization and racial trauma in the lives of People of Color. His account is made more powerful by his poignant narrative of racial trauma in his own life. But importantly, Dr. Hardy charts a hopeful path toward healing the hidden wounds of racial trauma and he paves the way for engagement across race to create a new voice for healers and organizations. A must-read for anyone seeking to heal, or help others heal, from racial trauma."

—**John A. Rich**, MD, MPH, director, RUSH BMO Institute for Health Equity, and author of *Wrong Place Wrong Time: Trauma and Violence in the Lives of Young Black Men*

Racial Trauma

Racial Trauma

CLINICAL STRATEGIES & TECHNIQUES FOR HEALING INVISIBLE WOUNDS

KENNETH V. HARDY

Norton Professional Books

An Imprint of W. W. Norton & Company
Celebrating a Century of Independent Publishing

Copyright © 2023 by Kenneth V. Hardy

All rights reserved
Printed in the United States
First Edition

For information about permission to reproduce selections from this book, write to Permissions, W. W. Norton & Company, Inc., 500 Fifth Avenue, New York, NY 10110

For information about special discounts for bulk purchases, please contact W. W. Norton Special Sales at specialsales@wwnorton.com or 800-233-4830

Manufacturing by Lakeside Book Company
Production manager: Gwen Cullen

ISBN: 978-1-324-03043-0
W. W. Norton & Company, Inc., 500 Fifth Avenue, New York, NY 10110
www.wwnorton.com

W. W. Norton & Company Ltd., 15 Carlisle Street, London W1D 3BS

1 2 3 4 5 6 7 8 9 0

*To my family who has lived and continues to
live the experiences that I write about.*

*To my ancestors, known and unknown, for empowering
me with the divine inspiration and clarity of purpose
to always climb the rough side of the mountain,
and the intestinal fortitude to stay in the race.*

AUTHOR'S NOTE

Throughout this book I will refer to the deaths of people of color—including the police-involved deaths of Breonna Taylor, Tamir Rice, Sandra Bland, Eric Garner, and Walter Scott and the killing of Trayvon Martin—as "murders," although I do not intend by this the legal meaning of the term "murder." None of those involved in these killings were convicted of murder—indeed, those involved in the deaths of Tamir Rice, Sandra Bland, and Eric Garner were not charged at all, and Trayvon Martin's killer was acquitted. Thus, technically and legally a murder never occurred in these cases. However, as a Black man who is haunted incessantly by these heinous acts, I walk and breathe daily feeling the weight and the deep dark despair of these untimely deaths. Living intimately with the inescapable pain and what these killings have meant and continue to mean for me and others in my community, it would feel like a white-washed act of dishonor, disrespect, and betrayal to morally and spiritually label these acts of terror in any other way than to call them murder. Thus, my use of the term "murder" in this book in reference to such killings is meant to reflect my personal moral–spiritual beliefs, and not as a legal term.

CONTENTS

ACKNOWLEDGMENTS

As I consider the wide range of significant professional initiatives that I have had the privilege to be involved in over the years, this book by far ranks very high among the most important and personally relevant. Writing it involved riding an emotional rollercoaster that often unexpectedly blurred the boundaries between past and present. At times, it conjured up painful memories that I thought were gone, but obviously had not been forgotten. It magnified the present by placing a spotlight on the racial division that plagues our contemporary world. I quickly learned by the time the preface was written that this was not just another ordinary initiative. Making a concerted effort to name that which had never been adequately named, but desperately needed to be, was no small undertaking. The project often felt emotionally weighty, and at times, I desperately needed many hands to hold it, coddle it, cuddle with it, and collectively embrace it to lift it over the finish line. Fortunately, I was surrounded by a community of support that provided varied and invaluable assistance every step of the way throughout the process.

The team at Norton has been nothing short of outstanding to

work with from start to finish. I would like to thank Mariah Eppes and Olivia Guarnieri for their embrace of this project and the support they provided during the relay race of getting it to and across the finish line. Thank you for your attention to the details, your patience, and partnership. I also would like to extend a very special and heartfelt thanks to Deborah Malmud, vice president at Norton. Deborah, I cannot find the words to express the depth of my gratitude to you for your belief in this project, your vision, support, and willingness to be a door-opener and an access-enabler.

I would also like to thank two key members of my team, Fifi Klein and Dhara Mehta-Desai, for their tireless and dedicated assistance. Many thanks to Fifi for the endless hours she devoted to assisting with the editing, formatting, wordsmithing, and lending her scrutinizing eyes throughout the process. These small, but not-so-small-at-all, contributions made a difficult and labor-intensive process appear simple and seamless. I want to thank Dhara for all the hands-on, last minute, faithful support and assistance that she incessantly and selflessly provided, from the proposal phase to the completion of the book.

Last, and certainly not least, I want to thank my beloved family for the unconditional love and support that they indefatigably provided, and that I relied on for sustenance, strength, and purpose. I am forever grateful for the seemingly endless, passionate, vein-protruding, hotly debated race-related conversations that we had and continue to have in the kitchen, car, living room, and almost anywhere else we congregate, which have provided a tsunami of inspiration for this book. Without your love, understanding, patience, and handholding, the completion of this work would not have been possible. I hope it will make each of you proud, as well as make a small difference in the world.

PREFACE

In the midst of finishing this book, I inadvertently stumbled across a poem (see pages xvi–xvii) from decades ago, scribbled on yellow tablet paper, sandwiched between papers in a file comprised of letters that I have received over the years from clients, workshop attendees, and former students. While rereading it for the first time in well over a decade, I had a poignant memory of the actual moment that inspired its composition. It was a day when the pangs and pain of working in a predominantly white organization had taken its toll. An organization that, although located in a richly diverse region, could never seem to find "qualified minorities" to hire. The reported lack of access, and not the lack of racial sensitivity and humility that permeated most of the place, was always their justification for the dearth of People of Color granted the privilege to work there. Through the commitment and dedication of a few "radical" white members of the leadership team, I was the first Black person, and in fact the first Person of Color, hired there. My presence was publicly lauded as testament to their goodness as white people, the openness and inclusiveness of the organization, as I was visible proof that they were not racist. After all, how could they be racist if they hired and welcomed me?

Throughout my tenure, a lot was said, but most impactful was all that was not said, at least not verbally. No one ever called me a nigger, although the term was casually and comfortably used in a few meetings, not in reference to any People of Color but to a white team member who felt like an outsider, which made the usage "acceptable" and it was treated with impunity. While often being assured that I was a valuable member of the team, I felt neither valued nor like a member. The words of embrace that were often used could not adequately conceal the tone, inuendo, coded language, and dispositions of discomfort and awkwardness they consistently and invariably conveyed. There was a powerful visceral and visible disconnect that was virtually impossible to address directly. The few attempts I made to address these issues were rarely received as an invitation for us all to engage in self-reflection and self-interrogation; instead, the onus was placed on me to examine my proclivity to play the race card, to figure out why I and others like me were so unjustifiably angry, difficult to work with, and inherently incapable of seeing the "big picture," whatever the hell that was! Sitting in countless meetings in which the lives of Black and other People of Color were treated as a casual game of whack-a-mole often left me enraged, but more often, deeply hurt. My colleagues didn't seem to understand that their nonchalant, often dismissive, and pejorative references to "warzone neighborhoods," and "lazy ambitionless people who were addicted to wanting something for nothing," "handout seekers," "wannabe radicals and revolutionaries," and a host of other derogatory racialized terms, referred to human beings, many of whom I interacted with daily outside of work. Many of whom had generously provided their backs and limited resources to help elevate me and other People of Color to overcome the walls of racism so we could be in such a meeting where we would be referred to in such callous and uncaring ways.

Back to the poem. The inspiration for it was from an intense meeting with my immediate supervisor, who sternly cautioned me about being "too emotional" in meetings. My tone, he admonished, was at times too impassioned and I needed to find a way to see the big picture because everything was not always about race. I felt not only deeply misunderstood but also incredibly invisible to him and my other white colleagues. Without any "empirical and objective" data or "proof," which many whites often demand regarding race, I was convinced that when he looked at me, he, like so many other whites, could only see an image of who he believed me to be. I began to reflect on how we, as Black people, are overly seen in some contexts and completely invisible in others. I started thinking about how I, as a Black man, am often just an image of man, and I started thinking, feeling, and scribbling.

As the poem might suggest, in one sense I have been mentally writing this book most of my life. Virtually every sentence, paragraph, and page have been carefully and internally etched in my psyche over the years. Pages have been written, rewritten, and reviewed innumerable times. Although this is my first attempt to pull it all together in one comprehensive and coherent document on paper in this format, "the data" have been painstakingly collected over decades. The sources have been many and varied, including conversations with great-grandparents who still wore the scars of the legacy of slavery, with parents who lived through the Jim Crow era in the past and with its painful remnants as an integral part of their contemporary lives, with clients, workshop attendees, and students, and, of course, my own lived experience as a Black man.

IMAGES OF A MAN

I AM A black man.... I AM MANY THINGS ....SOMETHIN[G]
And in many respects .... I AM CONSIDERED NOTHING at [ALL]

I AM SUSPECT ... CRIMINAL... A MENACE TO SOCIETY

I AM A BLACK MAN ... I AM MANY THINGS .... SOMETHINGS ... -
AND IN MANY RESPECTS I AM NOTHING AT ALL

I AM BRUTE, POWERFUL, AND ENDOWED ₹ DAUNTING PHYSICAL
MIGHT...

I AM IMPULSIVE, PRIMITIVE IN MY THINKING, ₹ INTELLECTUALL[Y]
LIGHT

I AM A BLACK MAN - - - -

I AM AN ABUSER OF BLACK WOMEN AND STALKER OF THOSE W[HO]
ARE WHITE

I AM THE SHADOWY, DARK, LOOMING UNIVERSAL SYMBOL OF PERI[L]
DURING BOTH DAY ₹ NIGHT

I AM A BLACK MAN

I AM DEPENDENT ON CIGARETTES, BOOZE, WEED, ₹ CRACK COCAINE

I AM WORTHLESS, WORKLESS, HOMELESS, ₹ BORDERLINE INSAN[E]

I ABANDON MY CHILDREN.... AM HEARTLESS... WITH LITTLE CAPACITY FOR PAIN

I AM THE SHAMELESS, FACELESS, SUBHUMAN SELDOM CALLED BY HIS NAME

I AM A BLACK MAN

I AM EMANCIPATED YET FOREVER CHAINED TO Legacy of SLAVERY

I AM TOLD TO WORK HARD, BITTER FREE, BECAUSE THERE IS EQUAL OPPORTUNITY

I AM A BLACK MAN

I AM A MODERN DAY SLAVE DRESSED IN A BUSINESS SUIT _ _ . NAUTICA, FILA, POLO, & TOMMY HILFIGER

I AM A CHILD OF AFFIRMATIVE ACTION OFTEN REGARDED as a NEW Kinda Nigger

I Am a black man and it doesn't seem to matter what I say, do, or who I Am n where I stand

Because you .... You seem to only be able to see the (an) Images of a man

THINKIN' BACK, THINKIN' BLACK

I am the first-born son of proud parents who were natives of the Old South. I was born and raised in the Northeast region of the United States, in a region of a state that was racially diverse but also rigidly segregated by race in ways that were much more sophisticated than what my parents experienced in the South. Blacks and whites shared the same land, occupied the same city, but lived in two separate and—though it is almost too cliché to say—unequal worlds. Neighborhoods and schools alike were segregated in every sense of the word. There were some racially integrated high schools, which were the places where the worlds of white and Black students converged and often clashed. We were foreigners to each other. Our knowledge of each other was relegated to stereotypes, innuendo, and a polite and acceptable distance. To each of us, the other was an "other." Interestingly, as powerful as these realities were, they were never acknowledged, never discussed. Yet the issue of race had a pervasive impact on virtually all aspects of school life. The white students, despite the fact that many of them lived less than a quarter mile away from Black neighborhoods, thought of themselves as better than the Black students. Unfortunately, many of the Black students, like myself, were also, at some level, convinced that whites were superior to us.

The places that Black people lived were officially called the "Projects." There were no whites in the Projects. Conversely, the whites lived in places referred to by names such as "Villages," "Complexes," and "Developments." There were no Blacks in places called Villages—and yet the only discernible difference between the Projects and these other places of residence was the name attached to them. Through the eyes of a child, these inequities were hard to understand and even more difficult to embrace.

These experiences, though never discussed or overtly acknowledged, were powerful markers of reality. They provided a rude awakening to the harshness of the world into which so many Children of Color are born. No matter how loving, secure, intact, or dedicated one's family is, the forces of racial oppression have a way of infiltrating the psychosocial interior of everyday family life. The forces of racial oppression erase and erode dreams, blemish innocence, and viciously assault one's sense of idealism. Yes, these are the realities of the anatomy of oppression and the concomitant invisible wounds that lacerate the heart, the soul, and the psyche. Sadly, neither their presence in the lives of those who are targeted nor the long-term deleterious effects that they have on every fiber of human life are ever acknowledged. Thus, the invisible wounds of oppression often remain invisible to both those who suffer from them as well as those who are responsible for inflicting them.

Racial oppression, regardless of the age of onset, is like an untreatable cancer. In a slow, deliberate, progressive way it makes its mark . . . it takes its toll . . . it maims, mutilates, weakens the spirit and the body. The effects are even more poignant and especially harmful for young, poor, minority children who are often ill prepared to understand the complexity of their (social) conditions. This was certainly true for me as a young boy. Throughout both my youth and my innocence, long before I finished high school or attended college, I was introduced, though I had no language for them, to the very concepts that I write about in this book. Long before I developed any conversance with the term *devaluation*, I knew what it meant and, more importantly, what it felt like to be degraded and disregarded. No, I didn't know words and terms such as *degradation* and *assault of dignity*, but I knew how it felt to be thought of and referred to in racially derogatory ways and denied access to opportunities because of my race. My lack of knowledge of these grand social–psychological concepts never once prevented my heart from weeping as I watched countless numbers of white men and women, who were half my father's age, quickly reduce him to nonhuman status by the cold, calculated, disrespectful, and belittling ways in which they spoke to him. I knew nothing about objectification, devaluation, or degradation back in those days, only humiliation—not as a concept, just as the powerfully painful unnamable experience it was.

Finding ways to make peace with humiliation is integral to the experiences of the racially oppressed. In many ways, humiliation and devaluation are at the core of virtually all the defining experiences of People of Color, the poor, and other oppressed and marginalized people. It is these core properties of the oppressed that give birth to many of the invisible wounds that will be discussed throughout this book. Growing up African American, my encounters, bouts, and hardships with humiliation and devaluation contributed heavily to this book long before I ever signed a contract. While the forces of racial oppression have been "generous" to me, in terms of providing me with life lessons to prepare me for this "project," there remain a couple of experiences that will forever be inerasable.

FRAGILE GUYS AND SUPERMEN

It was 9:35 p.m. on an otherwise quiet and uneventful fall Sunday night, but there was tension at the corner of Oak and Vine streets, where tempers were flaring, several revolvers were drawn, and an angry crowd was growing exponentially by the minute. As several police sectioned off a corner of the street to strategically contain their captive, several additional police cars, with red flashing lights and sirens that could be heard from blocks away, arrived at the scene. I was their captive.

I had been stopped by a police officer for—supposedly—

failing to come to a complete stop at a stop sign and for having a passenger riding on my motorcycle without a helmet. With my heart beating fast and my body on the verge of hyperventilating, I was overcome with fear, as I am anytime I am accosted by the police. My heavy breathing and the rapid palpitations of my heart had nothing to do with guilt or innocence, right or wrong, law or lawlessness. It was solely about Black and white. I was hyper-aware of race at that moment and of the strained relationship that has historically existed between the police and Black men. In a fruitless attempt to counteract and disguise my fear, I immediately assumed a hyper-compliant, hyper-polite stance that I often reserved for desperate situations where I had to interact with powerful, pro-racist whites who held absolute power over me. I flawlessly implemented all the lessons that had been passed on to me and to so many other Black children. All my responses to Officer Callahan, the policeman who stopped me, were of the "yes, sir," "no, sir" variety. But all my efforts seemed to matter little, as Officer Callahan continued to talk and interact with me in an aggressive and belligerent manner.

To make matters worse, I did not have the registration card for my motorcycle in my possession. However, the officer quickly verified, via the Department of Motor Vehicle's centralized computer system, that the cycle was legally registered to me. For some reason, none of this seemed to satisfy or comfort Officer Callahan. He told me that he was going to have my motorcycle towed since I didn't have proof of ownership. I stood quietly and rather stoically, as I was left with the discouraging notion that there was NOTHING that I could do to improve this situation. Officer Callahan then began to yell at me "Just who in hell do you think you are boy? Where are your [eye] glasses?" He was responding to a code on my driver's license that indicated that I am required to drive with corrected vision. My reply, "I am wearing contact lenses, sir." At which point, he took his heavy-duty flashlight, shining it in both of my eyes and said, "I don't see no damn contacts . . . Take one out!" I stood motionless, and I was confused about what to do next, so I made my first effort to reason with him. "Sir, my hands are dirty, and I really don't want to stick my dirty finger in my eye to take a lens out. I swear I have contact lenses on, please check again."

"Did you hear me boy?" he replied. "I said take out the goddamn contact, and take it out now . . . You don't fuckin' get to decide whether you take it out . . . Take the fuckin' contact out now!" Overwhelmed with fear, anger, and a profound sense of degradation, I reluctantly removed the contact lens. But even that did not bring an end to this developing nightmare.

As I was removing the lens, the truck arrived to tow my motorcycle. Officer Callahan looked at me and said, "Hook the bike up to the truck!" With tears beginning to form in both eyes, I said to him, "Sir, I am not going to hook the bike to the truck. I don't think that is my role."

"Did you hear me boy? I said hook the GODDAMN bike up to the truck, and do it NOW." This time I just stood quietly. He then stood toe-to-toe directly in front of me and poked me forcefully on my nose with his finger as he stated repeatedly, "Do you hear me boy? . . . Answer me boy!" He continued to poke me with his finger until my nose began to bleed. I was standing there in the middle of the street, with blood covering my upper lip and coldly dripping down and off my chin, surrounded by several officers while Officer Callahan continued to jab me with his finger calling me "boy." I cannot think of another time in my entire life that I have felt so humiliated, so dehumanized and degraded. While the entire group of onlookers who had begun gathering from the beginning seemed totally sympathetic to my situation, I still felt like a cheap spectacle or some kind of caged animal in a zoo. I was seething inside. I was inundated with thoughts such as "Why am I taking this shit? . . . Could it be any worse if he kills me? . . . Is this what I went to school all these years for? . . . What if this erupts into a riot? . . . My god, there are a lot of young people out here—too many to die."

I finally said, in a resolute manner, "Officer, you have just written me a ticket, you know my name; I will not answer you until you address me by name."

"Who in hell do you think you are talking to boy? . . . Answer me!" as he continued to poke me in the nose. "ANSWER ME! ANSWER ME! ANSWER ME!" I would not answer Officer Callahan, but I did answer an older Black woman who was just a few steps away from the encounter. I now had only a pool of blood and numbness in the region of my face where my nose ought to be. I was convinced that my nose was broken, and I was furious to be so defenseless at the hands on such unbridled and unashamed hatred and humiliation. Mrs. Jackson, an African American grandmother in her seventies, began to cry and asked rhetorically, "Why do these cops have to be so nasty to us? . . . Lord, why do they have to be so mean and full of hatred? I just don't understand it." Her quiet, godly voice and philosophical reflection amid all the chaos and the blood was exactly what I needed. I turned to Mrs. Jackson and calmly stated, "Miss, I understand it perfectly . . . . You see, they find these fragile guys, they give them a badge and a gun, and they become supermen over night!" As foolish as doing this was, for a split second my sarcastic and self-destructive analysis offered me some very short-lived, momentary relief. Officer Callahan became furious. He cuffed me immediately, threw me on the hood of his police car and began to beat me with his night stick. "Smart ass . . . . You are going to jail . . . . We will see how smart you are there."

My girlfriend, who was the passenger without a helmet,

attempted to retrieve my helmet from the street, only to be told to "leave it alone" as the officer kicked it down the street. Several bystanders were now yelling obscenities at the police and demanding that they release me. I was screaming from the blows across the back of my neck, lower back, and arm while also begging several young African American youth to stay cool and not get involved. I feared for their lives and mine. Officer Callahan was totally out of control and full of rage. And the crowd was becoming increasing disruptive as they witnessed what was a familiar drama on the streets of urban Black America: another cop, another Black man, and more Black blood shed.

I was arrested for terrorist threats toward a police officer, disorderly conduct, disturbing the peace, resisting arrest, and attempting to incite a riot. Through this all, I remained in a state of shock. To this day, I recall very little of the ride to jail. What I will always remember is the process of being admitted to the holding cell (a polite name for jail). The fingerprinting process provided a powerful and painful dose of reality. So did the mug shot. It hit me harder than any of the blows previously landed by Officer Callahan earlier that night. It occurred to me that I was a criminal. I am in jail. This was an embarrassing and terrifying experience for someone who had never had ANY prior brushes with the law. This was my first glimpse of the inside of a jail, and it was a gruesome experience. Once the arresting officers discovered that I had a doctorate, they began to taunt me. "Oh, we got one of those smart-ass niggers here . . . . No wonder he had so much to say," one officer stated, and I heard a group of them erupt into uncontrollable laughter.

My jail time was over within 24 hours, and I was released on my own recognizance. However, the complete ordeal lasted for almost two years post release.

I had watched this experience take a toll on my family of origin. My parents had conflicting views about what my legal strategy should be for resolution. My father was adamant that I should plea bargain. He thought that I should accept one of the prosecutor's many offers to plead guilty to a lesser offense and get probation. He was worried that I would be convicted, not because of guilt but because of race. Growing up in the South in the 1930s had taught him invaluable lessons about what he often referred to as "the white man's laws" and the "white man's justice." He believed, as his life experience had often taught him, that "fair trials" don't exist for Black people who are up against whites. He had too many memories of innocent Blacks, particularly males and many of whom were close friends of his, who had been convicted of "raping white girls" when in fact their crimes were perhaps looking at one for a second too long or simply speaking when they were expected to remain silent. On more than one occasion, my father reminded me "Kenny, take your freedom, because they want to see Black folks like you in jail . . . . Son, don't give them the satisfaction."

My mother, on the other hand, was outraged by the assault on my dignity, which she felt was a violation of the entire family. She urged me to fight this to the end no matter what the emotional or financial costs. She repeated something to me that I had heard her grandmother, my great-grandmother, say on many occasions: "Your name is more valuable than gold . . . . All you have is your name . . . . When you lose your name, you lose your dignity, and what are we and who are we without dignity?" She believed that a guilty plea, no matter how insignificant the charge, was tantamount to another public beating. Despite their undying support, I knew there was a subtle unspoken form of humiliation that plagued my parents throughout this ordeal. Although they never once uttered the words, I knew they felt powerless and defenseless as parents but also as Black people. After all, what could be more debilitating for any parent than to have to stand by helplessly and watch the flesh of your flesh be stripped of his humanity and sense of dignity and to know that there isn't a damn thing that you can do to rectify the situation. When it comes to parenting and race, this is part of what it means to be a Parent of Color. When it comes to "being" and race, this is part of what it means to *be* a Person of Color.

Eventually, after a series of unsuccessful attempts by the prosecutor to convince me to plea bargain and several trial continuances, my day in court arrived. It was a very emotional time for me. It was such a relief to finally to get to this point. It had been a long tumultuous journey, fraught with unending uncertainties. The trial, for a variety of reasons, had been continued and delayed at least a half dozen times. While I was aware there was a range of possible outcomes, it was still a tremendous relief just to get into the courtroom. At last, all the waiting, guessing, sleepless nights, and nightmares would finally come to an end, hopefully.

My family, along with my girlfriend and friends, showed up for the trial as they had for every scheduled court date. While I appreciated their presence, unbeknown to even them, they could offer me little reassurance because their faces spoke what they would not dare utter in words. They were petrified and they harbored the same fears, worries, and anxieties that I was feeling so intensely. As I sat waiting to take the witness stand, the throbbing sensation just above my eyebrows would not subside, nor would the anxiety that generated a perpetual grumbling growling sound from my stomach that seemed audible throughout Courtroom C. Unfortunately, my wait was not over. Officer Callahan was called to provide his testimony—an accounting that was laced with references to me as "lawless," "psychopathic," "liar," and "threatening." On this day, I was not nigger, boy, asshole, or any of the other derogatory terms that replaced my name the night of the arrest. According to Officer Callahan, I was an uncontrollable aggressor who had to be physically subdued by him and several other offi-cers. This was his sworn testimony under oath!

Fortunately, there were several eyewitnesses who were willing to testify on my behalf. Mrs. Jackson, the African American grand-mother who witnessed the entire situation from the moment I was stopped, agreed to testify. As she recalled the evening, citing both Callahan's words and mine almost verbatim, there was a stillness and somber feeling that permeated the courtroom. Her testimony, in ways that I could have never imagined, recreated the entire experience for me. It was excruciatingly painful. Without warn-ing, I began to feel the blows to the nose and the nightstick across my back all over again. I could again feel the cold clots of dark red blood streaming down my nose. I was not prepared for this moment. I began weeping uncontrollably and I had no idea why. It wasn't until over a year after the trial was over that I began to make sense of it all (a point I will return to later in this preface).

Mrs. Jackson's testimony was powerful and compelling. Her account of the event corroborated my claims and exposed numer-ous flaws and inconsistencies in Officer Callahan's testimony. In the end, I was vindicated, I guess. I received a unanimous "not guilty" verdict on all charges. However, before I could react to the verdict, Judge Hazlet, the presiding judge, quickly interceded and stated that he had a few final words for me. He turned to me, and in a terse tone of voice that was condescending and proselytizing he stated the following: "Dr. Hardy, you have dodged a bullet here today, and if there is a next time, you may not be so lucky. I don't care how many degrees you have or what you have . . . PhD, MD, or EdD . . . when you are on the street, young man, you better keep in mind that the streets are like a jungle and the police are the lions . . . . They are kings of the jungle . . . . Do you understand me?" Needless to say, I was stunned, but I was also enraged. Here I am, convicted of nothing, and yet it is me, not Officer Callahan, who gets a stern and belittling tongue-lashing from the presiding judge. I was still an emotional wreck, overcome with tears of joy, relief, pain, and furor. I felt every bit as humiliated and beaten by Judge Hazlet's lecture as I had by Officer Callahan's verbal and physical abuse. For a fleeting moment, I wanted to tell the judge exactly what do with his racially slanted advice. And yes, of course I knew there would probably be any number of costly consequences for doing so, but whatever the cost, it would be a small price to pay for my dignity. As I fought with myself over whether to speak up, I looked to the front row seats of the courtroom where my mother sat, wiping away tears and saying to me through verbal gesturing, "Kenny, please let it go . . . . Just let it go." After seeing my mother and feeling the intense pain she was feeling, I realized that my love and respect for her was more important than my sense of racial pride. After a protracted pause, I turned to the judge and I said, "I understand, Your Honor." Minutes later, with my family, I walked away a free and victorious Black man. But did I really?

For several years following this ordeal it was difficult for me to talk or write about any aspect of this experience. It was a traumatic event in my life, and it took me some time to both digest and deconstruct the complexity of it. Thus, the experience has helped me appreciate how, for the traumatized and the oppressed, having an experience doesn't necessarily translate into immediate understanding of the dynamics or long-term effects of such experiences.

My encounters with Officer Callahan, the judicial system, and the subsequent reactions and interactions with several of my white coworkers were also potent reminders of how intimately many Black people must live with humiliation and degradation. I so clearly understand why countless numbers of Black youth and other Youth of Color across this land proudly, brashly, and brazenly claim that they prefer "death over dis [disrespected]." I was ready to proclaim this, too, both that awful fall night and during Judge Hazlet's advice session. As a white colleague and friend once candidly reminded me: "Well Ken, in all honesty, this whole thing could have been avoided had you just sucked it up, done as the maniac asked you to, and not let your pride get in the way." While I appreciated my colleague Mark's brutal honesty, his comment was reminiscent of the kind of short sighted, racially uninformed advice that Black people must listen to from whites constantly. It was interesting to me that it never seemed to occur to Mark that the entire ordeal also could have been avoided if Officer Callahan could have seen me as human being, or if he had some modicum of awareness of his racially oppressive ways. Furthermore, it never occurred to Mark, as it rarely does to many whites, that maybe if my "pride" wasn't persistently assaulted, maybe, just maybe, "sucking it up" would be a much easier feat. However, when every fabric of the tapestry of one's life is interwoven with countless, nameless episodes of humiliation, degradation, and devaluation, issues such as pride, dignity, and respect take on a life-consuming significance.

There is seemingly no end to the humiliation that is attached to experiences like the one I just described. Humiliation that is connected not just to the pain of the actual experience but also to having to interact with, explain to, and be analyzed by well intentioned, racially uniformed, white colleagues and friends. In addition to Mark's advice regarding how I could have avoided the entire matter, there were also the "I don't know, Ken . . . I just can't believe that the police would just start beating you for no reason whatsoever" messages. Claims such as these that often left me feeling enraged and full of despair. I often found myself thinking, "Well of course you can't believe it. After all, it is not YOUR blood or your son's blood or the blood of your father or loved one littering the streets of America at the hands of overly aggressive police claiming to be colorblind when they are anything but! Of course you can't believe it! Because believing it may require you to perhaps connect to a piece of evil, ugly, unexamined racial bias that may be inside of you as well."

Despite my very strong feelings and thoughts, they remained mere private reflections, as is often the case with the oppressed. To express them seemed pointless—at least this was how I felt at the time. For years after the experience with Officer Callahan, I had difficulty trying to make sense of it all. Why could I not seem to let it go? No matter how much I thought about it, avoided thinking about it, talked about it, or avoided talking about it, gaining a comprehensive insightful perspective seemed elusive. It wasn't until three year later, after a terrible car accident and a near death experience, that I began to put the Callahan ordeal into a meaningful perspective.

THE CRASH

It was a rainy, unseasonably cold March night. I was traveling south on Interstate 95 when I noticed a northbound tractor trailer truck approaching the guardrail and heading in my direction. Although the large cigarette-hauling truck was moving very fast, especially for the current weather conditions, it appeared to cross the guardrail into my lane of southbound traffic in super slow motion. As I watched the truck traverse the guardrail, there was little I could do to avoid contact with it. I remember thinking at the time, "Oh my gosh, I am going to die!" The truck landed on my car, and I remember little else about the experience. I do remember glass shattering everywhere, especially from the windshield, leaving me with several facial lacerations. As I quickly descended into a cold, stark, unfamiliar, frighteningly dark place amid loud bangs, screeching tires, screaming voices, and flashing red lights, I remember trying to open the door on the driver's side of the car to no avail. The door had been pushed into the body of the car from the impact of the contact with the truck. With blood gushing everywhere, I managed to reach the handle of the passenger door and somehow drag myself from the car then fall to the ground. Fading in and out of consciousness, I laid on the cold wet shoulder of the highway, convinced of my impending death. As I lay there hoping . . . wishing that someone would stop to assist me, I began thinking about Officer Callahan. Although I was several states from where my past event with him had occurred, I was panicked that he would show up on the scene. I was worried that if I didn't die from accident-related injuries, he would probably kill me, and no one would know. I did not want to die that way. I did not want him to have the satisfaction of humiliating me again. Because I was only marginally conscious, I was convinced that the white EMS workers were, in fact, Officer Callahan. I did not want their help because I was suspicious of their motives. Yet, I desperately needed all the help they could provide me. It seems crazy when I read these words now, but at the time it all seemed so real.

I later realized that both the feelings I had and the predicament I imagined were familiar territory for many People of Color and other oppressed groups. I needed the assistance of the EMS workers to save my life, yet (as I imagined them to be Officer Callahan) I was afraid to trust them. It seemed like such a false choice: trust them and they kill me or don't trust them and die from untreated injuries. A perceived range of choices as narrow as this one is *delusion-inducing*. It is traumatizing. Experiences with trauma and oppression distort one's sense of reality, safety, and security. That in my case, my fears were grossly distorted because of the encounter with Officer Callahan doesn't change the fact that experiences like mine are commonplace for the traumatized and oppressed. Our lives are replete with circumstances wherein we are required to trust the good will of those who happen to look very much like those who have caused us great pain. We are expected to trust that the same hand that knocked us down is now altruistically extended to help lift us up. When we are appropriately hesitant, cautious, or suspicious we're dismissed as being untrusting, paranoid, or fixated with and committed to a stance of victimization. Seldom is any consideration given to the possible presence of a host of preexisting conditions related to negative and traumatizing experiences with domination and oppression. At best, this is a no-win situation for those of us who live along the margins of society. This is what it means to live with trauma and oppression; it is also what it means to live with invisible wounds.

It took me over a year to fully recover from the accident. I was officially declared medically disabled with regard to my ability to work, and I had to collect social security benefits to sustain myself. This confluence of being physically incapacitated and having to deal with a myriad of social services and medical facilities helped me to better appreciate the Officer Callahan ordeal. In fact, it was this experience that helped me to appreciate both the anatomy and the significance of invisible wounds.

While recovering from the accident, I began to notice a discernible difference between the response of others to my physical injuries (wounds) and to those that were less visible. My physical wounds were often the subject of much empathic conversation. I genuinely felt the empathy and compassion of virtually everyone around me. Not only did everyone exhibit unending curiosity about the details of the accident, but they also made numerous physical accommodations for me. For example, when I needed crutches to facilitate walking, those around me, without solicitation, moved chairs, cleared pathways and walkways, and opened doors for me. In a sense, they became partners in my healing process. As strange as it may sound, something about the consensual validation regarding my injuries and the warm embrace of a responsive community paved the way for my healing. It made everything easier, such as talking about the accident and discussing my fear that I would never again know life as I once knew it. It also made it easier to reach out to others when I was overcome with despair. At no point did I ever have to defend the legitimacy of my injuries or to explain why the healing process was so slow. The acknowledgment and acceptance by everyone who mattered and those who did not matter created a powerful healing circle.

Unfortunately, my injuries were not limited to the physical ones that garnered so much welcomed but unsolicited attention. The response to my invisible injuries could not have been more different. I had head injuries, a thoracic condition, and soft tissue damage, none of which produced discernible physical manifestations. Interestingly, the overall response to these invisible injuries was seldom one of compassion, innocent curiosity, or acceptance without suspicion. I was often quizzed about whether my complaints and conditions were an exaggerated, fabricated, or sophisticated posturing for a large insurance settlement. Because I "looked okay" to others, it was difficult for them to imagine that I could be *not* ok. Except for the times that I was suffering from a severe migraine headache, much of the feedback I received from friends, colleagues, and even some family members was peppered with suspicion and doubt about the authenticity of my ailments. I became frustrated with and tired of the countless innuendos suggesting that I was seeking some form of secondary gain—attention, financial benefits, or a prolonged absence from work—or that my condition was, in fact, psychosomatic.

Ironically, I *was* in a state of despair while all these grand psychological theories were being advanced. The suggestions of my malingering, even when they were stated jokingly, were hurtful and offensive. As they persisted, I found myself trying harder and harder to either deny or hide my aches and pains. I became increasingly less willing to talk about my headaches, about my fears of not being able to resume a normal life, and about anything related to the accident. Unfortunately, the healing circle that I once enjoyed had dissipated. I now knew only a circle of doubters that often left me feeling ashamed and shut down. My invisible injuries seemed to trigger impatience, doubt, and cynicism. Comments such as "OK, Ken, enough already," "It's time to move on with your life," "Are you sure you can't make it back to work, even if it is just for a few days?" occurred daily. These were the types of questions and comments that I had to endure if I agreed to talk about my condition. So, I stopped!

INVISIBLE WOUNDS

Thus it was the accident and its aftermath that really helped to crystallize the concept of invisible wounds for me. Before the accident, I had spent little to no time thinking about the phenomenon of wounds, especially those that are invisible. Similarly, I had not spent very much time thinking about wounds and the process of healing, even though I had practiced as a therapist for many years prior to the accident. As I struggled with my recovery from the accident, often living (with what had by then become) a familiar life of pills, physicians, physical therapy, medical and legal forms, lots of self-doubt, and perhaps even self-pity, I became fixated with the notion of wounds—especially invisible wounds. I began to realize that wounds were not just about pain or problems that one can easily see or readily solve. Wounds are really the products of conditions that can persist over time. They do not just disappear; they have a lingering effect, emotionally, psychologically, and relationally. Even when they are not visible, they exist. Wounds, whether visible or invisible, almost always leave scars, one of which is the fear of reinjury or rewounding.

These are the life lessons that the accident taught me. Fortunately, it also helped me to understand the dynamics of trauma and oppression better. Prior to my accident, I had seldom thought critically and deeply about the wounding capacity of the intersection of trauma and oppression. Thinking about it in this way helped me to understand all the emotions that I felt and still feel, even as I commit these words to this manuscript. Any time I find myself thinking about the Officer Callahan ordeal, I usually relive some portion of the experience.

Thinking about trauma and oppression as the crippling conditions they are also enabled me to come to terms with the fact that I suffered related wounds long before Officer Callahan entered my life. My dignity, and my parents' dignity, and the dignity of their parents, and the dignity of their parents' parents had been assaulted long before that night in November on the corner of Oak and Vine. Officer Callahan was not the first white person to wear the blood of a Black person on his hands and uniform, he is merely one member of a much larger clan. While it was his nightstick that delivered several stinging blows to my body, for the most part, he simply aggravated a myriad of preexisting wounds. As the son of parents who were raised in the segregated South, I/we sustained wounds long before meeting Officer Callahan. Although it wasn't my direct experience, I, too, as the first-born son of my parents, suffered the wounds from living vicariously through their experiences of having to drink from separate public water fountains, having to use the public restrooms with the signage "For Coloreds" while in "friendly" locations, "For Niggers" almost everywhere else. I felt their sense of pain and humiliation as if it were my own as they discussed being barred from the many beaches that surrounded them on the hottest of the sweltering hot southern days, particularly as their white counterparts swam uninhibited and with a sense of smug entitlement. I don't think the pain of living with such human indignities ever completely goes away. These are the wounds, the invisible wounds, that living with trauma and oppression demands that Black and other people of color make peace with, whether we want to or not.

Several years later it became apparent to me that the overwhelming emotions that I experienced during the final days of the trial, especially during Mrs. Jackson's testimony, were very much connected to invisible wounds. While some of my tears were most certainly in response to the exhilaration and relief that I experienced in finally having this ordeal reach a point of positive closure, there were also tears that had little to do with the joy of the moment. On the one hand, there was an incredible burden removed from my shoulders in finally knowing that I was not going to jail and I did not have to deal with lawyers, judges, missing time from work, and putting life on hold anymore. I did rejoice at the thought of reclaiming a portion of my life. Yet, on the other hand, I had emotions and tears that felt heavy and considerably less joyful. These tears were the ones that could only be explained though an understanding of invisible wounds. Although the tears oozed slowly down MY face, they were the tears of and for Mrs. Jackson, my parents, and all the other Black people trapped along the margins of society. My tears were in response to the pervasive sense of sadness and hopelessness that is often firmly attached to persistent dignity assaults, voicelessness, rage, psychological homelessness, and a host of other painful and hidden experiences, that is, invisible wounds. It is these wounds that this book is dedicated to naming, uplifting, and validating in a way that allows the trepid echoes from the margins to receive the spotlight and megaphone of the center, allowing the invisible to finally be made visible.

This book is divided into three sections. The first section provides an overview and analysis of the phenomenon of race and how it contributes to and nurtures the dynamics of racial oppression and trauma. It also provides an in-depth discussion of how racial oppression, as an incessant, life altering force, heavily contributes to the racialized trauma that is an inescapable, nonnegotiable dynamic that shapes the trajectory of the lives of so many People of Color. A major thesis of this section is that our society's denial about the significance of race, accompanied by widespread unacknowledged racial oppression, provide the roots for racial trauma that permeates the lives of People of Color, severely affecting their emotional and psychological well-being. These conditions are exacerbated by the dearth of attention that therapists, and the mental health field in general, devote to the understanding and treatment of racial trauma. To help address and ameliorate this gap, this first section provides the reader with a set of guidelines and principles that are vital to *becoming* a racially sensitive, trauma-informed clinician.

The second section consists of several chapters that provide the reader with a slow walk through the anatomy of racial trauma and seven invisible, but identifiable, wounds that are associated with it that therapists must be willing and prepared to address. Each chapter in this section is devoted to examining the intricacies of a singular invisible wound as well as highlighting its interconnectedness with the others. The final section consists of chapters that address concrete strategies and techniques that are necessary for providing effective racially sensitive, trauma-informed therapy and that demonstrate how these methods can be employed to help create a safe and sacred space for the invisible wounds of racial trauma to be effectively treated and ultimately healed.

Racial Trauma

IMAGES OF A MAN

A black man.... I AM MANY THINGS ....
IN MANY respects .... I AM CONSIDERED NOTH..

SUSPECT --- CRIMINAL... A MENACE TO SOCIETY

A BLACK MAN .... I AM MANY THINGS .... SOMETHINGS
IN MANY respects I AM NOTHING AT ALL

SECTION I:

THE DYNAMICS OF RACE, OPPRESSION, AND TRAUMA

CHAPTER 1

The Phenomenon of Race

During the beginning of the eighteenth century, Black scholar W. E. B. DuBois famously and insightfully predicted that "the problem of the twentieth century is the problem of the color line." DuBois's prophetic words from centuries ago still have resonance today and will very likely be true of the next century as well. While we have seen some steady signs of racial progress in the United States, we still seem to be a long way from People of Color being able to live untethered by the entanglements of racism and white supremacist ideology. The hope and optimism inspired by the 2008 election of the first Black U.S. President, Barack Obama, led many to naïvely and prematurely exalt that the country had entered into a new "post racial era," perhaps finally traversing the color line that DuBois had referenced. Unfortunately, it took little time for the election of President Obama to catalyze and expose the insidious racial venom and anti-Black sentiments that have pervaded American society for centuries. Caricatures of First Lady Michelle Obama as an ape and persistent claims that the President was born outside of the United States and was thus not a citizen, as well as unrelenting assertions that he was a jihadist terrorist in disguise, are just a sampling of the onslaught of racist allegations lodged against the President and his wife over his two terms in office. As Maya Angelou once stated: "When someone shows you who they are, believe them the first time" (Goalcast.com, para. 26). Perhaps this is at least part of who we are as a nation! Rather than constituting the dawn of the post-racial era, as it had been touted to be, the Obama presidency provided the world with a clearly developed snapshot of who we are: a racialized society driven by white supremacy ideology. For those who were dubious, the subsequent election of Donald J. Trump as the 45th President of the United States, President Obama's successor, should have removed all doubt regarding the racial psyche of the country. Trump started his campaign and electrified the predominantly white, working class, noncollege-educated segment of the electorate with his reliance on brash, racist tropes that publicly demeaned Mexicans and other racially oppressed citizens. During both his campaign and tenure in office, as his white nationalist, anti-Semitic, and pro-racist rhetoric amped up, so did his popularity among those who agreed with his defamations and slurs.

Given our racial history as a nation, it is both befitting and predictable that a self-proclaimed "nationalist," who publicly refers to white supremacists as "my people," would succeed the first Black President of the United States. In fact, the election of Trump, and his entire presidency, appeared to be a referendum on the Obama presidency. The shift from Obama to Trump was emblematic of a system trying to regain homeostasis. According to systems theorists, human systems will, after a disruption, a disequilibration, or efforts to change from the predominant order, always gravitate back to their previous steady state, or homeostasis. Unfortunately, racial bias, bigotry, and injustice are integral to the prevailing order in the "United" States. Historian Carol

Anderson (2016), in her book *White Rage*, and Yale Professor Dr. Jennifer A. Richeson (2020) make similar assertions and chronicle how significant advances toward racial justice are often met with backlashes. Their writings remind us that the passage of the Thirteenth, Fourteenth, and Fifteenth Amendments was followed by the rise of the Ku Klux Klan, lynching, and a new era of racial subjugation in the form of Jim Crow. The landmark legislation of the civil rights era was followed by Richard Nixon's "southern strategy" and the ascendance of racial dog whistles as a central tactic of American politics. In this regard, DuBois's words about the *color line* continue to be more than just random, meaningless, ill-conceived rhetoric.

Race has always been and continues to be a potent organizing principle in virtually all dimensions of our everyday experiences. It dictates in very concrete ways whether one's humanity is valued or devalued, how one lives, where one lives, and how long and whether one lives. It affects every stage of the human lifecycle, from conception to death. Consider the following examples:

- Black women are 3–4 times more likely to experience pregnancy-related deaths than their white counterparts. (Centers for Disease Control and Prevention, 2021)
- Black women are more likely than white women to experience complications during pregnancy and childbirth. (Centers for Disease Control and Prevention, 2021)
- For every 1,000 live births, 4.8 white infants die in the first year of life compared to 11.7 Black infants. (Centers for Disease Control and Prevention, 2021)
- According to the Census Bureau, the 2020 life expectancy projections are 77 years for Blacks and 80.6 years for whites. For Black women, life expectancy is 79.8 years, and for Black men, 74 years. For white women it is 82.6

years and for white men, 78.4 years. (U.S. Department of Health and Human Services, 2021)

Similar racial disparities can also be found in education, mental health, employment, health care, and other sectors of society, despite the racial progress that has been made. In fact, Richeson (2020) cautions about the perils of looking at racial progress in a vacuum, as a static process.

DENIAL OF THE SIGNIFICANCE OF RACE

Paramount among the many complexities associated with navigating the issue of race is the pervasive tendency to deny its significance. It can be argued that race is so significant that we cannot admit or acknowledge just how widespread it is in everyday life. Our tendency to deny the significance of race often makes it easy to overlook its significance in therapy, particularly when it is not indicated in the presenting problem or identified as a client's specific reason for seeking treatment. I was reminded of this dynamic during my ongoing work with Yoshi, a 32-year-old Japanese male who entered therapy with a presenting problem of loneliness and mild depression. There was absolutely no indication in his psychosocial history that suggested any race related struggles. However, as our sessions progressed, and I began to ask him pointed questions about race and particularly one that I routinely ask during the early stages of therapy: "How does your racial identity shape how you look at the world and how do you believe it impacts how you are perceived?" the therapeutic conversation shifted dramatically. It was quicky revealed that much of his experience of feeling lonely and depressed was closely tied to his racial identity. He went on to explain that as an Asian man he often felt unattractive and unappealing to women that he wished to date. He mentioned that he had tried several online dating sites and discovered that most women, even many of his race, are not interested in dating Asian men. Although race was not indicated as a presenting issue, it was very much an important and integral factor throughout the ensuing therapeutic process.

There are three principal ways in which the significance of race is often denied: a) the insistence and perpetuation of claims of colorblindness; b) selective mutism and the unwillingness to discuss race transparently, especially cross-racially; and c) an over-reliance on ahistorical analyses of race. Unfortunately, none of these strategies of denial holds great promise or potential for promoting greater racial understanding, transformation, or healing. The depth of the therapeutic experience that was created for Yoshi would have been significantly diminished if the potential significance of race had been denied and ultimately treated as a colorblind phenomenon.

Colorblind, Color Bind

Well-intended, disingenuous, and often repeated claims of not seeing race, buttressed by heart-warming clichés such as "there is only one race, the human race," are claims that deny the existence and/or significance of race as a critical intervening variable in human interactions. When the phenomenon of race is denied, it makes it easy to deny the existence of and realities of racially based privilege and subjugation. Adherence to assertions of colorblindness invariably culminates in the creation of *color binds*. For example, it is the denial of the significance of race that makes it convenient to blame the victims of racial discrimination, bigotry, and oppression for their plight. Essentially, the notion is that those who have failed to thrive and who barely survive are responsible for their lot in life. Rather than critiquing and interrogating the expansive individual and systemic racially based forces that smother the quality of life for the racially oppressed, the oppressed are instead blamed for their life circumstances. *Blaming the victim* exonerates the racially privileged from assuming any culpability associated with the suffering of the racially oppressed. Generally speaking, this insulates the racially privileged from feeling any moral imperative to help alleviate the suffering of the subjugated or to transform repressive systemic forces that bifurcate human beings, assigning some to inferior status while others thrive. It is what makes it possible for many whites not only to enjoy but to extol the vestiges of their freedom, liberty, and access to power and to feel little to no compassion, moral imperative, or empathy for those who are systematically denied. The denial also empowers the racially privileged to promulgate analyses of the racially oppressed that are designed to denounce the significance of race while, ironically, relying heavily on toxic racially based stereotypes to support their claims. Rather than the racially privileged acknowledging and highlighting the significance of race as a salient factor underpinning the despair of the racially oppressed, instead the explanations they cite frequently focus on what they perceive to be the deficits of the oppressed. Dysfunctional family structures, fatherlessness, laziness, lower intelligence, lack of ambition, and possession of an insatiable appetite for handouts are the rationalizations that are often manufactured by the racially privileged to help obscure, minimize, or deny the significance of race. Furthermore, these factors are often used as *evidence* of social deviance rather than being interpreted as the symptoms and byproducts of hyperexposure to the debilitating conditions of racial oppression. These are the major dividends associated with denying the existence and significance of race, which ultimately helps to maintain the status quo, especially for those who benefit most from it.

Unfortunately, one of the most crucial binds of denying the significance of race is that these crippling racially stereotyped projections become internalized by the racially oppressed, who are also simultaneously tasked with the burden of either disproving them or *allowing* them to become self-fulfilling prophecies. This is the lethality of these messages. Those who are racially oppressed find themselves either working assiduously to dispel and/or counteract these toxic internalized messages as a means of disproving them or surrendering, psychologically and behaviorally, to the messages and adopting them as if there are undisputable truths. Both responses are riddled with deleterious consequences. However, like most issues involving race, these issues remain deeply felt experiences that, for the most part, remain unspoken.

Selective Mutism Regarding Race

The dictum to not talk about race openly, honestly, and transparently is widely adhered to, even though it is to our individual and societal detriment. Sanctions against talking about race ultimately facilitate the denial that race is significant. Those who dare challenge the unspoken but widely acknowledged rule of remaining mute about race are often the recipients of ostracism and scorn and of accusations of race-baiting, excuse manufacturing, or playing the race card. The scathing and negative valuations affixed to those who dare name race in bold, honest, and explicit ways are not partial to race. Whites who break the code are often dismissed as opportunistic, left leaning, n*&^# lovers. In this context, even the privilege of being white often fails to protect many who speak up from serious harm or retribution. When members of a racially oppressed group speak with clarity and bravery about race, some form of costly punishment is virtually always levied. Colin Kaepernick, the former National Football League (NFL) player and former Super Bowl winner is a poignant and public modern-day example of this phenomenon.

In 2016, during the period prior to the start of the preseason game with the Green Bay Packers, Kaepernick remained seated while the U.S. National Anthem was playing rather than standing, as was customary. His decision to remain sitting was designed to protest and *speak out* against police brutality, systemic racism, and oppression. During the ensuing weeks of the season, Kaepernick continued to bring attention to racial injustice by kneeling during the anthem, a gesture that a white NFL football player and former U.S. military veteran with whom he had consulted assured him would still show respect for the flag.

Kaepernick's public statement against racial injustice was extolled by some whites and many People of Color but was staunchly criticized and condemned by the all-white NFL team owners as well as then President of the United States, Donald Trump. Although the NFL owners vociferously denied that Kaepernick had been ostracized and blackballed by the league for kneeling during the anthem, he was never selected by another team and thus never played another NFL game despite signing what was considered at the time to be a record-setting seven-year, $126 million contract in 2014.

The extreme and harsh punishment that was doled out to Kaepernick is not uncommon, nor is it reserved for the rich and famous. There are countless numbers of everyday People of Color with considerably less celebrity and wealth than Kaepernick who are also punished, relatively speaking, just as severely and harshly for having the temerity to talk openly about race. Many, on the other hand, feel compelled to remain silent, fearing punishment and/or reprisal. After all, one of the consequences, even if it wasn't conscious or intended, of meting out such unforgiving and strict punishment to someone of Kaepernick's pedigree was the transmission of a resounding message to the masses about the costliness of being too vocal about issues of race and injustice.

This was the same strategy that was used during slavery with the "noncompliant," "incorrigible," runaway slave. Not only was it common for the slave to be beaten, it was also considered necessary to do so publicly, with onlookers and in a way that ensured humiliation. Once again, the purpose was twofold: 1) to teach the runaway slave an unforgettable message, should the urge to escape arise again; and 2) to issue a fear-invoking admonition to those who had not yet attempted to escape but might otherwise be inclined to consider it.

The driving force that underpins the reflex to punish those who attempt to talk about race is the desire to deny the significance of race. Naming and talking openly about race are tantamount to acknowledging that it is a powerful organizing principle in our lives that warrants deeper attention, scrutiny, and corrective actions regarding inequities. The systematic and deliberate efforts to obscure and/or deny the significance of race are as varied as they are persistent. The adamance of some whites to denounce, vilify, and demonize the Black Lives Matter movement is yet another effort to detract and distract from the relevancy of race. Labeling the BLM movement "a group of anti-American terrorist thugs" is dismissive, disrespectful, and tactical. Categorizing the movement as terrorist activity, and then compounding the problem with the liberal and unapologetic use of dehumanizing and derogatory racially coded words for Black people could not be any more offensive and assaultive. Once again, the strategy is to deny the significance of race by delegitimizing the Black Lives Matter movement. Interestingly enough, the principal method for accomplishing this feat is racially stereotyping the activists associated with the movement. This is the crazy-making nature of the phenomenon of race. The effort to further eradicate the issue of race was also evidenced by whites—again—appropriating the inventions and terminology of Black people by insisting that "All Lives Matter," "Police Lives Matter," "Farmers Lives Matter," etc. What all these proclamations have in common—other than their lack of originality—is the erasure of race. For many whites, the logic is quite simple. If we simply acknowledge that ALL lives matter, this would ostensibly include Black lives and hence there is absolutely no need to racialize the matter of who matters. Of course, if life in the United States was racially equitable, judicious, and inclusive, there would indeed be no need for a Black Lives Matter movement. It is both interesting and ludicrous to observe how contentiously polarizing these racial issues are, while simultaneously continuing as a society to deny the significance of race. It is so "insignificant" that it remains one of the most emotionally laden, conflictual, and polarizing issues of our time.

Ahistorical Analyses of Race

Superficial discussions about race buttressed by arguments and analyses that are essentially ahistorical and void of context perpetuate the erasure of race and the denial of its significance. As Paul, a middle-class white male, informed a group of racially mixed participants attending a cross-racial dialogues workshop:

> I am sick and tired of everything being about race. I just don't walk around everyday thinking about myself as white. I am not a racist! I don't have a racist bone in my body, and I don't know any white people who do. I am so tired of hearing about white supremacy. There is no such thing! I think Black people spend too much time blaming everything on race when race has nothing to do with anything. It has NOTHING to do with what

you have or don't have. I think if you spent more time *doing* rather than *blaming* [white people] you would be better off. I was born poor; my family didn't have shit when I was growing up. I have my own company now because I worked my ass off. I didn't complain or expect a handout, I worked hard; and in this country, anybody who is willing to work hard, no matter they be Black, white, Asian, blue, or purple . . . if you are willing to work hard, you can make it. You know how I achieved things? I worked hard. I am a fighter and I worked hard to overcome my circumstances. I didn't sit around accepting shit and then blaming other people . . . you know, white people. Where is the fight? Where is the work ethic? You can't just sit around and blame white people! You will not make me feel responsible or guilty! I refuse to feel either!

Paul's assessment and disclosure were provocative, chilling, infuriating, and familiar. It was also extremely myopic, in that it was woefully lacking in understanding of the historical realities of race and racism. His ignorance of and/or refusal to consider the protracted history of racism and racial discrimination against Blacks in all areas of society for centuries conveniently allowed him to deny the impact of race and to simply base his entire analysis of "achievement and success" on individual motivation, effort, and work ethic. Unfortunately, this is the same message that the economically privileged preach to the economically oppressed: "just work hard and pull yourself up by your bootstraps" without any recognition that poverty and class oppression are systemic. While there will always be isolated individuals who are able to scale the walls of poverty or racism to achieve productive and sustainable lives, the critical masses will nevertheless be left behind until broad sweeping systemic change is implemented. The matter of race is no different, and this is the understanding that Paul's exhortation of the benefits, marvels, and transformative potential of rugged individualism seemed to lack.

Andre, a frustrated, irate, and obviously hurt Black man, tearfully yelled at Paul:

> I wish you could exchange places with me for one week. No, just one day, because you could not tolerate half of the bullshit that I have to contend with daily. You have NO clue what it is like to be a Black in this society where you are constantly treated like you are a threat, dangerous, or that you just don't belong! Every damn day, feeling like you have the weight of the world on your shoulders, constantly having to prove yourself to ignorant ass white mother fu$%#rs like you.

Even as Paul reflected on Andre's statement, it was abundantly clear, based on his reply, that his analysis of who and how he would be as a Black man was overshadowed by his whiteness. Paul retorted:

> I am not ignorant, and you don't have to prove shit to me, you have to prove it to yourself! If I were Black, my life would be as it is because, as I stated earlier, I am a fighter. I am not going to sit around feeling sorry for myself saying "poor me." I would do what I needed to do, and you damn sure would not hear me bellyaching every minute about how someone else, the white man, is keeping me down! This has nothing to do about race! Nothing! And, nobody—NOBODY—can hold you down unless you are willing to be held down.

For Paul, and many others like him, the contemporary absence of more overt symbols of racial discrimination and injustice mean that the racial playing field is level; that everyone, despite their hue, has equal opportunity and, more importantly, that the past is truly in the past; that advancement in society is merely a function of possessing the appropriate individual attributes and the willingness and ability to work hard. From this perspective, the absence of signage such as "Whites Only," "No Coloreds Allowed," or "No Blacks or Jews allowed," "Japs Go Home!" and so forth means that racism, anti-Semitism, and bigotry are artifacts of the past. The absence of such public markers, according to this view, is testament that not only have our ideals for equality been achieved, but centuries of assault and genocide of Indigenous people, the brutality of 246 years of the enslavement of Blacks, the Chinese exclusion Act, and Japanese interment are of no consequence to the everyday lives of People of Color nor whites. This perilous ahistorical view assumes that the colonization and genocide of People of Color around the globe is all about the past and that any claims of modern-day consequences are greatly exaggerated. Therefore, the absolution of contemporary whites, like Paul, who are the beneficiaries of these "crimes against humanity" is justified by the notion that they, personally, never owned slaves, or never conducted boarding schools, or were never responsible for the persecution of a Person of Color. The abject denial of our shared racially troubled and tumultuous past is the most expedient way to deny the realities of our contemporary racial struggles and to fracture any hope of this changing substantively in the future.

The ubiquity of race coupled with the concomitant compulsion to deny it provide the foundation for a nation in a state of social and racial stagnation. No matter how many defining racial moments and movements, racial restarts of a restart, nor transformative marches and protests there are, authentic racial progress has been much too slow for those who wait for soul salvation and the actualization of dreams deferred. Yet for those who prosper from the wealth of inequalities that permeate our society, the demand for racial justice appears to be far too precipitous, aggressive, unfounded, and gluttonous. The "Pauls" of the world would passionately argue that such a demand is the ultimate expression of entitlement. The prevailing view is that People of Color want too much, too soon, and are attempting to confiscate what rightfully belongs to whites as an extension of their inalienable birthright. This is perhaps why Donald Trump's presidential campaign pledge to "take our country back and make America great again" resonated so deeply with so many whites. For many People of Color, the denial and dismissiveness regarding the pervasive impact of race only serves to intensify the racially oppressive conditions that exacerbate the wounds of racial trauma. The emotional–psychological toll that many People of Color must pay for living in a racially oppressive society in which race is consistently denied is limitless and far reaching. How one thinks of oneself; interacts with others; feels a sense of freedom, safety, and belonginess; participates in family and other intimate relationships; and regulates emotions, whether sadness, anger, rage, or loss, are all affected by living under racially oppressive conditions that are denied by those who oppress.

The deeply entrenched and conflicting sentiments regarding race contribute heavily to the racial polarization and paralysis that is characteristic of our society. Many whites, for example, fervently believe that People of Color routinely, habitually, and self-destructively over-endow the significance of race, while People of Color remain unalterably convinced that whites hypocritically under-endow the significance of race while simultaneously employing it as a tool of discrimination and oppression. Each accuses the

other of weaponizing race for their personal gain. This is merely
one snapshot of a multitude of complicated, crazy-making racial
dynamics that shape our everyday racial interactions.

One of the most potentially efficacious tools for addressing, and perhaps commencing a process to eliminate, the racial
impasses that divide us would be to engage in honest, meaningful, soul-cleansing racial discourse. Unfortunately, this option is
generally not available to us because of our societal aversion, fear,
or allergy to talking about race. Many whites don't understand the
benefits of nor the need for enduring the breathtaking discomfort
often associated with talking honestly about race, while many People of Color are often dismayed and fatigued by the innumerable
aborted attempts to talk about race and other attempts that rarely,
if ever, culminate in substantive change. To talk about race would
require an acknowledgment of its existence, in all of its manifestations from most subtle to acute. Unfortunately, the only thing that
is more difficult than talking about race is acknowledging it. If People of Color and whites were afforded opportunities to have meaningful, progressive, and accountability-rich conversations about
race, several salient race related issues would warrant careful and
critical scrutiny and consideration. As frightening and futile as having these conversations might appear to some, it would position us
to grapple with several notable factors associated with the phenomenon of race, how we relate to it, how we are affected by it, and how
we could dismantle the detrimental byproducts of it. A prominent
reckoning of race would require us to start with the basics, many of
which are simultaneously simple and strikingly complicated.

There are several noteworthy organizing principles associated
with race that profoundly shape our racial interactions, relationships, ruptures, and inability to move forward as a society. This is
one of several reasons why it is important to address these issues

in therapy. In addition to denying the significance of race and withholding the strategies that we routinely employ to enable the process of addressing issues in therapy, there are a host of other unexamined dynamics that serve to prevent us from really grappling with the horrors and ugliness of race. The racial socialization process, whiteness as a dominant ideological framework, the racialized and implicitly coded *rules of engagement* that guide the everyday relationships between the racially privileged and the racially subjugated, and the widespread deleterious effects of racial trauma are rarely points of acknowledgment, discussion, or intensive scrutiny. Yet it is the synergistic interplay of these dynamics that helps construct the impenetrable relational and structural guardrails that facilitate the maintenance of the racial status quo. At the core, these dynamics ensure that race continues to be perceived and treated as a People-of-Color issue. As such, whiteness remains invisible and certainly beyond critique and the belief that as long as the current structure and distribution of resources are working well for white people, the system is perceived as "working" as perpetuated.

RACE AND THE SOCIALIZATION PROCESS

In terms of human development, it is universally understood that the process of socialization is critical to the viability of a well-functioning society. It is "the means by which social and cultural continuity are attained" (Macionis, 2016, p. 126).

The process is so vital to our collective existence and survival that we can dare rely on one faction of society to adequately fulfill this crucial and necessary function. Most social scientists contend that there are at least five agents of socialization that play a major role in shaping and transmitting the values and customs that are necessary for cultivating an orderly and fully functioning society. *Family, school, religion, peer group,* and *media* are the major agents of socialization in the United States. These agents are exceedingly influential throughout all areas of our society because they help to establish and reinforce cultural norms, values, and customs regarding every dimension of our lives, such as what we eat; our standards and practices for the instruments we use to eat; what and how we dress; how we ritualize and/or celebrate births, deaths, and other developmental milestones; as well as what constitutes "acceptable methods for transmitting" traditions and cultural practices on to our young. In other words, the process of socialization and the agents we adopt for transmission are fundamental to our existence as a civilized society, and there is no aspect of our lives— not even our attitudes, beliefs, and behavior regarding race or race relationships—that is free from these influences.

The literature devoted to exploring the various domains of the socialization process is voluminous and expansive in scope, which is befittingly consistent with the significant role that the process plays in our lives. Interestingly enough, amid the myriad topics that have been studied, researched, and highlighted, the attention devoted to racial socialization ranges somewhere between scant and nonexistent. When racial socialization is a focus of attention, it is usually within the context of a discussion about "ethnic socialization" and the focus is almost always on Children of Color. The way this issue is (not) addressed in the literature is compelling and deserving of a separate, more detailed, and critical discussion that is germane to a broader conversation about race but beyond the scope of this chapter.

Despite the dearth of attention devoted to the racial socialization process in the literature, racial socialization is a very potent and influential purveyor of our attitudes, beliefs, and behaviors regarding race and the ways our relationships are shaped by it. Although not commonly acknowledged, racial socialization is a prominent aspect of our lives, and each of us experiences it in some form or fashion.

RACE AND AGENTS OF SOCIALIZATION

Each of us is racially socialized, and the contours and underlying processes associated with our racial socialization is racially driven and depends on whether one is white or a Person of Color. It is commonplace for people of color, especially Blacks, to receive explicit, direct messages about race. While some overt and direct messaging about race occurs for whites, much of their racial socialization is implicit. Sociologists typically refer to what is described here as "explicit and implicit" agents of socialization, that is, *deliberate* and *unintended* methods of socialization. Deliberate socialization refers to messages that are delivered overtly and directly, for example, "honesty is a virtue"; whereas unintended socialization refers to messages that are indirectly, or implicitly, conveyed by what ones does, regardless of what one actually states. Thus, if a child receives a direct message from a parent about the virtuousness of honesty while also observing the parent lie, a mixed message is conveyed, with the message conveyed by an observable action impressing the most persuasive and enduring message.

White children are also racially socialized very early in life albeit most often indirectly and covertly. It is rare that white families socialize their children with an overt consciousness about their whiteness. Whereas Children of Color receive direct messages about being Children of Color, white children rarely, if ever, receive direct messages about being white. Instead, they are most often socialized to think of themselves as just "children," just "human," or in terms of their ethnic, religious, or gender identities. This is not to suggest that white children are necessarily oblivious to race, because in many cases they are not. It is just that, in most instances, their understanding of race is often centered around the recognition of People of Color's race. In other words, it is rare that white children and, later, white adults think critically of themselves as racial beings, that is, white, although they are quite adept at seeing and knowing that People of Color are racialized beings. While most Children of Color are acutely mindful of their racialized identity before commencing elementary school, many whites lack any concrete conceptual understanding of themselves as racial beings or of what it means to be white until much later in life, usually adulthood. During a racial humility training sponsored by her employer, Elizabeth, a forty-two-year-old clinical social worker and director of a family services agency serving mostly Children and Families of Color, expressed a common refrain of whites who are engaged in interrogating their whiteness. She tearfully and embarrassingly stated:

> I am a forty-two-year-old woman who works in a largely Black and Brown community, serving People of Color exclusively. Until today and until this workshop, I can honestly say, with lots of humiliation, that I have never once before ever thought about myself as being white. It is just something I never thought about. Why would I? I feel embarrassed and ashamed. I feel afraid to even think about how this omission and my blind spot has affected my work as a director working with Staff and Clients of Color. I don't know how to make sense of this.

If we were to briefly consider race and the five agents of socialization introduced earlier, the following is illustrative of how these agents either explicitly or implicitly shape our attitudes, beliefs, and behaviors regarding race.

The Family

In Black families and in other Families of Color, it is usually considered a fundamental imperative of child development and a strategy of survival for Children of Color to know that they are People of Color and that the world sees and will treat them accordingly. It is difficult for many Families of Color to trust that the world will judge their progeny by the content of their character and not by the color of their skin. Children in Black families are routinely given some version of what is affectionately known and referred to as "the talk," which is essentially lectures and lessons about what it means to be Black in a world that eschews Blackness while passionately denying it does so. Few Families of Color enjoy the freedom of knowing, perhaps even imagining, that their children will receive a warm, inviting, and comforting metaphorical embrace from the society at large. Instead, they live in incessant fear and anxiety that their child could be the next Brianna Taylor, Tamir Rice, Trayvon Martin, Ahmaud Arbery, Sandra Bland, or any one of the countless other victims murdered by police officers or white vigilantism for *living while Black*. Unfortunately, Black Families are worried and consumed not just about possible random anti-Black police aggression but also the type of treatment that their children will inevitably receive from some teachers and tutors, prospective employers, classmates, camp mates, playmates, and various other sections of society where they interact with those who claim to not see color but invariably do. Accordingly, Parents of Color can ill afford to just let their children be children, unencumbered by the weightiness of having to be *home-schooled* about the realities of living in a racialized society whose lofty ideals greatly exceed the pragmatics of everyday life. The racial socialization process for Children of Color starts early, usually around the ages of 4 and 5 years old, and it continues across and throughout their lifetime. Thus, it is rare that Children of Color grow up devoid of any awareness that they are indeed Children of Color.

Schools

Schools and the entire educational system are major agents of socialization, especially regarding race. Historically, Children of Color throughout all regions of the United States have been taught a *standard* (white) *curriculum* that has promulgated notions of white superiority and the inferiority of People of Color. Accounts of historical events have been taught in ways that blamed People of Color even as they were victims of colonialism, white inspired imperialism, slavery, internment camps, racist legislative policies, etc., while privileging the stories of white people. Similarly, the historical contributions that People of Color have made to the birth, growth, and development of the United States have been marginalized or, in some cases, completely obliterated from lesson plans and instruction. Countless numbers of Children of Color have been, and continue to be, educated in a system that reinforces the racialized and stereotyped messaging of the broader society, a dominant message deeply steeped in the myth of white superiority.

Unfortunately, the crucial role that schools and the educational system play in the racial socialization of young people has never before been as vehemently critiqued as it has been in the 2020s post-George Floyd era of racial reckoning. Efforts to infuse issues of race into school curricula and to offer an alternative to the centrality of whiteness, which has been the universal foundational approach to education, has been met with vociferous, sometimes violent, opposition from a large faction of white parents, including many white liberals. Many of these parents assert that they don't want their children enrolled in toxic educational environments that make them feel ashamed or guilty about being white. They express an unwavering fear that taking a more multiracially informed approach to education will damage the self-esteem of white children. Meanwhile, some of us would argue that the very conditions that white parents want to protect their children from are the exact same circumstances and outcomes that Children of Color have been subjected to historically from pre-K through the highest levels of our education system, and no one seemed to care or give a damn about it. Whether in large or small classrooms; in public, private, or parochial schools; in middleclass or lower income neighborhood schools, the educational experience for white children and Children of Color is one that socializes (indoctrinates) them to internalize the broader society's views about race and, ultimately, the supremacy of whiteness.

Religion

As a society, we rely on religion and religious institutions to provide us with a moral and spiritual compass. Religion, in concert with the other agents of socialization, helps improve our ability, as a society, to engage in moral and ethical reasoning, to shape our sense of spirituality, and to make informed decisions about "right" and "wrong." In addition to these important functions, religion, as a practice and as an institution, has unfortunately played an active role in racial socialization and in upholding and reinforcing white supremacist ideology. Interpretations of the Bible and other holy scriptures have been widely used to reinforce notions that support the deification of whiteness and the demonization of Blackness. Barring Blacks and other People of Color from various religious positions of authority (Dobner, 2013) within certain religious doctrines and places of workshop helped to reify the reality that People of Color were less than. In Christian religions, high-level positions, such as bishop, pope, and priest, just to cite a few, were historically off limits to People of Color and to women. Non-Christian religions, especially those that were practiced largely by People of Color, have often been treated and regarded as inferior and on the fringes of the "mainstream." To this day, the congregants and worshipers of many U.S.-practiced religions in their respective places of worship are largely racially homogeneous. There is no faction of society that is free of the influences of race and the promulgation of the centrality of whiteness as an organizing principle.

Peers

Peers and other informal social networks are also major agents of socialization. For some young people, peers—especially at certain critical stages of the lifecycle—may be equally or more influential than their families in the socialization process. Without a doubt, peers help to shape the attitudes, beliefs, and behaviors of those with whom they share close relationships and strong emotional bonds, especially during adolescence. Unfortunately, given how the dynamics of race play out in U.S. society and the pervasiveness of racial segregation that remains an integral dimension of everyday life, it is common for most peer networks, at all stages of the lifecycle, to consist of racially homogeneous groups. Freely having and participating in intimate cross-racial social networks is more the exception than the rule for people of various races. Homogeneous peer networks invariably become major agents of racial socialization and often major manufacturers of racially based stereotypes, misinformation, and *othering*. In those rare instances, where peer group exposure and participation are interracial, the people of color engaged in these relationships are often considered *exceptions* which pave the way for any preexisting dominant racial stereotypes and misinformation to remain unaltered.

The Media

There is no more influential, powerful, and pervasive agent of socialization than the media, especially in terms of racial socialization. Negative and stereotypical portrayals of People of Color in all media forms have been a common practice throughout the history of the United States. Whether on the big screen, small screen, in product advertisements, political campaigns, or, more recently, on social media, the denigration and the devaluation of People of Color, particularly Black and Indigenous People, have been everyday practices. This issue has been exacerbated by the historic and systematic discriminatory hiring practices that made it difficult, if not impossible, for People of Color to hold high-ranking and influential media-related positions where they could address and provide input on the negative and racist portrayals of People of Color. Because the imaging of People of Color has been consistently and powerfully shaped by these five major agents of socialization in the exact same way, with each contributing to and reinforcing the other, it has become easy to embrace these characterizations and belief systems as consensually validated "truths."

The fact that the racial socialization of many whites facilitates their ability to see others through a prism of race but not themselves tremendously impacts cross-racial relationships. This dynamic, in part, helps to perpetuate two prominent, recurring, white-supported notions: 1) that race is essentially a "People of Color issue" and 2) that People of Color overemphasize race— two judgments rooted in and exposing how People of Color and whites have been differentially socialized regarding race. Since our society caters to whiteness, and one of the many privileges of white privilege is to possess the *inherent* power and authority to name and define others' experiences, the white driven accusations about People of Color's preoccupation with and narrow focus on race is a potent castigating narrative that significantly shapes the attitudes, beliefs, and behaviors of People of Color. It also contributes to the inauthenticity that is often exhibited in many cross-racial relationships.

The cross-racial interactions between most whites and People of Color are often polite, measured, and arduous. They require considerable effort. We are all victims of our racial socialization, a process that has left us all with deeply internalized messages that make having authentic trusting relationships virtually impossible. Looking through the lens of a Person of Color, how is it even remotely possible to authentically trust and engage in a relationship with someone whom you know has been socialized to see you as a less-human and inferior being? How can whites live in a mostly racially segregated world in which much of their meaningful exposure to People of Color has been with the latter relegated to subordinate and inferior positions and yet ultimately treat them as fully franchised human beings? These unspoken dynamics persist with little overt, interracial, consensual validation of their existence. They provide a strong foundation for not only how we as a society (fail to) deal with race but also how we (fail to) deal with each other across that color line that DuBois spoke of. Considering these troubling realities, it is hard to imagine how the process of therapy, the efficacy of which is predicated on the cultivation of a trusting and intimate relationship based on a mutual bond of respect, could ever be executed without overtly attending to issues of race. The deeply embedded racialized scripts and history that we all carry with us cannot be cavalierly dismissed, ignored, or overcome simply because its "therapy." The racially based healing work that is desperately needed throughout society is also needed in therapy as well. Therapists working with Clients of Color, especially white clinicians, must be professionally trained and racially prepared to deliver racially sensitive, trauma-informed therapy. Until therapists and the mental health field at large recognize this is an ethical imperative, the process of therapy will remain a place where the line of demarcation between help, healing, and harm will be a thin one.

CHAPTER 2

The Dynamics of Oppression and the Roots of Racial Trauma

It is nearly impossible to understand the everyday experiences of People of Color without having an acute understanding of the phenomenon of race. When the intricacies of race are scrutinized, the dynamics and long-term deleterious effects of racial oppression and its relationship to trauma are magnified. Although the entangled relationship between racial oppression and trauma is virtually inextricable, some attempt to explain them as two semi-autonomous but interconnected phenomena is important.

THE DYNAMICS OF RACIAL OPPRESSION

Racial oppression is a complex, multifaceted, invisible, and emotionally and psychologically asphyxiating condition that is integral to being a Person of Color in a white supremacist society. The effects are long-term and are transmitted through generations, often in ways that are difficult to quickly identify. For People of Color, racial oppression is a life sentence to a wall-less prison in which all aspects of one's being are affected. It encroaches on the freedom of People of Color by prescribing and demanding how they should behave, especially if they wish to be accepted within the broader (white) society. Coates (2015) speaks poignantly of the impact of racial oppression as he notes:

> It is truly horrible to understand yourself as the essential below of your country. It breaks too much of what we would like to think about ourselves, our lives, the world we move through and the people who surround us. The struggle to understand is our only advantage over this madness. (p. 106)

The dynamics of racial oppression are also born out of racist and discriminatory policies, seamlessly and complexly integrated into the institutional structures of society, that have historically dictated where People of Color can live, attend school, work, and worship, for example. Racial oppression is a driving force that ensures that People of Color are virtually always relegated to the margins of societal institutions and trapped in places and spaces with few or no metaphorical exits. It is the tentacles of racial oppression that guarantee that the racial complexion and composition of most of our institutions get progressively whiter as you move from the metaphorical sub-basement to the penthouse of the organization. Predictably and historically, most People of Color are confined to the lowest levels of our institutional structures where, not coincidentally, working conditions are often deplorable and inhumane and the income and health benefits lag significantly behind those enjoyed at the top, which are always disproportionately occupied by white people. These are the suffocating realities of racial oppression.

There are two critical manifestations of oppression—primary and secondary—that affect the lives of People of Color in ways that most whites are unable to see or realize. Afterall, the *genius* of the dynamics of oppression is that it can be simultaneously devastating for those who are targeted while remaining invisible to the architects, overseers, and beneficiaries of it. The distinction between *primary* and *secondary* racial oppression is largely a matter of whether the imposing and sustaining forces are overt or covert. Primary-level oppression is often historically based and usually involves more overt inflictions of physical brutality. Secondary-level oppression, on the other hand, is often, though not always, tied in with contemporary experiences and the usually more covert barriers, constraints, and repressive conditions that hinder People of Color. While the forces of secondary-level oppression are often hidden and discrete, the effects of the condition are no less debilitating than their counterpart's. In fact, the distinctions drawn here are principally illustrative and explanative. In the actual day-to-day experiences of People of Color, these two manifestations of oppression are complexly intertwined. The effects of racial oppression, whether primary- or secondary-level, are often transmitted intergenerationally.

PRIMARY-LEVEL RACIAL OPPRESSION

Primary-level oppression usually requires the following conditions to fortify its effectiveness: 1) there is direct exposure to the physical presence of an *oppressor*; 2) the oppressor and the oppressed have differential access to power, privilege, and the allocation of resources; 3) there is a mechanism for promoting dehumanization and/or objectification; 4) there is a liberal use of physical force, coercion, and/or other forms of overt punishment; and 5) there is a mechanism for obliterating or severely hampering individual agency and advocacy.

The Physical Presence of the Oppressor

"Oppressor" refers to any individual or group who uses acts of emotional, psychological, and/or physical domination through the misuse and/or abuse of power exerted over another to impose one's will for personal gain or advantage. In this regard, the process of oppression strips or severely hampers one's sense of personal agency and freedom. In the context of race, the privileges that the racial socialization process bestows upon whites, while simultaneously assigning a status of subjugation to People of Color, help to consummate the role of the white oppressor. This status is encrypted into what it means to be white, whether individual whites embrace it or *choose* to rebuke it. The chronicles of history are replete with examples of how Black, Indigenous, and other People of Color have been terrorized and traumatized by whites' insatiable thirst for dominance and control. These acts of aggression and tyranny, whether in the form of pilfering land or holding human bodies in bondage, all required the physical presence of an aggressor, that is, the oppressor. The enslavement of Black Africans and the Jim Crow era that followed the abolishment of legal slavery are but two potent examples of major events that are the enduring symbols of primary-level oppression. Many of these practices were aggressively and violently enforced with the oppressor nearby to ensure adherence by the oppressed. A major factor that contributed to the *success, viability,* and *longevity* of the institution of slavery was the proximity that slave owners had with the enslaved, albeit not voluntarily for the latter. The actual physical presence of the slave master was an instrument of intimidation and social control. Often, enslaved Blacks were constantly surveilled by their captors as well as other random white people. Thus, the *presence of the oppressor* was ubiquitous, strategic, and purposefully ominous. It ensured that the oppressed would be hyperobedient, compliant, and more susceptible to being controlled. The imposing physical presence of the oppressor served as a constant reminder that dissent without deadly consequences was not even a remote possibility for the enslaved.

Just like during slavery, for all practical purposes, the oppressed continue to be carefully and methodically *taught* how to be obedient, fearful, and compliant. Unfortunately, the presence of the oppressor as an apparatus to suppress and oppress the growth, mobility, and life circumstances of People of Color is not limited to our disreputable past. It is also quite prevalent in our contemporary lives. The twenty-first century version of this dynamic has changed the venue from the old workplace—the plantation—to the contemporary workplace—predominantly white institutions. Nonetheless, whether in public or private, for profit or nonprofit, governmental or nongovernmental, whites, and mostly men, constitute the majority of *overseers* of most institutions. The significance of this is twofold: First, it means that the overwhelming majority of People of Color in the workplace administratively report to white supervisors who ultimately dictate their fate and progress within the institution or organization; and secondly, the standards by which People of Color are evaluated (judged) are those solidly grounded in white, Eurocentric, white supremacist ideology. As many Black and other People of Color understand, acknowledge, and accept, the quickest and most expedient pathway to success in the workplace is predicated on one's ability to perfect and demonstrate adherence to the values of white people. Not only do whites constitute the overwhelming majority of those occupying positions of leadership but they also have the greatest access to valuable institutional resources. More often than not, whites have the power to hire and fire, establish and codify the norms of the workplace; and they are often the architects of the *pernicious p's* of institutions that are the purveyors of institutional and systemic racism and oppression. The pernicious p's—policies, procedures, protocols, and (best) practices—are typically informed by an unexamined and unacknowledged ideology that is shaped by Eurocentric values. For instance, valuing cognition over affect, drawing strong lines of demarcation between the "personal and professional," and promulgating dualistic (i.e., either/or) thinking are but a few examples of how Eurocentric ideology is infused into the policies and procedures of organizational practices. Moreover, they often constitute the standard for what is defined as acceptable, normative, and ethical. Thus, what is often considered normal, professional, and even American is usually synonymous with white.

The Power to Define

Through the dynamics of oppression, whites enjoy the privilege and the power to define not only their respective experiences but those of People of Color as well. It is whites, not People of Color, who are the final arbiters of what is racist and what is not, what is normal, "standard," "professional," beautiful, or aberrant. Hence, People of Color are often systematically denied opportunities to freely define experiences and realities that are germane to their existence and livelihood. The power to define is a potent privilege and resource to possess, and it affords whites the opportunity to have it and never acknowledge that such is the case.

Greater and Differential Access to Resources

Accumulating, hoarding, and controlling access to resources is a principal mechanism by which primary-level oppression is established and maintained. Resources have both intrinsic and extrinsic value. According to Zimmerman and Bradley (2019), intrinsic value is a property of anything that is valuable on its own. This is in contrast to extrinsic value, which is a property of anything that derives its value from its relationship to an other, intrinsically valuable thing. Whiteness has, or is believed to have, intrinsic value in our society. Because whites are afforded the privileges of being white in a racially stratified society that tilts heavily toward the superiority of whiteness, being white is, in and of itself, a valuable resource. Being white provides white people with universal social capital. This access to social capital facilitates access to other resources. Historically, whites have, at least in the United States, had uninhibited access to other intrinsic resources, such as education, decent housing, healthcare, and countless other valuable resources, including being granted the benefit of the doubt. The 2021 white supremacist insurrection on the United States Capitol provided a compelling snapshot of white privilege and the currency of possessing white skin. The insurrectionists, armed with military style weapons and plastic zip ties suited for kidnapping, not only entered the U.S. Capitol illegally while searching for elected officials but also stopped to take selfie photographs with local police. These blatant exhibitions of white privilege confirmed what many People of Color already knew, so it was hardly shocking or surprising. The respectful and deferential coddling of the aggressive white mobsters by some members of law enforcement was in stark contrast to how a group of peaceful, Black, Black Lives Matter protesters were tear-gassed and aggressively manhandled in the same city just months earlier. This occurrence was yet another troubling reminder of how our society affixes a higher premium to the value and humanity of white life.

In contrast, white people, largely through instruments of racial oppression, have taken every conceivable measure to systematically strip Black people of their intrinsic value as human beings. They have done so by the enactment of racist and discriminatory laws, policies, procedures, and practices that deny Blacks equal access to basic human rights, such as the right to an education, personal freedom, voting, decent housing, and equal protection under the law. All the major societal institutions: political, educational, economic, and health have historically been and continue to be controlled by white people, both structurally and ideologically, where access by People of Color is often limited, monitored, and managed by the invisible forces of institutional racism. These tools of oppression have had a long-term and devastating effect on the well-being of Black people. Through the intergenerational transmission process, these conditions have affected the lives of Black people for generations by hampering their full participation in all facets of life. The denial of access to education, for example, not only affects how one thinks of oneself but also dictates how one participates in the economic marketplace, which in turn affects access to healthcare. Collectively, the limited access to these resources ultimately affects where one lives, how one lives, and how long one lives. The impact is limitless and systemic.

The relative access one has to resources also affects one's spiritual and psychological well-being. The denial of access to basic resources can deplete and diminish one's sense of self. Especially when the denial of resources is imposed in conjunction with other assaults inflicted on the mind, body, and soul of a being. The perpetual and systemic confinement to an inferior and dehumanized state of being can significantly influence self-perception. It can be challenging to have a positive and affirming self-image when consistently exposed to broader demeaning and devaluing societal messages. The unrelenting nature of these conditions often culminates in the transformation of "beings" into "things." Once a (human) being is relegated to the status of a "thing" (i.e., an inanimate object), all doors to harm, both internally and externally imposed, are wide open. The transformation of *beings* to things is another vital component of primary-level oppression.

Objectification

When the racial socialization process deems some human beings worthy of unbridled dignity and respect and others not, the foundation for the process of objectification is soundly established. Objectification paves the way for the inhumane treatment of others without remorse, empathy, or compassion. When one species is socialized to believe that they are inherently superior, a belief that is reinforced and reified by all facets of society, the objectification of others is inevitable. The process of objectification liberates one group of human beings and grants them the freedom and the sense of entitlement to capture, enslave, brutalize, and terrorize another group mercilessly—for centuries—and deprives them of the ability to see any portion of themselves through the eyes of those they have tormented. When the tortured, captured, and terrorized are regarded as either nonhuman or less human, it is easy to dismiss their capacity for pain and suffering.

Objectification is the process by which human beings are relegated to the status of an inanimate object or a feelingless *other.* Through the eyes of those who objectify, those who are targeted for objectification lack feelings and any other innate human characteristic. The objectified are perceived and treated as emotionless, faceless others who are merely pleasure-providing servants for the superior. The sole purpose of those who are objectified, at least from the perspective of the oppressor, is to satisfy the needs of those who oppress and objectify them by being tireless instruments of industry and intimacy in many cases. The objectification process, whether by design or by accident, allows the oppressor to disassociate and therefore perpetuate atrocities without the burden of remorse, empathy, or compassion. Interestingly enough, the objectification of others ultimately exposes the inhumanity of the oppressor by stripping them of their capacity for empathy, compassion, and decency by transforming them into feelingless, machine-like creatures. Menakem (2017) refers to this phenomenon as a type of soul injury that white people, with their history of oppressing others, must confront.

People of Color and especially Black people have a lengthy history of being the targets of objectification. Slavery relied heavily on the objectification of Black lives and bodies. Black women's bodies were treated as pleasure centers and reproductive machines by white slave owners for their pleasure and the continuation of cheap labor. Black men were treated as workhorses by day and breeders by night. Young Black children born into captivity were immediately groomed to assume the same roles that were imposed on their parents as soon as humanly possible. All these atrocities occurred against the wishes and consent of the Black people, and according to Leary (2005) "yielded stressors that were both disturbing and traumatic, exacting a wound upon the African American psyche which continues to fester" (p. 116).

Many of these degrading, barbaric, and uncivil behaviors were possible because Black people were stripped of their humanity and because the whites who oppressed them were powerfully disconnected from theirs as well. Blacks were considered objects, not humans. The total disregard for their humanity was exhibited by the fact that they were considered property and were routinely treated as such. Brutal public beatings, the routine rape of Black girls and women, the mutilation of body parts for attempted escapes, and the imposition of hard labor under extreme weather conditions were the various ways in which those enslaved were victimized through the process of objectification. Additionally, Leary (2005) estimates that between 1866 and 1955, more than 10,000 African Americans men, women, and children were lynched; many thousands more had been murdered by other means; and untold numbers of women were brutalized and raped. Leary (2005) goes on to note: "I don't remember reading about any counseling centers that were set up for freed slaves after the Civil War. The effects of the traumas were never addressed, nor did the traumas cease" (p. 96).

Punishment

The use and infliction of extreme punishment is a major tool of primary-level oppression and is intricately tied to the inequitable access to power and resources as well as to the process of objectification. The oppressor's use of meting out brutal and inhumane punishment ensures that the oppressed will not only live a life of obedience, compliance, and submission but one of fear as well. Lynching, whippings, physical mutilation, physical confinement, rape, and the denial of food and water are some of the ways in which the oppressed historically have been punished by the oppressor. During slavery, Blacks were routinely the recipients of public beatings and whippings. In addition to the physical pain imposed, this tactic was also an instrument of humiliation as well as emotional and psychological torture. No consideration was given to the psychoemotional trauma of those relegated to the devastating position of powerless and helpless observers. The main concern was inducing fear and promoting compliance. Fear paralyzes movement and action, whether self-advocacy or activism. It constructs an impenetrable invisible fence of self-containment that suffocates personal growth, development, and self-actualization.

Silencing

Silencing is a major characteristic of primary-level oppression, and it is one of the most sophisticated and misunderstood forms of punishment imposed on the oppressed. In many ways, silencing is an act of domination and interpersonal violence. It is an instrument of punishment that strips the oppressed of their ability to literally and figuratively speak or engage in acts of self-advocacy. Silencing is always achieved through acts of aggression, force, and domination. It is driven, sustained, and reinforced by provoking fear. After all, one cannot be coerced into positions or hypercompliance and acquiescence and simultaneously retain the ability to resist or advocate for oneself by speaking freely.

As an act of interpersonal violence, the process of silencing assaults one's soul and sense of self. It breeds powerlessness and an increasing sense of helplessness, often creating a state of involuntary mutism. When one has been silenced, self-advocacy and literally speaking on one's own behalf become very challenging endeavors. Voicelessness is the internalization of the process of silencing. Since it is intricately tied to fear, it is extremely difficult to overcome, especially without devoting deliberate and conscious attention to doing so. In more instances than not, when one has been silenced, one has also been dominated.

When subjected to the stranglehold of primary-level oppression, it was common for the oppressed to be required to bear witness to the cruel and harsh punishment of others (friends and loved ones) while simultaneously being forced to remain silent, docile, and disengaged. Coercing people to observe these inhumane acts while also imposing a "gag-order" was not only an act of social control but also a main tool for puncturing the dignity and hope of those who were confined to the role of "helpless onlookers." The survival of both the target of the punishment as well as the coerced observer was predicated on their respective ability/willingness to comply with the rules of domination and silencing. These are the roots and rudiments of silencing.

The potency and efficacy of primary-level oppression are fueled by the overt and widespread reliance on physical force, humiliation, acts of domination, and violence. It is the confluence and synergistic interplay of factors—such as the physical presence of the oppressor, who enjoys greater access to resources, the process of objectification, the propensity toward literally and figuratively beating the oppressed into compliance and instilling fear, and the process of silencing—that make this such a daunting and debilitating experience for those who are maligned by it. In many ways, it is the manifestation of primary-level oppression that paves the way for the emergence of secondary-level oppression.

SECONDARY-LEVEL RACIAL OPPRESSION

The use of the term "secondary" in this context does not represent a quantitative or qualitative difference between primary and secondary levels of oppression, but rather denotes the differences in the manifestation of the effects. Secondary-level oppression is often void of the overt brutality and overbearing nature of physical domination that often accompanies primary-level oppression, although in some rare instances, secondary-level oppression might involve varying degrees of these dynamics. The more significant point is that secondary-level oppression, with or without overt brutality, is every bit as crippling and harmful as primary-level oppression. In many ways, secondary-level oppression and its accompanying effects are difficult to detect and define. The effects are pervasive and insidious. The salient characteristics of secondary-level oppression are: 1) the physical absence of the oppressor; 2) an emerging identification with the oppressor; and 3) the internalization of toxic messages.

The Oppressor Within

Unlike primary-level oppression, the physical presence of the oppressor is not needed to ensure or perpetrate secondary-level oppression (Freire, 2005). The actual physical presence of the oppressor is not a determining factor in secondary-level oppression because the oppressed become the principal vehicles of their continued oppression. They do so largely by internalizing the mindset and worldview of the oppressor, a process that is largely unconscious. It is complexly interwoven into the impulse and desire to survive. Attempting to understand the psyche and intellectual proclivities of the oppressor is essential to survival. Carefully and studiously observing the behavior of the oppressor can render valuable information that is germane to survival. Thus, having the ability to reasonably anticipate and predict the calculated moves of the oppressor can be a key guiding principle for how the oppressed should (*must*) behave in order to survive. This process of acute attunement to the ways and being of the oppressor often culminates with the oppressed developing an *oppressor within* identity.

In many ways, the internalization of the oppressor or the development of an *oppressor within*, while less physically taxing for the oppressed, is infinitely more insidious, afflicting, and self-destructive. The fact that the barriers are more emotional–psychological, more deeply internalized, and often difficult for the oppressed to see or understand in a comprehensive way make the effects more challenging, destructive, and ultimately harder to overcome. The absence of an overbearing, heartless, mean-spirited, oppressive physical force dictating and restricting the movement of the oppressed makes it easier to blame the oppressed for the complexities and plight of their conditions—a view that can also be widely held by the oppressed themselves, thanks to the oppressor within process. The hallmark of secondary-level oppression is based in the oppressed internalizing the views, actions, and behaviors of the oppressor as self-fulfilling prophecies. It is the unconscious identification with the oppressor and the concomitant internalization of oppressor-promulgated negative messages that contributes to the development of the oppressor within.

Identification with the Oppressor

As noted earlier, becoming an astute observer of the psychology, behavior, and emotional tendencies of the oppressor is a common survival tactic for the oppressed. Hence, it is unreasonable to expect or assume that one could devoutly study these inclinations over a substantial period without beginning to unconsciously adopt some or all aspects of them. For decades, psychologists and psychiatrists have reported that it is common for those who have been placed in severely abusive and life-threatening circumstances, in close proximity to their aggressor, to develop a phenomenon some have referred to as *defensive identification.* The American Psychological Association Dictionary of Psychology defines defensive identification as "the process by which a victim of abuse psychologically identifies with the perpetrator of abuse, or with the group with which the perpetrator is identified, as a defensive strategy against continuing feelings of vulnerability to further victimization" (VandenBos, 2007, p. 262). Ana Freud (1936/1937) was one of the first clinicians/theoreticians to introduce the concept of "identification with the aggressor" to describe the same phenomenon whereby an individual identifies with someone who poses a threat or with an opponent who cannot be mastered. While the origins of these conceptualizations were rooted in efforts to understand the psychology of victimization shaped by experiences of torture, aggression, and abuse more generically, the application to the dynamics of racial oppression is worthy of consideration. While not always as discernible as other more overtly egregious acts of domination, racial oppression is a powerfully dispiriting aggressive experience. It is threatening to all spheres of one's being: emotional, physical, psychological, spiritual, and relational. For these reasons, it is imperative that the racially oppressed develop tactics for survival in much the same way that victims of other forms of abuse, torture, and life-threatening aggression do.

Much like other victims of aggression, the racially oppressed often develop an unconscious *identification with the oppressor* that in many ways functions very similarly to the process described earlier. Identification with the oppressor has two salient interrelated features. On the one hand, the racially oppressed begins to internalize, or introject, the myriad racist, self-defeating, and self-loathing views that have been projected onto them by the oppressor and the anatomy of oppression. This also includes the internalization of messages that deify the oppressor. Once these ideas have been unconsciously internalized, the oppressed begin to adopt the ways and being of the oppressor. In essence, the oppressed becomes an oppressed-oppressor. A more detailed discussion of this phenomenon will be discussed in Chapter 12.

Internalized Messages

The unconscious internalization of messages about the inherent inferiority of the oppressed and the corresponding superiority of the oppressor is inevitable and predictable. These messages are not only espoused verbally but also reinforced behaviorally and seamlessly and flawlessly incorporated into institutional structures that help reify and fortify them. For example, if People of Color are consistently referred to as unintelligent, and this is consensually validated by the white dominant society verbally as well as in how People of Color are routinely treated, this belief becomes relatively easy for People of Color to adopt and internalize. Understanding and internalizing one's alleged inferior intelligence facilitates the relative ease with which one can ultimately behave in accordance with how once has been defined or purported to be. Consider this benign example: for decades, Black men were not only discouraged, but were effectively forbidden, from playing the position of quarterback at all levels of organized football.The belief was that the quarterback position was one that required high levels of intellect and analytical thinking. Hence, it was considered aptly suited for the "superior-thinking, brilliant, analytically thinking white man" and NOT the more "physical, animalistic, athletic Black man." This belief permeated football at every level from middle school through the National Football League. It was such a widely held belief that talented, aspiring Black quarterbacks were reassigned to play other positions for doubt that they possessed the requisite intellect to effectively play the position. While there was absolutely no truth or empirical or anecdotal information to affirm the widespread ridiculous and racist claim, the belief was widely held and did affect the behavior and decision making of coaches and players alike.

This is but one minor example of the crippling effect of deeply internalizing the powerful, self-destructive, self-denigrating, racially pejorative messages that have been defined and promulgated by the white oppressor. Internalized messages ultimately become, either partially or totally, the reigning reality of the oppressed. The reliance on and efficacy of this tool of oppression eliminates the necessity for any physical oversight by the oppressor. The identification with the oppressor and the internalization of negative racially stereotypical, self-defeating messages effectively locates the oppressor deep within the psyche of the oppressed, thus guaranteeing that the oppressor within will actively participate in and perpetuate self-subjugation.

The process of racial oppression is a condition that is sustained and intense and endures over an extensive period. It is multidimensional and is induced and perpetuated at both the relational and institutional levels. The relationship between the relational and institutional dimensions is cyclical, they both affect and are affected by each other. The *institution* of slavery that has been discussed intermittently throughout this chapter is an excellent example of the interlocking nature of the relational and institutional dimensions of the dynamics of oppression. While the brutality of slavery was both imposed and suffered at the relational level, it was simultaneously supported and reinforced by a myriad of institutional structures throughout the United States and abroad, including state, federal, and international laws. The enactment of Jim Crow laws following the abolishment of slavery allowed the oppression of Black people to continue while offering cover for, and giving birth to, a new version of slavery that relied on institutional structures rather than whips and chains. The institutional dimension of the anatomy of oppression severely obfuscates the crippling nature of it as a debilitating experience. Thus, racial oppression, while widespread in its reach, often enjoys some element of invisibility that often affords some plausible deniability about its existence.

Even for those who are targeted and *held in captivity* by it, racial oppression can be exceedingly mystifying and function in a way that is analogous to being maligned by an undetected, undiagnosed malignant cancer that gradually eats away at the core of one's being. It is a vicious act of violence that pierces the psyche and soul of those who are affected. There are a plethora of visible signs of its effects, but no overt signs of an oppressor/perpetrator or any visible, concrete, measurable data available to implicate one. Both those who affect (the oppressor) and those who are affected (the oppressed) can be totally oblivious to and unsuspecting of the widespread effects the dynamics of oppression have on the everyday life experiences of the racially oppressed. In this regard, it is not uncommon for whites to attribute the plight and hardships of People of Color to respective "deficits"—absence of intelligence, lack of good morals, dysfunctional families, poor work ethic, lack of motivation and drive, and/or reliance on handouts. The range and enormity of white-promulgated explanations for the plight of People of Color rarely, if ever, includes race and racial oppression as critical intervening variables. Similarly, it is equally challenging to convince whites or invite them to entertain the ways in which they, as a collective, have benefitted, and continue to do so, from the systematic oppression of People of Color. It is some combination of denial and/or ignorance that allows whites to remain perpetrators, coconspirators, and willing and unwilling stalwart supporters of the domination and racial oppression of People of Color. Unfortunately, the inability to effectively address racial oppression at the relational level is exacerbated by the absolute ineptitude and recalcitrance of addressing it institutionally. The disproportionate number of incarcerated Black men, the high number of unarmed Black men killed by law enforcement, the low test scores in reading and math in young Black children, the high COVID-related death rates in Communities of Color, and the high prenatal morbidity rates for Black and other Women of Color are just a few examples of the toll that People of

Color pay for the relational and institutional manifestations of racial oppression. Coates (2015) asserts that the relational/parental reality of these conditions is that

> Black people love their children with a kind of obsession. You are all we have, and you come to us endangered. I think we would like to kill you ourselves before seeing you killed by the streets that America made. That is a philosophy of the embodied, of a people who control nothing, who can protect nothing, who are made to fear not just the criminals among them but the police who lord over them with all the moral authority of a protection racket. (p. 87)

This is the interplay and totality of relational and institutional racial oppression that constitute the centerpiece and foundation of racial trauma.

RACIAL OPPRESSION, TRAUMA, AND MENTAL HEALTH

Children and Families of Color experience virtually all the same "normal" everyday life struggles and challenges as do their white counterparts. Whether these are centered around workplace woes, the stresses and strains of having and raising children, finding a healthy balance between work and family life, child and adolescent issues, marriage and divorce, or health concerns, these are life circumstance that virtually everyone experiences across the human lifecycle, regardless of race. Unfortunately, many People of Color must also contend with and do so against a backdrop of racial oppression and trauma in addition to managing these stressors of everyday life. The inescapable, nonnegotiable prevalence of racial oppression and trauma that besiege the lives of People of Color contribute to the creation of an all-consuming toxic stress that is not only omnipresent but is also life altering as well, a type of toxic stress that permeates every aspect of one's life on virtually a minute-to-minute basis. To complicate these matters further, there are few opportunities for People of Color to seek redress. When psychotherapy is pursued as a possible avenue for redress, it often falls short of providing the therapeutic deliverables that are desperately needed. The therapists' awkwardness, reticence, and ineptitude in talking about race—coupled with a workforce of therapists who have been trained to be "colorblind" in models of therapy saturated in an ideology of whiteness that arrogantly proclaim to be universal, neutral, and objective, while achieving neither—often leave People of Color feeling underserved and left to find other remedies to address their racialized suffering, or they receive no relief at all. It is imperative that contemporary therapists who are being called upon to answer the ringing bells of a racial reckoning begin to revision and rethink the process of therapy. We do not live in a colorblind society and to naïvely hold onto this misguided mythology contributes to huge racial binds that help support the notion that therapy, too, is colorblind. Today's therapist must be willing, positioned, and poised to address matters of race in therapy in ways that are thoughtful, responsive, and shaped to address the ever-widening issues of racial trauma. To engage Clients of Color in therapy without, at the very least, some cursory knowledge of racial trauma and an accompanying skillset to address it borders on racial malpractice.

CHAPTER 3

Racial Trauma

Racial trauma is the byproduct of persistent hyperexposure to racial oppression, which is, as noted earlier, an all-consuming, crippling, and debilitating condition. As a product of long-term exposure to racial oppression, racial trauma is a fundamental, predictable, and inevitable life circumstance for People of Color, and as such it must be dealt with explicitly in any meaningful therapy. Unfortunately, as Hardy and Qureshi (2012) note, "rarely is unmasking and treating the hidden wounds of racial trauma a focal point of intervention. Instead, conventional approaches attend to family problems, individual psychological issues, behavioral problems, affect disorders, and substance misuse" (p. 25) and rarely, if ever, racialized trauma.

Racial trauma is a type of unshakable hybrid of *chronic* and *toxic stress* that People of Color, regardless of other sociocultural factors, are coerced to live with, often without a conscious recognition that they are doing so. There are aspects of racial trauma that are like both toxic and chronic stress, although the classical definition of neither of these experiences adequately captures the essence of racial trauma. The stress associated with racial trauma is not limited to childhood experiences and caregiver attachment issues, which are often associated with toxic stress. There are some aspects of chronic stress that offer some insight into the anatomy of racial trauma, in that both may involve the physiological and/or psychological reactions one might have to a prolonged internal or external stressful event that may or may not be currently present. Chronic stress can be activated by memories or events that trigger a recollection of the precipitating stressor. Thus, there are critical features of chronic stress that are embedded in racial trauma.

Racial trauma is comprised of the emotional and psychological residue from the constant exposure to ever-present, race-related chronic stress. Part of the mystique of racial trauma is that it is not readily apparent to some, nor why or how it manifests. The fact that there is no overbearing oppressor present, imposing their will, often obscures both the prevalence and harmful impact of racial trauma. In fact, the absence of the physical presence of an oppressor should not minimize one's understanding of the damaging effects of secondary-level oppression. Racial trauma is like a noxious invisible gas that slowly infiltrates the airspace occupied by People of Color. While its release into the atmosphere is not visibly apparent, the life altering effects of it are. There are four racially based societal factors that are trauma-inducing dynamics for People of Color. These factors are intricately interwoven, essentially invisible, rarely named, and seldom identified as the lethal, highly destructive, and pernicious trauma-inducing dynamics that they are. Not only do they create and nurture the social context of racial trauma, they also are instrumental in promoting the paralyzing, undetected, undiagnosed trauma symptoms that are experienced by many People of Color.

SOCIETAL RACIAL TRAUMA-INDUCING FACTORS

The four racial trauma-inducing factors are: 1) the ideology of whiteness and white occupation; 2) pervasive racially based judgments and valuations; 3) racially inequitable treatment; and 4) unacknowledged, unaddressed, unresolved relational injury and racial hurt. The collective interplay of these factors helps contribute to and create trauma-inducing conditions for People of Color.

Living Under White Occupation, Surveillance, and Over-Policing

The United States is a demographically diverse, multiracial society guided by a centrality of whiteness (Hardy, 2022). The norms, values, and mores that define the essence of what is considered "American" are narrowly defined by an ideology of whiteness. What is considered fundamentally "right" is almost perfectly aligned with that which is fundamentally "white." Unfortunately, People of Color are burdened with the unenviable task of having to be white-ish to thrive and survive in "American culture" (a synonym for white culture).

Metaphorically speaking, People of Color currently live, and have always lived, under a form of *white occupation* wherein their lives and every miniscule gesture, no matter how significant or insignificant, is under surveillance. Under white occupation, whites decide, for People of Color, what is considered normal, desirable, and valuable. Whites even get to decide and define what is and isn't racist, often in ways to negate the claims made by People of Color, the victims of racism. Broad freedom is granted to whites, while freedom is restricted for People of Color in subtle but obvious ways. Thus, the infinite freedom whites have to walk through a park, to sit for hours in coffee shops conversing and commiserating, to sleep in the common areas of college and university dormitories, to freely enter apartment buildings where they live, to walk their pets, and to take selfie photographs with police during an armed insurrection, among countless other activities, do not exist for People of Color and especially Black people. Living while Black or as a Person of Color under white occupation means living under constant scrutiny, where what you say and how you say it is always subject to white people's judgment and tone policing. It is whites, not People of Color themselves, who exercise the freedom to judge whether a Person of Color's behavior means what they claim it does. It is within the purview of the seemingly unlimited power of white people to decide what Black people mean by *Black Lives Matter* or what it **really** means to kneel during the National Anthem. Relatedly, it then becomes the duty and responsibility of Black people to acquiesce, capitulate, and accommodate the interpretations of whites or be labeled radical, belligerent, dangerous, terrorist, or anti-American. Once these labels are affixed and are done so without racial scrutiny or interrogation of whiteness, it nevertheless becomes the burden of Black people to prove that they are not the embodiment of the unfounded, uncritiqued, manufactured characterizations that have been imposed on them by whites. Interestingly, whites are rarely burdened with having to prove the accuracy or legitimacy of their accusations; instead it is the responsibility of People of Color to disapprove them, which—while living under white occupation—is nothing short of impossible.

Similarly, whites have historically engaged in tactics of racial segregation that have been successful in restricting the access of People of Color to certain activities and opportunities. When People of Color, in response to white-imposed segregation, created racially focused alternative activities, opportunities, and spaces, whites then declared and labeled People of Color racist for doing so. The claim of (reverse) racism is often followed by some form of punitive action, rebuke, or retribution. This is the power of the ideology of whiteness and what it means to live under white occupation. Living under the stronghold of white occupation requires People of Color to live in and under a constant state of alert. Not staying alert can have—and often has had—deadly consequences.

Another related dimension of living under white occupation involves the ways in which the white society operates as the tone police for People of Color. Through *tone policing,* whites are the self-appointed final arbiters of what the appropriate tone and intensity of affect should be for People of Color. It is whites who are empowered and have the privilege to decide whether affect expressed by People of Color is too much, just right, or lacking in appropriate decorum. Whether enjoying a family picnic in the park, standing on a street corner with a group of peers, or walking down the halls in any U.S. school, People of Color are not only routinely surveilled but also publicly policed and often reprimanded for the tone of their expressions, be they exultations, laments, or expressions of anger and rage. The tone policing of People of Color by whites is widely tolerated and is often codified into codes of behavior that are transformed into policies and procedures that govern what constitutes appropriate tone (and behavior) in the workplace and other institutions. People of Color are hypersensitive and conscious about their tone because they know it is virtually always under scrutiny and that once it is deemed unacceptable by whites, access to white spaces can be severely restricted. Whiteness, and the privilege that accompanies it, not only affords whites the opportunity to engage in tone policing, but it grants them *the right* to engage in full-scale production of negative judgments and valuations about all aspects of the lives of People of Color well beyond critiquing their tone.

Pervasive Negative Valuations of People of Color

The manufacturing and promulgation of negative valuations about Black life and all that is associated with it have been around since slavery. It is an integral dimension of all our agents of socialization, as previously noted, and is systematically perpetrated by the educational system, by law enforcement, by the entertainment industry, and by virtually all societal institutions. The negative valuation of People of Color in general and Blacks specifically is a reckless guilty pleasure for the white dominant society. The negative valuation of Black life is so pervasive that it is even subscribed to and advanced by other People of Color. There is not a single thread of the life of People of Color, and especially Black people, that is exempt from vicious, negative, and hard to dismantle negative valuations defined and imposed by whites. These negative valuations have severe consequences on the everyday lives of People of Color. For instance, they underpin and fuel the actions of police officers who quickly shoot and kill unarmed Black men based on a deeply held, unconscious, and internalized belief that the men are dangerous, threatening, and lawless. Even when the "assumed to be dangerous" Black man is a twelve-year-old Black child, such as in the case of Tamir Rice, who was shot multiple times within seconds of police arriving to the scene where he was playing with a toy gun at a public playground in Cleveland, Ohio.

The negative valuations that led to Tamir's unwarranted and untimely death, as well as those of other unarmed Black people, are the same as those that inform the behavior of some white physicians who administer less and/or lower dosages of medication to Black women during childbirth based on their racist beliefs that, compared to white people, Black people have higher thresholds for pain and their skin is thicker. It is the negative judgments and valuation of People of Color that erodes human compassion for the losses and indignities that Communities of Color must endure, whether they involve children confined in cages along the United States–Mexico border or Black and Brown children trapped in poorly funded, inadequate, urban schools.

Due to the negative judgments and valuations of People of Color, the proudly held democratic principle of *innocent until proven guilty* is largely reserved for whites. People of Color, by comparison, are often presumed guilty until they can demonstrate their exceptionality. Unlike their white counterparts, People of Color—especially Black People, who have historically been proclaimed to be shady and criminally inclined—often move about under a cloud of doubt about their innocence, regardless of the circumstances. This is in part why countless numbers of Blacks are routinely stopped for *driving while Black.* They invariably *fit the description.* How could any random Black person not *fit the description* when the description and portrait of a criminal in the United States is often purported to be quintessentially Black?

Negative judgments and valuations are difficult to shed once they have been affixed. They often create a "no-win," "can't-win," "no-option" double bind for People of Color. Consider the scenario wherein a Black man is stopped by the police for appearing suspicious or "fitting the description" of a criminal assailant. If the man responds indignantly because this a common recurring experience, by doing so he validates the negative valuation of the angry, petulant Black man with an attitude. If, on the hand, he remains calm and hypercompliant, he is then perceived as suspicious, deceptive, and cunning—views that are also embedded in the negative valuations of Black people. There is no way to shed the negative valuation, despite the tireless efforts of many People of Color who fruitlessly attempt to do so, often to the detriment of their health and well-being. The negative valuation of People of Color often paves the way for the dehumanization and marginalization that are integral to perpetuating and reinforcing trauma-inducing conditions.

Common Everyday Racial Assaults on the Lives of People of Color

Living life as a Person of Color under the occupation of whiteness often means living intimately with an unwelcomed barrage of racially laced micro and macro slights, insults, and assaults. These punctures of the soul include the negative valuations discussed in the previous section as well as routinely having your competency and/or humanity questioned and being deemed invisible when your worth is at stake and hypervisible when someone wants ammunition to validate a racial stereotype. All these common occurrences are further compounded by also having to bear witness to the daily decimation and destruction of Black and Brown lives without reason or accountability. There is no respite or hiding place from the onslaught of common everyday racial assaults on the lives of People of Color. There is no vaccine for this metaphorical virus. There is no acknowledgment, no concrete strategy or plan of action to address or ameliorate the suffering. Instead, many People of Color find themselves in a quasi-numb, stupor-like state, dreading but anticipating the next premature halting of a Black or Brown life while the white perpetrator walks away, again. The pain of it all cannot subside so long as the assaults persist. There is no healing from the past and none for the present until the threats cease. Unfortunately, People of Color are left to cope with the slow, persistent, life-threatening bleeding from the proverbial "million cuts" sustained from the common everyday assaults on the lives of People of Color.

Unacknowledged, Unaddressed, Unresolved Relational Injury and Racial Hurt

The common everyday racial assaults experienced by People of Color are compounded and exacerbated by historically based racial hurts that have been intergenerationally transmitted. Many of these historically based racial hurts have been downplayed, ignored, and even, in some cases, denied credible standing. Danny Lewis (2016), in a post for the *Smithsonian Magazine*, noted that

> few things compromised the core values of the U.S. Constitution and left as lasting a mark on American society as 246 years of institutionalized slavery and the subsequent discrimination of the Jim Crow laws that marked African Americans as second-class citizens. As such, few people were more deserving of a formal apology than the millions of Black Americans whose ancestors were forcibly brought to this country and had their freedoms stolen from them. (para. 11)

Unfortunately, it was not until 2008, almost 150 years later, that the U.S. government could offer a largely symbolic apology for slavery.

> The formal apology for slavery and Jim Crow issued by the U.S. House of Representatives in 2008 was unprecedented, even after decades of lawmakers trying to push the government to finally apologize. In introducing the resolution, Representative Steve Cohen (D-Tenn), noted that despite the government issuing an apology for interning Japanese citizens and later pressuring Japan to apologize for forcing Chinese women to work as sex slaves during World War II, the American government had never formally recognized and apologized for

slavery. While the apology was primarily symbolic, by officially recognizing its role in perpetuating the horrors of slavery and Jim Crow, the American government took a step forward in addressing and atoning for one of its greatest wrongs. (Lewis, 2016, para. 12)

This was a small step in the direction of promoting healing, but it falls far short of what is ultimately needed.

The institution of slavery and the vicious assault on Indigenous People by white oppressors have forever tainted and strained the possibility of having healthy and trusting cross-racial relationships, especially without a concerted effort to repair the relationship. These historical events are not easily forgotten and are major organizing principles for People of Color. As Coates (2015) noted, Black people can "never forget that for 250 years Black people were born in chains—while generations followed by more generations who knew nothing but chains" (p. 70). For many whites, on the other hand, these defining experiences for People of Color are nothing more than distant, detached, sterilized historical events that have little to no relevance to contemporary life or modern-day race relationships. We live in a society where there is a palpable and deeply ingrained relational strain between whites and People of Color, especially those who identify as Black and Brown. It is neither talked about nor overtly acknowledged but it is always lying, often quiescently, just below the surface until it is activated. People of Color often expend considerable energy attempting to manage and mask this strain during most cross-racial interactions. In fact, most cross-racial relationships involving whites tend to lack trustworthiness, goodwill, and authenticity. The absence of these crucial relational attributes makes the establishment of meaningful, trusting, and substantive cross-racial relationships with whites somewhere between improbable and impossible. It is nearly impossible to have more committed and engaged cross-racial relationships without white acknowledgment of and accountability for historically rooted racial assaults, injuries, and harms. Unacknowledged, unaddressed, unresolved historically rooted racial harm comprises a major toxic and racial trauma-inducing condition for People of Color to confront, contend with, and manage. It is difficult for People of Color to recover from the contemporary wounding of common everyday racial assaults when they aggravate, as they often do, the generational injuries and wounds carried from the previous generation(s). It is the confluence of these factors that contributes to the pervasiveness of racial trauma in the lives of People of Color.

These four societal trauma-inducing factors often *force* People of Color to adopt strategies to cope with them and the invisible wounds they help create. These strategies become organizing principles that facilitate coping and are also simultaneous expressions of racial trauma. An *organizing principle* is a basic construct that shapes the attitudes, belief, and behaviors, of an individual or group. In other words, one might conceptualize an organizing principle as a construct that shapes or significantly contributes to how one sees and experiences their external world. For example, the phenomenon of race might be considered an organizing principle for People of Color. This would certainly be the case from my perspective since I believe there is virtually no aspect of the lives of People of Color that is void of the influences of race in some way or another.

RACIAL TRAUMA ORGANIZING PRINCIPLES

There are seven organizing principles associated with People of Color's efforts to cope with the racial trauma that is often embedded in and triggered by the four societal factors previously discussed. The following organizing principles are both coping strategies and symptoms of racial trauma: 1) living under a constant state of alertness; 2) intergenerational transmission and residuals of historical trauma; 3) direct contemporary experiences with racial oppression, discrimination, and racism; 4) vicarious contemporary experiences with racial oppression, discrimination, and racism; 5) recurring and intrusive race-based thoughts and ideations; 6) living with a generalized state of race-based anxiety and suspicion; and 7) emotional dysregulation and hypervigilance. I believe that some or all of these organizing principles can be observed in varying degrees of intensity and salience among the vast majority of People of Color suffering from racial trauma.

Trauma often causes the body to stay in a constant state of alertness, even during the absence of an immediate threat or of potential harm. Unfortunately, through the eyes of many People of Color, and especially Blacks, it is often difficult to imagine many life situations wherein race and racism are not critical influential factors. Given this perception, many People of Color find themselves guided by organizing principles that serve to *prepare* them for the likely occurrence wherein they will be the target of racism. The adoption of these principles is constricting and potentially liberating at the same time. On the one hand, these preparations contribute to the creation of a kind of obsession or preoccupation with racial harm while simultaneously offering some potential partial immunity from it by ensuring that one is emotionally and psychologically prepared for it, if/when it occurs. Consequently, People of Color learn to live in a state of racial alertness. Therefore, a Person of Color is always aware of who they are, racially, and what this means in a white supremacist society.

Living in a Constant State of Alertness

The anticipation of being exposed to and harmed by racial slights and racism *demands* that many People of Color remain in a heightened state of (racial) awareness and on guard. Unfortunately, existing in a constant state of alertness produces prolonged stress that can and often does disturb the immune, digestive, cardiovascular, sleep, and reproductive systems. Yet, it is conceivable that the rewards of remaining in a high state of alert outweighs the costs of not doing so. At best, this represents a double bind for People of Color. Either one maintains a constant state of alertness and suffers the prolonged stress that this often produces, or one moves about the world free of prolonged stress and the state of alertness but at risk of being ill-prepared to "respond appropriately" to an unexpected racist act that requires a spontaneous (crisis management) response.

The necessity to live in a state of heightened and constant racial alertness is often precipitated by the following race-related factors: (a) knowledge and residuals of historical trauma; (b) experiences of personal contemporary racial injustices and personal triggers; and (c) exposure to racial injustices inflicted on the symbolic self. The following is a brief discussion of each of these factors.

Intergenerational Transmission and Residuals of Historical Trauma

The vestiges of primary-level oppression have a powerful, emotionally riveting, and enduring effect on the contemporary lives of those whose ancestors spent centuries living under conditions of servitude and subjugation. For Black and Indigenous People, one needs only trace their lineage back three generations to locate family members who were enslaved or viciously treated as savages. The remnants of our bloody and inhumane past are poignantly present for those of us who carry the historical and generational scars of racial bigotry, hatred, and degradation. For those who historically have been the targets of colonization, slavery, and racial injustice, it is impossible to forget, even when those who are associated by blood, group membership, or ideology with the perpetrators and oppressors have difficulty remembering. Bessel A. van der Kolk (2014), in his ground-breaking book, described the broad systemic impact that trauma exposure has on the brain, mind, and body, reminding us that *the body keeps the score* (which is also the title of his book). Borrowing from van der Kolk's view, it is not reasonable to expect or believe that it is possible for a people to endure 300–400 years of systematic human degradation and not transport the pain, scars, and stress in every cell of their bodies. This dynamic is often difficult for some whites to understand, so they flippantly ask: "Why do you people keep talking about slavery? You were never a slave. It is time to move on!" They, unfortunately, fail to understand that one does not have to *be in slavery* for slavery *to be in them.* How can Blacks in the United States get over slavery when we have not been out of slavery for as long as our ancestors were in it? How? How can Blacks overcome slavery and move on while continuing to live under slavery-like conditions? How is this possible? How can Black people overcome the legacy of slavery and move on when so many are the namesakes of those who held them in captivity? Would it be reasonable to expect Indigenous People to forget about the plethora of broken treaties and all the promises made and reneged by whites and the rape of native women as well as of the land they inhabited while traveling and living throughout the United States where there remain countless cities and towns and at least twenty-seven states (Russell, 2018) carrying the names of their ancestral tribes/nations? When the trauma of the so-called past is intimately and vividly married to the present, it is hard to dismiss, ignore, or deny the potency of the intergenerationally transmitted pain that obliterates the temporal differences.

The painful racial experiences of the past are also passed down through generations via family stories. Many Families of Color consider it a rite of passage and a racially sanctioned responsibility to prepare their progeny for the racial realities of the world in which they will be interacting. Many families work assiduously to protect their young by ensuring that they know who they are (racially), where they come from, and the complexity of the realities they will have to confront as Children of Color. Through a variety of methods, Children of Color are admonished and encouraged to be cognizant of the harsh realities that the world will not always be fair, will not always see their humanity, and will not always judge them by the content of their character, capabilities, and accomplishments. These vital life lessons, while necessary for survival, are also emotionally depleting and anxiety producing. They are not only born out of racial trauma, they contribute to it as well. This is the one of the many complexities of racial trauma and what it means to have virtually every facet of one's life impacted by it. In fact, it is the universality of racial oppression and everyday acts of racism that are the additional impetuses for People of Color to adopt a constant state of readiness. Being alert and adopting a constant state of readiness is a protective strategy that may help to diminish the impact of racial trauma, but it cannot completely shield one from it.

Direct Contemporary Experiences with Racial Oppression, Discrimination, and Racism

For many People of Color, encountering racial microaggressions, slights, and acts of racism, both overt and covert, are virtually everyday occurrences. These artifacts of living under racially oppressive conditions are an integral part of the everyday life experiences of People of Color. For many People of Color, the prevalence of these experiences highlights why it is prudent for them to put themselves on high alert if they aren't already and if they already are, reinforces why they should remain alert. It is (racially) safer to expect to be racially slighted, harmed, or discriminated against and have this belief disconfirmed than it is to not expect it and be additionally victimized by one's ignorance, naïveté, or failure to appropriately protect oneself.

Vicarious Contemporary Experiences with Racial Oppression, Discrimination, and Racism

Acts of racism toward one's *symbolic self* can be just as injurious as racist acts experienced by the *literal self.* As relational beings, we are equipped with two manifestations of the self, a literal self and a symbolic self. The former refers to the complex array of thoughts, emotions, and behaviors that are integral to one's direct being and experiences. The symbolic self refers to the self that is created in response to and in relationship to another that is bound by perceived shared experiences, tribal/group affiliation, affinity, and empathy. Thus, the symbolic self is the byproduct of having the capacity to see another's self as a symbol of one's literal self and vice versa. Thus, one can have a host of symbolic selves. It is commonplace for People of Color to see other People of Color as members of their respective racial tribe and thus as an extension of themself, or their symbolic self.

When People of Color witness the human degradation, maltreatment, and unjustifiable brutality and murder of their symbolic self, there are no degrees of separation. Emotionally, psychologically, and experientially, it is as if one's literal self is the subject of the assault. I recall watching the May 2020 murder of George Floyd with a sense of hopelessness and humiliation, and a bolt of raw hatred trying desperately to invade the regions of my heart. I, like the victim, experienced difficulty breathing. As he desperately sought rescue from his long-deceased mother with his impassioned plea during the waning moments of his life, I watched and clearly saw images of my head on his torso. With tears streaming, feeling asphyxiated, I desperately tried to stop watching, but neither my eyes, nor my soul would allow me. During those moments, I was inundated with the stories, the imagery, and the agony-filled memories of my painful encounter with Officer Callahan, I thought of and saw the faces of thirteen-year-old Tamir Rice, of Sandra Bland, of Breonna Taylor, of Eric Garner, of Rodney King, of Ahmaud Arbery, of Walter Scott, and of the countless others that I carry on my back, within my heart, and within my everyday consciousness as a Black person. Emotionally, psychologically, and experientially, fortunately and unfortunately, there is no line of demarcation between the literal and symbolic self. Hence, the Floyd murder and other similar experiences serve as powerful reminders to Black people, and perhaps other People of Color as well, that it is imperative that one remains racially alert while living under white occupation.

Recurring and Intrusive Race-Based Thoughts and Ideations

Living one's life under constant racially based surveillance while also experiencing and witnessing the long and all-encompassing tentacles of racial injustice is burdensome in numerous ways. It makes it nearly impossible for People of Color to not think about race in a comprehensive and perhaps even slightly obsessive way. This is another organizing principle birthed by exposure to and efforts to cope with racial trauma. Being forced to think constantly about race and to consider how one's moment-to-moment life is being affected by it is an important tip for life and living that People of Color must adopt. To live in a constant state of alert requires consistently thinking about race and actively examining how it might underpin certain actions or behaviors. Having ideations about race and thinking about it incessantly, even when one doesn't want to or doesn't consider it necessary, is a major response to as well as symptom and indicator of racial trauma. Our society's long history of racial oppression, repeated betrayals by whites, and the widespread existence of racism and racial inequities throughout society underscores why recurring, intermittently intrusive ideations about race are common for People of Color. The presence of these thoughts and ideations are adaptive and intricately aligned with survival, and they perversely help to contribute to the cycle of racial trauma as well. This is one of many reasons racial trauma is such a complicated phenomenon and one that is not easy to conquer.

Generalized State of Racially-Based Anxiety and Suspicion

As you, the reader, have probably already discerned, all the prominent organizing principles associated with racial trauma are highly interconnected. Each of them helps to both create and reinforce the other. Hence, one of the major consequences of being in a constant state of alertness and thinking recurringly about race is that these processes give way to varying degrees of race-related anxiety and some underlying and generalized suspicion. Whether worrying about being stopped by the police or being perceived as too angry or reinforcing one of the million negative and demeaning negative valuations promulgated by white people about People of Color or wondering if a loan, job, or some other opportunity was denied because of race, it all leads to the same emotional place: an underlying feeling of race-based anxiety. Although this anxiety is intensely felt and is often quite pervasive in scope, it may never be directly expressed, especially by Clients of Color in therapy. To fully engage with Clients of Color and provide effective, racially sensitive, trauma-informed treatment, therapists must be prepared to address these issues with depth, sensitivity, and a sense of racial humility. Living under dense clouds of racial oppression and white occupation often denies People of Color the *privilege* of knowing whether the adverse decisions they encountered were free of racial bias. The racially sensitive, trauma-informed therapist can help clients gain clarity about these complexities and ambiguities by creating space for deep racial exploration to occur throughout therapy. The process of living with racial injustice, constantly having to question how, when, and whether race is a factor in one's contemporary life tends to breed suspicion. Since race permeates virtually every component of People of Color's daily life, the suspicion is vast and quite generalized. Once again, conventional racial wisdom is that it is prudent and much safer to be unwarrantedly suspicious than to be regrettably free of suspicion that was warranted. Living with a sense of generalized racial anxiety and suspicion, like living in and under a constant state of alertness, is a major organizing principle for people who are racially traumatized. These experiences are often pervasive, complex, and intense, and they cannot *not* affect one's emotional stability.

Emotional Dysregulation

Ideations about race accompanied by anxiety, suspicion, and worry, while dutifully remaining on alert, create an emotional elixir that is potently disruptive to one's state of being. Because many People of Color know from their lived experiences that racism exists and yet witness it often being passionately and vociferously denied makes it difficult for People of Color to feel trust in most cross-racial interactions. The lack of certainty, confirmation, and consensual validation is genuinely crazy-making. I observed this dynamic during a recent meeting of group supervisors involving a white male member, Larry, and an African American female member, Sabrina. Each group member was asked to share their first racial memory. This was a semi-structured exercise, wherein the members could speak whenever they wished. Toward the end of the group, Larry turned to Sabrina (who *had* previously shared) and said: "I don't think you shared yet, why don't you go next?" At which point, Sabrina responded with a sense of unexpected rage. She stated: "What the hell leads you to believe that I have not gone? I know why you thought it . . . because people like you never see people like me. We are invisible to you! That is why you speak over us all the time; it is why you will reach over me in a supermarket, brush up against me on the subway and NEVER say excuse me . . . NEVER open your goddamn mouth! Of course YOU wouldn't know that I have already spoken. It would require you to see me, to see me as someone who is every bit as human as you!" Larry looked stunned and softly stated: "I am sorry, I realize I made you feel invisible." Sabrina replied: "It is the story of my life." Ginny, a white female group member who was obviously feeling protective of Larry and perhaps seeing pieces of herself in Sabrina's description of whites, decided to offer a lecture on diplomacy and decorum. In a very condescending tone, Ginny offered the following advice to Sabrina: "I can see you are upset but I don't know why you had to make it about race when it had nothing to do with race. He was simply being thoughtful and considerate, and he gets viciously attacked for it. I just think there is a right and wrong way to talk to someone and I don't think what you said or how you said it was right. I was raised to believe that you treat people the way you want to be treated, and I don't think you would appreciate being treated that way."

Constantly having to grapple with a range of complex and varied emotions connected to race is another major organizing principle associated with racial trauma and living life under a constant state of high alertness. It is impossible to live life imprisoned within the walls of racial oppression and trauma and not have intense fluctuating human emotions. Yet People of Color are not only routinely expected not to have or express intense emotions but are also scathingly castigated, even punished, when they attempt to express any emotion that whites experience as too extreme. These abhorrent, over-controlling, and oppressive behaviors contribute to a set of societal conditions that are primed for racial trauma and the invisible wounds attached to it.

INVISIBLE WOUNDS OF RACIAL TRAUMA

Unlike other manifestations of trauma, there is absolutely no escape or reprieve from racial trauma for People of Color. Our turbulent and troubled racial history, the force-feeding and imposition of whiteness on People of Color, the war on Black and Brown bodies, and the delicate ways in which racism is so seamlessly integrated into the structures and institutions of society ensure that racial trauma will continue to have lasting effects on the lives of People of Color. This is one of the many reasons why therapy with People of Color must absolutely lend serious consideration to the dynamics of race, racial trauma, and oppression even if/when these issues are rarely overtly discussed in the process. Just as racial trauma is inevitable, so are the invisible wounds associated with it, and thus the therapist must be prepared to provide competent and racially sensitive treatment. Even the organizing principles that have elements of protection embedded within them are contributing factors to racial trauma.

The wounds associated with racial trauma are difficult to detect for a variety of reasons. First, as noted in Chapter 2, there is no nomenclature or clinical nosology for racial trauma, and any condition or phenomenon that remains nameless ceases, for all practical purposes, to exist. The painful and paralyzing effects of racism and racial oppression are often trivialized or dismissed as People of Color's fascination with victimization. And finally, living with racial trauma is so integral to the experiences of People of Color that even those who struggle and suffer mightily with the wounds often remain oblivious to them as well. Thus, the invisible wounds of racial trauma are not just invisible to those observing, interacting with, and providing treatment to People of Color but also equally and compellingly invisible to the very hosts of the wounds. Since racial trauma can be intermixed with other traumatic experiences, sometimes sorting out, disentangling, and identifying the wounds of racial trauma from other underlying and preexisting conditions can be challenging; but it is critical work to do (this issue will be discussed in greater detail in Section II). All these factors are compounded by the fact that while racial trauma is a pervasive, crippling, and debilitating condition, it is essentially treated by those who have the power to name, as a nameless, language-less, subjective, nonexistent phenomenon. Whether named or not, the wounds of racial trauma are real, especially for those who are maligned by them. They vary in scope and intensity and are an integral dimension of the life of People of Color.

There are seven highly interrelated invisible wounds that are prominently and routinely associated with racial trauma: Internalized devaluation; an assaulted sense of self; psychological homelessness; voicelessness; loss and collective grief; orientation toward survival; and rage are the entangled invisible wounds that shape the everyday life experiences of many People of Color. Some of these may be more pronounced in one individual than in another due to unique or idiosyncratic circumstances; however, some trace of each of these types of wounds can usually be uncovered in most People of Color; each is often present in some form and in varying intensities. It is also important to note that while a particular wound may be more prominent, additional wounds are often present, though perhaps harder to detect.

SUMMARY

Racial oppression and racial trauma are intricately linked. It is the hyperexposure to racial oppression that feeds and breeds racial trauma. Both racial oppression and racial trauma share a common experience of pervasive invisibility that helps to fortify its effectiveness and continuance. A major difficulty in understanding and addressing racial trauma is that there is no language for it, and the subsequent lack of acknowledgment of both its existence and its effects is prevalent. The lack of language, acknowledgment, and understanding of the intricacies of racial trauma adds significantly to the emotional and psychological burdens carried by those who fall prey to it. Relying on and resorting to the dynamics of secondary-level oppression, many People of Color struggling with racial trauma ultimately begin to question or blame themselves when battling this unnamed, unacknowledged condition. This is one of many reasons why therapists treating People of Color must "think race" and consider the invisible wounds of racial trauma when, for example, a client speaks obliquely and confusingly about feeling like an "imposter." Racially safe and coded language such as this refers to a common emotional psychological condition expressed by many People of Color suffering from internalized devaluation and an assaulted sense of self (two wounds that will be discussed in detail in Chapters 6 and 7, respectively). This psychological condition is directly tied to racial trauma but is essentially nameless. As a result, the client can't clearly identify it nor hypothesize about its origins and, often, neither can the therapist. To further complicate matters, there are a host of societal forces that are trauma-inducing for many People of Color; these, too, are unnamed and unacknowledged. These are also the factors that require People of Color to live in a state of alertness, fear, and anxiety related to their vulnerability to racial oppression and racism. The effects of these experiences are emotional, psychological, and relational. Thus, the hyperexposure to racial oppression and a myriad of trauma-inducing societal factors that reinforce racial trauma contribute to a range of emotional, psychological, and psychic wounds that many People of Color must endure. Unfortunately, these wounds are largely invisible, which makes acknowledging and treating them a challenging endeavor. Seven core invisible wounds of racial trauma have been identified and will be comprehensively discussed in the forthcoming chapters. Addressing these wounds in therapy must be a fundamental component of the standard therapeutic protocol for working with Clients of Color. To do so effectively, therapists must be willing to talk about race explicitly, to engage their clients around a host of delicate race-related issues, and, most importantly, to develop the requisite competencies necessary for providing racially sensitive, trauma-informed treatment.

CHAPTER 4:

Race and Therapy

Despite the prominence of racial oppression in the everyday lives of People of Color and their continually living amid a host of societally based trauma-inducing experiences, racial trauma is rarely a focal point in mental health treatment. The *Diagnostic and Statistical Manual of Mental Disorders* (American Psychiatric Association, 2013) recognizes posttraumatic stress disorder (PTSD), but not racial trauma, as a diagnosable mental health condition. The contemporary, day-to-day, in-the-moment exposure to racial oppression, discrimination, and racism is one of several features that would differentiate racial trauma from classical conceptualizations of PTSD. Given the overall lack of attention devoted to racial issues in treatment, it would be rare for a Client of Color seeking therapy to explicitly request help with racial trauma, and it would be equally rare for them to not struggle, at some level, with the invisible wounds of racial trauma during their treatment. The rarity of these two scenarios is indicative of the difficulties and dilemmas associated with the intersections of race, therapy, and the treatment of racial trauma. Unfortunately, there is no nosology, nomenclature, or codified classification to acknowledge or validate the racially based suffering of People of Color. Leary (2005) argues for the acknowledgment of a diagnostical category of trauma centered around the lingering psychoemotional intergenerational effects of enslavement. She describes posttraumatic slave syndrome as a debilitating traumatic condition, unique to Black descendants of slavery. Leary (2005) maintains that the condition profoundly shapes the contemporary daily life experiences of Black people in multitudinous ways. In her view, posttraumatic slave syndrome (PTSS) is the inevitable consequence of centuries of abuse, violence, and inhumane treatment, for which no systematic opportunities for psychoemotional healing were ever offered or made available to the descendants of the enslaved. In a sense, the absence of recognition of racially based suffering as a mental health condition compounds the pains of racial trauma by devaluing or, at best, deeming invisible the experiences of those who are already racially devalued.

Racial trauma is a powerful, pervasive, and often debilitating phenomenon that is essentially nameless, which makes it virtually impossible for Clients of Color to adequately identify as an area of distress and for most clinicians to appropriately diagnose and treat it. Rarely explicitly identified as the focal point for treatment, racial trauma is ignored entirely, misidentified by a secondary symptom (i.e., a symptom associated with a symptom), or conflated with other conditions that are creating distress for a client. For example, internalized devaluation is often misidentified or misdiagnosed as "issues with low self-esteem"; rage is often diagnosed and treated as an "anger management problem"; and psychological homelessness is often conflated with and misinterpreted as "problems with intimacy and commitment." The clinical challenge is that the presence of racial trauma wounds does not de facto negate the coexistence of other underlying issues. However, the problem is that, when these underlying issues are presented and examined, neither race nor racial trauma is ever considered to be an integral part of the equation. As someone who has spent much of his career training clinicians, I know from experience that a deep and comprehensive exploration of the psychoemotional effects of racial oppression on the lives of People of Color receives scant attention at best in most educational and clinical training programs. To address the wounds of racial trauma, a keen focus on race and racial oppression is required, as is rethinking the process of therapy as so many of us have known and practiced it. Doing intensive and transformative clinical work with racial trauma requires a major shift in how the process of therapy is approached, structured, and executed. It is neither practical nor reasonable to assume that issues of race or racial trauma can simply be affixed thoughtlessly to an existing model of therapy that has been negligent of attending to race from its conception and throughout its evolution. Most therapy models and therapeutic approaches that populate the mental health field are inattentive to issues of race. The work of Nancy Boyd-Franklin (2003) and Resmaa Menakem (2017) are the notable recent exceptions. Hence, addressing racial trauma earnestly cannot be achieved by treating it like an addendum attached to an email or by taking a "pin the tail on the donkey" approach. On the contrary, the work requires, first and foremost, the therapist to 1) adopt a racial lens; 2) become racially-lingual by developing a proficiency to effectively engage in conversations about race; 3) develop a good working understanding of the invisible wounds of racial trauma; 4) engage in critical racially based self-of-the-therapist work; and 5) actively redesign the therapeutic space to accommodate a greater tension between *being* and *doing* in the execution of therapy.

ON BECOMING A RACIALLY SENSITIVE, TRAUMA-INFORMED THERAPIST

Developing a Racial Lens

Developing a racial lens requires deep personal transformational work. It involves a process of racially based self-examination, self-interrogation, and self-reflection. These are distinctive yet highly interrelated processes. *Self-examination* calls for engaging in a process of self-exploration regarding race. It necessitates being curious about the lifelong experiences that have been instrumental in shaping one's racial ideology and behavior as well as examining the racially based messages that may have been internalized during this time. The process of self-examination is ultimately about exploring what is there racially (i.e., internalized) but may have never been thoroughly and systematically explored. This process paves the way for *self-interrogation*, which is a slightly more difficult process. Self-interrogation moves beyond the process of simply exploring to critically questioning one's racially based attitudes, beliefs, and behaviors. It is an invitation and opportunity to be brutally honest with oneself about oneself, especially in terms of one's racially based history and biography. Rather than engaging in acts of deflection, distraction, or denial, the process of self-interrogation is most effective when it leads to critical (racial) *self-reflection*. Colloquially, this process is best described as demonstrating the ability and willingness to sit in ones "poopy pamper." It sets the stage to reflect on the following questions: 1) Who am I racially? 2) Who have I been racially? 3) What are the potential schisms between what I believe and what I do or fail to do? 4) Who is it and how is it that I wish to be racially as I move forward? 5) What is the work that I need to do to *become* who I wish to be, before I can actually *do* the work I wish to do? Self-examination, self-interrogation, and self-reflection play a crucial and fundamental role in developing a racial lens.

The development of a racial lens is crucial to providing racially sensitive, trauma-informed therapy. It is a dynamic process that is fluid and ongoing. There is a beginning, but there is no identifiable end point. The lens is developed, cultivated, and refined over time. The methodology one employs to facilitate the development of a racial lens is quite varied and, in some ways, parallels the process of becoming a therapist. It is developed by participating in a combination of ongoing and comprehensive didactic experiences, such as lectures, trainings, and conferences as well as intensive self-of-the-therapist work. It also involves acquiring direct, face-to-face, hands-on clinical experience with addressing race in therapy while actively engaging in racially focused clinical supervision or some other closely related experience. In addition to these initiatives, positioning oneself to have sustained experiences interacting with people outside one's respective racial group is also of vital importance. In other words, the process requires so much more than reading a book or watching videos, which are important but woefully insufficient for meeting the rigors of the task at hand. Developing a racial lens requires consistent ongoing work, and it is essential work for all therapists who are committed to working intensively with Clients of Color and racial trauma.

The development and adoption of a racial lens augments the therapist's preexisting clinical knowledge about human suffering, particularly as it pertains to race and racial trauma. It inspires critical questioning of the myth of colorblindness and how this notion is an impediment to providing racially sensitive, trauma-informed therapy. In fact, possessing a racial lens is the antithesis of colorblindness. At its core, having a racial lens means one is intentional about seeing, acknowledging, and considering the significance of race in the analyses of virtually all human interactions. It also heightens a therapist's awareness and sensitivity to the impact of racial oppression and the psychoemotional pain associated with it. Developing a racial lens means seeing more clearly the ways in which the phenomenon of race is a powerful organizing principle that informs and potentially shapes virtually all aspects of our lives. With a racial lens, one embraces the notion that we all are racialized beings and that *how* we are racialized carries both tremendous meaning and heavy consequences for how we function throughout society. To this end, rather than adhering to the archaic notion of the therapist as a tabula rasa, seeing through a racial lens helps the therapist to recognize that even they are racialized, and this can be germane to the therapeutic relationship and/or process. Watts-Jones (2010) argues that it is important for therapists to be mindful of how various dimensions of their social identities, including but not limited to race, potentially impact the therapeutic process. According to Watts-Jones (2010), the therapist's

> location of self is about integrity in our work, a way of developing a greater skill with addressing issues of intersectionality inside the therapy room and demonstrating an awareness and interest of how issues of social status—those positioned as superior and inferior and their respective entitlements and losses—operate in the lives of the clients outside the room. (p. 418)

It is worth noting here that the impact of the therapist's racial location could be facilitative and/or prohibitive. The more important point is that it is prudent for the therapist to be both mindful of race and curious about its potential impact on the therapeutic process, even if it doesn't readily render anything significant. Being considerate and reflective of the potential impact of race throughout the therapeutic process significantly enhances both the relational integrity and the racial sensitivity of the process.

Another benefit of developing a racial lens is that it enables and empowers the therapist to address or debunk several racially based misnomers that often hamper the process of therapy, especially with Clients of Color. The development of a racial lens allows the therapist to rethink and, in many instances, reject the following rarely scrutinized racially based *misconceptions*:

1. Race is a concept relevant only to and for People of Color;
2. Race is a social construction, and therefore it need not be attended to;
3. Race is relevant in therapy only when People of Color are involved;
4. The racial identity and background of the therapist are irrelevant to the process of therapy;
5. Race is not an issue in therapy unless the client indicates that it is;
6. If/when race is an issue in therapy, the client will indicate that it is;
7. Race should be introduced as a topic of discussion in therapy only when the client raises the issue;
8. Racist comments expressed in therapy are best ignored, especially if they are tangential to the presenting problem or the process of therapy;
9. Talking about race in therapy is tantamount to inappropriately infusing politics into therapy;
10. Therapists who raise issues about race are acting on their personal agenda;
11. It is easier to address racial issues with interracial couples and mixed-race families;
12. Race is not an issue for interracial couples and mixed-race families;
13. When race is pursued with interracial couples or fam-

ilies, it is the Members of Color who must be vigorously engaged;

14. Trauma is trauma, and if a therapist works with trauma,
there is no reason or need to focus on racial trauma;

15. Therapists of Color can and/or should work only with Clients of Color.

These racially based beliefs and misguided therapeutic operating
principles are produced and assigned credence in the absence of
a racial lens. The development of a racial lens uniquely positions
the therapist to consider the racialized context in which Clients
of Color live and the ways in which it may be clinically relevant to
the therapeutic relationship and process and the formation and
maintenance of the presenting concern(s). Further, a racial lens
ensures that the therapist is also consciously and actively engaged
in a process of self-examination and curiosity about their respective racial context and its relevancy to what is or isn't occurring in
the consulting room.

As therapists begin to see the world through a lens of race,
the process of incorporating conversations about race into therapy becomes more seamless and considerably less arduous.
Viewing the process through a racial lens helps the therapist to
see more, to be more racially curious, and to generate a natural and incessant flow of racially grounded questions that are
authentic, substantive, and intimacy-building. It extricates the
therapist from being sidetracked and/or distracted by the usual
internal questions that many therapists have regarding "When
is the appropriate time to raise the race issue?" "How do I introduce race without being offensive?" or "What if I say the wrong
thing?" These are the types of frequently occurring internal
questions that often result in some therapists choosing caution,
self-protection, and avoidance of racial engagement which often

culminate in Clients of Color being either underserved, in the best of cases, or retraumatized, in the worst of circumstances. It is challenging for therapists to talk openly, honestly, fluently, and confidently about that which they cannot *see* (conceptualize) or which they don't fully understand. There is a strong positive correlation between possessing a racial lens and enhanced fluency in talking effectively about race in therapy. When a therapist's visual acuity has been sharpened to see the subtleties of race, conversations tend to become more fluent and less onerous. When race is a regular part of our conversations, it is easier for it to be a regular conversation.

Talking About Race: Becoming Racially-Lingual

It is very difficult to talk about that which is invisible or hard to see and comprehend in its full complexity. In this regard, the development of a racial lens makes talking about race a little less cumbersome. Obviously, effectively addressing racial trauma in therapy is nearly impossible to do when merely talking about race at all is a challenge. Developing a proficiency in talking about race— or becoming *racially-lingual,* as I prefer to think about it—is an integral component of the fundamental preparatory work that an aspiring racially sensitive, trauma-informed therapist must accomplish. This is no small feat, given the awkwardness and vacillation between the loud silence and emotional volatility that often characterizes most everyday efforts to discuss race in society. Both in and out of therapy, there is no shortage of ineptitude when it comes to having meaningful, substantive, and engaging conversations about race. The lack of experience and success in talking about race outside of therapy, coupled with the failure to develop a racial lens, are major barriers to effectively addressing race in therapy. Consequently, racial issues in therapy are often ignored or addressed in a very hypercautious, cursory manner. Therapists tend to struggle with how to introduce race into the therapeutic discourse, with what to say, with how to manage fears and anxieties about saying the wrong thing, and with how to respond effectively to racial microaggressions in an effective way. The lack of knowledge regarding these and other related issues often leaves therapists feeling trapped into offering superficial, trepid responses to race related issues, if they respond overtly at all. Often, when a response is offered, it lacks conceptual depth, racial sensitivity, or a sense of curiosity that invites a deeper conversation.

One of the many clinical benefits of developing a racial lens is that the therapist is much more adept at seeing and understanding the intricacies of race and of its potential connection to the presenting problem and/or the therapeutic relationship, which makes hypothesizing about race a much more fluid process. In this regard, developing a racial lens alleviates burden on the therapist of having to laboriously search for "appropriate" questions to ask or comments to make. Instead, what the therapist can see, coupled with what they know, serves as an incubator for producing racially based questions, hypotheses, curiosities, observations, and reflections that can be effortlessly and naturally incorporated into the process of therapy.

While the process of seeing and developing a racial lens is instrumental in facilitating the ability to talk about race in therapy, it is by no means a panacea. Having the ability to incorporate race-talk skillfully and effectively into the therapeutic process requires more than simply becoming more conversant with the language of race, although this is an incredibly important task to learn and master. The task of effectively talking about race also involves personal development.

There are six critical relational factors that therapists must master to enhance their ability to effectively integrate and navigate racial issues in therapy. These relational factors represent *metaphorical muscles* that must be exercised and developed, otherwise they atrophy and serve as a major clinical impediment to working with racially traumatized clients. The six muscles are: 1) intensity; 2) intimacy; 3) transparency; 4) authenticity; 5) congruency; and 6) complexity. As these muscles continue to develop, so does our ability to have difficult conversations that are progressive and sustainable.

Intensity—This critical relational factor is the metaphorical muscle that refers to both the willingness and capacity to develop an increasing level of comfort with discomfort. It means deliberately and metaphorically "stretching" oneself beyond one's normal and customary comfort zone. When making the effort to enhance the capacity for intensity, it is imperative to have an unrelenting and resounding commitment to asking one more racially based question than one is comfortable asking or making one more statement than one is comfortable making. When we verbalize only what we are comfortable stating, we tend to just do what we always do, even when there is compelling data to confirm that repetitively "doing what we always do" is not effective. While doing what we always do promotes comfort through familiarity, it offers little support to promoting a deeper and more sustainable conversation. Surrendering to the silence that is often considered the solution to the fear of saying the "wrong" thing only serves to perpetuate the status quo. It forecloses virtually all possibilities for discussing race and ultimately unintentionally further marginalizes the issue of race in therapy.

In cross-racial conversations, both in and out of therapy, intensity is often difficult to achieve for two principle interrelated reasons: 1) whites tend to conflate "comfort" and "safety"; and 2) People of Color withhold the expression of deeply seated authentic feelings that add intensity to a conversation for fear of reprisal by whites. Sometimes People of Color also worry that they will express their underlying, often suppressed and accumulated, unexpressed feelings in a way that is construed by whites as "threatening." When whites express feeling "unsafe" in a cross-racial conversation, it is usually virtually impossible for the conversation to continue. This dynamic unfortunately contributes to and perpetuates the ultra-polite, cautious, guarded, and nonsubstantive conversations that often characterize so many of our attempts to effectively engage with each other cross-racially. The inability or failure to "lean into conversations" about race often strips the therapeutic process of the type of trust, safety, and intimacy that are so critical to the process of change.

Intimacy—This critical relational factor is often entangled with the intensity muscle. In fact, in some ways the successful "exercising" of this muscle is predicated on the strength of the intensity muscle. The intimacy muscle is highly germane to promoting and sustaining meaningful and progressive challenging conversations. It refers to the ability to express empathy and vulnerability as well as the ability to *be* vulnerable. In its purest form, it means approaching the conversation with a spirit of openness and non-defensiveness. The presence of intimacy helps to underscore the important role of reciprocity in relationships—the notion that we are in this together, even in the face of stark differences. It helps to exorcise blame and deliberate shame-inducing responses from the conversation and ultimately from the relationships as well. Intimacy is often the emotional barometer and regulator that adjusts to the ebb and flow of the conversation.

In progressive, difficult conversations, intensity and intimacy are often virtually inextricable. When intimacy is increased in a conversation, it contributes to an increase in intensity. This process usually allows for a deepening of the conversation. The reverse process is NOT true. Thus, it is possible to heighten intensity in a conversation without any corresponding increase in intimacy, and these types of conversations that are prone to rapid escalation without any possibility for meaningful resolution. A major guiding principle that should be exercised is that whenever and wherever intensity is increased, it is essential for intimacy to increase as well. Intimacy is the connective tissue, the relational glue, that holds the interaction together, especially in the wake of increased intensity. Relational intensity devoid of intimacy is seldom productive and is virtually always destructive and hurtful to all involved. Thus, the demonstrated ability of the therapist to infuse elements of intimacy into the therapeutic process, especially during race related conversations, is of paramount importance. For example, the traditional therapeutic approach, in which the therapist "has license" to ask clients (especially Clients of Color) a wide range of difficult, personal, imposing, and penetrating questions without disclosing any information such as the potential origins of the questions, is strongly contraindicated when providing racially sensitive, trauma-informed therapy. The adjustment that is needed is not one that would require the therapist to indiscriminately share random personal information with a client. Instead, the development of the intimacy-muscle positions the therapist to be emotionally present and appropriately share relevant information that will ultimately foster a greater level of therapeutic trust and empathy and will deepen the relational bond. For instance, the therapist who shares the following with a client would be using both the intimacy and intensity muscles: "As a white therapist, I am devoting more time and space in my work to having real conversations about race, and yet there is always a part of me that is sitting with a little bit of fear and anxiety about saying the wrong thing. I won't let it stop me, and I want you to know I will be holding myself accountable; however, if by chance I miss something, I hope you will let me know how you have been impacted."

Transparency—Intimacy is difficult, if not impossible, to express if one is unable to be transparent. Though it is possible to be transparent without being intimate. Consider the aforementioned example in which the therapist acknowledges the "fear and anxiety of saying the wrong thing," which conveys transparency and vulnerability. The therapist could have stopped short of disclosing this information and noted only that they are "devoting more time and space to have real conversations about race because [they] think it is really important to do so," which would be an example of transparency devoid of intimacy.

The transparency muscle, when properly exercised, requires the therapist to be willing to show oneself and to be seen. At its core, this muscle rejects the notion of the therapist as a blank slate. It presupposes that the therapist is a living, thinking being who affects what happens in the process of therapy and may, on occasion, be affected by it as well. Transparency is the major vehicle by which intimacy is achieved. When one is transparent in a conversation, there is openness, a willingness to admit, own, and exhibit all parts of oneself. Intimacy is the vehicle that allows for the authentic expression of this to occur. There is a willingness to engage in a process of self-reflection and self-interrogation. It is the willingness to be transparent that makes it possible for the therapist to be known and visible to clients. Here, again, the development and exercising of the transparency-muscle is not to suggest that therapists should indiscriminately place every thought or feeling they experience on full display. Rather, it means that the therapist participates in the therapeutic process and relationship as a thinking, feeling, emotionally accessible human being and not a stoic, emotionally detached, preprogrammed robot, fiercely holding onto false claims of being a tabula rasa.

Transparency involves an interlocking, two-step process. On the one hand, it involves possessing the willingness to *show one-*

self, to let down "professional" guardedness, and to demonstrate a willingness to question longstanding sacred therapeutic principles rooted in white ideology that sanction objectivity and emotional detachment. Hence, it challenges the notion of the therapist as an apolitical, blank-slate, flawless tactician uninfluenced by the broader sociocultural context in which one is embedded and practices. In other words, transparency involves appropriately risking exposure of those parts of who we are as clinicians that might be considered potential vulnerabilities. The other aspect of transparency centers on the willingness to be *seen.* It is possible to show oneself but not want to be *seen.* When this occurs, it makes it difficult to embrace feedback regarding how one is perceived by those with whom one is interacting. The recipient of the feedback insists, often in an unaccepting and argumentative manner, "Well this is not how I see myself . . . . I am not who you say I am nor how you see me," rather than making a concerted effort to consider and conduct an analysis of the possible schism in perceptions. This is the part of transparency that is entangled with the intimacy muscle.

Another dimension of transparency centers on those who *want* to be seen and ultimately understood while also being reticent to show themself. The lack of comfort with intimacy and transparency makes it difficult to open up enough to show oneself, despite the underlying desire to be genuinely understood. It is virtually impossible to have meaningful race-related conversations when one or more of the participants are withholding parts of themselves from the conversation. It is a major impediment to the therapeutic process and relationship when it is the therapist who takes such a stance. The lack of transparency in a conversation not only affects intimacy and intensity but also makes another critical relational factor—authenticity—difficult to achieve.

Authenticity—In short, this muscle refers to demonstrating the ability to say what you mean and mean what you say. Authenticity helps to promote transparency. Conversely, it is difficult to be authentic if/when one is unwilling to be transparent. This is why simply providing therapists with "skills" regarding what should be said is often limited and short sighted. It is quite possible to know "the right words to say" and still have the conversation, and ultimately the therapeutic relationship, fail to prosper because the "how it was said" overshadows and/or negates the "right" words that were said. Throughout every fabric of society, race relationships have historically been marked by an unwillingness or an inability to talk about race in a clear, direct, uncoded, and unambiguous way. Many of our experiences in society, especially cross-racial ones, have been characterized by guarded, euphemistic, and inauthentic approaches to talking about race. Unfortunately, therapy has been a microcosm of how society as a whole engages with race. When one fails to be authentic, whether in therapy or in life, the ability to communicate congruently is inhibited.

Congruency—The development of this muscle is achieved when what one is thinking, saying, and exhibiting behaviorally are perfectly aligned. In other words, there is a compelling compatibility and coherence between what is conveyed verbally and nonverbally as well as in what one appears to be thinking. While it is difficult to truly know what another is thinking, it is surprisingly easy to detect when someone's thoughts and verbal disclosures are not tightly aligned. A lack of congruency compromises one's ability to be authentic, and the absence of authenticity compromises congruency. Once again, this underscores just how interrelated all the relational factors (muscles) are. The presence or absence of the congruency muscle is critical to building a strong therapeutic alliance with Clients of Color. Since so many acts of racism have been, and continue to be, subtlety perpetrated and often in direct contradiction with what might otherwise have been conveyed, articulated, or promised, many People of Color have learned that what many whites *say* regarding race is not nearly as revelatory and trustworthy as observing what they *do*. Boyd-Franklin (2003) noted that Black families often operate on "vibes," which is an intuitive sense of knowing. My great-grandmother, the grand-daughter of a slave, who didn't have Boyd-Franklin's academic pedigree or clinical acumen, often referred to "hunches" that she had in dealing with white people. It was commonplace for her to base the trust she invested, or neglected to invest, in whites based on a "hunch" or an intuitive sense that she often said "something is telling me." Vibes, hunches, and the "something is telling me" phenomena are all based on lived experiences in which the words and deeds of many white people have been lacking in congruency. It is perhaps what inspired the words of the great poet Maya Angelou (n.d.) when she stated: "People will forget what you said. People will forget what you did. But people will never forget how you made them feel." In this vein, therapists can be taught all the right words to articulate, but if they are expressed in ways that are perceived as inauthentic and/or incongruent, the delivery of racially sensitive, trauma-informed therapy will be a nonstarter. The schism between what is spoken verbally and what is conveyed nonverbally is often one of the major obstacles to effective cross-racial work. The therapist's ability to reconcile this split is often facilitated by the development of the complexity muscle.

Complexity—This critical relational factor is vital to conducting and sustaining difficult conversations. It refers to the ability to simultaneously hold together two seemingly disparate thoughts or feelings. It is the ability to embrace complexity that allows a therapist to acknowledge and remain open to the possibility that they can initiate an action with a client that can be simultaneously well intentioned and hurtful. In other words, the complexity muscle allows the therapist to be open to the possibility that they can say the all the right words and a client still may be offended by what they experience as a lack of authenticity. And one can be passionately committed to conducting an antiracist practice and behave in ways that support a racist ideology. Thus, it is complexity that enables us to see "the good that is contained in the bad" and vice versa. Complexity facilitates the promotion of *both/and* positioning in difficult conversations and helps to avoid the traps of *either/or* thinking that often prematurely forecloses possibilities and stifles interactions. The complexity muscle also strongly encourages the therapist to be just as vigilant in analyzing themself as they might be in analyzing another (the client). The development of the complexity muscle allows the therapist to stay authentically engaged in the relationship, despite the gaps that might exist between their noble intentions and the adverse consequences that a client may experience. It is the complexity muscle that potentially enables a therapist to sit comfortably with the discomfort of their incongruity, for example. In other words, a well-developed complexity muscle empowers the therapist to "accept and explore" possible misalignments that exist between their actions and their words regarding, for example, issues of race.

A crucial interplay exists between and among these relational factors. Thus, it is neither prudent nor sufficient to rely on one independent factor to completely transform a difficult conversation. The commitment to effectively participate in a difficult conversation also requires similar dedication to developing some facility with and/or mastery of incorporating these critical relational factors into one's modus operandi. The development and refinement of the six critical relational factors, which function as metaphorical relational muscles, are essential to increasing the ability to talk about race in therapy and to explore the invisible wounds of racial trauma in a comprehensive manner.

Understanding the Invisible Wounds of Racial Trauma

The entire next section of this book will be devoted to promoting a comprehensive understanding of the invisible wounds of racial trauma. Thus, the discussion here will be brief and is intended to introduce the wounds that will be highlighted in subsequent chapters. The seven invisible wounds that will be described in the ensuing sections are commonly shared experiences for many People of Color, although they may vary in intensity, mode of expression, and how they manifest. While Chapters 6 through 12 will present the wounds in a linear fashion with seemingly clear lines of demarcation between and among them, the real-life manifestations of the wounds are infinitely more complex, multidimensional, and difficult to discern. It is difficult to convey, in print, the nuances of the wounds and how there is a type of symbiotic relationship between and among them, such as how a client's arrogant-appearing bravado can be simultaneously rooted in a deep sense of internalized devaluation, rage, and underlying anxiety about survival—none of which is overtly acknowledged by the client or therapist.

In the day-to-day lives of People of Color, invisible wounds are not only delicately and complexly intertwined with each other, they may also be compounded by the presence of other threads of sociocultural oppression and trauma associated with other marginalized identities in addition to race. People of Color's lives are neither monolithic nor solely defined by race, although race is powerfully significant. It is often the case that People of Color who also identify as female, gender queer, nonbinary, transgender, poor, or working class or who are living with a disability (visible and nonvisible) must navigate very complicated lives marred by other forms of discrimination, bigotry, and hatred in addition to grappling with racial trauma. For example, Black transgender women must struggle not only with racial trauma but also with the steady and horrific assaults of transphobia. Unfortunately, this is often the case even within some areas of the Black community and other Communities of Color. Intersectional sociocultural trauma is a form of complex trauma that results from the concurrent exposure to and suffering from multiple layers of sociocultural traumas that are simultaneously separate and interconnected. The racial trauma wounds experienced by People of Color living with a disability or those who identify as female, queer, transgender, or poor are often exacerbated by other forms of sociocultural trauma and oppression. For example, a gay Puerto Rican, Latino male may very well find himself plagued not only by wounds of psychological homelessness from being a Latino and Puerto Rican, but also by wounds from ostracism for being gay, the latter quite possibly occurring even within his and other Communities of Color. The intensity and severity of psychological homelessness will be very different for a gay Man of Color than for a Man of Color who enjoys both the privilege and protective factor of being, or being perceived as a cisgender, heterosexual man.

It is imperative that therapists who are committed to providing racially sensitive, trauma-informed therapy have a deep understanding of the intricacies of racial trauma and the myriad ways it is often entangled with other manifestations of sociocultural trauma. The therapist must be equipped to see and address the whole of a client's suffering while also zeroing in on, with laser pinpoint precision, the wounds of racial trauma and the overall pervasive impact of race and racial oppression on the client's everyday life experiences and functioning.

Having a comprehensive understanding of the invisible wounds of racial trauma empowers and equips the therapist to work intensively with racial trauma. It provides the therapist with the insights they will need to see the symbiotic nature of the wounds, the web of toxic stress, and the entanglement of intersectional sociocultural trauma wounds, and to "surgically" disentangle them when necessary.

Developing a comprehensive understanding of the anatomy of racial trauma is a necessary and daunting task for all therapists. For many Therapists of Color, this process often involves coming to terms with and confronting the fact that as therapists who have been People of Color much longer than we have been therapists, we are not immune to racial trauma nor the wounds associated with it. Thus, positioning oneself to work intensively with racial trauma requires engaging in some form of process devoted to healing oneself. There is similar work that white therapists must commit to as well. White therapists must spend time interrogating whiteness and their historical relationship with it. They must also be unrelentingly committed to exploring, coming to terms with, and confronting how their metaphorical bloody fingers and footprints are deeply etched on the souls of People of Color and are connected to their racial trauma. White clinicians must also be willing to deeply question and explore how to authentically engage in a relationship designed to promote racial healing while bearing the visage of the "harmer." This type of racial transcendence is possible for white therapists; however, it requires being committed to doing deep self-reflective work. For white clinicians and Clinicians of Color, these important preparatory and developmental processes require an ongoing commitment to thoroughly engage in racially based self-of-the-therapist work.

"Self"-of-the-Therapist Work

(Note: References to "self" are placed in quotations to indicate that I use this term only to achieve linguistic accuracy. If I were establishing fidelity with what I believe conceptually, I would use "selves of the therapist" because I consider it a more accurate reference.)

Since the bulk and heart of most clinical training take a colorblind approach, therapists interested in working with People of Color and treating the invisible wounds of racial trauma must commit to participating in comprehensive, racially focused self-of-the-therapist work. This type of work not only enhances the therapist's ability to develop a racial lens and become racially-lingual, it also assists the therapist in developing racially "trained eyes."

When therapists' eyes are trained, they become more self-inquisitive. They are not only curious about their clients' lives and the process of therapy but become curious about themselves as well. They begin to ask as many self-reflective questions about themselves as they may ask clients (Hardy, 2018, p. 8).

It is through ongoing self-of-the-therapist work that one begins to engage in the racially based process of self-examination, self-interrogation, and self-reflection as well as to develop a keen sense of who one is as a racial being.

This ongoing work is a place and space where white clinicians are encouraged to seriously explore what it means to be white and, especially, a white therapist. It also offers a place for Therapists of Color to be supported and encouraged while exploring how racial oppression, racial trauma, and internalized whiteness may affect both their professional identity and their clinical work with Clients of Color. The potency of high-quality self-of-the-therapist work is that it is personally transformative. Through a comprehensive process of self-interrogation and self-reflection, it helps the therapist to develop a deeper understanding of one's personal beliefs, biases, and emotional reactions. The work is largely experiential and serves as a type of social laboratory that enables the therapist to learn not only cognitively but also by doing and experiencing. It is the focus on race that differentiates this particular approach from the other more traditionally focused self-of-the-therapist methods.

Racially focused self-of-the-therapist work is essential for therapists of all races who are committed to working with racial trauma and Clients of Color. The centerpiece of the work is devoted to helping clinicians develop a multidimensional view of the self (Hardy, 2018) as a prerequisite to working with Clients of Color. This view enables the therapist to see themself more complexly, which entails coming to terms with the notion that one is neither a tabula rasa nor simply comprised of a singular self. Instead, it becomes clear that the therapist is shaped by their social context and is comprised of multiple selves.

The concept of the *multidimensional self* is based on the assertion that what we conceptualize as "the self," an undifferentiated entity, is really the product of threads of multiple semi-discrete selves. Thus, there are multiple dimensions that comprise the self. For example, each of us has dimensions of selves that are significantly shaped by race, class, gender, sexual orientation and identity, religion, ethnicity, family of origin, and so on. One could argue that each of us has an infinite number of selves, each providing us with a prism through which we see the world and through which we believe we are seen. A therapist who insists on seeing themself as an emotionally focused, psychodynamic, behavioral, group, couples, or individual (or some other narrow and rigidly defined category) therapist only, for example, is unintentionally setting up a major barrier to providing effective, racially sensitive, trauma-informed therapy. Ignoring and/or remaining oblivious to one's social location (Watts-Jones, 2010)—whether it be male, heterosexual, cisgender, able-bodied, middleclass, Sikh, etc.—and to how such contextual variables inform who one is, what is seen or not seen, and how one may be potentially perceived by clients contributes to major therapeutic impediments.

Performing racially focused self-of-the-therapist work acquaints the clinician with their multiple selves while also accentuating the salience of the racial self. Through this process, the therapist develops a sense of self as a racial being, which sharpens their ability to develop a racial lens, talk about race, and become more intimately acquainted with the intricacies of racial trauma and the ways in which one's racial background and identity are shaped by either racial privilege or subjugation. It also facilitates the therapist's ability to establish a greater appreciation for how a client's racial background and identity are also attached to positions of privilege or subjugation and how these experiences may impact all aspects of the client's life. For a more detailed discussion of this work, the reader is referred to *Antiracist Approaches for Shaping Theoretical and Practical Paradigms* (Hardy, 2016).

For white clinicians, the major task of this work involves developing a critical understanding of white privilege, unpacking what it means to be white, and increasing one's capacity to decipher the varied ways in which the ideology of whiteness is embedded throughout many of the standard practices of psychotherapy. This task is crucial for many whites who mistakenly assume that the nonracially based oppression they experience from having membership in one or more nonracial minoritized groups absolves them of addressing their white privilege. This miscalculation and misunderstanding about the nature of white privilege by some whites, regardless of their personal exposure to other forms of sociocultural oppression, often hampers their ability to work effectively with People of Color and racialized trauma. Too often, it, unfortunately, leads to the faulty and somewhat dangerous act of equalizing suffering, such as equating the class oppression associated with growing up as a poor white person with the racial oppression associated with growing up as a Person of Color. It is vital for white therapists to have a growth-producing place and opportunities to explore the full anatomy of the "centrality of whiteness" (Hardy, 2022) and what it means to be a white clinician working with racially traumatized People of Color. In fact, it is also important for Therapists of Color to engage in this work, although the focus is different.

The complicated dilemmas that many Therapists of Color must confront and negotiate are seemingly endless, yet they are rarely overtly acknowledged or addressed throughout the field. Therapists of Color live their lives as People of Color before becoming, while being, and after being a therapist, and unfortunately they are not shielded from racial oppression simply because they are clinicians. Since People of Color are generally not afforded many opportunities to understand, address, or metabolize racialized trauma, it lives valiantly in most of us, regardless of who we are and how or where we are stationed in life. The core of the racially focused self-of-the-therapist work that Therapists of Color must engage in centers on understanding, addressing, and unpacking the intricacies and residuals of racial trauma. Additionally, this work must also address the inherent tensions that invariably exist between being in a position of power and privilege as a therapist while also occupying a racially subjugated position as a Person of Color. The opportunities to be emotionally triggered by working with racially traumatized clients, whose race related struggles and wounds may mirror the therapist's, constantly present the Therapist of Color with potential emotional triggers, leaving very little time and space for processing and/or reflection.

Racially focused self-of-the-therapist work can provide Therapists of Color with a zone of safety in which to breathe. This metaphorical breathing room offers a type of sanctuary for Therapists of Color in which they may name, acknowledge, and have validated their respective invisible wounds of racial trauma and their effect on the therapist's work.

For white clinicians and Clinicians of Color, doing the work that is crucial to participating in racially focused self-of-the-therapist work usually cannot be achieved through the more classical approaches to clinical supervision. It also should not be awkwardly tacked onto the self-proclaimed colorblind approaches to self-of-the-therapist work that highlights the importance of the family of origin while concomitantly remaining woefully and inexplicably silent and inattentive to issues of race. Even if therapists are not under supervision and/or in training, it is incumbent on them to remain engaged in a process of racial self-examination, self-interrogation, and self-reflection. The following questions—15 for white clinicians, followed by 15 for Clinicians of Color—may be useful in beginning that process.

These sample questions are important for white therapists to explore in their ongoing work toward becoming better equipped to provide racially sensitive, trauma-informed therapy with Clients of Color:

1. What from my lived experience as a white person qualifies me to work with Clients of Color? What from my lived experience as a white person could make me a danger to working with Clients of Color? What from my lived experience as a white person could be an asset for me in working with Clients of Color?

2. What is an aspect of my racial history that should give me pause about working intensively with racially traumatized People of Color?

3. What is an aspect of my racial history that contributes to my preparedness to work intensively with racially traumatized People of Color?

4. What cross-racial experiences have I had with People of Color in which I, the white person, was a) in the numerical minority; b) not in charge nor in a position of power; and c) in a space where the norms and mores of People of Color defined the experience?

5. As a white person, what meaning do I attach to my answer to and reflections on questions 4 and 5?

6. How often over the course of my career have I, as a white person, been responsible for (administratively or organizationally) reporting to a Person of Color who was *not* responsible for reporting to another white person?

7. What shame inducing and/or unresolved racial issues are deeply rooted in my family of origin that I have yet to completely reconcile, come to terms with, or address?

8. What is a racially based stereotyped message that I once believed and now reject but still finding myself periodically acting, thinking, or behaving as if I believed it were true?

9. What are at least two deeply subtle and internalized dimensions of white superiority that I still have difficulty releasing or letting go of, despite my efforts? What meaning do I attach to my answer?

10. Have I ever admitted to myself that I have, at some point in my life, used derogatory and/or racist terms to refer to Black, Latinx, Asian, and/or Indigenous People? If/when asked this question by a Colleague or Friend of Color, could I, would I, or did I answer honestly?

11. What aspect of my own trauma or suffering inspires me to work with racial trauma?

12. What life lessons can I extract from my experiences with trauma, oppression, and or personal hardships to inform

my clinical work and increase my efficacy with People of Color and racial trauma?

13. What residuals from my personal trauma, oppression, or hardships pose the greatest threat to my work with people with racial trauma?

14. What is the one question that I, as a white clinician, would absolutely dread a Client of Color asking me?

15. What was the most dominant and recurring emotion I experienced while answering these questions?

The following questions are designed to help facilitate the self-interrogation process for Therapists of Color:

1. What are the circumstances or conditions that often activate me to question whether I am an imposter?

2. What are the subtle and highly sophisticated ways in which I still make too much effort to please white people?

3. What is the profile of the Person of Color within my race that I dislike, struggle with, or hold contempt for? What meaning do I attach to this?

4. How would my life change and what would my life be like if/when I permanently stopped code-switching? Or, how did my life change and what is it like now that I am no longer willing to code-switch?

5. At what age and/or stage of life will I be prepared to irreversibly commit to releasing *all* the energy that I devote to pleasing, accommodating, or taking care of white people?

6. What do I need to change in my life and/or self-perception to wholly embrace all my race-related rage?

7. How do I or will I channel my race-related rage?

8. When I have somber thoughts or emotions connected to

> racial injustice, who are my tears for, who or what is my pain connected to, and whose race-related grief am I honoring, holding, and/or transporting?
>
> 9. What pride issues do I hold about being who I am racially?
> 10. What traces of anti-Black racism remain embedded in me?
> 11. What traces of anti-Indigenous bias remain embedded in me?
> 12. What traces of anti-Asian racism remain embedded in me?
> 13. What traces of anti-Latinx bias remain embedded in me?
> 14. What traces of bias do I hold toward light-complexioned/white-passing, mixed-race People of Color?
> 15. What is the race related survival strategy that runs through my blood, that was passed onto me from those before me, that still serves me today, and that I will certainly pass onto the next of my ancestral kin?

Positioning oneself to address race and racial trauma effectively in therapy requires considerable (self) preparatory work and personal will. It requires ongoing work that extends well beyond the mastery of skills and techniques divorced from racial self-interrogation and self-of-the-therapist work. It requires the therapist to continually strive toward becoming racially sensitive and trauma informed, with the clear understanding that this is a process without a finite end point. Becoming a racially sensitive, trauma-informed therapist is the precursor to providing racially sensitive, trauma-informed therapy.

SUMMARY

Historically, most psychotherapy approaches have not devoted substantive attention to the issues of race and racial trauma in a comprehensive way. The paucity of attention devoted to race means that therapists committed to working intensively with

People of Color and racial trauma must commit to engaging in racially focused preparatory work. This chapter identified several critical developmental steps and preparatory processes that therapists must accomplish to ensure that they are duly equipped to provide effective racially sensitive, trauma-informed treatment. This chapter identified the steps of developing a racial lens; becoming racially-lingual; understanding the invisible wounds of racial trauma and the intersections with other sociocultural trauma; and engaging in racially focused self-of-the-therapist work as important precursors to providing racially sensitive, trauma-informed therapy. The successful negotiation of these critical steps paves the way for the therapist to be more emotionally present with Clients of Color and to take a more active and racially sensitive therapeutic posture when addressing the invisible wounds of racial trauma.

CHAPTER 5

Therapeutic Principles

It is a challenging endeavor to address race and racial trauma issues thoroughly and effectively within the existing parameters of most traditional approaches to therapy. A *neglect of context,* which is the failure to seriously consider the relationship between human suffering and the sociocultural context in which it is often embedded, permeates most traditional models of therapy. This is especially true regarding the notable role that race plays in our society, which makes it difficult to fully address the psychoemotional impact that race and racism have on the lives of People of Color. When the suffering of People of Color is divorced from the racialized context in which it is embedded, the therapist's ability to provide effective, racially sensitive, trauma-informed therapy is severely curtailed. Hence, working with racial trauma wounds requires some revisioning of how the process of therapy is structured, executed, and, most importantly, how it conceptualizes the intertwinement of human suffering, racial oppression, and trauma. In this vein, there are several interrelated core principles that provide a conceptual foundation for providing racially sensitive, trauma-informed treatment that helps to operationalize the revisioning process that is required.

These principles comprise a quasi-meta framework that enables the therapist to address the invisible wounds of racial trauma in a thoughtful and racially sensitive manner, whether they are designated as the presenting problem or not. This is particularly important since, as noted earlier, there is no codified language for identifying racial trauma, even though it may be an organizing dynamic in treatment and even if/when it remains unnamed.

The core principles provide the groundwork for structuring a client's therapy and how it will ultimately be approached. It sets the stage for addressing racial trauma wounds in a comprehensive, wholistic, and systemic manner. The major emphasis of this therapeutic work is largely on *soul work*, a focus that helps to restore all the parts of one's being that have been nicked, bruised, and decimated by the forces of racial trauma and oppression. The point is, the therapist's drive to fix a specific presenting problem should not overshadow the client's need for the space to process their being, to promote a type of *spiritual liberation,* and to sit quietly and perhaps uncomfortably with themself and the complexity of their conditions while the therapist bears witness. This type of process is so vitally important because many People of Color, despite the enormity and prevalence of racial trauma in their lives, have very few sacred places where dedicated time and space are granted for the sole purpose of metabolizing the emotional strains and stresses of racial trauma.

The core principles that undergird this therapeutic work and that help to shape it are:

1. Racial trauma work is relationship work.
2. Race must be named explicitly, with the therapist functioning as the broker of permission.

3. Racial awareness enhancement must be threaded through-out the process.

4. The creation of the therapeutic milieu as a racially safe, sacred, and self-reflective space is imperative.

5. The therapeutic process must be centered on racially oriented restorative and transformative work.

6. Space for deep emotionally focused work, expression, and catharsis must be seamlessly integrated throughout the therapeutic process.

7. The naming and promotion of self-love is a necessary and important dimension of the work.

8. The invisible wounds of racial trauma must be named and addressed.

9. Treatment protocols must be expanded to include nontraditional therapeutic aids and racially sanctioned healing practices.

10. Storytelling is a key component of the work and must be named explicitly.

Attending to and integrating these principles throughout the therapeutic process is not a linear process, with a predetermined start- and endpoint. These principles are fluid, seamless, and malleable to the evolving therapeutic process.

CORE THERAPEUTIC PRINCIPLES

The Centrality of Relationships

Adherence to this principle requires the therapist to not just high-light and work with relationships in the most concrete sense but also to be guided by *relational thinking* as well. The enduring focus on relationships enables the therapist to constantly entertain and explore the client's network of relationships, including family, friends, and a myriad of other social networks. It invites the therapist to explore how race was managed within a client's family of origin and the racial dynamics that have been transmitted intergenerationally. The therapist must not only be skilled in working with relationships but also possess the willingness and ability to think relationally. In a society and field that highly value and routinely reward individually oriented thinking, engaging in relational thinking is, by no means, an easy feat. At its core, it involves exploring and remaining curious about the (potential) connections between the client's past and present, affect and cognition, racial trauma, and other forms of sociocultural trauma, to cite just a few examples. Operating with this principle in mind, the therapist recognizes that a core component of racial trauma work is relational work, which will necessitate including family members, friends, cultural and community healers, and others into the therapeutic work, with the client's permission and endorsement, of course. It also means that the therapist, as a matter of practice, priority, and principle, recognizes the significance of communal approaches to addressing racial trauma and works assiduously to ensure that they are an integral component of the therapeutic protocol. Whether in the form of affinity groups, healing circles, or intensive racial sensitivity groups, communal engagement work is critical to the healing process. The focus on the centrality of relationships reminds the clinician that the work does not exist in a vacuum and should not be isolated. The therapist must be a willing collaborator and must recognize that commitment to a relational approach is tantamount to embracing the notion that "it takes a village" to work effectively with the wounds of racial trauma. The timing of and the pace for expanding the relational network of the therapeutic process must be dictated by the client's willingness, progress, and movement. Those who are invited to be a part of the process are not there to receive therapy or work on a problem or to serve as a proxy-therapist for the client. Instead, they are strategically invited to provide testimonials, to offer consensual validation, to offer communal affirmation, to bear witness, and, most importantly, to help fortify the client's sense of community as a means of counteracting invisible wounds such as psychological homelessness.

The cultivation of the therapist–client relationship is also a critical dimension of this process, as it always is in therapy. It is through this relationship that the client may also experience, and perhaps even further hone, relationship skills that may have been frayed or obliterated as a result of experiences with racial trauma and oppression. For example, whether dealing with rage, the orientation toward survival, or an assaulted sense of self, all these wounds can have a dramatic effect on how a client communicates and participates in relationships. Unfortunately, the development of good, effective relational skills is seldom enough to conquer psychological homelessness, or any other trauma wound, though it helps. The therapeutic emphasis on self-love is also critical to addressing and ameliorating deep feelings of not belonging, of devaluation, or of an assaulted sense of self. Since these wounds are tied inextricably to race, it is important for the therapist to center race in the therapeutic process.

The Centrality of Race and Therapist as Broker of Permission

Conducting racially sensitive, trauma-informed therapy requires the therapist to have the willingness and requisite skills to discuss issues of race, whether they are connected to the presenting problem or not. Part of the purpose behind developing a racial lens is to enhance the therapist's ability to see how race can be threaded within, buried under, and/or alongside a host of other issues that otherwise may be difficult to discern with racially untrained eyes. Therapeutic conversations about race don't necessarily have to center around a process of uncovering and/or discovering deep underlying racial issues or secrets; the goal and purpose are much more modest. The goal is to provide a sacred place where conversations of race, regardless of magnitude or severity, can be conducted sincerely, authentically, and respectfully. It is the therapist's responsibility to jump start these conversations. In other words, it is the role and responsibility of the therapist to be the broker of permission (Hardy, 2016).

Unfortunately, in both our personal and professional lives, we tend to operate under a metaphorical gag order with regard to talking about race honestly, openly, and authentically, especially in cross-racial spaces. The volatility and explosiveness associated with talking about race create caution, trepidation, and high levels of anxiety that feed avoidance of engaging in conversations. Admittedly, the process of therapy has not been immune to the effects of the racial gag order under which society operates.

It is important for the therapist to take an active and proactive role in introducing and acknowledging race in the therapeutic process. The therapist must do so by refraining from asking the client to self-disclose about race before it has been established that it will be safe to do so. Therapist-generated questions such as "How does it feel to be in therapy with me as a(n) [your race] therapist?" should be staunchly avoided. The reliance on such a question would represent a failed attempt at assuming the role of broker of permission because it places the burden of initiating self-disclosure about race on the shoulders of the client, the least powerful person in the relationship. It is a completely different matter if the client initiates the disclosure from the outset, without a prompt from the therapist. A more effective and racially just way for the therapist to execute the broker of permission role would be to take the initial responsibility of introducing the phenomenon of race into the therapeutic process. Ideally, this should be done in the most seamless and benign way possible. Locating and identifying oneself racially is one of many ways this task can be accomplished. The ultimate purpose of this process is to convey to the client not only that it is permissible to talk about race here but also that it will be a natural and integral part of the work they will be doing together. The seamless centering and acknowledgment of race early in the evolving therapeutic process is a critical preliminary step toward establishing therapy as a racially safe and sacred place for engaging in intensive race-related work. It also potentially demonstrates some baseline awareness and sensitivity to issues of race, which can never be taken for granted.

Racial Awareness Enhancement

Since the effects of racial oppression and trauma are so insidious, it is often difficult for those who are perpetually harmed by it to fully comprehend all the ways in which one's life may have been affected. The wounds of trauma, as is the major topic of this book, are often invisible and complexly entangled with an assortment of other issues and conditions. These wounds do not exist in a vacuum and can often affect other areas of one's life without there being an understanding of a direct association with racial trauma. For these reasons, it is important for the therapist to maximize the use of the therapy space by "connecting the racialized dots" for a client, such as by assisting a client in understanding the full anatomy of rage, how it is distinctive from anger, as well as both the functional and dysfunctional aspects of it, etc. By executing this function, the therapist is ipso facto enhancing racial awareness. The point here is not to suggest that People of Color need to be taught about race. Instead, the main point is that it is imperative for the therapist, largely by thinking relationally, to see the big picture and the multitudinous ways in which race, racial trauma, and the struggles of everyday living are often complexly interwoven. For instance, it may be difficult for a Client of Color to see the connections that may exist between being racially devalued and the effects of this on their capacity for self-love, which in turn may contribute to their difficulties in an intimate relationship or marriage.

Ideally, the process of enhancing racial awareness should be a seamless part of the therapeutic process. While it is intended to be somewhat didactic, it should occur within the natural flow of the therapeutic process. Petite lectures and the racial genogram are two major techniques that can be used to implement the principle of enhancing racial awareness. Both can be integrated into the therapeutic process without being disruptive or promoting discontinuity. Chapter 13 is devoted to strategies and techniques and will provide a full description of both approaches as tools for enhancing racial awareness. The willingness of the therapist to initiate, guide, and participate in conversations about race can have a strong positive effect on the therapeutic milieu.

The Creation of the Therapeutic Milieu as a Racially Safe, Sacred, and Self-Reflective Space

Part of the efficacy of all therapeutic work rests on the ability of the therapist to create a safe and sacred space that affords clients the freedom to explore, think, and feel in a growth-enhancing environment. Fortunately, these types of therapeutic environments have been accessible to People of Color, although they have not always been expansive enough to invite and include deep reflection and exploration of race-related issues. When race is introduced, it is often as a slight aside to the main presenting problem or is treated as an ancillary issue of limited significance. I vividly remember how often I, as a client in therapy, brought up issues of race with my white therapist, with whom I had a significant connection, and it never seemed to gain any traction. She always politely acknowledged it, but there was no substance, depth, or authentic curiosity or pursuit of the issue. I quickly concluded that therapy was not the place to delve deeply into issues of race even though it was highly germane to my life experiences and intimately connected to why I was in treatment.

Addressing issue of race and the invisible wounds of trauma attached to it does require the therapist to center issues of race and to ensure the therapeutic milieu is a racially safe and sacred place. This requires the therapist to treat race as an organic component of the process, avoiding the tendency to treat it as a one-and-done, cursory, check-off-the-list type of issue. It also requires the therapist to utilize and incorporate the six relational factors (muscles) into the therapeutic process. In so doing, the therapist demonstrates the ability to engage in conversations about race with intimacy, transparency, congruency, and authenticity while also embracing the intensity and complexity that these engagements often entail. The creation of a racially safe and sacred space for Clients of Color to reflect in contributes to the formation of a foundation that paves the way for racially focused restorative and transformative work to occur.

Focus on Restorative and Transformative Work

Restorative work centers around the notion that racial trauma and oppression strip People of Color of their livelihood and liveliness. Racial oppression, for all practical purposes, is tantamount to experiencing an insidious form of interpersonal violence. It can "lacerate the spirit, scar the soul, and puncture the psyche," (Hardy, 2003, p. 25). Thus, a critical dimension of racial trauma work demands that the therapist take a deliberate, proactive role in assisting Clients of Color to reclaim and restore all that has been stripped (lost) as a result of living life under racially oppressive conditions. The scope of this work is extensive and may include restoring dignity, one's sense of self, and one's love for self. Much of what has been stripped away, diminished, and/or annihilated is integral to the core of one's being, that is, one's soul. As hooks (2001) cautions, "as long as Black folks normalize loss and abandonment, acting as though it is an easy feat to overcome the psychological wounds this pain inflicts, we will not lay the necessary groundwork for emotional well-being that makes love possible" (p. 31). The zone of impact of these assaults often involves mind, body, and soul. Thus, the restorative work that is needed must also address all these domains as well. The work must, in some respects, be devoted to restoring the soul.

Promotion of Self-Love

Providing opportunities for the client to try new ways of being in relationship with themself is also a key dimension of thinking and working relationally. Racial trauma is like an aggressive form of cancer that rapidly metastasizes. It decimates virtually all facets of its victims' lives, emotionally, psychologically, and behaviorally. Internalized devaluation, psychological homelessness, and the assaulted sense of self are all wounds, for example, that can be counteracted by the promotion of self-love, which can be a long and tedious process. First, there is a metaphorical thousand-piece puzzle that must be reconstructed to highlight how one's sense of self has been assaulted and thereby punctured and, in some cases, has destroyed one's capacity for deep self-love. When the whole of one's being has been perpetually and historically assaulted, it is relatively easy to not love oneself. hooks (2001) asserts that

> the practice of self-love is difficult for everyone in a society that is more concerned with profit than well-being, but it is even more difficult for Black folks, as we must constantly resist negative perceptions of Blackness we are encouraged to embrace by the dominant culture. (p. 71)

The assaults on the dignity of People of Color, and Black people specifically, are often multidimensional and usually start very early in life. Consequently, the therapist must work at a slow and methodical pace to explore and uncover all the race-related assaults that have contributed to the sense of internalized devaluation and the assaulted sense of self that a client is experiencing. For so many People of Color, the wholesale societal denigration of the physical traits—hair texture, eye shape, complexion, lips—or other attributes—character, intelligence, work ethic, morals, life choices, ways of talking, overall ways of being—of the members of their group makes self-love nearly impossible. The prevalence of white supremacist ideology throughout our society has historically legitimized and mainstreamed the rampant denigration of virtually all aspects of Black and Brown life. Therefore, therapy must be a safe, sacred, self-reflective place where all deeply internalized self-deprecating messages can be properly explored, challenged, and deconstructed. In fact, "it takes courage and vigilance to create a context where self-love can emerge" (hooks, 2001, p. 56). The investigation into the race-related assaults in each client's life must be broad, multifaceted, and inclusive of family members, friendship networks, clergy, colleagues, and others. It is common for clients to be unaware of all the messages, experiences, and relationships that have contributed to the internalized devaluation and assaulted sense of self that wreaks havoc on the soul. Thus, the struggle with self-love is not always expressed in direct terms; in fact, some People of Color may deny it is an issue while simultaneously disavowing major parts of who they are racially. "Self-loving Black people," according to hooks (2001, p. 73), "work to fend off white colleagues' attempts to pit them against each other." This same notion can be applied to People of Color in general. The disavowal of one's racial self, whether the literal or symbolic self, is the ultimate unconscious expression of an impaired sense of self-love. It is important for the therapist to explore these issues with a modicum of delicacy and sensitivity because they rarely exist without particles of shame that are deeply entangled with devaluation. Exposing a client's shame or behaving in a fashion that triggers feelings of disrespect will almost certainly provoke premature termination of therapy.

Once a therapist assists a client in developing a comprehensive understanding of the forces that undermine self-love and has highlighted all its ramifications, the next vital step involves gradually beginning to plant the seeds for the promotion of self-love. There are two major strategies that can be used to facilitate this process: 1) the use of the Validate-Challenge-Request (VCR) approach and 2) the "as-if" technique. Both techniques are designed to be restorative in nature, that is, they restore one's sense of racial self-affirmation. These techniques will be discussed in greater detail in Section III.

Space for Deep Emotionally Focused Race Work, Expression, and Catharsis

There is deeply rooted complex pain associated with racial trauma. These emotions are often as confusing as they are complex. The expression of these emotions, which contain a mixture of shame, solemn grief, rage, anger, and despair, can be very intense. The damaging-to-the-self messages that People of Color often receive and attempt to live by to ensure the comfort of whites—such as "be a strong person of color"; "don't come across as too angry"; or "don't make everything about race and don't be too hyper-sensitive about it"—lead to the suppression of so many complex emotions. In a sense, racially focused trauma-informed work is intensive, emotionally focused relational work. The therapist must not only contribute to the creation of a space where deep, raw, unfiltered emotions can be expressed but also demonstrate the ability to hold the range of painful feelings that erupt. White therapists must be able to fully participate in this process without allowing guilt, shame, fear, or unexamined and unaddressed internalized racial messages co-opt the process. For instance, the white therapist who is prone to therapeutic paralysis by the presence of Black rage will not be able to offer the cathartic and growth-producing experience their client may need for healing and transformation. Therapists of Color, on the other hand, must be at an emotional, psychological, and experiential place where they can hold the complex trauma-saturated emotions of clients without being dysregulated by their own racial trauma wounds. In all cases, it is crucial for the therapist to have done their self-of-the-therapist work so that they can encourage, inspire, provoke, and hold the deep emotions that surface in the context of conducting intensive racially based trauma work.

Addressing the Invisible Wounds of Racial Trauma

Regardless of the emotions that are generated, the overarching goals and objectives of the therapeutic process must be geared toward addressing the invisible wounds of racial trauma. This must be an intentional focus of the therapy whether racial trauma has been explicitly identified as a component of the presenting problem or not. It is exceedingly uncommon for invisible wounds to be explicitly identified and rare that they are not connected to the presenting problem. This is one reason that an integral part of addressing the wounds of racial trauma involves the process of *naming* them. The purpose and power of naming are twofold: 1) naming reifies the wound and 2) it provides the client and therapist with a shared language with which to talk about the wound. In other words, naming is instrumental in making the invisible visible, the unspoken spoken, the unacknowledged acknowledged, and the unnamed named! Embedded within the process of naming is an invitation for others as well as oneself to *see, affirm,* and *consensually validate* that which has largely been felt but unseen prior to this process.

Addressing the invisible wounds of racial trauma also means that the therapeutic process is designed and being executed to accomplish the following goals, when indicated and appropriate: counteract devaluation and promote self-love; repair relational ruptures and restore a sense of community; promote and support the reclaiming of one's voice; acknowledge loss and create a space for expressions of mourning and grief; rechannel rage; and transform habits of survival into strategies for survival.

Attending to the invisible wounds of racial trauma may be conducted in conjunction with other clinical work that a client may be engaged in, or it may constitute the sole focal point. In either case, it is important that the therapist is mindful of the wounds and makes a concerted effort to devote ample time, effort, and energy to addressing them. This aspect of the work will require the therapist to be amenable to expanding the therapeutic protocol to include nontraditional approaches to healing and transformation, a topic I will now address.

The Use of Nontraditional Therapeutic Aids

The spirit of this principle is not based on a novel idea and is likely one that some therapists may already randomly employ in their clinical work. However, it is important to highlight it here because these nontraditional therapeutic aids are vital to promoting the effective engagement and treatment of People of Color. The use of nontraditional therapeutic aids can expand the scope of therapy from a just-talk process to one that incorporates racially attuned healing practices that do not rely exclusively on speaking or conversing as the nucleus of the therapeutic experience. The use of dance, movement, song, poetry, music, deep breathing, and other mediums can be powerful dimensions of the racial-trauma healing and transformation process. Using the therapy session to sit in solitude and listen to inspirational music that speaks to and for the soul can be a powerful intervention. Encouraging and including dance or other expressions of movement can be quite the catalytic agent for exorcising trauma from the body. Exposing clients to and asking clients to read or openly recite the work of Activists and Healers of Color can be an uplifting and liberatory experience for Clients of Color. Lengthening what is often considered to be the "standard and sacred one-hour therapeutic hour" to create more time to watch relevant short videos with clients can inspire salient trauma-based soul work.

If the therapist is too committed to and indoctrinated into what are considered the *standard principles of clinical practice*, the integration of these nontraditional racially/culturally based therapeutic aids will be challenging. Historically, music, poetry, prose, and other art forms were the only avenues available to People of Color for giving voice to their oppressive experiences, since speaking up directly was not an option and was often life threatening. Thus, these outlets hold a special place in the lives of many People of Color. Raheim (2019) notes that "songs are pervasive across cultures and serve a myriad of functions in the human experience" (p. 449). Raheim further asserts that "given the many functions of songs, they can serve as a valuable tool in therapeutic practice and organizing with individuals, groups, and communities, especially those who are targets of historical and emerging forms of oppression and marginalization." This is one of the main reasons why the Black church has been such a beacon of hope, healing, and transformation for so many Black people. The Black church has always offered spiritual hymns promoting faith, hope, and healing; spiritual grounding through the spoken word (i.e., sermons), and a sense of community. The Black church has historically and robustly provided Black people with something the field of psychotherapy has woefully neglected to do, and that is a safe place to metabolize racial trauma.

Racial and cultural storytelling, which are essentially songs without music, can also be used as a powerful therapeutic tool for addressing racial trauma once a therapist can operate free of the shackles of "managed care," of the rules of "best practices" (often a synonym for "white practices"), and of "standard principles of practice," which were neither designed for People of Color nor implemented with People of Color in mind. Incorporating creative nontraditional, racially and culturally attuned strategies into the therapeutic process empowers the therapist to *actually* do what so many of us claim to do, that is, meet clients where they are and need to be met.

Providing racially sensitive, trauma-informed therapy to Clients of Color requires some measure of revisioning, expansion, and reconceptualization of the ways in which so many of us, as clinicians, have been trained to think about therapy. Efforts to work effectively with racial trauma, and to authentically engage Clients of Color in the process, require so much more than devoting cursory attention to race and/or participating in periodic casual, measured, and trepidatious race-centric conversations.

SUMMARY

This chapter outlined several critical therapeutic principles that therapists must be knowledgeable of and resolute about installing within their processes of therapy to enhance the efficacy of their clinical work with Clients of Color. These principles provide a foundation for shaping the strategies and techniques that therapists can employ to help facilitate their effectiveness in working with the invisible wounds of racial trauma.

SECTION II:
THE INVISIBLE WOUNDS OF RACIAL TRAUMA

CHAPTER 6

Internalized Devaluation

The chapters of Section I discussed the widespread ways in which People of Color are routinely hyperexposed to a superfluity of circumstances and experiences that potentially devalue all aspects of their lives. In fact, People of Color are born into a group that is systematically devalued in society. White people are the racially privileged and "valued" group, and People of Color are commonly understood to constitute the racially subjugated and "devalued" group. Racism, racial oppression, and discrimination are the tools that are routinely relied upon to reinforce this positioning as well as messaging throughout all segments of society. It is impossible for People of Color to be consistently exposed to an onslaught of devaluing messages, practices, and treatment without internalizing some or all of them. This is especially true when many of the acts and messages of devaluation have been sanctioned by state and federal laws as well as standard operating procedures of many societal institutions. School segregation, redlining laws, voter suppression, discriminatory hiring, and promotion/retention policies designed to marginalize and/or exclude Blacks and other People of Color are a few examples of the ways in which the proclaimed inferiority of these groups have been incorporated into, and ultimately supported by, institutional policies, practices, and procedures. When People of Color are consistently devalued at the individual and institutional levels, internalization of the devaluation is inevitable. Internalized devaluation is one of several potent and life-altering hidden wounds associated with racial trauma. Its effects are multifaceted and range in intensity and manifestation.

DEFINING CHARACTERISTICS

Internalized devaluation is a largely unconscious process, although it may have some conscious aspects. This devaluation relies on the incorporation of negative racial valuations into the mainstream of one's psyche to significantly influence patterns of behavior, both those that are volitional as well as those that are, for the most part, reflexive. Internalized devaluation is analogous to rampant, untreated cancer in that it attacks other spheres of one's functioning as a human being. It assaults one's sense of dignity and how one perceives oneself. It also emotionally, psychologically, and behaviorally/interpersonally affects individuals and groups. In each of these experiences, the underlying driving forces are centered around the assault to one's sense of dignity and the incessant pursuit of respect as an attempt to mediate the condition.

EMOTIONAL/PSYCHOLOGICAL MANIFESTATIONS

Internalized devaluation profoundly shapes and distorts how one perceives oneself as well as the group in which one belongs. One feature that makes this condition so devastating and difficult to detect is that the negative valuation messages can be consciously questioned or rejected on the surface and simultaneously internalized unconsciously. This process often contributes to the creation of secondary symptoms that often are not considered to be associated with the primary condition at all. In fact, this is often the case when a Person of Color has a major emotional outburst in response to feeling disrespected by an action or event that a naïve onlooker might judge to be relatively minor. Take, for example, the white cashier who approaches a cash register and says: "I will take whoever is next" and then immediately turns to a white patron. The Person of Color standing there becomes enraged, regardless of whether they were next in line or not. The trigger for the explosive affect is a visceral reaction to internalized devaluation that the Person of Color may or may not be aware of at the time. The deeply stored internalized negative messages that suggest "I am less than, invisible, and not worthy of a momentary pause or your consideration that I might be next" activate the underlying trauma. To the cashier and other onlookers, the reaction seems extreme and/or emblematic of the unjustified, unbridled anger and fury of yet another Person of Color. Internalized devaluation creates a state of mind in which the Person of Color believes and expects their worth, value, dignity, and personhood to be constantly called into question (best-case scenario) and flatly devalued and rejected (worst-case scenario). It creates an exhausting, psychologically and emotionally taxing condition in which People of Color are constantly wondering whether they are doing enough, educated enough, and working hard enough and, the deeply buried unconscious sentiment, whether they are good enough. On the other hand, internalized devaluation also leads to a great deal of second guessing and self-doubt wherein some People of Color are never quite sure of their reactions, views, or behaviors. These psychological processes are dizzying, disorienting, and mentally disruptive. The persistent underlying and daunting questions generated by internalized devaluation can exist and persist unconsciously, even if they have been answered consciously. The following vignette, about my 30-year-old client, Xiomara, provides a prime example of this dynamic.

Vignette: "Am I Doing Enough?"

Xiomara is the 30-year-old, oldest of six children, daughter of Mexican immigrants. The family moved to the East Coast from Mexico when Xiomara was 11 years old. She is the clinical director of a behavioral health agency in Princeton, New Jersey, where she also attended graduate school en route to receiving two master's degrees, one in public health and one in mental health. She was seeking therapy for anxiety, sleeplessness, and unspecified problems she was experiencing at work. She reported that she often felt nervous, and she couldn't remember the last time she had a night of peaceful and uninterrupted sleep. She noted that she loves her work but has been losing interest in her job over the past several months. She stated: "Since being promoted to director, I have been wondering whether this is the right move for me. Maybe I should have stayed doing direct services. I just feel exhausted, burned out, and constantly wondering whether I am doing enough." The theme of "not doing enough" continued to come up in our therapy sessions, although Xiomara could never fully explain the impetus for her worries about not doing enough. She was not receiving feedback from her supervisors that her workload or quality of work was less than satisfactory. I noticed that she repeatedly expressed very subtle messages that suggested internalized devaluation, so I often asked her: "doing enough for whom or to do what?" Each time, with a look of defeat, deflation, and puzzlement she nervously smiled while tearfully shaking her head and softly saying: "I don't know, it's just a feeling I have.

Maybe it's just me . . . I have always put a lot of pressure on myself." A critical juncture in the therapy occurred when I asked: "Is it that you feel like you aren't *doing* enough? Or is it that you feel you aren't *good enough* and you are worried that you are an imposter?" The slow-moving tears that once crawled from her eyes began to stream more steadily as she sat motionless and seemingly stunned. After a few seconds, she acknowledged that maybe it was more that she didn't feel good enough. She went on to express that she was anxious all the time and worried that her colleagues thought of her as a "diversity hire." "Do you think they would hire a Mexican for the director if they were not trying to prove they were not racist?" She went on to share the childhood messages she had heard since her family immigrated to the States, messages that said she had to be twice as good as "the Americans" (whites). I assured her that I was born and raised here in the United States, and I, too, had received those very same messages, almost verbatim. Clinically, I was certain that much of her fatigue and burnout were precipitated by all the intense psychoemotional energy that she was expending to prove to herself and to others that she belonged and was worthy of the position she held. Yet, there was also a part of her that wasn't completely sure. Additionally, she worried that if she somehow wasn't successful, it would make things bad for all other People of Color.

Xiomara's case is not at all unique to her nor to immigrants from Mexico, although it is rather common among racially traumatized People of Color. The internalized devaluation that she was struggling with was certainly "in her head," but it was not only in her head; it also came from powerful external messages that intensified the internal messages. I don't doubt that she, like so many People of Color in similar positions, had been asked seemingly benign questions by whites, such as "Oh, how did you get the director's position?" The question can be simultaneously innocent, racist, and trauma-triggering. One question with this potential for harm would be sufficient for triggering the internalized devaluation. While it could be a consciously innocent question posed by a curious white colleague, it is commonly infused with the implicit bias that white people earn jobs and People of Color are given them.

Vignette Analysis

As is common in cases of racial trauma, Xiomara made no overt mention of race in describing her presenting problem. However, by examining her presenting problems and related complaints through a racial lens, I was able to hypothesize that her emotional struggle with "not doing enough" was very likely tied to racially based feelings of inadequacy, that is, internalized devaluation. I was relatively certain that beneath the anxiety and questions she had about whether she was "doing enough" was a much deeper nagging sentiment that unconsciously speculated that "maybe if I were better, I could be doing more, and because I am not doing more, maybe this means I am unworthy, or worse, an imposter." There was a pivotal moment in the therapy when I asked: "Is it that you don't feel like you are *doing* enough? Or is it that you don't feel you are *good enough* and you are worried that you are an imposter?" The explicit naming of feeling like an imposter and later connecting it to devaluation seemed to free her to openly explore this painful internalized message and to talk about it more uninhibitedly. It was also important that I explicitly acknowledge and name race, her Mexican identity, and her status as an immigrant. It conveyed a very clear and powerful message that it was appropriate to incorporate these factors into our work. Over time, she felt free to openly discuss all dimensions of her background and to develop a keen understanding of how race and a bevy of negative and self-destructive messages had been deeply internalized, blocking her focus both at home and at work.

The wound of internalized devaluation often leaves People of Color privately questioning not only their worth, value, and fit but also whether they are a fake or some version of an imposter. Over the years, I have worked clinically and as a colleague with absolutely brilliant People of Color who are overcome with what seems like self-doubt regarding their capabilities. Many had multiple—sometimes triple—bachelor's and master's degrees that didn't provide the internal affirmation and validation needed to offset the crippling messages and experiences of devaluation that inundate their everyday experience as People of Color. It is important to note and is worth saying here that internalized devaluation is not some random family of origin-rooted self-esteem struggle.

Those struggles may and do exist for People of Color, as they do for many of us, regardless of race. Internalized devaluation is a vicious assault on the soul. It is the result of years and generations of psychological tyranny and terrorism. It is stitched into all areas of People of Color's lives—how we are demeaned physically, intellectually, educationally, economically, emotionally, and in terms of our overall humanity.

There is an intergenerational dimension to internalized devaluation that affects how many Parents of Color parent, which affects child development. The admonitions from Xiomara's and from my parents to always strive to be "twice as good as white people" is indicative of the intergenerational dimension of the wound. White children are afforded the luxury and privilege to just be children, while their Counterparts of Color, at every developmental stage, have to play and grow up with the weight of the symbolic chains of racial degradation and oppression firmly clasped around their necks, wrists, and ankles. The psychological manifestations of internalized devaluation are far-reaching. How one perceives oneself and believes how one is perceived is markedly shaped by the wound of internalized devaluation. As one might expect, there are a host of very complex emotions that are tied in with the psychological aspects of the wound.

Internalized devaluation is the direct result of external devaluation, which is something that happens *to* you. External devaluation involves a puncturing of the soul. It is a process by which an individual or a group is stripped of the essentials of their humanity, that is, their dignity (Hardy, 2013). The use of aggressive metaphors here is intentional because of the emotions connected to this process. There is no one definitive emotion that defines or is characteristic of internalized devaluation. Instead, there is a complex array of emotions, some of which may seem contradictory, that are integral to and that accompany the wound. Sadness and despair, shame, humiliation, hurt, destructively entitled self-righteous anger, and anxiety are common emotions associated with internalized devaluation.

There are dimensions of internalized devaluation that center around deep feelings of despair, sadness, grief, and, in some extreme cases, depression. The process of *de-valuing* involves the stripping away or removal of a person's sense of dignity, which involves a significant form of loss, including the loss of respect. There is a powerful circular relationship between loss of dignity and loss of respect. When dignity is compromised so is respect, and when respect is compromised, so is one's sense of dignity. Stripping any human being of dignity and respect fosters a sense of dehumanization, which is another loss. When one is dehumanized—that is, reduced and relegated to the status of an object—all things are possible. The degrading atrocities that People of Color have had to endure over the years have been emotionally and psychologically catastrophic. The underlying sense of loss, despair, and degradation embedded in these experiences are seldom of concern or interest to the perpetrators of these heinous acts, nor to disinterested bystanders. But to those who are locked out, stepped on and over, and whose lives are blanketed in devaluation, disrespect, and dignity assaults, the pain is palpable. The interesting issue about devaluation is that when you are devalued, all aspects of your life are devalued—in life, in death, and all places in between. Thus, the despair, sadness, loss, and grief that underpin internalized devaluation are often ignored or dismissed and remain largely unacknowledged and untreated. Societal disconnection, isolation, emotional resignation, and use of legal medication or substance misuse and abuse often become principal strategies for coping.

Shame is another powerful emotion that is a byproduct of internalized devaluation. It is usually born out of critically examining one's inner self. In fact, many psychologists, including Tangney and Dearing (2002), maintain that shame is a composite of the negative emotions generated in connection to the entire devaluation of the self. Once devaluation is internalized, it ravages one's sense of self, leaving little for one to hold in an affirming, self-assuring, positive regard. The process of devaluation defines and exposes one's sense of worthlessness, and the internalization process provides it with a home. Once devaluation is internalized, it becomes a fundamental component of one's being and a robust negative perception of oneself. The situation rapidly shifts from recognizing *"I have been devalued, and therefore I am treated as less than"* to believing an unshakable internalized truth that *"**I am less than.**"* A devastating omission occurs that turns *"I have been treated as if I am less than"* into *"**I am less than.**"* Unfortunately, internalized devaluation guarantees the latter! It is the embrace of these perceptions that fuel strong feelings of shame—feelings that are often too shameful to admit, acknowledge, seek help for, or to make a concerted effort to ameliorate. To do so, after all, would only calcify and reinforce one's feelings of devaluation and, ultimately, shame. It is often shame-inducing and humiliating to acknowledge that one is struggling with shame. Humiliation is another emotional state associated with internalized devaluation. It is often closely aligned with shame but warrants a separate discussion.

Humiliation

When one is devalued, one is essentially dehumanized. Humiliation is often a tool of dehumanization. Because People of Color are routinely dehumanized, they are also routinely humiliated, and routine humiliation is central to the process of dehumanization. Simply stated, humiliation refers to the process or act of being publicly embarrassed, shamed, harassed, or denigrated. Unfortunately, People of Color are humiliated by whites as a way of life. The constant and insidious over-policing of Black and Brown people not only by the police but also all other white people is a major source of humiliation. Whether in Starbucks, movie theatres, parking lots, street corners, or on their own property, People of Color, and Black People in particular, are always the subjects of public scrutiny, embarrassment, and disrespect perpetrated by entitled white law enforcement and civilians alike. Black people are often placed in awkward public social situations where we are expected to gleefully offer "proof" that we belong or that we are where we are supposed to be. It is reminiscent of slavery when Blacks were required to travel "with papers" or former Arizona Sheriff, Joe Arpaio's, strong armed tactics during the Obama Presidency years to enforce immigration laws by having members of his force systematically stop members of the Hispanic and Latinx community to check their "documentation."

The widespread humiliation of Black people is so widespread and commonplace that this entire book could be devoted just to this one issue. From elementary age Black children removed from the classroom by the police to the Black male high school wrestler whose hair was cut on the gymnasium floor immediately preceding a wrestling match because his dreadlocks were considered inappropriate to the Black teenage girl who was aggressively tackled by a white male police officers in public while still in her bathing suit to the two Black male business associates arrested for sitting in Starbucks, these real-life examples represent a very small sample of the everyday acts of humiliation that Black people in particular must endure. This does not even take into account the humiliation associated with having to witness the countless, ruthless, and unnecessary twenty-first century public lynchings of Black people. Strong feelings persist because so do the acts of humiliation. This is one of the reasons so many Black people find it really difficult to talk with white colleagues and friends after murders like those of Breonna Taylor and George Floyd. Whites often want to talk about that single experience, and most Black people are overwhelmed and inundated with a stockpile of accumulated intense emotions that vacillate between shame, humiliation, and rage—and what they feel in the moment is NOT about this one experience. One brief conversation about "THIS awful experience" offers no solace or soothing to the deeply rooted pain, degradation, shame, humiliation, and hopelessness that most Black people are experiencing in those moments. This is how trauma works. This is how racial trauma works: every murder brings back the pain of all of the previous murders, often dating back to ancestors. Not only do the shame and humiliation experienced by People of Color go unacknowledged, but there are very few places, if any, where these intense emotions can be validated and metabolized. When one is devalued, all aspects of their existence are correspondingly devalued. This is why so many People of Color, especially Blacks, live in a constant state of racialized hurt. The injuring process is constant, but the healing process usually is not.

Racialized Hurt

Although seldom named as such, race-related hurt is a common and recurring emotional experience for people who are racially traumatized. Like the other emotions described in this section, it is a major component of internalized devaluation. It is hard to identify because it is entangled with shame, humiliation, and despair. In therapy sessions with clients, as well as during intensive experientially based racial sensitivity groups, People of Color recalling painful personal experiences with racism can often very easily and readily identify the anger they felt in response to a given situation. However, it always requires a bit more effort to get them to locate, identify, name, and embrace the underlying hurt that is inevitably attached to the experience. I think this is the case for several reasons. First, racialized hurt is a constant state of being; it is ever-present because its source is ever-present as well. It is a low-grade, nagging, persistent, and steady state of mental distress. It is a persistent pesky ache. Living with it is analogous to being forced to live with recurring physical pain: the hurt is always there, but you adjust to it as an invariable way of life. In other words, People of Color tend to find a way to live with it, so it is not always readily identifiable. Secondly, acknowledging hurt is infinitely more vulnerable than acknowledging anger. Embracing that one is hurting or has been hurt is very challenging for anyone suffering from internalized devaluation. It is often considered tantamount to admitting that one is weak, fragile, or flawed—fears and feelings inextricably tied to internalized devaluation. This is an example of how internalized devaluation can involve the systemic interplay of a range of emotions that are exceedingly complicated to comprehend and even more complicated to manage. At times, the anger and rage provoked by racial injustice is a more momentary dominant emotion, and it may be slightly easier and emotionally safer to acknowledge.

Destructively Entitled Self-Righteous Anger

The type of anger experienced in relationship to internalized devaluation is unique in that it is characterized by threads of self-righteousness and destructive entitlement. It is a trauma response inspired by an awareness of one's internalized devaluation and the efforts to push against it. Hence destructively entitled self-righteous anger is an act of resistance. The difficulty is that it is executed from a state of emotional dysregulation, so it is rarely interpersonally productive. The self-righteousness is a psychological overcompensation, therefore it is more performative than reflective of substantive change. It is fueled by an underlying fear of surrendering to one's devaluation, therefore the self-righteousness is a fight for one's liberation and elevation and is a push back against one's marginalization. Destructively entitled self-righteous anger often represents the beginning stage of rage, another wound of racial trauma that will be discussed in Chapter 10. Once again, destructively entitled self-righteous anger is a radiant emotion, very much connected to internalized devaluation, that is relied upon to counteract devaluation while simultaneously giving birth to another wound: rage.

Destructively entitled self-righteous anger is often misunderstood in both lay and clinical circles. It is not the type of anger that is indicated for anger management treatment protocols. It is intricately tied to traumatic suffering, experiences of internalized devaluation, and destructive entitlement (Boszormenyi-Nagy & Spark, 2013). According to the tenets of contextual family therapy theory, destructive entitlement is a concept that focuses on relational ethics, that is, issues of fairness and justice that take place between people in relationships. Entitlements, in Nagy's view, are rights that can be earned and accrued by benefits, privileges, or contributions that serve another (i.e., constructive) or by suffering (i.e., destructive). Consequently, destructive entitlement posits that when a person has been repeatedly harmed, denigrated, or dehumanized, either individually or as a member of a targeted group, that person *earns or accrues the entitlement* to see others as less human or as undeserving, while perceiving themself as owning the right to have their needs met. According to contextual theory, this is one of the unfortunate consequences of abandoning relational ethics as a guiding principle in all types of relationships. When one is maligned by the invisible wound of internalized devaluation, there is a sense of momentary empowerment and self-actualization that occurs with expressions of destructively entitled self-righteous anger. Predictably it is often short-lived and followed by flashes of despair, remorse, and withdrawal. For many, this can become a lifelong pattern that contributes to emotional *stuckness* and conflict-laden, strained, intimacy-averse, interpersonal relationships.

Vignette: Monique

Monique is a 54-year-old dark-skinned African American woman who was a very successful and prominent attorney before returning to graduate school to become a clinical psychologist. Despite success in her career, Monique's life as a Black woman has been a challenging one. As far back as she can remember, she was mercilessly teased about her complexion. She has poignant memories of being called "Boo" as early as elementary school, an unwelcome nickname that followed her uninvitedly to high school. This nickname was assigned to her because, she was often told, she was so dark that she was scary. Her home life was no exception: She described her family as loving and unconditionally supportive but as never missing an opportunity to ridicule her for being so dark. She was often prohibited from playing outside in the sun with other kids. This was her parents' effort to shield her from the risk of getting even darker during the sweltering summer heat of her native New Orleans. She has painful memories about not being allowed to wear her favorite color, red, or any other color that was not considered a good blend with her dark skin. Her lighter complexioned sister, Tina, who was often touted as the beautiful one, had no such restrictions. The tribulations of Monique's childhood continued throughout her adolescence. She recalls always being the last girl to be invited to dance at parties and being shunned by her classmates regarding her Senior Prom. She attended but did so with her first cousin Maurice, an experience that she still describes as humiliating, although she appreciated his generosity. College life at Tulane University, where she attended undergraduate school, presented a new set of obstacles for her to overcome as she found it racially challenging being in a predominantly white environment. Until college, she had always attended all Black schools. She described feeling like "pepper in a saltshaker" during her entire academic career. She found it daunting, infuriating, and frustrating to deal with the racism on campus, the stares from white students and professors that she often interpreted as communicating: "Hey Black girl, what are you doing here? Who let you in?" She recalled the many times she had to sit through classes and listen to white students and white professors make viciously racists comments. She has vivid memories of the October during her sophomore year, when she witnessed two classmates talking openly and glibly about dressing up as Klan members for Halloween. In therapy, she spoke incessantly about the internal conflict she felt being on a college campus that was once a slavery plantation and in many ways still was. She joined a sorority that helped her create a sense of community and cultivate close relationships with other Black females, women with whom she is still closely connected. Following graduation from Tulane, Monique decided to attend an HBCU for law school and enrolled at Howard University in Washington, DC. While in law school, she began dating Thaddeus, a dark-complexioned Black man from Bermuda, whom she eventually married. She indicated that she loved Thaddeus deeply, in part because he was the first man she had ever dated "who didn't have 'issues' being with a dark-skinned sista." They dated steadily and exclusively throughout law school. Shortly after graduating from law school and after 18 months of marriage, they had their first daughter, Gabrielle. Monique was pregnant two years later with a second daughter when she discovered that Thaddeus was having an affair with a white female lawyer from his practice. Monique reported that she was beyond emotionally devastated and found it hard to recover. If it were not for her children, she very likely would have ended her life. She stated: "As a woman and as a Black woman, I had never felt as devastated, hurt, worthless, and betrayed as I did during this period of my life." Monique and Thaddeus, after a number of failed attempts to repair their relationship in therapy, eventually divorced. They have retained a cordial relationship and are actively engaged coparents. Monique has worked hard to stabilize her personal life, and her work life has also been fraught with setbacks and challenges. On two occasions in the three years before coming to therapy, she was asked to submit her resignation from two executive level clinical positions. Her pursuit of therapy was inspired by a Corrective Action Order (disciplinary action) issued by her current employer. Monique's difficulties at work are almost always centered around "her attitude and affect." According to the Corrective Action Order, "she routinely shows up late for meetings, even those she is hosting and always without remorse, accountability, or any demonstrable regard for others' thoughts, feelings, or needs. When confronted, she is routinely dismissive and angrily cites white privilege, racism, and differential treatment of her as a Black woman as the culprit." The referral from her Employee Assistance Program noted that "Monique is a brilliant and intellectually gifted employee who seems to struggle with the everyday interactions with coworkers. She is often hypercritical of others in ways that are often belligerent, hostile, and unforgiving while simultaneously granting broad latitude to herself for her misgivings and usually without the faintest signs of remorse or personal accountability."

Monique's case provides an excellent and poignant illustration of the invisible wound of internalized devaluation compounded by the manifestations of destructively entitled self-righteous anger. The detailed description of her background provided in the vignette is there to help facilitate readers' understanding of the complexity of these wounds and how they develop over an extended period. The peculiarities of Monique's work-related behavior are difficult to comprehend without some understanding of the profound sense of devaluation she has experienced over her lifetime, from both whites and People of Color. None of this is offered to excuse or justify her behavior, yet until one actively considers what has happened to her, one is only likely to understand the anatomy of her suffering in behavioral terms. This line of thinking inevitably leads to dead-end clinical assertions such as "she is a bad person, behaving badly, and deserving of punishment." Much of Monique's previous therapy focused on her family history and marital dissolution, both no doubt significant life experiences that should be considered. However, none of her previous treatments explored the underlying and deep sense of racially based devaluation and trauma that she has experienced since birth. There is no doubt that she has strong residual anger, perhaps even rage, about her failed marriage. But what about the anger, despair, and destructive entitlement generated from living a devalued life as a woman and dark-complexioned Black person? And never have these issues been addressed in a thoughtful, caring, and comprehensive way. Being forced to share her husband and his affection with a white woman certainly intensified the pain of the affair: betrayal and underlying hurt that she has been unable to overcome.

Monique's work situation is complicated, as the workplace often is with regard to race. The complaints contained in the referral form from her EAP provider all sounded familiar. The references to her tone and attitude were a central component of the report and are typical claims levied against People of Color, especially in the workplace. The legitimacy of the claims as well as the potential racial underpinnings of the characterization must be seriously considered. This situation obviously warrants both greater scrutiny and more discussion, but this particular angle is outside the purview of this chapter.

I will add that, as Monique's therapist for over a year, I did get to experience some of the behavior that was alluded to by her employer. She was often 10–20 minutes tardy for sessions, and she often expressed frustration when I would not extend the session or she didn't have ample time to explore an issue that was pressing for her. On more than one occasion she maintained: "I feel like my concerns and what I need help with are less important to you than finishing our sessions on the exact minute that they are scheduled to end. If it is the money you are concerned about, I will pay you the extra money!" It was clear that she felt disrespected by my insistence on honoring our schedule and that she never once considered that there was anything about her behavior that could be interpreted as disrespectful. This is the essence of destructively entitled self-righteous anger. As mystifying and potentially off-putting and infuriating as it can be, it is critical that it is treated as the racially based trauma wound that it often is.

Vignette Analysis

Entangled with Monique's sadness and despair about the dissolution of her marriage to her first love were the invisible wounds of racial trauma that scarred her life long before she went on a first date. The early stages of her therapy with me were designed to provide her with a safe place to mourn the loss of her first love, Thaddeus, as well as to explore the intangible losses that she has experienced as a dark-skinned Black woman. She was devastated by her husband's deceit and infidelity, as any spouse would have been, yet the fact that his mistress was white made the pain of it even more severe. Initially, she was reluctant to acknowledge this to herself or to me because, as she later noted, it was "just too painful, embarrassing, and shame provoking" to own. As her therapist, I had to hold her, firmly and metaphorically, with one hand and gently push her to explore the deep pain of how it felt to grow up feeling unattractive because of her skin tone and then have her beloved husband and father of her children affirm those early messages with his actions. I frequently reminded her that, because she was never really granted the psychoemotional space (not even her previous couples therapy) to explore the severe underlying damage and rejection she had endured—early on and throughout her life—as a Black woman, she never had a moment to acknowledge or grieve the assaults to her sense of dignity or to understand or examine the anger and rage associated with these experiences. It was critical for Monique's healing that our work together focused not only on her very painful divorce and struggles with coparenting but also on the racial trauma wounds that were intricately interwoven into these other stressful life circumstances.

BEHAVIORAL/RELATIONAL/ INTERPERSONAL MANIFESTATIONS

As the vignette with Monique hopefully demonstrates, internalized devaluation not only affects one emotionally and psychologically but also significantly informs what one does, how one behaves, and, ultimately, how one navigates interpersonal relationships. Internalized devaluation creates both an insatiable hunger for "respect" and a correspondingly explosive, allergic-type reaction to any deed, gesture, or behavior that can be remotely construed as disrespectful. The organizing principle of respect and the underlying dynamics associated with the acquisition of it are major relationship informants and contaminants. In other words, the quest to receive respect and avert disrespect is often a major driving force in relationships. It is, by no means, the only force, however it a significantly potent one.

Consider the consistent and resolute message from Xiomara's parents that she had to be "twice as good as the Americans." This was a parenting strategy informed by the realities of devaluation and efforts to achieve respect and thwart disrespect. This parental message is not based on their fears or questions regarding whether she is "as good as the Americans" but rather of the racist perception of others that she isn't. As noted earlier, I grew up on a heavy diet of the very same messaging.

The efforts of Monique's parents to manage and monitor her exposure to the sun to prevent her from getting even darker was a parenting strategy rooted in internalized devaluation. The fact that her parents associated "too dark" with "not good" is indicative of an internalization of devaluation. Even part of Monique's attraction to Thaddeus was fueled by internalized devaluation, both in terms of his acceptance of her dark skin as well as the rejection she had experienced by other men solely based on their internalized devaluation of their and her Blackness. In therapy, Monique even confided that while she deeply loved Thaddeus, she was initially ambivalent about having children with him because they both were dark and would very likely produce dark-complexioned children. She felt a deep sense of shame and embarrassment about these feelings and had never shared them with anyone before, not even Thaddeus. She remembered fantasizing about marrying someone lighter who could produce lighter complexioned children because she didn't want her children to suffer the same effects she did for being dark-skinned. Unfortunately, she felt that lighter-skinned men saw her not as a potential life partner but as a sexual object only, a view likely precipitated by the racial stereotype that associates dark skin with sexual promiscuity. A couple of white men did show interest in her, but she quickly rejected those overtures because she decided never to date a white man "due to history." She stated: "I could never have a white man touch me without thinking about slavery—never!" She continued to, graphically, state: "The mere thought of a white penis penetrating me shuts down my entire body and sends me into a chronic state of shock and disgust. When I think about all the Black women who have been raped by white slave holders, I feel it would be disrespectful to all who came before me." Monique's deeply rooted raw feelings about her involvement in an interracial relationship with a white man highlighted the pervasive impact of racialized trauma and how widely it affected her contemporary life. The entire dating and courtship phase of her life occurred against a backdrop of race and, ultimately, internalized devaluation, both hers and others'.

Internalized devaluation and the quest for respect were also major motivating factors underpinning how both Xiomara and Monique approached their respective careers. Both had acquired multiple graduate degrees and endured all the hard work and anxiety that such stellar achievements require because they were perceived as tickets to being respected and to counteracting devaluation and disrespect. It was not surprising to either of them that having more formal education, more graduate degrees, and, in Monique's case, more practical work experience than their white counterparts did not afford either of them any material advantage. What is commonly understood but rarely stated is that the accumulation of academic degrees is often needed to compensate for the lack of white skin. The realities of devaluation and the wound of internalized devaluation are almost always critical intervening variables in most interactions and relationships.

Those who suffer from internalized devaluation don't seek therapy or other forms of help for this condition, yet the bulk of my clinical work with both Xiomara and Monique centered around it. In fact, internalized devaluation is seldom mentioned because there is no language for it, which makes it difficult to identify or discuss. Usually treatment is sought for a visible, underlying behavior associated with internalized devaluation. For example, it is the incident of the young Black teenager, full of bravado, who physically attacks another youth walking down the school corridor for accidentally brushing up against him, as he boastfully declares "I rather die than be dissed," that we would respond to, not the underlying internalized devaluation that makes being respected worth dying for. It is Monique's belittling of others that we see and respond to, not the ways in which her life of constant racial belittlement has pushed her to a place of destructively entitled self-righteousness, disguised as self-respect. The broader point here is that behavioral and interpersonal interactions fueled by internalized devaluation are never identified as such and that they require a comprehensive understanding of the dynamics of racial trauma and an ability to see the invisible wounds that are, invariably, connected to it.

SUMMARY

Internalized devaluation is a core invisible wound associated with racial trauma. It is the byproduct of devaluation, which is a process by which an individual or a group is essentially stripped of their humanity. Internalized devaluation, a largely unconscious process, can manifest psychologically, emotionally, and/or behaviorally/interpersonally. In this regard, it can, and often does, affect the whole of one's life, particularly in ways that may not be readily evident to observers, to people with racial trauma themselves, nor to clinicians whom clients see for assistance.

CHAPTER 7

Assaulted Sense of Self

The wounds of internalized devaluation and an assaulted sense of self are intricately entangled. Both are injuries to the self and both affect one's overall being. It is difficult to possess a clear, cogent, and healthy sense of self when one is consistently on the receiving end of devaluation and acts of racially based psychological domination. Consistent and prolonged exposure to racial oppression and the subtle forms of psychological domination it usually entails assaults People of Color's sense of who they are and their perceptions of who they can ultimately become. Due to widespread racial oppression, the totality of People of Color's existence is often systematically shaped, controlled, and defined by the judgmental whims of white people. For many People of Color, living with and under a constant stream of racially based negative valuations and the threat of unfair and unreasonable punishment contributes to a state of internal conflict and an assault on one's sense of self. An assaulted sense of self, very much like internalized devaluation, is a life altering and potentially incapacitating invisible wound of racial trauma that has multifaceted effects on the lives of People of Color.

DEFINING CHARACTERISTICS

An assaulted sense of self is intermixed with internalized devaluation. It is the culmination of consistent exposure not only to devaluation but to acts of domination that may be physical, psychological, interpersonal, or some combination of these. The acts of domination often involve targeting the core being of People of Color by discounting and denigrating the essence of their racial identity and personhood.

Both possessing and exercising the power and privilege to define another individual or a group's life experiences is the ultimate manifestation of domination. Similarly, the reverse is also true: the inability to define oneself may be the ultimate expression of powerlessness and submission to domination. People of Color, living under white occupation, must not only know what is important to whites but also acquiesce to it whether it is consonant with their values and authentic identity or not. Virtually all aspects of People of Color's lives are sharply shaped and influenced by the behavior and values of white people. When the very survival of People of Color is predicated on living in accordance with "what is white," or in adherence with what one is expected to be to comply with white-imposed standards, it is hard to have a clear sense of one's authentic self. As Eun-Kyung, a Korean American psychologist once shared in our therapy session:

I have spent much of my entire life twisting myself into a pretzel to be acceptable to whites, to fit their image of a model minority, to not be hypersensitive, to smile when I wanted to cry, to remain silent while my heart screamed. I have spent so much of my life performing for whites, I really don't know who I am, and I worry for what this means for my Asian-American daughter. I don't want her to grow up having to be the *caged-in*

Asian that I have been. As an Asian, and especially as a clinician who should have known better, this breaks my heart, and I am ashamed of myself.

Eun-Kyung's thoughts, feelings, and reflections highlight the burden and pain of an assaulted sense of self. It is neither rare nor surprising that Eun-Kyung would blame herself and her "bad choices" for her current state of distress. It is often difficult to see the powerful, pervasive, and rather sophisticated ways in which racial oppression, and all that it produces, leaves many People of Color with limited choices.

When *the self* of People of Color has been badgered, abused, and pierced at its core by racial oppression and white domination, along with the utter disregard for their personhood, it is hard to not be *clearly confused* about the essence of one's being. To be defined, as People of Color, one has to also be dominated, and to be dominated is to essentially be defined. An assaulted sense of self is the culmination of being both dominated and defined by both white people and an overarching white supremacist ideology.

Assaulted sense of self, as an invisible wound of trauma, is often composed of the following major characteristics that are the results of being *defined* (Hardy, 2019):

- Distorted self-image
- Emotional dysregulation (overcompensation, rage, unacknowledged hurt)
- Focus on what/who I am *not* rather than who/what I *am*
- Internalization of crippling messages
- Negative valuation of self
- Exaggerated need for respect
- Disavowal of cultural self (rejection of parts of one's cultural self to accommodate the oppressor)

Distorted self-image—difficulty cultivating and/or the inability to cultivate a clear and definitive sense of self, independent of having to factor in what white people think, believe, or perceive.

Emotional dysregulation—the range of vacillating emotions that are often generated by having to self-monitor, hyperperform, or repress parts of oneself in order to be perceived as *acceptable* to white people and in white spaces; a state characterized by emotional flooding, vacillation, and/or paralysis.

Focus on what/who I am *not* rather than who/what I *am*—People of Color often carry the burden of defending themselves against assertions, projections, and negative valuations from white people. In other words, white people freely define, and People of Color are left to defend. The burden is laid on People of Color to prove that they are *not* who whites claim them to be. The process of defending almost always requires People of Color to focus on *what* they are not rather than *who* and what they are. For example, when whites indiscriminately define Black People as criminals, it becomes the burden of those same Black people to prove that they are not.

Internalization of crippling messages—Even when the negative messages imposed by whites on People of Color are soundly rejected by People of Color, the messages are nevertheless internalized. After all, defending against a negative message requires one to know what the message is, and often being aware of the negative message goes hand-in-hand with some degree of internalization.

Negative valuation of self—This is the consequence of an internalized message. One begins to treat the message *as if* it is true, either in relationship to one's literal or one's symbolic self.

Exaggerated need for respect—As noted in Chapter 3, the heightened and persistent demand for respect is always a byproduct of and reaction to devaluation and an assaulted sense of self.

Disavowal of one's cultural self (rejection of parts of one's cultural self to accommodate the oppressor)—As a strategy for coping and surviving, the oppressed, that is, those who have been defined, will frequently reject parts of who they are, especially those parts that have been rejected by the oppressor. These rejections are visible in People of Color who go to great lengths to significantly alter physical traits they have that align them with their respective racial group. Whether bleaching one's skin to make it lighter, having eyelid surgery, or trying to significantly alter the texture of one's hair, the underlying motivation for these behaviors in some People of Color is the rejection of those parts of oneself that conflict with what is regarded as the white ideal. The roots of these self-loathing, self-rejecting behaviors are usually unconscious.

The interplay of these factors constitutes the emotional, behavioral, and psychological manifestations of an assaulted sense of self and what it ultimately means to be systematically defined.

EMOTIONAL/PSYCHOLOGICAL MANIFESTATIONS

W. E. B. DuBois, in his 1903 publication, *The Souls of Black Folk*, introduced the concept of *double consciousness* to describe the internal conflict that Blacks were forced to live with in the post-slavery United States. According to DuBois, double consciousness involved the psychological challenge of Blacks having to see themselves through the prism of their white oppressors, being mindful of the ways in which they are perceived with contempt, and to balance this with how one perceives oneself. Years later,

Fanon (1952/1967) wrote a detailed analysis of a similar theme in a book called *Black Skin, White Masks*. The common thread for both theoreticians and writers was the focus on the mental conflict and anguish that is invariably involved in having to function within the parameters of dual identities. Unfortunately, little today has changed regarding this racial conundrum. Blacks and other People of Color must live with a double consciousness regarding how they see themselves as a racial being and how they are perceived by whites as a racial being. Whites, on the other hand, have the luxury and privilege to live their lives freely and only be concerned with how they see themselves, which rarely includes seeing themselves racially.

The thoughts, beliefs, and behaviors of People of Color, especially when interacting with whites, are often measured, guided, influenced, and tempered by consideration of how they will be perceived (judged) by whites. After all, whites and white supremacist ideology define what is normal, beautiful, intelligent, creative, suspicious, etc. In other words, to be white is to be the rule maker, norm setter, and the ultimate definer of reality for all of society. Conversely, to be a Person of Color means to be "ruled" and defined. It is the expectation, role, and duty of People of Color to comply with the dictates of whites, regardless of the emotional, psychological, familial, or existential costs involved. While these rules and roles are pervasive and generally understood by many whites and People of Color throughout society, they remain implicit, although compliance is demanded. The lack of explicit messaging coupled with the prevalence of punishment for noncompliance makes this a very stressful and disorienting experience for many People of Color. The following is derived from an article posted on TheCut.com, recounting what, as of the time of that publication, was known about the death of Elijah McClain, one of countless stories that could be included in this chapter to illustrate the point about the power to define and what it means to be defined:

> In August 2019, police officers in Aurora, Colorado, approached 23-year-old Elijah McClain as he walked home from a convenience store. The Aurora Police Department later said that a 911 caller had reported a "suspicious person" in a ski mask, and that when officers confronted McClain — who was not armed and had not committed any kind of crime — he "resisted arrest." In the 15 minutes that followed, the officers tackled McClain to the ground, put him in a carotid hold, and called first responders, who injected him with ketamine. He had a heart attack on the way to the hospital, and died days later, after he was declared brain dead.

The article went on to refer to McClain's family's belief that the officers' use of excessive force led to McClain's death and noted that "a report commissioned by the Aurora City Council suggests that police lacked the legal grounds to stop McClain and to forcefully detain him." Body-cam footage of the arrest that was released three months after McClain's death reportedly does not show very much of the officers' actions, "because all of their body cams allegedly fell off during the arrest." But, the article says, the body-cam audio reveals disturbing details, including an officer who can be heard admitting McClain had done nothing illegal prior to his arrest; another accuses McClain of reaching for one of their guns. McClain, meanwhile, can be heard asking the officers to stop, explaining that they started to arrest him as he was 'stopping [his] music to listen.' He gasps that he cannot breathe. He tells them his name, says he has ID but no gun, and pleads that his house is "right there." He sobs, and vomits, and apologizes: "I wasn't trying to do that," he says. "I just can't breathe correctly." One of the officers can also be heard threatening to set his dog on McClain if he "keep[s] messing around," and claiming he exhibited an extreme show of strength when officers tried to pin back his arms.

McClain's autopsy reportedly raised questions and the coroner listed his cause of death as "undetermined." Some news reports mentioned in the article on TheCut.com said that the officers were trying to restrain a "violently struggling" McClain. An attorney for the family reportedly responded, "Whatever the [autopsy] report says, it's clear that if the police had not attacked Elijah McClain, he would be alive today."

As TheCut.com reported, after an independent report commissioned by the Aurora City Council was released, Elijah McClain's mother, Sheneen McClain said, "My son's name is cleared now. He's no longer labeled a suspect. He is actually a victim." Ms. McClain was quoted as saying, "I looked at everything that happened to him because it's my responsibility," she added. "Even in death, he's still my son. His name, his legacy. All that matters" (TheCut.com, 2020).

(As of this writing, three police officers and two paramedics are facing criminal charges connected to Elijah McClain's death.)

Unfortunately, there is absolutely nothing new or unique about this story. McClain, like countless other unarmed, peaceful Black men, is dead because *he fit the description* of what white society defines as dangerous and suspicious. When Blackness is defined as dangerous, thuggish, threatening, and menacing, how can any Black man, or any Black person, NOT fit the description? We are white people's definition of the description. We are the universal face of what is defined as "suspicious." This is what it means to be defined. And being defined assaults one's sense of self: It means constantly searching to find the balance between who I am, who I wish to be, and how I wish to be seen, while having to be extremely mindful of who I am projected to be and how I am seen. Losing sight of either point of view, especially the latter, can be costly, even deadly. Being coerced to live and exist within the confines of a state of double consciousness is emotionally over-taxing, and peace of mind is both an unaffordable and an unattainable luxury. There are extraordinary psychological and emotional costs associated with this delicate, life-preserving, life-altering, coping mechanism. It perpetually gnaws away at the emotional, psychological, and spiritual well-being of People of Color.

Managing a fractured, compartmentalized sense of self that is often in a state of flux is a heavy, emotionally laden experience. Living a life in which one's authentic self (i.e., who one genuinely is racially) is under a constant state of siege while also having to juggle and balance multiple versions of oneself requires boundless energy and effort. Calibrating the incongruities between what one authentically feels and wants to express with what one is *expected to feel and express* requires immense emotional and psychological effort, energy, and restraint. For example, many Black and Brown people work assiduously to avoid expressing any emotion that could be remotely construed by whites as anger because they are keenly aware that they have been narrowly defined by their counterparts as being "too angry." It is understood intuitively and experientially that whites control the anger meter, and it is their birthright to decide just how much anger is too much for a Person of Color to express. Thus, more often than not, anger, or any other strong emotion, experienced by Black and Brown people is denied expression or is minimized. "I am just trying not to show up as 'the angry Black woman,' 'the angry Latina,' or 'the threatening Black or Latino man'" are familiar and recurring refrains from People of Color, especially when in white spaces, even when they *are* feeling the very same emotions that they are attempting to convincingly deny. The incessant management and monitoring of the various dimensions of the self can be quite demanding and emotionally overwhelming. Thus, fatigue, especially mental fatigue, is a major emotional consequence of grappling with an assaulted sense of self. In fact, People of Color often cite not having the "emotional energy" or the bandwidth to continually invest in white people or white spaces. These feelings often propel many People of Color to, in their work settings, do as Jalen, a 35-year-old Black male accountant, asserted: "I simply show up, keep my head down, and get the work done. I just don't have the energy to deal with white people who don't want to change or see my humanity. I am done, bro!" Not surprisingly, there was an unforeseen inherent risk and unfortunate twist involved in Jalen's strategy for coping with whiteness in his workplace. Despite his resolve to remain self-contained, he was not exonerated from the surveillance, interpretation, and the tendency of his white coworkers and Administrators to carefully scrutinize and ultimately criticize his behavior. Jalen's decision to "simply show up, keep his head down, and get the work done" was ultimately perceived and defined as his refusal "to be a team player," "aloofness," and an "exhibition of an angry and arrogant disposition," according to his immediate white male supervisor. People of Color, and especially Black people, who refuse to or are remiss in adhering to the unspoken racial rules of the workplace often find themselves the focal point of harsh critiques and/or disciplinary actions. It is common for Black women, especially those in white works spaces, to receive relentless "invitations" to smile, "straighten their faces," or explain why they look so "mean." People of Color are seldom free from the judgments and negative valuations of whites. Ignoring these defining and intrusive judgments is not an option, thus People of Color must meet this demand for attention and all the ongoing (emotional) work that this involves.

Emotional/mental fatigue is omnipresent for many People of

Color, and it is often laced with an undercurrent of despair that can easily spiral into hopelessness and despondency in some cases, anger and frustration in others. There is also an ever-present, low-grade anxiety that People of Color must contend with daily. Being burdened with having to live down or defy racial stereotypes that are imposed on you is tremendously anxiety producing, especially when they can never be completely disconfirmed in the eyes of the universal white "jury." Having to live in the in-between places of one's (authentic) racial self and one's institutional-inspired self (i.e., an adopted white-appeasing self) is not only challenging to negotiate but is also besieged with anxiety. It is an experience beset with inner turmoil, anxiety, conflict, despair, and fury connected to having to lock one's authentic racial self in the background to make oneself more palatable in white spaces. With an assaulted sense of self, the self becomes bifurcated, which is another manifestation of DuBois's and Fanon's notions of double consciousness and the Black skin/white masks phenomena, respectively. People of Color must, by necessity, adopt, develop, cultivate, and effectively manage an authentic *racial self* and an *adopted white-appeasing self*.

The *authentic racial self* refers to both how one perceives oneself racially and how one believes they are perceived by members of the racial group to which they belong. It is also a state of being in which one feels the freedom to behave and act in accordance with the dictates, mores, values, and culturally based idiosyncrasies of the racial group or groups to which one has a mutually agreed upon shared membership. Most often, the authentic racial self is inextricably tied to a shared understanding between the individual and the group about one's racial and family history, shared racial identity, phenotype, and country/nation of origin.

The adopted white-appeasing self, on the other hand, refers to a manufactured self that a Person of Color adopts to make themself more acceptable to whites. In this process, the values, preferences, and ways of being of whites are adopted by People of Color so they will appear more "mainstream," "more cultured," "more American," "more professional," and, ultimately, more "white-ish." It also implicitly requires People of Color to relinquish any and all parts of their authentic racial selves that create any tension with them being white-like or "being a good fit." It is important to note here, that the development of an adopted white-appeasing self is a fully integrated dimension of the self, thus it is not to be confused with "racial code-switching," which is more linguistically oriented. Code-switching is an instrument often employed by the adopted white-appeasing self, and yet they are not the same. Code-switching refers to the tendency and ability to alternate between two or more different linguistic styles to facilitate cross-group communication. It is performative and, for Black people and many other People of Color, it is skillset intimately and intricately tied to survival. The adopted white-appeasing self is a state of consciousness that is much more phenomenological and psychological than code-switching in its orientation and development. Like code-switching, however, it is *not* connected to an unconscious wish to be white nor a subscription to false notions of white superiority. Instead, it is a tactic of survival. Both the authentic racial self and the adopted white-appeasing self constitute a self that is bifurcated along these dimensions.

Becoming acutely acquainted with and managing a bifurcated self is pragmatically useful, though it is also emotionally burdensome and, in some cases, overwhelming. Over the years, I have had numerous conversations with white clinicians who are curious about this phenomenon, and their queries are often framed in terms of "the real self or the fake self." I frequently remind them that, unfortunately, there is no fake self! Moreover, there is a strong case to be made that, in the purest sense of the term, there is no "real self" either. There is a bifurcated self. The (authentic) racial self is often compromised by the fact that it must accommodate, coexist, and at times contend with an adopted white-appeasing self. In *safe*, People of Color-affirming spaces, that is, those comprised exclusively or predominantly of People of Color, there tends to be more latitude, comfort, and safety for the uninhibited expression of one's authentic racial self. However, even in these settings, the white adopted appeasing self is not nonexistent, just dormant. Thus, the potential for it to trickle through inappropriately is always a possibility. Blacks and other People of Color who are assailed as "acting white" or "not being Black, Indigenous, Latinx, or Asian enough" by other People of Color are usually expressing some breakdown in their management of the authentic racial self and their adopted white-appeasing self. The reverse dynamic can also occur, wherein the authentic racial self may seep through and be exposed in a white space where the presence of the adopted white self is not just preferred, but required.

As noted earlier, both the physical energy and emotional labor that are required to effectively navigate and manage the bifurcated self are enormous. Yet most People of Color are so accustomed to and adept at existing in and managing dual identities, while living simultaneously in dual worlds, that on the surface, it all appears effortless. However, beneath the surface, out of the view of the naked and pragmatic eye, there is, in addition to the anxiety and fatigue discussed previously, an abiding sense of despair, frustration, and fury. The emotional underpinnings of the invisible wound of an assaulted sense of self are almost as invisible as the wound itself. Once again, the reader is reminded that invisible wounds are often as invisible to their carriers as they typically are to the perpetrators.

The sinking feeling of despair that is often associated with an assaulted sense of self wound is directly connected to a series of intangible losses (which will be discussed in greater detail in Chapter 11). The often-inextricable ties between trauma and "intangible losses" are essentially metaphysical and of an existential nature (Hardy, 2007). They are invisible and are not easily concretized or measured. Nevertheless, they are quite emotionally impactful and require the same process of grieving that is common for more overt and tangible losses.

The intangible losses that undergird the despair associated with an assaulted sense of self wound are centered around the loss of spontaneity and freedom to be as one wishes, consistently and universally, and a loss of inner peace and tranquility. Additionally, there is the loss of one's core self, which compromises both the freedom and clarity to *really* know who one is and could be without the presence of an overshadowing, bifurcated self. It is the sentiment that Eun-Kyung expressed when she reflected on her life and the tremendous amount of energy she devoted to (re)shaping herself into the image that she imagined whites wanted her to be. Her actions and "choices" undoubtedly made her more palatable to whites, for which she was rewarded in terms of career advancement. However, none of this was now significant enough to erase the sadness she carried from all of the lost years spent suppressing, maybe even denying, her authentic racial self. She was saddened by the forfeiture of opportunities to invest in her spiritual growth, development, and self-actualization as a Korean American woman. And finally, she was also struggling with both anxiety and the loss of satisfaction, assurance, and peace of mind in knowing whether her beloved daughter, Cho, would ultimately respect her in spite of her assaulted sense of self.

Eun-Kyung's circumstances and story are like those of most People of Color suffering from an assaulted sense of self. When a safe and racially sensitive space is provided, all the painful and emotionally saturated stories of intangible loss, regrets, grief, and mourning, come to the surface. They highlight all that is unseen, yet potently experienced and felt, in the lives of People of Color. Eun-Kyung's worries about what her daughter will think, whether she will hold her in respect, and whether she, as a parent, possesses what is needed to raise a proud, self-confident, Asian daughter is a common experience for many Parents of Color. Monique, too, had recurring concerns about her two daughters and how she could prepare them for the hostilities and disrespect they will likely face as Black females who have been, as she often states, "cursed with their mother's dark skin." The emotional weight of internalized devaluation and an assaulted sense of self is virtually always present and prevalent in the everyday lives of People for Color, even when it is neither explicitly mentioned nor visible to the racially oblivious eye.

BEHAVIORAL/RELATIONAL/ INTERPERSONAL MANIFESTATIONS

The relational, behavioral, and interpersonal manifestations of an assaulted sense of self are generally replete throughout most cross-racial and intraracial interactions. As is often the case with racial trauma and the attendant invisible wounds, these dynamics occur frequently and openly; however, they remain far removed from the consciousness of many of us. Operating within the confines of a state of double consciousness and a bifurcated self means always being attentive to and conscious of one's self-perception as well as how one is likely perceived by others. This dynamic alone can make one appear "suspicious," and this phenomenon is compounded if one has other characteristics of—that is, one fits the description of—people who are routinely defined and perceived as suspicious. And usually any efforts one makes to discount the notion that they are suspicious increases others' perception that they in fact are suspect. On the other hand, ignoring that one is perceived as suspicious also reinforces others' suspicions. This double bind, no-win proposition is a common, everyday occurrence for many People of Color, especially Black men. Living with a gut full of anxiety, frustration, and fear is the only "option." My clinical work with 28-year-old Ahmed has been centered around his ongoing struggles with this daunting dilemma.

Vignette: Trapped

Ahmed is a 28-year-old, Black, male. He is a very successful graphic artist, and he suffers from incapacitating levels of anxiety, both on and off the job. He decided to enter therapy after a non-encounter encounter he had with a white woman while walking down a side street in Alexandria, Virginia, just before dusk one fall evening. This experience was a breaking point for Ahmed because it mirrored many similar ones that he had experienced over the past year. He recalled that he and the white woman walked toward each other, headed in opposite directions but on the same side of the street; he noticed his heart begin to race because he sensed her fear of him. He noticed her nervously clutch her bag as he began to have a flight of ideas about what he should do. In a state of panic, he wondered if he should stop walking and look in a nearby window or cross the street or try looking her in the eyes and warmly smiling and say hello. He quickly realized that none of these would likely reassure her nor himself. He noted that he felt stuck in time as they continued to converge. At the moment when he decided he would just jay walk and cross the street, he was immediately frozen by the thought of a cop driving by as he did so. He reported that he then worried about what would happen if the cops came by. Also, unfortunately for him, there were two white women on the opposite side of the street, which nullified the option of crossing. He eventually took his cellphone out and pretended to be on a call as they nervously passed each other. Later that night, he reported having horrible nightmares of being beaten and shot by a cop responding to a 911 call indicating that he had robbed a white woman. He woke up in state of anguish, rage, and disappointment. He lamented: "I am sick of this shit; I am sick of living like a f*&^ing criminal. Every f*&^ing where I go, I have to do cartwheels to prove to racist ass m*&%#$ f^&*%s that I am not going to hurt them. I am the one who should be worried about being attacked . . . even killed." "Doc," he went on to say, "I feel trapped, I feel like a trapped animal. We are guilty no matter what . . . even when we are found innocent. We are trapped even when we are found innocent—it's only good to the next white encounter."

During my sessions with Ahmed, his emotional state constantly vacillated between rage and despair. There were moments when his profanity-laced expressions could be heard throughout our office suite while tears simultaneously filled his eyes. His perception and feelings of being trapped were insightfully profound, because he was. He was trapped within the narrow prism of how society perceived him as a young Black man, and he was also trapped within the walls and by the limitations imposed on him by an assaulted sense of self. As a Black man, he was trapped by the mandate to perform—to continuously look for and discover ways to assure white people that he was not who they suspected him to be. The more time he actively engaged in searching for fail-proof ways to reassure whites that he was not dangerous, the less time he had available for knowing and discovering who he really was, could be, and aspired to be. This is one of the major behavioral manifestations of an assaulted sense of self. For those who are maligned and wounded by it, spending an inordinate amount of time proving who and what *you are not*, rather than who and what *you are*, is a customary and predictable practice. This is what happens when one is defined! There was little to no time for Ahmed to demonstrate that he was a loving, gentle, and spiritual soul because he had to constantly prove what he was not. There was virtually no time for him to show his skills as a graphic artist because his time had to be devoted to who and what he was not. This is why living with an assaulted sense of self is so exhausting and simultaneously infuriating. Not every Person of Color has to deal with overriding levels of anxiety attributable to how they are being perceived, or perceiving how they are being perceived, while walking down a sparsely populated street, but virtually all People of Color have to deal with some version of this dynamic. It might be how one is being perceived while in a meeting, driving, dining out, or several other benign activities where one is subject to white surveillance and judgment.

It is unclear whether the white woman that Ahmed encountered was indeed concerned about any potential danger his presence posed to her. However, given the racial and gender dynamics of our society, it would not be shocking to discover that she was concerned about his Blackness, maleness, or both. What is slightly clearer is Ahmed's internal process. Regardless of whether she perceived him as dangerous, he perceived her as perceiving him as dangerous, and this is a consequence of an assaulted sense of self and of living in a society that has the proclivity to freely judge Black people in such a narrow and prejudicial manner. Ahmed's desperate efforts to find a solution that would comfort the white pedestrians on that street in Alexandria that evening was his adopted white-appeasing self in full activation. It is somewhere between robustly challenging and impossible for People of Color to have a sense of impeccable clarity about who they are racially when so much of their energy, time, and attention must be devoted to anticipating and responding to what white people think, feel, and perceive. There was a major part of Ahmed who felt sickened by and furious with, what he described as, his desperation to make the white woman feel safe. While at some level, he understood his sense of panic, he nevertheless wished that he had responded with more integrity and less reactivity. This is the bind. It is also a critical dimension of an assaulted sense of self.

The disavowal of one's racial self is another complex manifestation of an assaulted sense of self. It typically involves one or more of the following tendencies: 1) a rejection of one's literal self and a conscious or unconscious wish to be white; 2) a disavowal of one's symbolic self, that is, the rejection of members of one's respective racial group; and 3) a rejection of one's literal and symbolic racial selves.

DISAVOWAL OF THE LITERAL SELF

The disavowal of the literal racial self essentially involves rejecting all, or parts, of who one is racially. It can be a total rejection of one's personhood as a Person of Color or it can involve a repudiation of specific traits often aligned with one's racial identity. It is a response to internalized devaluation and the racial demonization and denigration of one's racial self. The disavowal process is often unconscious, although there are instances where it is very much conscious and intentional. The following two vignettes provide slightly different manifestations of the disavowal of the racial self.

Vignette: Pei Shan—"More Beautiful Eyes"

Thirty-two-year-old Emily, an immigrant from Taiwan, entered therapy to address marital tensions in her relationship with her white husband of five years, Jason. Over the course of their marriage, Emily had taken extraordinary steps to fit into U.S. culture and to make herself increasingly more "Americanized." She had successfully undergone eye lid surgery shortly after she and Jason were engaged. When I asked her what motivated her to get the surgery, she replied: "I just wanted to have more beautiful eyes; I think my eyes are more beautiful now." In her opinion, her pursuit of "more beautiful eyes" had absolutely nothing to do with race, whiteness, or anything of the sort. From her perspective, it was simply a decision based on her notions of beauty. She also confided during treatment that "Emily" was not her birth name, but one she had adopted after arriving in the United States. Her birth name, Pei Shan, was only used when she was in the presence of her parents, extended family, and her inner peer circle that was comprised of other immigrants from Asia. Her husband, Jason, knew her only as Emily. Not only did she have an American name, but their 2-year-old biracial son, Cory, was also given an "American" name. Emily reported that as Cory gets older, she thinks more about losing herself and her identity. In fact, this has been a source of tension in their marriage. She reported that she was overcome with guilt and sadness because she felt ashamed of her parents because they spoke very little English. She reported feeling increasingly guilty and unsettled about deliberately keeping their son isolated from his maternal grandparents. She indicated that she and Jason had begun to fight regularly over which grandparents should be the principal babysitters for Cory. The nascent struggles in their marriage, according to Jason, have taken him by surprise. "I am the same person she married five years ago," he laments. Jason has reported on several occasions that he resents the insertion of race into the therapeutic conversations in their couples therapy sessions. In his view, none of what they are experiencing has to do with race.

Although neither Emily nor Jason overtly identified race as an issue, it seemed to be connected to some of the tension points in their marriage. From a racial standpoint, Emily's behavior was incredibly consistent with an assaulted sense of self and efforts to disavow one's authentic racial self. Without overtly stating it, Emily has made a concerted effort to disavow her Asian identity and to replace it with a whiter version, which she understands and refers to as becoming "more Americanized." She has adopted a white, European name, not a non-European "ethnic" name, such as Takeya or Tawanna. She has replaced her birth eyes with European eyes, has a white husband, and a half white son with a European name. She has also distanced herself from her slow-to-assimilate Taiwanese parents. Jason, on the other hand, perceived his wife's actions as "normal and understandable." When asked in therapy whether he had considered adopting a Taiwanese name, he immediately rejected the notion and laughed hysterically. He went on to point out that it was a ridiculous question because "no one would ever take it seriously, it is obvious I am not Asian." When I asked about his son's name, he responded: "Look we are in America, he was born in America, he is American, and it makes sense he would have an American name." The purpose of my questions regarding these issues was not to suggest or coerce Jason to consider adopting an Asian name but rather to invite him to consider the potential particles of white supremacist ideology that underpinned the issue of names and the process of naming.

These are very sensitive and delicate issues to discuss in and outside of therapy. The observations and critiques of how race was playing out in their marriage were not an indictment of interracial marriages. In fact, for the record, I am in solid support of people having the freedom to marry whomever they love and wish to, without regard to race, class, gender, sexual orientation, or any other critical dimension of diversity. Thus, I am not against interracial marriage, although I am staunchly against racial erasure. In Emily and Jason's marriage, virtually everything associated with her Asian identity had been erased. Jason never asked nor encouraged his wife to engage in the erasure, but he didn't need to. Emily's feeling of "losing herself" was reflective of the erasure. It is very likely that Emily wants to be white or white-like and that Jason unconsciously wishes for her to be white-like as well. Yet, despite changes she made with her appearance or name or how much she endeavored to disavow her Asian-ness and exchange it for whiteness, in the eyes of the larger world, she remained some version of an "other." At some point, she will receive implicit and explicit messages that she is too white-approximate to be perceived and trusted as an authentic Asian woman and too Asian to ever be fully embraced and accepted as a white woman. These are the dilemmas associated with an assaulted sense of self. For the most part, Emily's disavowal of her authentic racial self was largely unconscious. She never consciously or overtly stated: "I hate being Asian, and I want so desperately to be white," even though this is the message that most of her actions conveyed. These dynamics inevitably contribute to racially based relational ruptures that are difficult to resolve. Regardless of whether individual, couple, or family therapy is the treatment of choice, therapists must be willing and prepared to address these very difficult and thorny racial trauma issues as the salient clinical matters that they are. Failure to do so invariably leaves clients, particularly Clients of Color, underserved and their lives chronically maligned by unacknowledged and untreated invisible wounds.

Some People of Color, on the other hand, are consciously aware of their desire to disavow all, or parts, of who they are racially and can readily admit it to themselves and others. This was certainly the case with a highly acclaimed Black female collegiate gymnast, who openly discussed her assaulted sense of self without even labeling it as such. Nia Dennis, a 22-year-old, Black collegiate gymnast at University of California Los Angeles (UCLA), gave a public and candid interview to Yahoo Life (February 24, 2021) about her struggles as a Black female gymnast. She shared:

> "For a long time, I wanted my skin color to be different. For a long time, I wanted my hair to fall down, and I didn't want it to stick up straight. For a long time, I wished the chalk didn't show up on my legs . . . . I wasn't even accepting who I was, so it was so important for me to figure out who I was as a woman, so that not only I could see myself but also so others could see me." (Justich, 2021, para. 2)

While she doesn't overtly state a desire to be white, it was embedded within her "wish list." All the features that she wanted to possess, it goes without stating, are those that are connected to whiteness and society's view about what constitutes beauty. On the other hand, all the traits that she wished could be different, or that she disavowed, are those that have been devalued by white society.

In some respects, the disavowal of the literal self is the consequence of the adopted white-appeasing self overshadowing the authentic racial self. The racialized concepts of "banana," "Oreo," and "coconut" all refer to the process whereby the authentic racial self has been repudiated and supplanted by an ever expanding adopted white-appeasing self. Each of these terms refers to People of Color, namely Asians but also Black and Brown People, who are phenotypically People of Color on the outside but essentially white or white-identified internally. The terms are universally considered derogatory and are usually used within and by Communities of Color. The disavowal of one's racial self is a consequence of racial oppression, internalized devaluation, and an assaulted sense of self. While the disavowal of the literal self is often welcomed by and endearing to whites, it concomitantly contributes to huge within-group relational strains between and among People of Color—race related strains and ruptures that are often characterized by lack of trust, within group suspicion and conflict, anger, and rejection. People of Color who are perceived as over-identifying with whites and as disavowing their authentic racial selves are often the ostracized and disavowed by members of their respective groups. The disavowal of the literal self almost always inspires the disavowal of the symbolic self as well. After all, rejecting who one is racially facilitates the rejection of others with whom one shares a racial identity. Thus, the disavowal of one's symbolic self is another salient feature of an assaulted sense of self.

DISAVOWAL OF THE SYMBOLIC RACIAL SELF

The disavowal of the symbolic self is a very complex, multidimensional, and, at times, perplexing phenomenon. On one hand, it can be centered around a full embrace of one's authentic racial literal self and a simultaneous rebuke of members of one's racial group who are perceived as a plague and affliction to the well-being of it. While there is no underlying desire to be white, the repudiation of the members of one's racial group, that is, one's symbolic self, is ultimately informed by a preoccupation with what is considered desirable and acceptable by white standards. Kettie, a former client, was the personification of this phenomenon.

Vignette: Hood Rats

Kentavious, who prefers to be called "Kettie," is a forty-two-year-old Black, gay, cisgender male. He is the executive vice president for diversity, equity, and inclusion at a Fortune 500 company in New York City. He is originally from inner city Baltimore, where his family lived in poverty for much of his childhood. Kettie often proudly credits his humble beginnings and childhood hardships for providing him with what he affectionately describes as "the intangibles to be successful." While Kettie often speaks proudly about growing up in Baltimore, he rarely misses an opportunity to provide a scathing critique of its residents, whom he often refers to as "conniving, ruthless, wanna-be-nothing, do-nothing, hood rats." When I expressed curiosity about his use of such derogatory terms to describe his former neighbors, he responded: "Look Doc, you are a smart man, and you know better than many that all of your skin folk ain't your kinfolk. I call it the way I see it. *Those* people don't want anything, to be anything, and all they do is make people like you and me look bad." Kettie would often use his personal escape story from poverty, as well as homophobic and racist practices in Baltimore, to discredit and denounce any consideration that the "hood rats" that he despised and disowned could possibly be the victims of racial trauma and oppression. He once exclaimed: "The only thing they are victims of is wanting something for nothing, acting as if the world owes them something . . . and to be honest, the women are just as bad as the dudes. It is why I stay away. I used to go back to get hooked up by my old barber, and the last time I did, I was petrified the entire time. I have nothing in common with those brothers. To be honest, I hate to even refer to them as brothers because we have nothing in common." Kettie continued to draw parallels between the "brothers back in B'more" (as he refers to it) and some of the Black and Latinx staff at his Fortune 500 company, who he also described as having a "the world owes me something" mentality.

Kettie is a proud Black man who embraces his racial self, and yet he has very complicated relationships with other Black and Brown people. He often seems ashamed of or embarrassed by other Blacks, especially those who seem to reify white imposed stereotypes. He acknowledged in one of our sessions that he often feels irritated with Black coworkers who insist on talking about basketball "as if it is the only sport out there or that everyone should care about it." I don't have access to his coworkers or his old friendship network back in Baltimore; however, I imagine that they very likely struggle with him racially. It would not be surprising to me if they too were fully engaged in a process of disavowing the symbolic self that he represented to them.

I would imagine that some People of Color in Kettie's life would regarded him as the quintessential Oreo. He is unapologetically and irrefutably "Black on the outside," but some of his views about other Blacks would be construed to be quite white-approximate. Although it may not be overtly apparent, much of Kettie's struggles with and disdain for some versions of his symbolic self are centered around white approval. People of Color are rarely free from the influences of whites, even when whites are not physically present. The relational ruptures that undoubtedly and inevitably exist between Kettie and other Blacks will be rooted in whiteness, yet this will remain invisible and unacknowledged. Many of the early stages of my clinical work with Kettie were devoted to exploring his deeply seated issues of racial shame and hurt while placing our therapeutic conversations within a broader frame of racial trauma. One of the goals of the treatment was to help him understand that the racially based traits that he despised in other People of Color, both at work and at home, were in fact parts of himself that he had learned not only to hate but also to disavow. These unexplored issues were significantly affecting his ability to execute his professional role at work and to have fulfilling personal relationships both within and outside of the workplace.

SUMMARY

The intricate entanglement of internalized devaluation and an assaulted sense of self creates a stronghold on the lives of People of Color maligned by racial trauma. Rather than having a fully integrated, wholesome sense of self that provides an anchor for one's life, many People of Color are burdened with a bifurcated self that must be constantly juggled, adjusted, and monitored to survive in a dual world. Like most invisible wounds of racial trauma, an assaulted sense of self affects all aspects of People of Color's lives, including their relationships with each other. These are very complicated interpersonal and intrapsychic phenomena. The impetuses for disavowing all or parts of one's racial self can be quite varied in depth and scope; and regardless of the underlying reasoning, these behaviors have a tremendous impact on one's emotional wellbeing and interpersonal functioning.

CHAPTER 8

Learned Voicelessness

Voicelessness entails so much more than an inability to speak. It also involves the stripping of: personal power, the freedom to exercise personal agency, and the ability to speak and advocate for oneself. In a sense, this is what Ahmed was experiencing as he searched for solutions to assure and comfort the white woman he encountered on the street that he was not a dangerous Black man. At its core, voicelessness is the consequence of being silenced and stripped of personal power.

DEFINING CHARACTERISTICS

As noted in Chapter 2, *silencing* is the principal mechanism by which voicelessness is invoked. It is a very sophisticated process that can be deceptive and can take many different forms. There are at least five different silencing strategies that People of Color regularly contend with: 1) white domination and the power to define; 2) white denial and dismissive behaviors; 3) white intimidation; 4) covert white expectations of gratitude; and 5) white recruitment of surrogate silencers. The common unifying thread for each of these is the way in which these strategies, both individually and collectively, effectively silence the voices of People of Color.

SILENCING STRATEGIES

White Domination and the Power to Define

The links between domination, the power to define, and racial oppression have been discussed in detail throughout the first three chapters of this book. However, it is important to reference them here as well. The links involve the misuse and abuse of power to suppress (and repress) the will and ways of being of an individual or group for one's personal gain and benefit. Throughout all areas of society, the lives of People of Color are dominated and defined by white people, white spaces, and a white supremacist ideology. Whites, not People of Color, usually decide when a claim of racism is legitimate or not, when an allegation of unfairness is really unfair, and whether the racial realities and assertions of People of Color are "really racial" and "really based on reality." This is the power of domination and the ability to define others' experiences. It also demonstrates what it is really like to have the power and ability to reshape another person or group into your image of them and to know that they have little recourse. These are the dynamics that often plant the seeds of silencing. Our society is replete with examples of the white dominant society defining the experiences of People of Color in ways that ultimately promote some form of silencing. For example, the more former U.S. President Donald Trump and other prominent white politicians and leaders *define* the Black Lives Matter movement as a violent terrorist group, the more reluctant some Blacks are to publicly demonstrate their support for it. A similar dynamic occurs with the assertion and definition of the "angry Black person." Many Black people are so cognizant of and influenced by the definition that they work assiduously to avoid expressing any emotion that could be even remotely construed as an affirmation of the damning definition. Voicelessness is always a consequence.

White Denial and Dismissiveness

The process of domination and defining is not a multidirectional phenomenon. It is very much unilateral. Whites have the power to define others and themselves as well. Regardless of the setting or circumstance, whites often vociferously deny and/or dismiss most attributions People of Color make about racism, racial inequities, or about race in general. There is virtually nothing more challenging for People of Color than trying to engage some white people in substantive and meaningful conversation about race, white accountability, and white supremacy. The futility of this experience often leaves many People of Color questioning whether it is a productive use of time and energy. Denial and dismissive behavior by whites usually sends a message that issues of race are manufactured by race-obsessed People of Color who are self-indulgent and myopic. In many ways, the tendency to deny and dismiss the racial disclosures advanced by People of Color is an extension of domination and the power to define others' experiences. People of Color not only lack the power to rebuff the definitions imposed on them by whites but also are simultaneously unable to convince them to consider how *they* are perceived and experienced racially. The fact that whites have the power and ability to simultaneously define themselves and People of Color is a notable display of power and a potent tool of silencing.

White Intimidation

Among the many powers and privileges possessed by white people is the freedom to punish People of Color freely, independently, and often without cause. The propensity of white people to punish creates a culture of intimidation that many People of Color must live with daily. The culture of intimidation is reinforced by the rapidity with which law enforcement is solicited by whites to take action toward People of Color, especially Blacks, for activities that do not constitute legal violations for white people, such as for sitting in a public coffee shop, for walking on the side of the street to avoid an icy, snow covered sidewalk, for entering one's own apartment, for having a picnic in a public park, ad infinitum. Living one's life under constant surveillance within a culture of intimidation produces trepidation, suspicion, and fear to exercise one's voice. People of Color must be hypercautious about what they say and how they say it in an attempt to avoid disrupting the comfort that so many whites feel entitled to enjoy, and the loss of which could trigger a premature summoning of law enforcement or some other potentially punishing overseer. The bottom line is that it is very risky to freely exercise one's voice and personal power in a culture of punishment and intimidation where one, based on skin color alone, is presumed guilty until proven innocent. It is not just the fear of the punishing potential of law enforcement but also the ongoing sense of intimidation by other whites in positions of power, such as supervisors, employers, landlords, or random surveillance civilians. It is very difficult to freely exercise one's voice and personal agency when one is not free of scrutiny, surveillance, and the threat of punishment.

Covert White Expectations of Gratitude

This strategy of silencing seems benign and hardly malicious or harmful, which is what makes it so powerfully effective. Yet, it is a potent mechanism of manipulation and silencing. It involves a different type of power and perhaps even intimidation. It is a tool that is frequently employed by liberal, well-intentioned whites who intend no harm but harm is often committed, nonetheless. The harm is usually connected to the fact that the covert expectation of gratitude promotes voicelessness. It is not uncommon for many liberal whites to remind People of Color, usually in covert ways, that they are different from other, more racist whites and that they are deserving of a pass from being held accountable for their whiteness. Again, this is rarely, if ever, stated directly, though the sentiment is clearly expressed. The covert expectation is that People of Color should be loyal to and extend latitude to them because, as whites, they have been generous to and supportive of either People of Color or the cause of racial justice. The underlying message is: "How can you do this to me, after all I have done for you?" This is a common dynamic underpinning the behavior of whites, for instance, who have supported Colleagues of Color in the workplace or have directly spoken out against racism and racial injustice. The dynamic is compounded by the fact that many People of Color often do feel a deep sense of gratitude and yet feel silenced by the potential that their white supporter may perceive them as disloyal or ungrateful and may withdraw future support. The thought and feeling of potentially losing the support of a white supporter, which could conceivably be the only support one has, is threatening and slightly intimidating. Remaining silenced is the compromise.

White Recruitment of a Surrogate Silencer

This strategy is closely aligned with the covert expectation of gratitude. Once a Person of Color has been silenced by covert expectations of gratitude, they become ripe for recruitment to be a "surrogate silencer." This position is often assigned to and performed by People of Color who are racially aligned with whites philosophically or who feel indebted to them. These People of Color must also demonstrate a willingness to assume an active role in silencing other People of Color. Once again, the silencing process is very sophisticated and difficult to discern because of its subtleties. Surrogate silencers are proxies for white people, and they rarely overtly discourage other People of Color from speaking or engaging in self advocacy. Instead, they exert consistent and deliberate efforts to promulgate positive race-related messages that attest to their white colleagues' good (racial) intentions and racial openness and sensitivity as well as other messages that enable the surrogate silencer to be elevated above, officially or unofficially, People of Color who do express uncomfortable and/or dissenting views about race. The voice of the surrogate silencer, to the extent that is has been endorsed by whites, will always overshadow, negate, and silence the voices of other People of Color. In this regard, the surrogate silencer performs exactly as designed. Moreover, an additional attribute of the voice of the surrogate silencer is that it is often relied upon to "respectfully" and "sensitively" "disprove" or counteract claims of racial bias and racism lodged by other People of Color. The conventional wisdom is that if the surrogate silencer, who *is* a Person of Color, has categorically dismissed, discredited, or denounced a claim of racial bias or racism, it is, ipso facto, neither racial nor racist. Although not always easy to detect, voicelessness is inevitable. Interestingly, some degree of voicelessness continues to be an emotional and interpersonal hurdle even for the surrogate silencer.

Regardless of the strategy that is used, silencing is an act of aggression, domination, and interpersonal violence. When one has been silenced, one has also been dominated and systematically denied one's ability to speak and engage in self-advocacy. Thus, voicelessness, too, ultimately becomes a strategy and learned response to coping with domination and oppression. It enables one to survive the suffocating forces of oppression while concurrently contributing to the reinforcement of one's oppression. It is important to emphasize here that voicelessness, as a learned response, is a painful lesson that is *learned* intellectually, experientially, emotionally, and intergenerationally. The teaching of voicelessness is seldom overt or unidimensional. Hence it is deeply internalized, often reflexive, and can operate unconsciously because of its powerful connection to trauma. Those who are racially traumatized have not *chosen* to be silent and are not just innately silent; they have been forced into silence, and voicelessness is the byproduct of having been silenced. They have "learned" that their voicelessness has the potential to protect them from further harm; thus, it becomes a survival strategy. Nevertheless, it is important to keep in mind that Voicelessness, while "learned," is ultimately the consequence of something that has happened to you, not just that which describes who and/or how you are.

CHARACTERISTICS OF VOICELESSNESS

There are six salient characteristics associated with the invisible wound of learned voicelessness that warrant careful consideration. An examination of these characteristics is vital to understanding the complexity of voicelessness as well as its underlying debilitating effects. The six critical characteristics are:

1. It is nonvoluntary.
2. It is a byproduct of domination and degradation.
3. It has a relational dimension.
4. It has an intergenerational component.
5. It features a spiritual death/physical death dilemma.
6. It is connected to the phenomenon of rage.

The following paragraphs offer a brief discussion of each of these characteristics and how they affect those who are targeted.

Nonvoluntary

It is important to distinguish voicelessness from being quiet: the former is forced, and the latter is volitional. Being quiet is voluntary, thus it is the willful exercise of a choice. Voicelessness, on the other hand, always involves coercion and is nonvoluntary. The coercive force may be overt, such as a direct threat or punishment, or it may be covert, such as acts of intimidation as discussed earlier or an implied threat or punishment. Voicelessness is the result of an imposition of one person's will over another's. No one ever chooses to be silenced and ultimately deemed voiceless.

Domination, Marginalization, and Devaluation are Crucial Elements

The gravity of one's sense of voicelessness is often proportional to the degree to which one has been dominated, marginalized, and/or devalued. These acts of interpersonal violence can range from physical force and violence to the imposition of psycholog-ical terror by publicly shaming, humiliating, or ostracizing those who are targeted. Once exposed to any of these processes, it is pre-dictable that the traumatized and oppressed will internalize their marginalization and devaluation, thus their voicelessness becomes mostly internally driven and seemingly less dependent on external forces. This powerful dynamic almost always lends itself to the mis-guided notion that the voiceless are in fact responsible for their voicelessness and that it can be conquered if only they chose to be more assertive.

The Presence of a Relational Dimension

Voicelessness is commonly experienced individually, however there is also a strong relational dimension that is always operative. First and foremost, there is always the very powerful and influential, one-sided relationship between the oppressor and the oppressed, that is, the silencer and the silenced. Although "the relationship" may not always be readily apparent, it is, nevertheless, always a contributing factor to the voicelessness experienced and exhibited by those who are voiceless. The relational dimension of voiceless-ness also dictates how those who are affected by it interact with others across a variety of contexts. For example, voicelessness shapes how parents who are affected by it parent their children. Many cross-racial collegial relationships in the workplace are sig-nificantly impacted by the ways many People of Color often feel racially silenced on the job. And finally, broader race relationships throughout society are routinely affected and shaped by the relent-less efforts of People of Color to express their voices and attempts by certain segments of the white population to silence them. The relational impact of voicelessness is widespread and far reaching, even across generations.

Intergenerational Factor

People of Color have been the targets of racial domination and oppression for generations. Unfortunately, being silenced has been a way of life for many People of Color. As a result, acts of silencing and voicelessness also have been around for generations. As such, voicelessness has been strongly connected to survival and transmitted from one generation to the next. Understanding the complexities of voicelessness has always been an integral component of the racial socialization survival tool kit advocated by many Families of Color.

Death/Death Dilemma

As briefly referenced earlier, voicelessness is a survival tactic employed by people who are racially traumatized and oppressed to shield them from further harm but its employment concurrently increases their exposure to (more) domination and oppression. When one is silenced, there is a failure and/or inability to resist one's domination and oppression. There is always a potential cost that the voiceless pay for speaking, and there is also a cost to remaining silenced. This is the spiritual death/physical death dilemma; regardless of what action one takes, one pays a cost. Voicelessness often offers its victims a false choice: speak up and risk punishment or the annihilation of your physical self or remain voiceless to protect your physical self but risk the spiritual death of your soul. Both "choices" are attached to a deadly consequence. In either case, "death" is the only option!

Rage

No one can be systematically silenced for lengthy periods of time and not experience rage, which is the other side of voicelessness. Rage is a deeply rooted, intense emotion that is born out of degradation, domination, and voicelessness. Rage is the emotional reminder of the injustices that one's body and soul have had to endure. It is a significantly more intense version of the destructively entitled self-righteous anger that was cited in Chapter 6. Rage will be discussed in depth in Chapter 10.

The confluence of these six characteristics contribute to and bolster the host of psychological, emotional, and relational/behavioral/interactional manifestations of learned voicelessness.

EMOTIONAL/PSYCHOLOGICAL MANIFESTATIONS

The origins and effects of voicelessness are extremely difficult to concretize or identify for many of the reasons already cited. In most cases, there is no menacing other invading the space of People of Color and preventing them from speaking. As Markieff, a Black cisgender male, mentioned during an affinity group discussion at his job: "It's not like somebody is saying you can't talk about race, but as a Person of Color, you grow up knowing that there are certain places, certain situations, and certain people where a conversation about race is just better off not being had."

On the surface, everyone enjoys and benefits from the "American ideal" that espouses freedom of speech. Unfortunately, our nation's history is an ongoing example of how and why the ideals of our country have not been applied equally to all. How can we say we believe all "men" are created equally and simultaneously justify designating some as "masters" and others as "slaves"? Can we truly stand for freedom and justice for all while some have the freedom to dictate the fate of others? Is it fair and just for some to exploit and manipulate the laws of the land to create redlining legislation that ensures that Black and other poor People of Color are trapped into living in dense residential areas heavily polluted with toxic chemicals from industrial plants from within the same area? Historically, whites have been empowered to make decisions that affect the fate and welfare of People of Color without remorse, reprisal, or accountability. This is what it looks like and what it means to silence a people. Power and powerlessness are closely aligned with voicelessness. It is rare that one exists without the other. Thus, People of Color do not just suffer from voicelessness but from a sense of powerlessness as well. It is a vicious and enervating cycle that is psychologically limiting and quite harmful. The more one's voice is silenced, the more powerless one feels; and the more powerless one feels, the more one sinks into a place of voicelessness, and self-advocacy becomes impossible and unimaginable.

Silencing the voices of People of Color is a very sophisticated and dynamic process. Again, it is rare that People of Color are overtly prohibited from speaking or engaging in self-advocacy. Instead, People of Color live under the unrelenting control, domination, and intimidation of white people and a white supremacist ideology. Through (negatively) defining the experiences of People of Color and then threatening to punish by withholding resources or other goods and services, whites implicitly demand compliance, cooperation, and silence. Whether attempting to speak out against racial injustice or attempting to name white supremacy, People of Color are often quickly admonished by whites about "playing the race card" or "being too preoccupied with race." These assertions are often designed to silence the voices of People of Color and to reinforce voicelessness. I am reminded of a "helpful and benevolent tip" I received from a CEO of a predominantly white organization on the eve of starting my racial equity work with his executive leadership team. During the first fifteen minutes of my interview, Mr. Whelan said:

"We are excited to embark on this journey with you. My team is eager to get started, and I just want to give you one helpful tip that I hope you will seriously consider. If you want to retain buy-in from the team, this is not a place for you to come in talking about white privilege, because I don't believe in it and neither does my team. I grew up very poor in Wilmington, Delaware. My family had nothing when I was growing up, nothing but hard work, and we certainly were not privileged. We watched a couple of your YouTube videos, and some of your language, quite honestly, gave us pause. However, rather than not retain you, I thought I would just let you know out of the gates that the white privilege language would be a nonstarter here. So, I really hope we can avoid that path because it would really turn our team completely off, and I know this is not what you would want."

I understood completely that the "helpful benevolent tip" was not a tip but a mandate. There was absolutely no room for discussion, debate, or compromise. The message was clear and quite familiar—either comply with the mandate or withdraw my candidacy as a potential consultant. The interaction with Mr. Whelan was a classic example of how the subtle but sophisticated dynamics of silencing and voicelessness operate. Unfortunately, and fortunately, I have had extensive experiences with exchanges like the one with Mr. Whelan. On the one hand, it is replete with dilemmas that often feel like a double bind; there is no way to really win, only to escape. I responded by reassuring him that: "I agree with you that, given the time and resources that you and your company are devoting to this initiative, it is important for it to start on a positive note and with your team's full buy-in. I also want to genuinely thank you for your willingness, honesty, and investment in this process by engaging with me in a conversation about the not-so-easy-to-talk-about topic of white privilege and alerting me to how the concept will be perceived and received by the group. The degree of candor and straightforwardness you have put on full display here is exactly what I hope I will take to the meeting with your team. Thank you."

Unlike Fox News Journalist Laura Ingraham, who urged National Basketball Association (NBA) superstar LeBron James to "shut up and dribble" in response to his advocacy for racial injustice, Mr. Whelan didn't say to me "Shut up," however he did clearly define for me what he thought, as Ingraham did with James, the appropriate parameters of my speaking would be. These are the seemingly benign types of everyday acts of silencing that breed voicelessness. I didn't believe I could, in good faith, with any degree of honesty and integrity, promise Mr. Whelan that his request would be acted upon. Nor did I openly reject it. Instead, I acknowledged that we were having an open conversation about his thoughts about white privilege, and it was my goal to bring the same degree of honesty and straightforwardness to the meetings with his team.

It is challenging to thoroughly conceptualize the impact and effects of voicelessness without considering it within the context and in relationship to the other wounds of racial trauma within which it is embedded. Keep in mind that voicelessness is simultaneously intertwined with internalized devaluation, an assaulted sense of self, and other intense experiences rooted in racial oppression and domination. The interplay of these wounds often places people with racial trauma in a state of quandary and indecisiveness. Constantly second-guessing oneself and experiencing paralyzing levels of self-doubt become an integral part of everyday functioning. Spontaneity is often compromised by having to pause to consider what is or isn't appropriate to say or do, or how to act or not act, or whether one's authentic racial self or adopted white-appeasing self should be engaged. It is difficult to take definitive and spontaneous action when there is so much that must first be considered and negotiated internally. Furthermore, it is hard for People of Color to have clarity of thought and perception when their expressed views are constantly denied, modified, or dismissed by whites or a surrogate silencer. It becomes more expedient, safe, and conciliatory to just remain silenced. However, internally, these accommodating, survivalist, go-along-to-get-along decisions are often fraught with a cascade of deeply complex underlying emotions.

Beneath the seemingly resolute and quiet (silenced) demeanor of most People of Color is a metaphorical suitcase full of deeply complicated and suppressed emotions; it is the emotional baggage of voicelessness that is always lugged around everywhere and at all times. These emotions are firmly suppressed because the rules of racial oppression require them to be. They often range from fear to rage. It is humanly impossible to live one's life on the receiving end of domination, under a constant threat of punishment and where one's dignity is used for target practice, and not have a range of mixed and complex emotions. Fear is a major and predictable emotion associated with learned voicelessness. It is the fear of reprisal and attempts to avoid it that push one toward voicelessness. Silence is considered "golden" because "seeing but not seeing" and "keeping your mouth shut" are proven strategies to avoid saying the wrong thing and/or, ultimately, being punished. In white spaces, there is also voicelessness mixed with fear that is born out of internalized devaluation—the fear of being judged as racist, too race obsessed, too emotional, or playing the race card if one speaks up about race. Or the fear and worry that one will be perceived as not smart enough, articulate enough, or objective enough to be respected by whites. All the white-imposed negative valuations that have been projected onto People of Color live inside them like a bad, indigestible meal. These internalized toxic messages provide the basis for the fear and anxiety that many People of Color experience and that often undergird their voicelessness.

The fear that is often associated with voicelessness is commonly laced with anxiety. The internal dialogue that many People of Color have while vacillating between questions about whether one should risk speaking or remain silenced is tremendously anxiety producing. To speak or not to speak is the issue that generates considerable anxiety because, as noted earlier, there is a cost either way. The recognition that there is no consequence-free option often contributes to severe feelings of hopelessness, powerlessness, and despair. Oddly enough, this cluster of feelings makes it easier to acquiesce to voicelessness. Hope is energizing and hopelessness is energy-depleting. When one has been taught repeatedly that their voice is essentially *on mute* and that exercising it will not change anything, it is easier to surrender to both voicelessness and the oppressive conditions responsible for it. Historically, this has been a primary motivating factor, for example, regarding the low percentage of People of Color routinely participating in and voting in the electoral process. The country's long and troubled history of denying Black people the right to vote coupled with widespread voter suppression schemes and political gerrymandering have denied or marginalized the voices of Black and other People of Color in the election process for centuries. It has sent a very strong message that the voices of Black and other People of Color are insignificant and inconsequential to the electoral process, but they are not. Even when the voices and votes of People of Color are counted, it doesn't seem to benefit them nearly as much as it does their white counterparts. This has discouraged a large segment of Black and other People of Color from voting, and these people have major questions regarding the utility of participating in the process. Of course, not voting only guarantees the continuation of their voicelessness. The signs saying "Your Vote Is Your Voice" that now often appear in Neighborhoods of Color during election seasons have been a powerful and effective racialized message designed to challenge historically based voicelessness.

Powerlessness, hopelessness, and voicelessness often feed off and reinforce each other in ways that make overcoming these dynamics personally daunting and overwhelming. In fact, feeling overwhelmed is a recurring emotion for those grappling with voicelessness. As noted earlier, the constant self-doubting, second-guessing, swaying back and forth between wanting to speak and fearing to do so, and holding onto to what should or needed to have been expressed but wasn't create an overwhelmed state of being for many People of Color. Many harbor all these emotions for extended periods of time with very few outlets to discuss or metabolize them, especially in ways that are racially affirming, cathartic, and emotionally liberating. As is the case with internalized devaluation and an assaulted sense of self, despair, sadness, and even depression are emotional states that are commonly associated with voicelessness. The losses of personal agency, power, and the freedom to represent oneself openly, congruently, and transparently constitute major intangible losses. These emotions are often exacerbated and intensified by the tendency of People of Color to blame themselves or to assume too much responsibility for their voicelessness, which is often understood in nonracialized ways and attributed to generic personality traits, such as being too shy, really quiet, or lacking in self-esteem. This dynamic eventually propels some People of Color to devote considerable time, effort, and energy to seeking personal psychological solutions to a systemic, socially constructed problem. Not surprisingly, emotional burnout and full-scale energy depletion are often the rewards they receive. This is not to suggest that personal development work is contraindicated or futile; the point is that there must also be an awareness that although voicelessness may be individually experienced, it is systemically born, nurtured, and reinforced. Thus, the condition, as it affects the lives of People of Color, is rarely, if ever, solely and independently due to their respective human frailties, deficiencies, or personality shortcomings. Yes, People of Color, like any other people, can and do experience hardships that may affect their personality development; however, consideration of these should never obscure or negate acknowledgment of the experiences that are deeply rooted in racial oppression and trauma. Clinicians must be prepared to do both.

As People of Color become more acutely and consciously aware that voicelessness is a trauma wound that has been inflicted by chronic exposure to abusive, repressive, and oppressive racial conditions and is not a product of their doing or their shortcomings, rage is often ignited. Rage and voicelessness are complexly entangled. The greater the depths of one's experiences with prolonged periods of voicelessness, the greater the intensity one's rage will be. The greater the intensity and expression of one's rage, the more difficult it is to see and appreciate one's ongoing struggle with voicelessness. The verbalization of consistent enraged outbursts, which require "speaking," are often divorced from our understanding and conceptualization of voicelessness. Remember, voicelessness involves much more than one's literal ability to speak or utter words. The presence of one's voice does not necessary eliminate an underlying and ongoing struggle with voicelessness. This is one of the many complexities of voicelessness. The complexities involving rage and voicelessness are further compounded by efforts to silence rage and the voices of those who express it, which virtually always intensify as rage intensifies. As efforts to silence rage increase, so do the intensity and expression of rage. This becomes a never-ending cycle that is excellent for momentary emotional catharsis for people with racial trauma, but that, over time, is harmful to People of Color, who are usually subject to harsh punishment, criticism, ostracism, and emotional burnout. These are the People of Color who are often labeled "hostile, uncooperative, race-baiting, non-team players." There are no corresponding characterizations for whites who label, overstep, and disrespectfully and routinely encroach on the lives of People of Color, denying their humanity and denying that they are denying it! When voicelessness transforms into rage, which it often does, it has severe consequences on interpersonal relationships.

BEHAVIORAL/RELATIONAL/ INTERPERSONAL MANIFESTATIONS

The relational, behavioral, and interpersonal manifestations of voicelessness are wide ranging in scope and impact. Like all invisible wounds of racial trauma, voicelessness powerfully guides and shapes one's behavior and relationships. Many of the behavioral and interpersonal manifestations of voicelessness are difficult to detect because they are complexly interwoven with other wounds and complicated behaviors. For example, as noted earlier, rage and voicelessness are inextricably linked. Hence, an uncontrollable and inexplicable outburst of rage may have as much to do with voicelessness as it does with anger, yet this analysis or conclusion seldom garners consideration. Similarly, though powerlessness is an integral part of voicelessness, it is often misperceived as a mere lack of assertiveness, drive, or ambition rather than the secondary wound of racial trauma that it is. These are but two examples of how voicelessness can be interwoven with other psychological conditions, which can impede our ability to accurately understand and appropriately identify it. This is critical because how voicelessness is perceived will ultimately dictate how and whether it is addressed. If voicelessness and the powerlessness that often accompanies it are perceived primarily as a lack of assertiveness, this will ultimately shape how they are treated. Thus, one might consider assertiveness training as a viable remedy. Assertiveness training is a marvelous remedy for addressing and overcoming a lack of assertiveness; however, it is a profoundly ill-suited and ineffective strategy for addressing the entanglement of voicelessness and powerlessness that are rooted in racial oppression and trauma. Understanding how voicelessness is intertwined with other complicated behavioral, psychological, and relational phenomena is of paramount importance.

Voicelessness is also a potent invisible force shaping and affecting the interpersonal relationships between and among People of Color. In fact, the within-group relationships among People of Color can be massively strained as a result of voicelessness. This dynamic can, and often does, occur outside the awareness of those involved. Overcoming voicelessness requires considerable personal soul work and healing. It is a long-term developmental process. Not everyone recognizes their voicelessness, makes significant strides in overcoming it, or even has a means of challenging it, which means the personal development process can vary substantially from person to person. Because racism and racial oppression are ever-present in the lives of People of Color, the race-related stakes are always high. As a result, People of Color are always living under enormous pressure related to race relationships, racial equity, and injustice. In other words, People of Color live in a state of racial trauma. There is little margin for error, and even less room to metaphorically breathe. Many People of Color who have achieved some modicum of success in overcoming some degree of voicelessness expect, and in some cases demand, that others within their community also exert their voices to overtly speak out against racism and injustice. Some People of Color, particularly those at a different stage of development, may not be at place where they can do so, even if it is what they desire. This creates a tension between those who are mired in voicelessness and those who have begun to exercise their voice; the result is often strained and conflicted within-group relationships.

Within-group relationships also become strained as a result of a slightly different scenario from the one aforementioned. There are many instances of People of Color, struggling with voicelessness, expecting more vocal members of the group to be better advocates by asserting their voices more assertively. This dynamic also occurs in the workplace where Staff of Color, for example, expect, wish, want, and demand that Administrators of Color push past their respective voicelessness and be more vocal and proactive regarding racial injustice. Former President Barack Obama was faced with a similar dynamic during his presidency when large segments of the Black community, including Dr. Cornell West and Ta-Nehisi Coates, wanted him to exercise his racial voice more broadly and effectively. All these examples highlight the sophisticated complexities of voicelessness and its fusion with racial oppression and trauma. Less powerful People of Color demanding those in positions of power speak up and overcome their voicelessness represents more than just a selfish and pointless criticism; rather, it emanates from a place of desperation and a search for hope. There is an understandable and unrealistic sense of hope that is generated when People of Color see their symbolic selves in positions that historically have been reserved for whites only. There is comfort and an intuitive belief that the Person of Color in the position of authority understands and knows what is needed and therefore should deliver it. Unfortunately, the sense of hopefulness, though understandable, is unrealistic because Administrators of Color, like the first U.S. President of Color, regardless of position and status, are still People of Color and *are not* extricated from the stranglehold and stronghold of voicelessness. For Administrators of Color, like my client, Xiomara, dynamics related to the intersections of voicelessness, internalized devaluation, and an assaulted sense of self may generate many internal questions that they grapple with on a daily basis in their new position. As she incessantly pondered "Am I doing enough?" she never stated " . . . for my people" or "for People of Color," but this was an underlying concern for her. She understood that her voice was both expected and needed. At the same time, she also knew that there was a major part of her voice that was silenced and that maybe this was part of what made her a "good fit" for her new position (at least in the eyes of white colleagues and supervisors). These internal questions often prove to be fertile ground for breeding self-doubt, competency insecurities, and, in some cases, self-contempt.

The within-group tension that centers around voicelessness is also often conflated with an assaulted-sense-of-self wound. When People of Color in positions of power fail to live up to the hopes, wishes, and demands of their racial counterparts with less power, this dynamic invariably leads to questions about what it means to be a Person of Color and who is an authentic Person of Color and who isn't. Rather than fully understanding and appreciating that People of Color in positions of power and authority are also voiceless to varying degrees, people often label them Oreos, bananas, and coconuts. These allegations are rarely, if ever, advanced from a place of mean-spiritedness but rather from a place of deep disappointment, despair, hopelessness, and their own assaulted sense of self. Yet, those who use such unflattering labels often lack the comprehensive understanding of racial trauma that such an analysis would require. Since People of Color in positions of power are not immune from an assaulted sense of self, the within-group allegations about being a sellout, Uncle Tom, or betrayer of one's people are not easily dismissed, ignored, or disregarded. Unfortunately, there are no winners in these situations, save the benefits reaped by white people. The pitting of People of Color against one another is an old and well tested strategy that has been brilliantly successful in perpetuating the silencing and powerlessness of People of Color for generations. It is the strategy that helped to pulverize the Black Panther party decades ago as well as other movements that were designed to empower and de-silence the voices of Black and other People of Color. Thus, the within-group tension, conflict, and relationship strains and ruptures are predictable given the defining principle of secondary-level oppression, which is designed, as was indicated in Chapter 2, to ensure that *the oppressed become the vehicles of their own subjugation.*

Another within-group fracture interspersed with voicelessness and secondary-level oppression is the shame, fear, and disapproval that some People of Color feel toward members of their group who have overcome degrees of their voicelessness and who attempt to hold white people racially accountable. People of Color who are uninhibitedly outspoken often earn the ire of some of their racial counterparts because they are perceived as "too" angry, "too" aggressive, and "too racially obsessed" or "radical"; all messages that have been extracted from and unknowingly internalized from the negative valuations perpetrated by white people. There is also a dimension of disavowing boisterous People of Color by others within the community that has to do with traumatic fear and anxiety. The trauma and terror that has been lodged against People of Color, especially Black People, has created an innate fear and anxiety that is easily activated by white people feeling upset or threatened. Some People of Color's desire for more vocal People of Color to avoid making white people uncomfortable is ultimately about safety and self-preservation. A historically based belief and an internalized trauma response are activated for many People of Color when whites feel upset or threatened. It is a type of prodromal sign warning that People of Color will likely experience some form of punishment if whites continue to feel threatened and are not comforted. The interesting point to remember here is that none of these tense, intense, often highly contentious dynamics and relationships necessarily requires the physical presence of a single white person. In many cases, whites are conspicuously physically absent but nevertheless central to the dynamics.

Voicelessness also has a profound impact on what occurs within the psychosocial interior of Families of Color as well. It informs how Children of Color are socialized racially, how parents' parent, and, in some instances, how family interactions are carried out. Children of Color, particularly those who are Black, are raised with the police in mind, and unfortunately, they are also the only children for whom this is necessary. They are taught that their survival on the streets of America is predicated on their willingness and ability to manage their movement and voices as well as their proficiency at it. They are taught how important it is to remain polite, silenced, deferential, and cooperative no matter how much they are demeaned, disrespected, violated, or denigrated by whites. When these same children enter adolescence with a "chip on their shoulder" from being caged in, denied of the human dignities they see accorded to white children, hardly anyone thinks about what it must have been like for them to live the formative years of their lives muzzled like a ferocious canine, while other children were free to be children. As hooks (2001, p. 29) notes, "repression often turns pain into rage." Many of these young people are treated in school and by other societal systems not as the victims of an insidious form of trauma, where their voices and sense of agency have been neutered, but rather as bad kids, thugs, and criminals. The only pathway to managing and mitigating these confining perceptions in ways that are acceptable to "(white) mainstream society and institutions" is to acquiesce to being silenced and to adopt a white-appeasing self, even as a young person. It is seldom mentioned or considered that the sacrifice these young people experienced early in life was a spiritual death that makes navigating the normal developmental tasks of adolescence exceedingly more complicated.

The markers and remnants of voicelessness also show up in the homes of many Families of Color in the unleashing of one's authentic voice after having suppressed it all day at school and work. This can take on many forms, ranging from openly sharing one's sense of despair, hopelessness, and emotional fatigue to overt expressions of anger and rage. This latter point is particularly and poignantly true for Men of Color, where the home may be the only safe space to openly express strong emotions without the risk of triggering premature and impulsive signals to law enforcement. There are also the cross-generational conflicts that erupt, precipitated by the differing views that some Parents of Color and their late adolescent children have about dealing with being silenced. Increasingly, many contemporary young People of Color are rejecting the notion that adopting a white-appeasing self or that acquiescing to being silenced by whites is necessary. They are increasingly more boldly vocal and actively resistant to being silenced. While many Parents of Color understand, and perhaps even marvel at, the cou**rage** of their progeny, there is a corresponding heightened sense of worry, anxiety, and fear rooted in their historical understanding of how whites typically respond to Black and Brown racial resistance. In some instances, the intrafamilial differences about silencing and voicelessness make for interesting mealtime conversations and vein-protruding debates. There are other times, unfortunately, where the differences can lead to major relationship ruptures that are difficult to repair. My long-term clinical work with Lloyd, a 66-year-old Black, cisgender male was such a case.

Vignette: Sellout

Lloyd sought therapy for depression and in hopes of repairing his relationship with his two sons, Lloyd, Jr., age 30, and Odom, age 28. Lloyd is a retired executive from a Fortune 500 company, where he had a very successful and accomplished career. He is very financially secure but has a myriad of health issues including hypertension, COPD (chronic obstructive pulmonary disease), and diabetes, which interfere with his quality of life. Frankie, his wife of 40 years, died from breast cancer a year after his retirement. Lloyd reported that he is deeply troubled about his relationships with his sons and desperately wants to improve the quality of their relationships. According to Lloyd, "I know they love me, they know that I love them, but I know they don't respect me. I know this because they have told me as much. I have so many regrets for the ways in which I have embarrassed and disappointed them." With his voice cracking noticeably, he went on to say: "I don't know that *I* respect me. I don't blame my boys. They see me as a sellout, an Uncle Tom . . . and you know what Doctor Hardy? I don't think they are wrong. There was so much I had to give up to survive in corporate, I did it so that I could have the best for my family. Both of my sons have college degrees from the best universities in this country. They couldn't have had that without the sacrifices I made. LJ (Lloyd, Jr.) recently told me that watching me at the retirement party the company gave for me made him sick to his stomach. He said he and his wife were embarrassed and humiliated. He was so angry with me that I didn't see him for two weeks following the event." I listened attentively and could sense the deep pain and life regret that he was carrying. I could only imagine the emotional, psychological, and familial sacrifices that he had to make to survive as a Black man in corporate America. Perhaps Lloyd stated it best when he said, "I now realize that I had to give up everything in order to get what I have. I made a pact with the devil. I gave up my voice, my values, my sense of self, and my sons. All for what? So, I could be the exceptional and acceptable Negro! I don't blame my sons. I think the last straw for LJ was my willingness to sit silently, and . . . maybe I even laughed, as two white senior VPs, who'd obviously had too much to drink, mocked the way Congressman John Lewis spoke, and then capped it off by saying '*And Lloyd, this is why it has been so great to have you as a colleague because you speak English, and we can understand you.*'" Lloyd noted that he was offended and that he noticed his wife, his sons, and their partners were as well, but he didn't acknowledge it at the time. When I asked him why not and what was going on for him internally, he stared at the ceiling and reflected: "I didn't know what to say. I have heard comments like that my entire career and I never said anything. I couldn't. You get used to it . . . it comes with the territory. I didn't say anything because I have never said anything. Mike and Tom [the two VPs] would never expect me to say anything, they wouldn't even know what to do with it because I have never said anything." Lloyd began to cry as he stated: "I can never forget the look of disappointment and humiliation on my boys' faces. They needed their father to be a strong, proud Black man and I let them down. I really let them down, and I don't know that this can ever be repaired. I don't know if they could ever forgive me or whether they even should. This wasn't the first time I probably disappointed them, not the one hundredth time; this has gone on since they have been in the world. I used to tell them that these were the sacrifices that I had to make so they could benefit from them, and they will likely have to do the same for their families. I don't even believe this bullshit anymore myself. I would NEVER want them to be who I had to be or who I am. All a man has, at the end of the day, and especially a Black man, is his pride. And when you give that away, who the hell are you?"

My sessions with Lloyd were both powerful and painful. So much of his story was reminiscent of the untold stories of countless numbers of People of Color, especially Black people, and Black men in particular. Voicelessness often denies People of Color the freedom and right to tell their own stories uninterruptedly, without censure, sometimes even when in therapy. The pivotal retirement dinner incident that Lloyd and his family will remember for the rest of their lives is probably nothing more than a distant, vague memory for Mike and Tom, the two white vice presidents. I would imagine that from their perspective, the John Lewis comment was nothing more than "good fun," and there was no harm intended and therefore none done. For Lloyd, his family, and for me as his therapist, it was reminiscent of an old-fashioned, seventeenth century lynching wherein a Black body was hung from a rope tied to a tree, in public, with loved ones looking on with agony, despair, fury, disgust, and, above all, silenced and voiceless. For those whites, it was amusing, entertaining, and void of human compassion.

It is difficult to divorce Lloyd's health issues from his voicelessness and other wounds of racial trauma. In some ways, the intersections of his physiology, biology, psychology, and ecology seem to be intricately interrelated. Unlike for his depression, diabetes, elevated blood pressure, and COPD, there is no medication readily available to help ease the pain of the indelible scars and suffering of racial trauma. Just as it is possible for some or all these medical conditions to be passed onto LJ and Odom, so may the wounds of racial trauma. It remains unclear how LJ and Odom will navigate their lives as Black men, whether they will remain silenced when they believe they should speak or how the racial trauma wounds of their father will infiltrate their lives. The answers to these questions are unknown and unclear, however the known and is abundantly clear issue is that they cannot *not* be affected by his or their respective exposure to racial oppression and the trauma it births.

Vignette Analysis

Lloyd was experiencing deep pain and grief related to the recent loss of his wife of 40 years, his declining health, a long history of assaults to his sense of dignity and respect, and especially the loss of the embrace of his sons. His suffering, like that of so many People of Color, was a rich elixir of family of origin issues, life cycle challenges, and racial trauma. Although his clinical needs were multiple and varied, what he needed most was an opportunity to release decades of toxic, self-eroding, suppressed, racially based experiences that haunted him and had built an impenetrable wall between him and his boys. The tactics that had allowed him to survive and ascend in the white man's world didn't easily translate to the intimate needs of life at home. Instead, they had reduced him to a mere image of the man, husband, and father he had hoped to be. What he needed, and what I knew I needed to provide for him, was a safe and validating landing place where his shame, hurt, and stories of suffering, struggle, and survival would not only be acknowledged but validated as well. He needed a place where he could tell *his* racial story in his own words, through the prism of his life and that of his forebears and his successors alike, free of restraint, interruption, devaluation, or editing. Doing so allowed him to relinquish a heavy burden that he had been carrying for much too long and that was undoubtedly connected to his hypertension medical condition in ways that he had failed to realize. He desperately needed a sacred place to engage in a type of racial cleansing process, a place where all the indigestible chunks and crumbs of racial hurt and indignities that he had swallowed over the decades could be regurgitated, before he could ever hope to repair the relational ruptures with his children and possibly find peace, solitude, a sense of home, and wholesomeness in his life. Therapy allowed him to do this.

As Lloyd's therapist, I knew it was important to create ample space for the exploration of race and his complicated history with it. An integral part of this process involved uncovering the barrage of deeply embedded deleterious messages he had internalized regarding what it meant to be Black. This was undoubtedly the most painful and humiliating part of the process. Lloyd had never before allowed himself to consciously examine what all the messages meant and how they had profoundly shaped his life; and now he was sharing his inner most shameful and humiliating experiences with a virtual stranger. My task was to bear witness, to metaphorically stand in this very fragile place with him, authentically validating both his experiences and his feelings, while also gently but firmly encouraging him to dig deeper into his exploration. During several of our sessions, Lloyd insightfully described himself as a man who had been frantically running away from the harmful racialized messages that defined him as a Black man. On numerous occasions, I reminded him of this disclosure when he would claim that he had gone as far as he could in his process of self-exploration. I continuously reminded him of his tendency to run, avoid, deny—to "go along to get along"—and that I needed him to push himself to go deeper in exploring the racialized trauma that was sabotaging his life, especially his relationship with his sons. I often reminded him that the racial trauma that kidnapped his life did not occur overnight, and neither will the efforts to overcome it. Our work continues.

SUMMARY

Voicelessness is a complex, little understood, often misunderstood pervasive wound of racial trauma. It affects all aspects of one's existence and has stark emotional, psychological, relational, and behavioral effects that are concurrently ubiquitous and invisible. Voicelessness is often invisible because the tools of oppression and domination and the ability to define and silence others that produce voicelessness are subtle and systemic, and therefore remain somewhat hidden and undetectable. Voicelessness not only has powerful lifelong and life-altering effects on cross-racial relationships but also can be equally as harmful to the relationships between and among People of Color and within families. Overcoming voicelessness, or at the very least finding effective ways to mediate it, is critical to the liberation of one's soul and to healing the wounds of racial trauma.

CHAPTER 9

Psychological Homelessness

Lloyd, who was introduced in the previous chapter, in many ways personifies the wound of psychological homelessness and demonstrates how all the invisible wounds of racial trauma can be intertwined. Although he lives in an upscale, quaint, gated community in a picturesque southern Connecticut suburb, he is essentially homeless, at least psychologically. At the age of 66, retired, widowed, and estranged from his two sons, Lloyd is not only haunted by the racially based decisions he made to fit into and survive in white-dominated corporate America, he is also battling a myriad of existential questions regarding who he is as a Black man, father, and grandparent. While this type of introspection and reflection is developmentally appropriate for his stage of life, it is severely compounded by the issue of race. The nagging, inescapable feeling that he sold his soul is as painful for him as it is daunting. He has a beautiful house, a generous pension, and a host of other accoutrements that are a testament to his success, yet psychologically he is without a home. Unfortunately, psychological homelessness is common for many People of Color and is yet another debilitating nameless condition.

It is critical to have a keen understanding of the multifaceted notion of "home" before exploring the powerful connections that exist between race, racial oppression, home, and the invisible wound of psychological homelessness. Home is not just a physical place. It is a concept, a sense of one's being. It is an integral part of one's lived experience that is tightly tied to one's history, system of meaning making, and ancestral tribe. McGoldrick (2019, p. 96) asserts that

> home is a place where we should be able to own our cultural heritage and not have our deepest stories denied. . . . Home is about much more than where we live physically. It is not just where we sleep, and it is not just the nostalgic home of our childhood or our wished-for childhood. It is a spiritual and psychological place of liberation. Home is a space, where we could all belong—with each other—strengthened by what we take from those who have come before us, creating a safe haven for those who are with us in our time, and ensuring that we leave a safe space for all those who will come after us.

When the psychological and spiritual meaning of home is considered, the following factors are prominent and have considerable resonance: a) freedom; b) familiarity; c) unconditional love and acceptance; d) safety and belongingness; and e) spiritual rootedness and moral/ethical guidance. When one feels a sense of home, all these critical factors are vibrantly operational and highly interrelated. They have the power to fortify a sense of home or, in their absence, massively compromise or disrupt it. Thus, home is not just *a place* but an experience. It is a state of feeling free to be who and what we believe we are, not a coerced and/or compromised version of it. Home is the temple of our familiar; a *place* and experience where we feel seen, understood, and validated. It is where the life story we tell is understood, whether we tell the abridged or unabridged version. Feeling and experiencing a sense of safety and belongingness are also essential dimensions of home in the spiritual and psychological sense. Safety, both emotionally and physically, ensures protection from harm, attack, or the infliction of undue pain and suffering. It is the coexistence of safety, freedom, and familiarity that enables one to feel a deep sense of belongingness. It is the sense of belongingness that allows one to feel supported, emotionally, physically, and psychologically embraced, and metaphorically held. Home also equips one with a moral and spiritual foundation that facilitates one's ability to answer four of life's most challenging existential questions: 1) Who am I? 2) Whose Am I? 3) What do I believe in and stand for? 4) Who and how do I wish to be? These are critical existential questions for each of us to ask of ourselves and, ultimately, to have some idea about how to answer. Although they are all questions framed in terms of "I," they are fundamentally relational questions. They are questions whereby the answers are deeply rooted in relational connectedness that demands a *self in relationship to other* analysis. In other words, the questions require an analysis of the individual in relationship to one's group or groups.

Who Am I? Who Am I reflects an existential search for a greater and more comprehensive understanding of the essence of one's being. It takes into account one's history, connectedness, and rootedness with those with whom there is a shared sense of community. This question invariably paves the way for other similar and related questions, such as "Whose Am I?"

Whose Am I? This question is an extension of the "Who Am I?" query. It endeavors not only to provide clarity to the first question but to build on it as well. "Whose am I?" is principally a question about belongingness. Who do I belong to? Where and whom do I come from? Who are the those that constitute the embodiment of my soul, my sense of being, beyond superficial descriptors?

What Do I Believe in, What Do I Stand For? This question is important because answering, even just pondering, it helps to clarify the ethical and moral imperatives that guide one's life, especially in relationship to one's community. Perhaps a more accurate wording of this question is: "What do we believe in, and what do we stand for?" The "we" is a reference to one's tribe, those to whom and with whom one belongs.

Who Is It and How Is It That I Wish to Be? The potency of this question resides within the question. It makes clear that who it is and how it is that one wishes to be is a matter of choice. At least it should be. As one answers this question, one has the ability to choose to live in concert with who one knows oneself to be as a part of a greater whole or to succumb to and stray toward a different path, whether by choice or coercion.

It is the sense of home and connection to one's community that determines how easily or difficult these critical existential questions are to answer. Unfortunately for many People of Color and other oppressed groups, finding a sense of home is a desirable yet seemingly unachievable task in the United States and perhaps even throughout many areas of the world. McGoldrick, who has written extensively about the concept of home, points out that finding home is challenging due to the constraints imposed by social inequities. She acknowledges that

> historically, certain of us, especially those who are white, have found our safety at the expense of others. We seek safety that

> jeopardizes others or denies them their own sense of belonging
> and spiritual connections. For the most part, we do this
> unwittingly. (McGoldrick, 2019, p. 96)

Colonialism, racism, and oppression have been powerful forces in disrupting and destroying both the psychological and physical homes of many People of Color. The U.S. Government's absolute denial and refusal to grant statehood to geographical territories that are inhabited by large numbers of People of Color, such as Washington, DC, and Puerto Rico, is a denial of home in the most literal and concrete sense. Unfortunately, the assault on People of Color's sense of home can be directed toward one's psychological home as well. In fact, the decimation, disruption, and destruction of home, can often be experienced both psychologically and physically. Systemic weaponry such as zoning laws, redlining policies that confine People of Color to areas of cities and towns with poor and toxic levels of air quality, and standard practices that force them to live adjacent to deadly environmental waste all physically and psychologically disrupt home for many People of Color. These conditions, and many others like them, are instrumental in inflicting the hidden wound of psychological homelessness.

DEFINING CHARACTERISTICS

Psychological homelessness is a chronic state of psychoemotional and existential disconnection that assaults and destroys one's sense of safety, connectedness, security, and feelings of belongingness. People who are psychologically homeless live under a constant state of threat and insecurity. Psychological homelessness helps to create and exacerbate the state of hyperalertness that many People of Color live with daily. In fact, most People of Color don't have the luxury of living with an enduring sense of security;

when security is experienced, it is exceedingly fleeting. Feeling safe and secure is situational and circumstantial rather than a presumed and constant state of being. The psychological costs and the manifestations of psychological homelessness are extensive.

EMOTIONAL/PSYCHOLOGICAL MANIFESTATIONS

Psychological homelessness shatters one's sense of safety, security, and belongingness. It is intertwined with an assaulted sense of self in that it has the power to contribute to the distortion of one's self-perception. It is challenging to develop a clear, solid, and sustainable sense of self when one is psychologically homeless. It is equally as difficult to establish a sense of connection and belonging when one's sense of self is compromised, shattered, or assaulted. Many People of Color, especially Black people, feel like foreigners or visitors in their homeland of the United States. Many Blacks and other People of Color are often made to feel like, and are often treated as, Americans with an asterisk. This is why it is common for Asian Americans and other People of Color born and raised in the United States to be continually asked: "Where are you from? . . . No, where are you REALLY from?" Or for People of Color to be routinely and tersely told by white Americans to "go back where you came from." It is hard to feel at home when historically one has been and continues to be treated as a marginalized other, where access to the American Dream is a right for some but is conditional for others.

The search for home and the incessant efforts to reconcile psychological homelessness have been major (unconscious) driving forces underpinning the many names that Black people have used to self-identify the over decades. Over the course of time, Blacks identified as "Negro," "Colored," "Black," "Afro-American," and "African American." Latinos/Hispanics have undergone a similar process, over the years identifying as "Hispanic," "Latino," "Latin," "Spanish," "Chicano/a" (in some regions), and "Latinx." These shifts in how to describe oneself is more than a frivolous semantical exercise. At their core, they represent a deeper desire for groups to self-identify as well as expressions of an existential struggle with belongingness, how one sees and defines oneself, *who* has the power to define, and, ultimately, the continuous bout with psychological homelessness. In the case of Black people, the quest to find home is so intense and unrelenting that most Black people are willing to claim the entire vast continent of Africa as a home identifier even though it leaves as many questions about identity unanswered as it answers. Most African Americans and other Blacks remain unsure of their ancestral tribal roots due to enslavement. For many, this uncertainty has created a deep and daunting sense of yearning.

I have vivid memories of emotionally struggling with recurring questions about my rootedness throughout my life. Yet it was during my tenure as a professor and clinical trainer in family therapy at Syracuse University where I felt the sensation most consistently and recurringly. The program had a very strong self-of-the-therapist orientation. As such, both graduate students and faculty were constantly encouraged, perhaps even expected, to engage in a process of personal exploration regarding the person that underpinned our work as therapists. It was customary for the students to construct and publicly present their family genograms in didactic classes and clinical supervision many times throughout their training. One class we offered was a 4-hour intensive group experience where students were actively engaged in deep self-exploratory work. Each student had to conduct a detailed personal genogram presentation. As a Black professor, there were two dominant responses that I often had to these experiences. First, I was always impressed with and amazed by the incredibly detailed records of family history that many white students had. The white Mormon students consistently had stellar records of their family history that were comprehensive and beyond comparison. As some white students traced their lineage back to the Mayflower, I was in awe. I was also in a deep sea of agony and despair as well. My focus as a professor was often disrupted and interrupted by a stubborn, deep, penetrating, and piercing feeling of pain and sadness that the Black part of me was experiencing. I was invaded by a flurry of intrusive thoughts that had to do with questions about my sense of being that placed me in a constant fight with myself and the process. I was always left with so many unanswerable questions regarding who I am and whose I am. Who am I, beyond the first-born son of a Black father with an Irish-Scottish surname, Hardy, and the son of a southern Black mother with the maiden name of Eikenberg? Where did those names come from? Who were my parents before they became "Hardy" and "Eikenberg," respectively? These questions continuously haunted me. These persistent nagging questions and the accompanying existential crisis that they provoked led me on a journey to find answers, a journey that is often undertaken by many Black people, and one that, at least pre-ancestry.com, often proved fruitless. I tried unsuccessfully to trace my lineage back through slavery, a process that requires knowledge of the names of all slave owners who may have owned my family members. The inaccessibility of this information made a successful search impossible.

My insatiable thirst, quest, and search for home was reminiscent of the efforts that many Black friends, clients, and family members have reported. Their experiences have centered around visiting Africa in hopes of finding the ever-elusive home; only when they arrived there, they discovered that the locals perceived them—African Americans—as much *too* American to be authentically African, thus they were again deemed "other," which viscerally reinforced that they are essentially homeless. This dynamic is also true for other People of Color who are "American" but who have roots and bloodlines that connect them to other ancestral territories. Many of these people's lives and identities are uncomfortably sandwiched between two worlds, and they never feel a sense of belonging to either. As a result, the search to find that "missing, unnamable, ever-elusive something else" is continuous.

The search for a sense of home never ceases. It often involves constantly looking for an elusive "something else" that is hard to find, because, in part, it has never been fully experienced. Many People of Color ultimately try to find that sense of home through a variety of alternate means, whether starting a family, purchasing a "home," or actively pursuing other activities that provide a hint of safety and security. Unfortunately, these experiences provide only partial and/or temporary fixes to the underlying and unrelenting sense of yearning that accompanies psychological homelessness. No matter how much status or material wealth one achieves as a Person of Color, some degree of psychological homelessness will always be a factor. Material possessions and well-being fall far short of providing a viable substitute for "home."

We should not forget how much of an issue some people made of "home" relative to former U.S. President Barack Obama's birthplace, citizenship, and racial identity. There were even Black Americans who, early in Obama's candidacy for the presidency, questioned whether he was "Black enough" to represent their interests. Others, like former U.S. President Donald Trump, continued to question whether Obama was even an American citizen. Former President Obama's stature and privilege did not protect him from exposure to the manifestations and consequences of psychological homelessness, neither as an office seeker nor as the office holder. Some questions about who he was and whether he belonged persisted throughout his time in office. In her memoir, *Becoming*, former U.S. First Lady Michelle Obama provided a very chilling account of the pain and fears associated with the Donald Trump–inspired claims that her husband and U.S. President Barack Obama was not a U.S. citizen, a claim that she described as "crazy and mean spirited with its underlying bigotry and xenophobia hardly concealed" (Obama, 2018, p. 352). According to Obama,

> the people who tried to define us as "other" had been doing so for years already. We did everything we could to rise above their lies and distortions, trusting that the way Barack and I lived our lives would show people the truth about who we really were. (Obama, 2018, p. 353)

Those maligned by psychological homelessness live in a betwixt state of being, where there is always, metaphorically, one foot here and one foot there, with no firm footing in any one place. This dynamic requires one to endure the constant pressure of having to "prove" that one belongs, often to no avail. Continually trying to "prove you belong," always questioning whether or not you do, and entertaining the notion that "maybe if I behave a certain way, talk a certain way, etc., I will demonstrate that I belong" are markers of psychological homelessness.

The four critical existential questions discussed earlier are nearly impossible to answer thoroughly and adequately for those experiencing psychological homelessness. Home is a type of respite for the soul. It affords one the opportunity to retool and refuel after facing adversity. It is a source of psychic energy that allows those who are racially maligned to keep on keeping on, to keep pressing forward against seemingly insurmountable odds. When in a state of psychological homelessness, all these personal psychological resources are compromised, if not completely depleted. The challenges of living with and constantly negotiating this and other invisible wounds against a backdrop of depleted psychoemotional resources can be emotionally overwhelming. Unfortunately, because the wounds of racial trauma are largely invisible, the complex emotions attached to them are often misunderstood, misdiagnosed, and/or falsely attributed to deficiencies in one's racial makeup.

Anxiety and restlessness are two dominant emotional experiences that are often associated with psychological homelessness. The expression of these emotions is usually subtle and can easily be overlooked, yet there is always a persistent, strong undercurrent that is omnipresent. It is very difficult to lower your emotional guard in the absence of feeling safe, secure, and a sense of belongingness. Living under a state of hyperalertness obliterates any reasonable chance of relaxing or just allowing oneself *to be*. As described throughout this book, People of Color live under the constant scrutiny and surveillance of the critical and condemning eyes of white people, a relentless gaze that often communicates, with a resounding sense of resolve, "you are other, and you do not belong"; thus it is reasonable that People of Color feel anxious, restless, and fearful. Even People of Color with celebrity and extensive coffers of privilege are not exempt from the emotional manifestations of the wound of psychological homelessness. They experience the fear, anxiety, and restlessness either in connection to their literal self, that is, experiences that they have had directly, or in connection to their symbolic self, such as feelings connected to and generated by the experiences of family members, other loved ones, and other members of one's race. This is one of the many reasons why, in the aftermath of George Floyd's murder in May of 2020, it was commonplace to see Black celebrities from all walks of life visibly emotionally distraught during interviews. Many were crying as if they had experienced the loss of a close family member, and, symbolically and vicariously, they had. Regardless of one's circumstances or relative possession of privilege, the recurrent and persistent undercurrent of race-related anxiety, fear, and restlessness is always present.

There is also a dimension of the anxiety and restlessness that is associated with the perpetual search for home. The *necessary* burden of constantly seeking and searching for a place, external or internal, where one can feel a strong sense of belongingness, without any reassurances that it exists or can or will be found, is tremendously anxiety-producing. Some of the anxiety produced by the search is from an intuitive understanding that what is being sought has never been experienced in a significant or sustainable way. One might experience momentary flashes of it when attending, for example, an event that is comprised of all People of Color. These experiences, while greatly appreciated, are usually short-lived and nonsustainable. Thus, the search for home is a yearning; an endless quest to find that elusive something else. Even though what is being sought has likely not been fully experienced, it is believed to be far preferential to the current state of psychological homelessness that most People of Color live in. Maybe it is as simple as People of Color desiring the opportunity to live life in a way that is comparable to that of their white counterparts, perhaps a life wherein one did not have to be on constant alert or to live fearfully or with the anxiety of waiting for the next police shooting, personal attack, or some other blatant display of racism.

Living with fear, anxiety, and a sense of restlessness without the comfort, tranquility, and peace of mind that a home affords means that many People of Color live day-to-day with strong feelings of vulnerability. Home is a buffer against adversity. Obviously, when one has no home, there is a de facto absence of the buffers required to provide a fortress against threatening levels of vulnerability. The type of vulnerability being described here is closely related to the sense of powerlessness that accompanies the learned voicelessness that was discussed in Chapter 8. It is the type of vulnerability that is produced by knowing and coming to terms with the chilling feelings of ineptitude and powerlessness that Parents of Color feel with regard to protecting their children from law enforcement or others who are prone to quickly prejudge them as criminals, as suspicious, or as "fitting the description." It is the vulnerability associated with knowing that one is susceptible to being shot and murdered while sleeping, walking, running, sitting in the park with a toy rifle, or just being Black, Asian, or any other Person of Color. It is the type of vulnerability that is rooted in knowing that there is no safe haven, no respite, no retreat, no escape from these assaults. Essentially, there is no home place, only hyperexposed vulnerability.

The widespread feeling of vulnerability is generated not just by the defenselessness against the powerful external forces of racism and oppression but also by the internal feelings of aloneness and loneliness. The sense of aloneness and loneliness referred to here is directly and specifically in relationship to race. This is not a reference to what one might feel or experience in a personal intimate relationship. Instead, it refers to what it feels like to exist in a world where you know you are despised, cannot and very likely will never be completely embraced as a fully franchised and respected human being. It refers to what it means and feels like to be *the only one* or *one of very few* in predominantly white spaces, wherein you are essentially invisible, voiceless, and homeless. It is easy to feel alone and lonely when it is difficult to tell your version of your story uninterruptedly, without whites or their surrogate silencers attempting to edit, censor, silence, or finish it for you. There is a powerful overlay of homelessness and voicelessness. Yet, the feeling of aloneness and loneliness are not just calcified and reinforced by the silencing of People of Color voices but also by a dismissal and repudiation of their human value as well. There is something remarkably isolating about internalized devaluation. In fact, one of the main coping strategies to deal with the shame, embarrassment, and humiliation associated with internalized devaluation is to isolate oneself, to keep parts of oneself hidden and sealed off from others, especially those who are prone to scathing judgments. While self-isolating and self-barricading behaviors address and "protect" one's wounds of racial trauma, they simultaneously reinforce the deeply penetrating and painful feelings of aloneness and loneliness that are central to psychological homelessness. Knowing that others who are like them are having similar feelings of aloneness and loneliness is often comforting and reassuring to People of Color. At least they know they are not alone in feeling alone. Unfortunately, the opportunities to participate in these types of intimate, transparent, soul-rejuvenating, home-building, affirming, within-group experiences are far too few and can hardly compete or keep pace with the onslaught of assaults to People of Color's sense of home.

When opportunities to have one's feelings and experiences consensually validated, especially by those who are compassionate and embracing, are denied or simply unavailable, the feelings of aloneness and loneliness can quickly become compounded by sadness and despair. A significant portion of sadness and despair is triggered by feelings of hopelessness and the difficulty believing that things will ever substantively change. Hopelessness is a plausible emotion to feel, at least momentarily, as we watch innocent Asians assaulted and murdered on the streets and subways of America for just being Asian or Black men, women, and children shot and murdered for just being Black or the thousands of Latinx children caged in putrid living conditions along the United States–Mexico border. It is hard, at times, to feel hopeful when your literal and symbolic selves seem inescapably trapped amid a menacing and relentless life of madness that is not of your making. And no one seems to really give a damn!

There are also some threads of hopelessness that are tied to the internalization of the negative valuations that have been espoused and securely planted into the psyches of People of Color through racial trauma and oppression. Since People of Color are often blamed for their racial victimization, it is not uncommon for some to internalize these messages and blame themselves as well. The sadness and despair in these cases is often generated by the Person of Color lamenting that it is their deficiencies alone, and not their exposure to racial oppression, that are single handedly responsible for their plight and sense of psychological homelessness. This particular manifestation of sadness and despair is often expressed through self-loathing and self-contempt for one's literal self and quite possibly for one's symbolic self as well.

BEHAVIORAL/RELATIONAL/ INTERPERSONAL MANIFESTATIONS

As one might reasonably expect, living in a state of psychological homelessness severely affects the day-to-day interactions and relationships of those who are affected. The ever-present sense of feeling racially unsafe, insecure, and tolerated rather than authentically accepted often leaves People of Color mistrustful of white people and white spaces. People of Color often approach whites with a sense of guardedness, suspicion, and anticipation of being surveilled, targeted, or devalued. To enjoy and facilitate some modicum of inclusion and (false) sense of belonging, many People of Color work extra hard to be flawlessly performative to that end. Exercising restraint in what one says, especially regarding race-related issues, managing one's tone, taking on the role of surrogate silencer, code-switching, shunning notions of racial hypersensitivity, and wearing a happy, smiling, welcoming, nonangry face are some of the *minor* accommodations that People of Color often make to feel included in white spaces. Paul Lawrence Dunbar's classic poem "We Wear the Mask," published in 1895, poignantly describes the emotional and psychological labor that Black people must expend to be embraced by white society.

We Wear the Mask

By Paul Laurence Dunbar

We wear the mask that grins and lies,
It hides our cheeks and shades our eyes,—
This debt we pay to human guile;
With torn and bleeding hearts we smile,
And mouth with myriad subtleties.

Why should the world be over-wise,
In counting all our tears and sighs?
Nay, let them only see us, while
We wear the mask.

We smile, but, O great Christ, our cries
To thee from tortured souls arise.
We sing, but oh the clay is vile
Beneath our feet, and long the mile;
But let the world dream otherwise
We wear the mask!

This poem was originally written to describe the racial accommodations required of Black people following emancipation from slavery, and, unfortunately, it is still painfully relevant in the twenty-first century. Black and other People of Color must wear "masks" to be incorporated into a white world that otherwise refuses to see, dignify, or respect their humanity unless they are white-like. As many People of Color intuitively understand, even then the acceptance by whites is conditional and often transactional. It is rarely an authentic acceptance where People of Color are fully embraced on their terms as nonwhite human beings with a unique culture, way of being, history, and racial perspective. Instead, the acceptance is, often, based on the degree to which People of Color are willing to forego who they really are, cater to and accommodate white ways of being, develop an adopted white-appeasing self, and become the quintessential GEMM (Hardy, 2008), the Good Effective Mainstream Minority, which I have referred to in previous writings. White people's demands that People of Color become GEMMs are seldom explicit. Instead, the pressure applied is often subtle, nonverbal, and embedded in the dynamics of most cross-racial relationships. The following is a list of implicit *demands* that People of Color must fulfill to become GEMMs and, ultimately, acceptable to whites.

1. Always smile, regardless of how much you hurt and what you feel.
2. Always demonstrate that you have a good attitude, because your attitude will dictate your altitude and the degree to which you are accepted. Being one of the "good ones" is always an asset.
3. Avoid expression of any intense emotion that might be confused with or construed as anger. Just keep smiling and never expose your anger and rage.
4. Never discuss race UNLESS the views you are expressing are compatible with the views of the white person/people with whom you are speaking. Remember, *you* "playing the

race card" is never appropriate, but it is absolutely acceptable when whites play it when accusing you of doing so.

5. Avoid using incendiary language that makes white people feel "unsafe." Understand that the use of words like "white privilege," "white supremacy," "white people," and "racism" (unless its "reverse racism") are inappropriate because they make some whites feel unsafe.

6. Always use white euphemisms and deracialized language, such as "some people," "some cultures," "other ethnicities," or "the dominant group," to avoid naming white people and terms such as "people who look like me" or the "non-dominant group" to avoid direct references to People of Color. Retaining some level of vagueness in the racial language you use can be quite beneficial to being accepted.

7. Avoid expressions of *racial hypersensitivity* and don't be offended by an innocent and funny racial joke or whites' usage of racially insensitive language. In other words, prove that you are a good sport and that you can take a joke!

8. Accept that your verbal disclosures in meetings and others interpersonal settings will not be acknowledged nor considered valuable or brilliant until they have been endorsed or reiterated by a white person.

9. Always be willing to acknowledge and state in the presence of whites that "there are racist People of Color too." Demonstrate that you are fair in acknowledging that there are good and bad people on both sides!

10. Avoid extensive (public) interactions with groups made up exclusively of People of Color, regardless of how much whites congregate exclusively with other whites. It is critical that YOU demonstrate your cross-racial acumen and that *you* are not cliquish, racially discriminatory, or exclusive.

These mandates are stated somewhat sardonically to highlight their utter absurdity. However, they are extraordinarily intrusive, demanding, demeaning, and psychoemotionally taxing. They are also ridiculously impossible to comply with in a way that fosters healthy and meaningful cross-racial engagement. Yet, some semblance of compliance does afford some People of Color with a sense of pseudobelonginess in white spaces. GEMMs are often warmly embraced by whites because they are congenial, non-threatening, non-race-obsessed, and easy to talk to in general. For the Person of Color, on the other hand, the entire experience is rooted in racial oppression and is emotionally and psychologically debilitating. No one willingly submits to becoming a GEMM. Becoming a GEMM is deeply rooted in the efforts of the racially oppressed to survive and to experience a sense of belonging in a white dominant and oppressive world where equity is often an ideal and seldom a measurable and sustainable practice. Unfortunately, becoming a GEMM does not, as many soon discover, protect one from the suffering associated with psychological homelessness because they are often estranged and disconnected from their racial roots.

My clients Lloyd Jones and Eun-Kyung, both of whom I referred to in earlier chapters, provide excellent examples of how making racial accommodations to fit in can be costly in other areas of one's life and can intensify their struggles with psychological homelessness. The accommodations that Lloyd made at his job to fit in, to be embraced by whites, and to be widely respected as one of the good ones—the GEMM—came with a very high cost, especially at home with his sons, LJ and Odom.

At age 66, Lloyd is battling depression that is undoubtedly connected to the death of his life partner of 40 years but also very strongly connected to his search for home in the spiritual, existential, and psychological sense. His lack of clarity about who he is as a Black man after being whitewashed in corporate America haunts him daily. Our sessions are inundated with his recollections of very painful memories associated with the ways in which he, in his words, "compromised his soul," as by often feigning laughter at racist jokes told by a coworker or administrative superior at his former office. He recalls with impeccable clarity the many times he should have spoken up about race but failed to do so. Lloyd keenly understands that he engaged in these self-annihilating behaviors not only to fit in but also to survive. His sons have been very honest with him regarding the respect and gratitude they have for him as a hard worker as well as for the comfortable life he has provided for them. On the other hand, they have been equally transparent with him about the shame, disappointment, and anger they feel toward him as a Black male role model. Lloyd has several times read to me a letter that his oldest son LJ sent to him. The pain he obviously feels with each word is fresh and palpable every time he reads it. The phrase that moves him to tears every single time is: "every time I watch you interact with white people, especially white men, I wonder where is the strong Black man I used to know, love, and respect as my father? How did this spineless, fearful, and deferential dude take over my dad's body?" The sting of LJ's feedback understandably makes it difficult for Lloyd to grasp the deeply seated hurt and disappointment buried beneath his son's toxic words. At this stage of his life, Lloyd is in a ferocious wrestling match with himself. He has incessant questions about who he is and how he wants to be as a Black father of adult Black male children. In many ways, Lloyd understands that he has been "too white" for his sons' comfort and that the person and father they wanted and needed him to be racially likely would never have been fully accepted in the workplace. Like most parents, he wants the best for his children. He is clear that he does not want his children or grandchildren to be forced to relinquish who they are racially as he did. However, he worries intensely that if they don't compromise, adjust, and accommodate, the white world will be punishing, unforgiving, and harshly discriminatory. When he thinks about the racial double binds that his children and grandchildren will inevitably have to confront while also trying to reconcile how he dealt or failed to deal with his, it intensifies his despair and depression. His sense of psychological homelessness is magnified by the homelessness that he fears his children and grandchildren will inevitably have to experience. This is the intergenerational entanglement that is often associated with psychological homelessness.

Eun-Kyung, the daughter of Korean immigrant parents, spent much of her formative years with her parents' assistance, shaking off and shedding anything that publicly connected her to her Korean roots. She worked hard to cultivate a well-manicured "Americanized self." She adopted a European name, never spoke Korean in public, and met all the unspoken mandates of becoming a GEMM. These credentials, along with her doctorate degree in psychology from a prestigious northeastern university, helped propel her to the top of her profession. Professionally, she is internationally recognized as a prominent psychologist. However, personally, she is, in her words, "absolutely unhappy, disappointed, and lost." Like Lloyd, Eun-Kyung is deeply concerned and worried about her daughter, Cho. She desperately wants her daughter to have what she never had: a deep, meaningful, and substantive connection to her Korean roots. She worries that neither she nor her husband is aptly prepared to provide Cho with the type of cultural grounding they want her to have, although they are fervently committed to it. Other than their families of origin, both Eun-Kyung and her husband are fairly disconnected from other Asians, let alone Koreans. As is often the case with psychological homelessness, Eun-Kyung never feels quite "Asian enough" when in the presence of other Asians, regardless of ethnicity and/or nationality; and she, despite all the racial accommodations she has made, is often painfully reminded that white-like is not white when in the presence of whites. She grapples daily with the inconvenient truth that she doesn't feel like she belongs anywhere. Eun-Kyung was emotionally devastated and distraught after she took Cho on a long-awaited and much-anticipated trip to Korea for the first time. She said she had expected it to be an opportunity to get reacquainted with her Korean roots as well as to introduce Cho to their shared cultural heritage. She was disappointed when her daughter consistently rejected the local Korean cuisine and only wanted to eat at McDonalds. Eun-Kyung also had another rude awakening and epiphany when she noticed that every time she entered a store, or any other business establishment, as a patron, she was always greeted in English, although she speaks Korean fluently. She was stunned and dismayed that she was immediately and consistently perceived and treated as an "American," an identity that she had spent her entire life cultivating and one that she, in the moment, regretted because it overshadowed her homecoming.

This is what it means to teeter on the fringes and to be stuck betwixt, in the never-comfortably-fitting-anywhere world of psychological homelessness. Having an authentic, completely transparent, and intimate relational interaction is almost always a monumental endeavor when one is beset with psychological homelessness. The mask wearing, the surrender to the pressures of racial accommodation, and the process of GEMMification create a level of dissonance within oneself that has far-reaching relational consequences. It becomes exceedingly difficult for one to be authentic and transparent in intimate and personal relationships if one is genuinely unknown and foreign to oneself. Psychological homelessness strips one of the ability to answer some of life's most challenging questions: Who am I? Whose Am I? What do I believe in and stand for? Who is it and how is it that I wish to be? When these questions are virtually unanswerable, the devastating consequences are not just individual, they are relational as well. Thus, psychological homelessness is a condition that is experienced individually but has far reaching ramifications throughout one's network of relationships. Lloyd's complicated relationship with his eldest son, LJ, is an excellent example of the how psychological homelessness can contribute to the disruption of an intimate relationship. Lloyd's interactions with his sons are often overshadowed by the deep sense of shame and regret he has about certain "choices" that he made in his life regarding race. Choices that weren't always "choices." His sons, on the other hand, are trapped between their feelings of admiration and love for him as their father and their disappointment and disgust with what they perceive as his rejection of, or discomfort with, his Blackness. In young Black men, these conflicting feelings, views, and experiences are hard to reconcile. Lloyd, his sons, and even Eun-Kyung are all searching for that elusive "something else," which is often a major indicator of some underlying bout with psychological homelessness. Eun-Kyung traveled to Korea in hopes of rediscovering loss pieces of herself that she could begin to pass onto her daughter only to return to the United States feeling more confused and less psychoemotionally grounded. Attaining the sense of home she was seeking, and naïvely thought would be easy to capture by going to Korea, proved to be more challenging than she had anticipated. As noted earlier, existing within a perpetual state of yearning is a major and predictable feature of psychological homelessness.

ANALYSIS OF EUN-KYUNG'S STORY

Eun-Kyung struggled in our initial session to find the right words to clearly and adequately convey the baffling condition that characterized her life and fueled the constant anxiety that she felt about her life and particularly the future for her daughter, Cho, as Korean Americans. One of the most devastating elements of racial trauma is that it often places the sufferers of it in a gut-wrenching conundrum because they can't make logical sense of the intense underlying feelings they are experiencing, and they often find it difficult to describe. In therapy, one of the most critical interventions the therapist can make involves naming the condition. Doing so has the benefit of establishing a common language between the therapist and client, and it frees the latter to attach a name to an otherwise nameless phenomenon. In the absence of naming, most clients either dismiss the legitimacy of their pain and suffering or, more importantly and unfortunately, blame themselves.

Throughout our first two sessions together, I listened carefully as Eun-Kyung unknowingly described in perfect detail the salient features of psychological homelessness as she described her life. After listening to this segment of her life story, I said, "It sounds to me like you are really entangled in an intense battle with a condition that I often associate with racial trauma called psychological homelessness. It is what so many People of Color must deal with as a consequence of feverishly trying to fit into two separate worlds, only to find that they do not comfortably fit into either." Before I could fully complete the "petite lecture" I wanted to offer about the condition, she began to cry with deep body-altering sobs that often left her grasping for air. There was something about naming the experience that immediately removed key bricks from the wall of the dam that had kept her blocked from all the deep emotions she had about feeling like she was everywhere but belonged nowhere. These feelings were intensified for her when she thought about the possibility of Cho replicating this same pattern, and she wanted better for her daughter. By assigning a name to the phenomenon, and especially one that spoke to the essence of her experience, Eun-Kyung was immediately able to release the self-blaming and self-doubting intrusive thoughts that she had been having and that were also a major source of anxiety for her. The process of naming is not a metaphorical, magic therapeutic pill; however, it is a critical first step in the racial trauma healing process.

SUMMARY

Psychological homelessness is a common and recurring invisible wound of racial trauma experienced by the racially oppressed. It compromises one's sense of belongingness, safety, and security and relegates one to living a marginalized existence, often trapped between two or more worlds while never feeling authentically embraced by either. It is the experience of all *hyphenated-Americans* of Color who are always perceived to be too Black, Asian, Latinx, Indigenous, South Asian, or multiracial/biracial to be regarded as authentically American and too American to ever be fully embraced by one's race of origin. The relentless effort to find viable ways to live in both worlds is the very factor that often spearheads psychological homelessness, which is individually and relationally destabilizing. For example, consider the complications embedded in the situation of the family who immigrates to the United States from Guatemala and who forbid their 5-year-old son, Eduardo, from speaking Spanish in public to facilitate his assimilation. Thus, he speaks only Spanish at home to his non-English speaking parents and only English outside of the family. At some point during Eduardo's school age years, he becomes ashamed of his parents' poorly spoken, broken English as well as of their insistence on holding onto Guatemalan culture. He doesn't want them to come to his school or to be with him in public. The parents in turn, become increasingly concerned about Eduardo becoming "too American," as he is commonly known as "Eddie" outside of the family. Eduardo/Eddie is forced to live in two worlds, both of which place incredible and often undeliverable expectations on him. His dark skin, Indigenous physical features, and slight accent are stark reminders of his outsider status outside of the home, and yet his style of dress, mannerisms, command of the English language, and his adopted name are painful reminders to his family that they "have lost him" and that he is "no longer one of [them]." These dynamics are often the source of tremendous pain, conflict, and emotional cutoff in families who do not have an understanding of the intricacies of psychological homelessness. The need to belong is a basic human need, and when it is denied, psychological homelessness is inevitable.

Rage

Of all the complicated wounds associated with racialized trauma, rage is by far the most complex and difficult to conceptualize. It has many different faces, contours, modes of expression, and behavioral manifestations that add to its extraordinary complexity. It is misunderstood similarly by those who are beset with rage as well as those who observe, invoke, or are tasked with responding to it. In its more intense manifestations, rage can be frightening to those who are finding it difficult to manage as well as to observers and/or to its intended targets.

Rage covers a wide spectrum of expressions, which further magnifies its complexity. There are expressions of it that are laced with aggression, volatility, and a heightened state of agitation and explosiveness. On the other hand, it can also be expressed in less overt, emotionally demonstrative ways that are equally intense and all-consuming as the more overt expressions. The more subtle expressions of rage usually involve a type of silent seething. There is no fist pounding, vein-protruding yelling nor overt expressions of hostile, anger-laced discord. To the contrary, this version of rage represents a type of metaphorical "slow boil" that remains slightly beneath the surface of overt expression, thus it is easy to overlook, dismiss, or miscalculate. Our conventional perception of rage often centers around a set of behaviors that are driven by strong, threatening, seemingly uncontrollable affect. Obviously, a much more comprehensive, sophisticated, and nuanced understanding of the phenomenon of rage is necessary, especially for those interested in engaging with clients with racial trauma.

DEFINING CHARACTERISTICS

Regardless of how it is ultimately expressed, rage is a raw, sustained, and intense emotion that occurs over a protracted period. It is often closely interwoven with experiences of marginalization, degradation, loss, and voicelessness. In one way or another, each of the invisible wounds discussed up to this point of the book is entangled with rage and is a major contributor to it as well. Rage is the predictable byproduct of continued hyperexposure to merciless acts of domination coupled with devaluation, assaulted sense of self, psychological homelessness, and the systematic and relentless stripping of one's voice and self-agency. In fact, these experiences often serve as the incubators for rage. Thus, the seeds of rage are, with every act of humiliation and injustice that they experience and are routinely coerced to endure quietly and passively, firmly planted within the soul and psyche of people with racial trauma.

Rage is a type of emotional ledger that "records" all the racially based slights, injustices, and maltreatment that People of Color experience, both literally and symbolically, over the course of a lifetime. Hence, it is a universal experience for People of Color, and it is ever-present in some form or fashion, albeit in varying degrees of intensity. It represents a type of gradual (emotional) "nuclear" build up that is constantly reinforced and fortified by the dynamics of oppression and the insistence that the authentic affective experiences of People of Color remain both silenced and suppressed. It is the consistent, steady, and on-going build-up of intense emotion, inextricably connected to degradation, marginalization, humiliation, and silencing, that differentiates rage from anger.

Recognizing the critical distinctions between anger and rage is important. Unfortunately, whites have weaponized the notion of the "angry Black person" or "angry Person of Color" to the point that many People of Color work hard to deny any feelings of anger or the expression of any emotion that might be construed as it. When the justifiable rage of People of Color is reduced to a broad, sweeping, overly simplistic, reductionistic label of "anger," it denies and defies the historical suffering and persistent racial oppression they have endured. Hardy and Laszloffy (1995) offer the following analysis of the distinctions between anger and rage:

> The critical distinction between anger and rage is related to time and intensity. Anger tends to arise "in the moment," generating intensity that usually leads to an emotional release that quickly reduces tension. When it is denied expression, the intensity associated with it festers, and eventually is transformed into rage. Thus, suppressed anger acts as an incubator for rage. (p. 58)

Anger is often a temporary, episodic emotion that has a fleeting quality associated with it. **Rage** on the other hand, is a deeply rooted emotion that is "aged" because, as previously noted, it occurs over time, often without an opportunity for release. Rage is the culmination of something (or somethings) that has (have) happened to you, literally and/or symbolically. It, unlike anger, is often transmitted intergenerationally and can be experienced vicariously through the experiences of others (the symbolic self). By all measures, it is a response that is deeply rooted in trauma.

In addition to its distinction from anger, there are a few other noteworthy defining characteristics of rage. There are four critical and salient properties of rage that must be considered to fully comprehend its depth and scope. Regardless of its level of intensity or root cause, rage can be: 1) suppressed and/or repressed; 2) internalized and/or externalized; 3) functional and/or dysfunctional; and 4) complexly entangled with voicelessness and powerlessness. The careful consideration of these underlying properties of rage further helps provide a more thorough understanding of how deep and personally consuming the experience is for those who are mired in it.

SALIENT PROPERTIES OF RAGE

Suppressed and/or Repressed Rage

Rage can be suppressed, which is a conscious process, or repressed, which places it beyond the scope of one's consciousness. The dynamics of racial oppression virtually force People of Color to either deny their rage entirely or to "avoid burdening white people with it" by not expressing it. The suppression of rage involves People of Color taking direct, definitive, and intentional actions to conceal, deny, or minimize any overt expressions or acknowledgment of rage. Failure to do so often culminates in some form of punishment, censorship, or ostracism. Suppressing rage also ensures an intensification of the very rage that is being suppressed.

Repressed rage, on the other hand, results from a much more unconscious process and is often the culmination of repeated punishment, reprisal, or previous trauma associated with the expression of rage. It is as if the human body and psyche intuitively understand that rage is so objectionable and toxic that it must be completely sealed off and buried from one's realm of consciousness. In these instances, there is a lack of conscious awareness of rage, which may be expressed and experienced through another "more acceptable" affective experience, such as despair. Since repressed rage is unconscious, its existence is beyond the awareness of those who suffer from it. The repression of rage is also a self-protective mechanism that facilitates emotional containment and some simultaneous distancing from the alleged negative and undesirable aspects of the phenomenon. Repressed rage tends to be internalized and is rarely expressed externally.

Internalized and/or Externalized Rage

Rage can be expressed and/or directed internally or externally. Internalized rage is directed toward oneself, either the literal or symbolic self. As mentioned earlier, repressed rage is often internalized, and it is seldom expressed in ways that involve a strong, raw, intense emotional expression. Internalized repressed rage often looks strikingly similar to despair and depression. It can also be expressed through a wide array of self-soothing, self-destructive behaviors, such as substance abuse, elements of addiction, self-mutilation, or a range of other self-defeating behaviors. On the other hand, the repudiation of and aggression toward members of one's biological or ancestral family would be an example of internalized rage directed toward one's symbolic self. Again, the self is the intended target, however, in this case it is the symbolic self. Internalized rage differs from externalized rage in that the latter is predicated on the overt expression of raw, intense affect that is outwardly directed. While it is unlikely that repressed rage would ever be expressed externally, suppressed rage often is externalized, usually in subtle, discreet, and indirect ways.

Functional and/or Dysfunctional, Constructive/Destructive

It is important to note here that technically rage, in and of itself, is neither *functional* nor *dysfunctional* but rather the way it is experienced, managed, and expressed can be. Rage is a potent source of energy, and how, where, and when it is directed can ultimately dictate its functionality and/or dysfunctionality. Rage is often the fuel that drives the vehicles of social activism and the quest for racial justice. Stoute (2021), a Black psychoanalyst who specializes in working with rage clinically, acknowledges how her rage as a Black woman mobilizes her work. She notes,

> my rage is well-encapsulated, stored in my mind; it protects my sense of self and fuels my drive to write, because Black Rage, as an adaptive construct, promotes defensive sublimations. The activated Black Rage construct serves a protective function as I work to modulate the reactive rage while living in a racist society that assaults my consciousness daily. (Stoute, 2021, p. 270)

As Stoute affirms, rage can be, and often is, a powerfully transformative emotion when it is regulated, properly channeled, expressed, and targeted. Thus, *functional rage* is often regulated and generally meets the aforementioned criteria. The functional dimensions of rage have little to do with how loud one speaks, the persistence or intensity of one's affect, or whether one is civilly obedient or disobedient. Instead, it is based on whether rage has a vessel for expression and the extent to which it can be discharged, guided, and directed free of blockage, misplacement, suppression, or repression. When rage is regulated, it can be a potent source of spiritual energy that liberates the soul and imbues one with a sense of personal empowerment. It can be constructively channeled. This approach to the expression of rage is embodied in a type of rage that I refer to as "righteous rage," which will be discussed in greater detail later in this chapter.

On the other hand, rage can be paralyzingly dysfunctional and immobilizing when it is denied expression, lacks a vehicle for discharge, or is displaced or misguided. When this occurs, rage is often dysregulated and is an emotionally intense state of being whereby an individual is completely overwhelmed by and consumed with a painful and deep sense of grief, despair, and destructive entitlement that is overshadowed by a sense of uncontrollable and unmanageable fury. Dysregulated rage can also be a source of energy, although it is often self-destructive and misdirected. It usually allows for the activation of one's voice and momentary flashes of self-empowerment. However, unfortunately these experiences are often short-lived and nonsustainable because of the destructiveness inherent in the experiences of dysregulation. The rage-induced looting and the destruction of physical property perpetrated by some factions of protesters during racial demonstrations following the murders of unarmed Black and Brown men by the police is a potent example of dysregulated rage. The protesters who cross the moral, ethical, and legal lines of their constitutional right to assemble by engaging in destructive behaviors are usually governed by a tsunami of intense emotions (rage) that have accumulated over time and for which there have been no viable pathways for discharge. Fortunately, and unfortunately, the public protests afford legitimate opportunities for the expressions of rage that are usually either unavailable or denied. Unfortunately, protesters are often trapped in a chronic state of dysregulation or as I prefer to say: *dysragelation*. This is one of the major defining characteristics of self-righteous rage, which will be discussed in greater detail later in this chapter.

The ability to reason and, in many cases, to physically relax are all severely compromised during a state of dysregulated rage. It is a highly disembodied state that makes the a priori assessment and appraisal of personal consequences for one's actions nonexistent. It creates and contributes to a temporary state of nihilism. The "choices" that one typically makes during a heightened state of dysregulated rage are inevitably self-destructive in one way or another. What matters most during these moments is the release of rage, which is often a complex mixture of anger, frustration, hopelessness, despair, voicelessness, and an assaulted sense of self that has been bottled up, contained, and building in intensity over an extended period. Unfortunately, and understandably, during moments of dysregulated rage, there is very little attention extended to what the consequences of one's seemingly impulsive and enraged actions might render. There is a willingness to "die" (literally and/or spiritually), to barter death for dignity. It is only the profoundly devalued and dehumanized that would treat death with such seeming frivolity. But then again, it is only the profoundly devalued and dehumanized that live their lives in a cesspool of disrespect, where blatant acts of dehumanization are a common occurrence and death appears to be an upgrade in status. This was my state of mind during that the encounter with Officer Callahan on that unforgettable November evening described in the preface of this book.

When there is a dearth or denial of proper channels for authentic engagement and the expression of (constructive) rage, the alternative will always be to disintegrate into dysfunctional/ destructive expressions of rage. The silencing of rage only ensures a rapid escalation and deepening of it.

Voicelessness and Powerlessness

The pervasive dynamics of racial oppression often deny People of Color adequate opportunities to give voice to their rage about the experiences of inequality and racial injustice that permeate our society. Too often, People of Color feel silenced, cajoled, and placated when they attempt to constructively engage with white people and white systems about racial injustice. For all practical purposes, People of Color are essentially silenced. It is the systematic suppression of the voices of People of Color by whites that often underpin the seemingly inexplicable, senseless, and "mob-like behavior" expressed by some People of Color, especially during public protests and racial demonstrations like the ones connected to the 2020 murder of George Floyd. The rage expressed by People of Color during experiences of racial unrest is palpable, understandable, and (functionally) cathartic even when the vehicles for and targets of the expression might be (self) destructive, misguided, or misdirected. From the vantage point of the oppressed, the expression and discharge of rage is empowering. At the very least, it affords an opportunity to challenge and overcome one's sense of voicelessness and powerlessness, even if only temporarily.

Voicelessness and powerless are highly interlinked and constitute the major roots of rage. It is the state of voicelessness that essentially deems the voices of People of Color muted. As noted in Chapter 8, voicelessness is the result of being silenced, which is an act of interpersonal violence. When invoked and widely executed, it strips People of Color of their rights and the ability to speak on their behalf. People of Color often "choose" to remain silenced or, more accurately, acquiesce to being silenced as a strategy for survival. The more silenced People of Color are, the deeper their sense of voicelessness and, consequently, the more intense their rage. The perpetual and systematic relegation of People of Color to voicelessness inevitably punctures their sense of personal agency; in other words, it breeds a sense of powerlessness. Hence, many People of Color are trapped and their voices are silenced, which means that they are not heard, and their needs are neither met nor responded to, which in turn strips them of virtually all opportunities to successfully self-advocate. This dynamic reinforces powerlessness and makes reclaiming one's voice and speaking up seem futile. It is this escalating sense of hopelessness and frustration, associated with the vicious cycle of voicelessness and powerlessness, that fuels rage. The internal emotional container that is used to hold and store all the blocked, unexpressed hurt, degradation, and frustration has a limit. When that limit is exceeded, there is either an internal implosion, in which the person breaks down emotionally, or an external explosion of rage. When anger, hurt, and frustration are continuously denied expression, rage is usually the consequence; when rage is consistently and systematically denied expression, violence is often, unfortunately, a predictable consequence. The violence can be directed internally toward oneself, literally and/or symbolically, completely externalized, or some combination of the two. Rage cannot be easily addressed or eradicated when the racially inequitable conditions responsible for it are allowed to persist. Thus, many People of Color must learn how to live in a perpetual state of rage with all the extraordinarily complex emotional and psychological underpinnings associated with it.

EMOTIONAL/PSYCHOLOGICAL MANIFESTATIONS

Simply stated, People of Color live *in* rage and consequently must learn to live *with* rage in a state of *en*rage. Living enraged and always on the precipice of outrage is a nonnegotiable, lifelong, emotionally taxing experience. Being enraged creates an inescapable psychoemotional quandary for many People of Color because the expression of rage, or outrage, is rarely tolerated in any fashion and seldom goes unpunished. People of Color, and especially Black people, have historically been stereotyped (defined) to be angry, barbaric, and prone to violence. This stereotypical assignment has been used throughout all areas of society as a tool of oppression and has served to advance the agendas of whites. U.S. presidential candidates and other political office seekers have effectively used images of allegedly scary, threatening, angry, and potentially violent Black People to influence election results. Law enforcement often relies on the same racist and stereotypical reasoning to justify the excessive use of force against Black and Brown people who are perceived to be "threatening," "angry," and "violent." Whites in office suites, company board rooms, and in factories all share a common bond in "not feeling safe" in the presence of emotionally demonstrative People of Color. The long-standing, racially oppressive historic and efficacious strategy of defining Black people as angry and threatening has created a deeply rooted fear and anxiety within People of Color of being perceived as angry and threatening. Black people intuitively understand, and both historical and contemporary events have proven, that just being perceived as angry by a white person can lead to deadly consequences. Being incarcerated within the narrow walls of such a crippling stereotype that requires constant acknowledgment is not only emotionally exhausting, it is also rage-inducing at its core. Herein lies the double bind. To disprove the stereotype and to increase one chances of survival, one must submit to it, which, on the other hand, only intensifies rage. If the rage is ever expressed, the legitimacy of it is never scrutinized, only the fact that it reifies the notion (stereotype) of the angry Black person. Emotionally and psychologically, Black people and other People of Color expend a considerable amount of psychic energy, anxiety, worry, and effort attempting to monitor and effectively manage this untenable condition. The need and desire to survive almost demands that People of Color become adept at holding, living with, and managing two very conflicting sets of complicated emotions. Surviving means having to live with a blazing and justifiable cauldron of internal rage, rooted in endless experiences of racial injustice and degradation, all the while having to cater to comfort-seeking whites by trying not to appear angry. This dynamic is the hallmark of what it means to live amid impenetrable racially oppressive conditions, where racialized trauma is a predictable outcome. The vicious cycle of being enraged and silencing it to reduce racial trauma only to have the "solution" further intensify the condition and to thus require further silencing is emotionally overwhelming, confusing, and paralyzing. Living life on this "hamster wheel" generates several other complex related emotions that People of Color must regularly contend with.

Unfortunately, there are countless numbers of People of Color, largely due to internalized devaluation, who believe that there is something inherently wrong with or flawed in them because they feel what they understand as *intense anger.* Their adherence to the white-promulgated stereotype often becomes a major source of underlying anxiety. Solutions to this quandary are often hard to find, largely because the anatomy of the problem is grossly misunderstood. The omnipresent race-related rage that consistently looms slightly below the surface on good days, quickly becomes treated, understood, and embraced as a personality trait rather than a response to racial injustice. Not only do processes such as anger management and/or psychotherapeutic approaches that are not race-centric usually fail miserably, they also unwittingly contribute to the enhancement of anxiety and, in some cases, the sense of degradation and despair that an individual may be experiencing.

Degradation, which severely diminishes one's sense of worth through the eyes of self and other, is a critical dimension of rage. It is often transacted and promulgated through a host of societal actions, inactions, words, and behaviors. For example, the Black Lives Matter movement, which was preceded by the "Black and Proud" movement decades earlier, was born out of and in response to the degradation and devaluation of Black life as evidenced by the number of unarmed Black people who are routinely murdered by Police officers with virtually no accountability or responsibility. The devaluation of Black life is put on full display for the entire world to see, which is not only degrading but humiliating as well. Black and Brown bodies being a commodity has been an integral part of the culture of the United States historically. The incessant degradation of People of Color is further illustrated by the myriad ways in which whiteness is elevated in our society while all other hues are marginalized and pathologized. In most sections of our society, whiteness is considered better, preferred, and synonymous with "normal," "human," and "American." As noted in Chapters 2 and 3, to be a Person of Color ultimately means to be born into circumstances wherein you will be regarded as less than and will be relegated to a life sentence of devaluation, degradation, marginalization, and humiliation. The complex, choking, and pent-up emotions that are inevitably associated with these experiences sow the seeds of rage. Thus, it is virtually impossible to live a life under perpetual emotional, psychological, and behavioral racial assault and not experience some degree of rage. To ignore the significant psychological impact of these experiences on the lives of People of Color by reducing and attributing the enormous complexity of these issues to simply "having anger issues" is itself a blatant act of degradation that can be a major precipitant not only of rage but of despair as well.

Despair virtually always underlies and is intermingled with rage. Despite its prevalence and prominence, it is seldom acknowledged or addressed. Though other emotions may be entangled within the web of rage, the intensity, rawness, and force of most expressions of rage often overshadow and obscure the other salient and related emotions. Through the eyes of naïve and unsophisticated observers of rage, it is hard to see and appreciate the dignity assaults, hopelessness, powerlessness, and voicelessness that overt expressions of rage often mask. The more overt expressions are often both the antidote and catalyst for disrupting feelings of despair and hopelessness. This is in part why it is common to see someone who is yelling in an angry, boisterous, and loud voice simultaneously be crying hysterically. Rage and despair are frequently intermixed. It is often a sinking sense of despair that is the dominant emotion that immediately surfaces following a rage outburst. It is important to note that the expression of rage does not *cause* despair. Instead, it is a fundamental component of rage that is virtually always lingering in the background and slightly below the emotional surface. The despair that is often accompanies rage is also attributable to the depth of loss that inundates the everyday lived experiences of People of Color. Loss is deeply rooted in the historical and contemporary experiences of People of Color, and despite its prevalence, it is seldom consciously acknowledged. Living intimately with loss, as many People of Color are required to do, also means living with an incessant and nagging sense of race-related hurt and pain.

The deeply rooted pain that virtually always underpins rage is often ignored and underappreciated. The race-related pain that is often a component of, and complexly fused with, rage is not a sharply pointed physical pain. It is a diffuse, hard to pinpoint psychic pain that appears unnamable because it is embedded in both the past and the present and is believed to foretell aspects of the future. It is inextricably connected to one's literal and symbolic self. It is a subtle but piercing pain that is saturated in grief, intermittently numbed by anger, and fortified by the legacy of trauma and oppression that neither the mind nor the body can forget. It is a pain that is continually aggravated by the innumerable societal reminders that "fairness and justice for all" is an ethical/moral ideal that has been systematically denied to generations of People of Color. Acclaimed Black poet Langston Hughes acknowledged this complex mixture of hurt, pain, rage, and justice denied in his poem "Harlem," which was published in 1951. Hughes asks: "What happens to a dream deferred?" (Rampersad & Roessel, 1994, p. 426).

Whether these deeply internalized complex emotions "fester like a sore, or just sag like a heavy load, or explode" (Rampersad & Roessel, 1951, p. 426), there are no good options. They do not adequately address or ameliorate the underlying and deleterious effects of racial oppression and trauma. Even the relief that is achieved from the overt expression of rage is often tenuous. Any relief is often short-lived because expressions of rage are often limited by punishment, reprisal, silencing, or some combination of each of these. Unfortunately, one is ultimately left with a reservoir of unnamed hurt and pain that is often grossly overlooked, unacknowledged, and unaddressed. It should not be surprising to anyone that the attempted containment of these complicated emotions, for which there are few appropriate channels for expression and discharge, would likely stultify the execution of effective race-related interactions.

BEHAVIORAL/RELATIONAL/ INTERPERSONAL MANIFESTATIONS

Since, as noted earlier, some degree of rage is always present for People of Color, finding ways to manage it is an ongoing and challenging endeavor. Rage is a powerful filter through which many People of Color see, experience, and interact with others, especially whites. The efforts to manage and/or mask rage in white spaces, and particularly in the presence of white people, require continual focus and energy. Some People of Color find it necessary to detach and/or withdraw from cross-racial interactions because it is the only way for them to regulate and manage rage. The withdrawal, in many instances, is not intended to be hyperbolic, antisocial, or arrogantly aloof; instead, it is a survival strategy. It is a way of keeping a container on rage to avoid being overwhelmed and consumed by it or having it explode and, subsequently, being punished, ostracized, or stereotyped for expressing it. The management and expression of rage is always replete with countless double binds and dilemmas wherein one is forced to select from "choices" that usually range from bad to worse. For example, one can voluntarily withdraw from certain interactions to keep one's rage appropriately suppressed, while suffering silently with all the internal struggles that accompany it. Or one can "choose" to engage, risk having one's rage activated, and then be left with the "choice" to suppress it while being triggered or to express it and then be ostracized, critiqued, or overtly punished. This is one of the reasons it is common for the Person of Color who is perceived to be hypercompliant, GEMM-like, quiet, easy-going, easy-to-get-along-with to also have a bulging sense of intense suppressed rage. Rather than representing an absence of rage or an eagerness to please, the hypercompliant behavior is actually a control valve for managing rage because it may not be safe to either acknowledge or express it. Unfortunately, one of the many dilemmas associated with the management and expression of rage is that the hyper-compliant Person of Color can and will often inevitably be the target of others' rage for their unwillingness or inability to address issues of race more overtly. The following vignette highlights the hidden racial subtleties and dilemmas of this dynamic.

Vignette: No White Problem Here

Dr. Clarice Larsen, a white president and CEO, of a behavioral health organization in a large urban city, retained me as a consultant to address "racial issues in the workplace." In her preliminary meeting with my team, she reiterated several times that it was important we know that her organization was unique because their racial issues were *not* Black versus white or white versus any other color. She proudly asserted:

> I am really happy and relieved to announce that we don't have a Black–white problem here, and thank God for that! Our problem is a Black and Black, People of Color–People of Color issue, and my white staff, fortunately, have learned how to just stay out of the way, even though none of us quite understands why there is so much within-group angst and bickering. Our executive leadership team is committed to addressing this issue and concurs that our problem is Black and Brown versus Black and Brown. We have two groups of People of Color who seem to always be at odds with each other. We have a very small contingent of very angry, race-baiting Staff of Color who have appointed themselves the spokespeople for all Staff of Color, and we have a group of very hard-working People of Color who show up every day and just want to get their work done. The latter group is not interested in playing the race card,

getting in the middle of racial politics in the office, or accusing all the white staff of being white supremacists. The former group is quick to constantly point out how this policy is racist or that action was biased, and then they get miffed when the other People of Color disagree with them or choose to not get involved in the counter-productive, divisive interactions. At the end of the day, those people just want to show up at work and get their jobs done. I don't know why this should cause angst, do you? I just don't understand it, and I am hoping that you and your team can find some answers for us.

Dr. Larsen's knowledge and understanding of the racial landscape of her organization was quite limited and myopic. She was oblivious to the ways in which her exclusively white executive leadership team, the preponderance of white staff, and the subtle but pervasive manifestations of silencing, voicelessness, and rage were wreaking havoc on the entirety of day-to-day interactions in the organization. Contrary to her view, there was as much of a *white issue* within the organization as there was a *Black and Brown* issue. In fact, as I once mentioned to her, there are few circumstances where "Black and Brown" issues exist devoid of "white issues." After conducting a series of racially segregated affinity groups with the staff, the entanglements of the Black, Brown, and white issues were identified.

A disproportionate number of the white staff shared Dr. Larsen's view that there was a small group of angry, sometimes hostile, People of Color who were "race-baiters" and "rebel rousers." Through the eyes of the white staff, these staff were described as the see-the-glass-half-empty type who could never be pleased and who were not content unless they were being divisive. According to Dr. Larsen and the executive leadership team, "the disgruntled group of People of Color constantly complained that 'nothing had changed,' despite the considerable diversity related changes that had been consistently implemented throughout the organization over the past several years." The view of the executive leadership team was passionately shared by many white staff participating in the white affinity groups. In other words, they believed that there was a group of Staff of Color who were perpetually dissatisfied, regardless of what diversity related changes were implemented throughout the organization. These staff were routinely described as "hard to please," "pessimistic," and "ungrateful."

The People of Color affinity group, on the other hand, started off quite contentiously as the tensions and conflicts within the group were quickly and passionately put on full display for our consulting team. Just as Dr. Larsen had indicated, there was quite a bit of discord expressed within the group. However, it appeared a bit more complex than she had described. There was passionate unanimity within the group regarding what was described as "racism within the organization." The exclusively white executive leadership team was often referred to as one of the numerous examples of what one participant referred to as "the reign of white supremacy at Genwright Behavioral Health." The unanimous sentiment and cohesion of the group became splintered when some participants expressed disappointment with and criticism of those in the group whom they perceived as "white enablers" who were unwilling to hold "white people accountable." Next I share the highlights of the People of Color Affinity group meeting and how it was shaped by the manifestations of race and various expressions of rage.

Vignette: White Enabler or Black and Proud?

The mood in the room was emotionally intense yet simultaneously somber. The tenor of the meeting was polite but quickly changed from congenial to conflictual when a Woman of Color,

Marsha, who had been included in a group that was disdainfully referred to as the *white enablers* of the organization by another participant, was quite visibly offended and outraged by the characterization. She immediately stood up and began to angrily state in a loud assertive voice: "I am no white enabler; I am a very proud Black woman and resent the allegation. None of you know me that well, you don't know who the hell I am, what I am or what's in my heart. How dare you f^&*ing judge me! I see the same racist shit here that everybody else sees. I said no more than ten minutes ago that this place is like a god-damn plantation! I see it! I feel it every day I walk through those doors, but at the end of the day I have three children . . . three Black children, who I worry about second-to-second and who I am raising on my own. So, I must show up here daily, swallow my pride, and be nice to a bunch of white folks here who treat you like you are invisible one day and their servants the next. I have to show up and swallow all of this shit because I have to think about my little ones, to do whatever I need to do to make sure they survive." At this point, she begins to sob uncontrollably. She goes on to say, while sobbing, clinching her fists, and shaking her head in a slow rhythmic way with her eyes closed, "and then to have you—my own people—throw me under the bus, accuse me of being some goddamn, f^&*ing white sympathizer hurts. It really HURTS! What do you want me to do? What do you . . . want . . . me . . . to do? I need this job! I can't afford to be labeled some Black Lives Matter radical. I cannot risk getting a bad performance evaluation or to be issued a corrective action plan like some of you. I am sorry that I have let you all down. I am so sorry."

The air in the room was heavy, there was not a single dry eye anywhere in the group. Marsha's rage, pain, and sense of powerlessness were palpable. Her powerful personal disclosure resonated with everyone in the room, even her detractors. In many ways, all of our stories, including us as a consulting team, were some version of her story. In fact, Barbara, the woman who had originally referred to some members of the group as white enablers, was the first to immediately reach out and firmly hug and hold Marsha closely as they both cried inconsolably. The meeting, although indeed very painful, was also cathartic. It acted as a release valve that enabled all the participants to say what needed to be said, share what needed to be shared, and hear what needed to be heard by each of them. The communal sharing and consensual validation that they were all having similar experiences, albeit expressed very differently, enabled them, as a group, to begin to purify and solidify their relationships with each other. "Marsha," I said, "thank you for loving yourself enough to express all that toxic rage and hurt that you just expressed to us. It needs to be discharged, otherwise it will destroy you and yours. It was a gift to each of us, as you provided us with a window into your soul; and I think it invited of all of us here to take a look into ours as well."

This brief vignette provides a wonderful illustration of the complexity of rage and how two or more individuals affected by it may respond differently. Both Marsha and Barbara were overcome with rage and a host of other emotions attached to it, yet they managed the rage very differently, which had a negative consequence on their relationship. Marsha marveled at the ways in which Barbara could so freely and openly express what they both felt about the workplace. There was also an element of Barbara's "boldness" and the threat of a punitive backlash from whites that created a level of fear for Marsha. Barbara, on the other hand, had some low-grade resentment that Marsha, and others, remained quiet and were consequently deified by the white staff while she was demonized as angry and hostile. This unfortunate dynamic served only to intensify Barbara's rage toward the likes of Marsha as well as her white colleagues. Meanwhile, Dr. Larsen lacked the type of comprehensive knowledge or understanding of silencing, voicelessness, rage, and racial trauma that would have enabled her to fully recognize the complex racial dynamics that were playing out throughout the workplace. It was difficult for Dr. Larsen to understand or appreciate the level of rage that a significant number of the Staff of Color felt in reaction to what they experienced as racially oppressive practices within the organization. More specifically, it was difficult for her to fully understand the ways in which Barbara was deeply committed to the organization and simply wanted People of Color to be treated more equitably and humanly within it. Barbara's rage was precipitated by and rooted in what she and other People of Color perceived as racially based, unfair, unjust, and inequitable treatment in the workplace and throughout all of society. Unfortunately, the longer these underlying conditions are allowed to persist, the more intense the rage becomes, and ultimately it can affect a wide range of relationships, within the organization and beyond.

The extent to which rage manifests relationally, how and whether it is expressed, and what its overall impact will be is ultimately dictated by several factors, such as whether it is suppressed or repressed, internalized or externalized, and regulated or dysregulated. It will also depend on the type of relationship the enraged people have with their rage. There are three principal types of rage, each rooted in the common experiences of protracted hyperexposure to racial degradation and injustice and each with a distinct impact on how it is expressed behaviorally and the way it ultimately shapes relationships.

The three types of rage are: 1) quiet rage; 2) self-righteous (destructively entitled) rage; and 3) righteous rage. Each of these was briefly alluded to earlier in this chapter, however a more expansive explanation follows. There are both distinctive differences and considerable overlap between the types. For instance, they all share a deeply seated emotional intensity that is inextricably tied to experiences of degradation, marginalization, and silencing. The major differences are attributable to the relative relationship that one has with one's rage, how it is metabolized, how it is expressed, and how it affects interpersonal relationships. These types are not fixed and are often contextual and situational. Here is a closer look at the three types of rage and some of the major characteristics that distinguish one from the other.

Quiet rage is an intense emotion that is often expressed indirectly and usually in ways that are not immediately attributable to rage. It is self-consuming and requires constant effort and energy to keep appropriately harnessed and somewhat disguised. It is always activated but remains slightly below the surface of overt congruent expression. It is typically expressed in subtle and indirect ways, unless a stronger and more direct response is provoked. Obstinance, resistance, and stubbornness and abstinence from interacting, cooperating, and participating with others can all be potent indirect expressions of quiet rage. The voice of quiet rage is often communicated behaviorally and interpersonally and may not involve the utterance of a single word. In this regard, it is often misunderstood, miscalculated, and dismissed as rage. The anatomy of quiet rage is difficult to grasp conceptually because it lacks the more overt and obstreperous qualities that are customarily associated with anger and rage. It is "quiet" because of the perception (and quite possibly the reality) that it isn't safe to express it in overt ways. People of Color who suffer from quiet rage generally appear interpersonally reserved and guarded in cross-racial relationships. They are physically present but emotionally somewhat detached. This demeanor is often critical to the management and effective regulation of rage. Although this type of rage can be intermittently suppressed, it is often channeled in ways that are often measured, methodical, and strategic. There is a quiet and unabating tenacity associated with it. In the People of Color affinity group, Marsha exhibited many of the characteristics of quiet rage. She was about as enraged as Barbara, though there were likely some degrees of difference in the intensity of their rage and certainly in their respective modes of expression. In fact, it was Marsha's detached demeanor and refusal to publicly express her rage that led Barbara and others to perceive her as a white enabler. Although Dr. Larsen perceived Marsha as the ideal worker, in some respects she was less emotionally committed to the organization than was Barbara, who was a relentless vocal critic and was often perceived as a problematic troublemaker. Marsha, on the other hand, managed and contained her rage through remaining somewhat emotionally disengaged from her coworkers and from the workplace in general.

Marsha's channel for her rage was her children's future. She was narrowly focused on ensuring that her children would be well positioned and better equipped to combat racial oppression and racism than she was. She was also very focused and strategic about getting her work done to facilitate her transition to a higher position with another organization. In many ways, she was every bit as critical of the racism in the workplace as her counterpart, Barbara. She expressed it differently. It was her quiet rage that steadily fueled her passion, energy, and tenacity to persevere, despite working in a place that she referred to as a "plantation." Far removed from the spotlight of the People of Color versus People of Color issues at Genwright Behavioral Health, several of Marsha's Colleagues of Color unanimously described her as a powerful source of inspiration behind the scenes. They reported, privately, that she was, especially with Black women she trusted, a powerful voice of Black female empowerment, which is why she found the label of white enabler so condescending and hurtful.

Marsha's emotional reaction to Barbara's insensitive words was understandable and yet the interaction between the two of them was a reminder of how rage can infiltrate a relationship and be an aggravating factor between two parties with a shared racial view and varying degrees of rage. It was also a further reminder that there is no one typical and/or predictable way to express rage. Just as rage varies in degrees of intensity, it also varies in terms of how it is expressed. Quiet rage, for example, is often expressed in measured ways. It is expressed, and often perceived, as a type of low-voltage rage, based on how it manifests. Thus, it is the intensity of expression, not the depth of the experience, that distinguishes it from other types of rage. On the surface, quiet rage looks very different from self-righteous rage, which is a high-voltage, deep, intensive emotion that is virtually always expressed overtly and in some version of an outburst or, stated differently, outrage. While *quiet* and *self-righteous* rage share some common foundational factors, the way each is expressed could not be more different.

Self-righteous rage, especially in terms of how it is expressed, is the antithesis of quiet rage. It is virtually always overtly externalized, and no effort is made to conceal, diminish, or downplay the forcefulness of the strong affect attached to it. Again, like all other types of rage, the genesis of self-righteous rage is rooted in experiences of racial degradation, marginalization, and silencing. However, the response to these effects of oppression is to develop a sense of *destructive entitlement*, that is, an ideology rooted in the belief that "the world has not been fair to me, so therefore I deserve to now be treated equally and fairly regardless." This strategy for survival, and the sentiment attached to it, is understandable, though the way it is usually expressed and approached invites, unfortunately, only more unfair, rejecting, and harsh treatment from others. Self-righteous rage is often expressed with strong elements of narrowly focused condescension, condemnation, and criticism, all engulfed in a flurry of fury. Self-righteous rage occurs within a constant state of chronic affect dysregulation. The state of chronic dysregulated affect coupled with the painful and debilitating underlying effects of racial oppression significantly obscure and narrow the view of those who suffer from self-righteous rage. Their worldview is markedly egocentric. All aspects of one's life are perceived through the lens of racial oppression, racial degradation, and racial injustice. The world is dichotomized into "us versus them," and the emotional consequence of this view is unbridled self-righteous rage. There is seldom a middle ground, "you are either with me or against me" is the organizing principle that informs most interpersonal relationships of those with self-righteous rage. Deeply rooted, unacknowledged, and untreated hurt and pain often supplant the capacity for emotional sensitivity to others. The egocentric, unbridled, often belligerent expression of self-righteous rage is momentarily self-soothing but relationally injurious.

The high-level intensity of self-righteous rage is usually a by-product of race related degradation and emotional injury that is further complicated and compounded by other non-race-related deeply rooted hurts and relational injustices that may have occurred in one's life. Family of origin related abuse, neglect, abandonment, and/or hurts associated with membership in other societally stigmatized groups are often connected to self-righteous rage. Thus, the gravity and overwhelming nature of the rage is commensurate with the gravity and depths of global suffering that one has had to endure. Unfortunately, the torrent of non-self-reflective belligerence that is often relentlessly directed toward others often obscures the deeply rooted pain that undergirds the behavior.

The relational consequences of self-righteous rage are far-reaching and unfortunate. Because the high-voltage type rage is always front and center, it becomes an integral component of one's overall persona. Those who suffer from self-righteous rage are often perceived as "toxically hostile, belligerent, abusive, and disrespectful." Sadly, much of their behavior often involves many of these emotional features as well as corresponding self-destructive behaviors. Their underlying pain and desire to belong, to be valued, and to be respected are often hopelessly obscured by the perpetual expression and ferocity of their rage. People of Color suffering with self-righteous rage, despite their life circumstances, are less interested in and less adept at managing their rage through masking and suppression. For these people, employing subtle and indirect means of expressing rage is never even a remote consideration, even when there is some potential material gain for doing so. With self-righteous rage, the emotional build-up is so intense that it can be evident in how one speaks, behaves, and participates in relationships. It is neither concealed nor compartmentalized. The gravity and intensity of rage that the person lives with are reflected in all domains of their being. It is conveyed via facial expressions, tone of voice, and the overall varying degrees of perceived abrasiveness in their interactions with others, especially whites. Interpersonal relationships are often marred by others' fear of what is often considered to be an imminent outburst of rage, which may or may not be an accurate prognostication. Nevertheless, demonstrative expressions of rage often serve, and may be interpreted, as a warning sign that one should proceed with caution. The presence of the smallest glimpse of rage tends to have a significant impact on how relationships are negotiated. Often, relationship interactions remain superficial due to the underlying fear that others often have that authentic, substantive engagement could trigger an explosive rage response. The interpersonal-relational dynamics associated with self-righteous rage are among the most complex and challenging to effectively negotiate of the various types of rage. The deep sense of under-lying hurt and pain as well as the remnants of rage from other non-race-related injustices, often are grossly overshadowed by the intensity and expression of rage-laced self-righteousness. Hence, for those besieged with self-righteous rage, the underlying hurt, pain, and deeply inflicted wounds of internalized devaluation and voicelessness are simplistically perceived and labeled as "having anger issues." Consequently, interpersonal relationships with others are often strained, ambivalently attached, superficial, and characterized by caution and trepidation. Unfortunately, the fragility and superficiality of these relationships unwittingly serve to further intensify self-righteous rage due to what is often experienced as unjustifiable and inexplicable relational rejection, isolation, and ostracism by others. Self-awareness about the adverse effects that one's destructively entitled rage has on others is often woefully lacking.

Matias, a 28-year-old Latino client, exemplified the profile of self-righteous rage. He was born and raised in the Bronx, New York City, where he was raised by a single-parent mother. His relationship with his father has historically been strained because Matias thought his father preferred Matias's older brother and rejected Matias because of his complexion. Matias said that his father always questioned whether Matias was his son and often directed the anger and questions he had about Matias's paternity toward him. He was convinced that the anger and mistrust that his father expressed toward him was connected to issues he had with his wife, Matias's mother. In addition to the strained relationship with his father, Matias also has a highly conflictual and contentious relationship with his brother. As a light complexioned, half-Puerto Rican, half-Dominican, Matias has often had to live between several different worlds, often with devaluation, disrespect, and discrimination as driving forces. He is an outspoken social justice activist who is well known throughout New York City political circles. He entered therapy because of difficulties with Lucia, his girlfriend of three years. The conflicts in this personal relationship seem to closely mirror those he has at work and in public life as an activist. Lucia loves him but admits that she is growing tired of his self-absorption and his "anger issues" that often feel mean, bordering on hostile. She explained that any request that she makes of him to be a more engaged and loving partner is met with a slew of anger-laced rants about how she doesn't understand him as a Latino man who must constantly walk around with the white man's hands around his neck. She reports that when she reminds him that she is Latina and lives in the same racist world, "he blows a gasket. He begins to yell and threatens to end the relationship because I have lost my roots and don't understand." She says he is very "sensitive to issues of racial equity and social justice when he has been disrespected but is largely clueless of all the ways he is disrespectful, condescending, and unreasonable." This dynamic is the hallmark of self-righteous rage.

When I pursued these issues with Matias in therapy, he quickly accused me of taking sides and dismissing his plight as a Man of Color. During one session, he told me, in a rather terse and annoyed tone, "Damn Doc, you been hanging around too long with too many of those white dudes; now you are getting into the tone policing." I responded, "I trust that you will hold me accountable and not let that happen, because it is a real issue for us People of Color. I love your rage and the passion and energy it provides for you; I simply want you to be in a position to control it rather than have it control you. When it controls you, it will destroy all aspects of your life, even your relationship with Lucia."

Vignette Analysis

Over the course of treatment, my goal was to encourage the couple to think of Matias's emotions as "rage," which I associate with hurt, pain, and trauma, and not anger. Once the mindset and the language are accepted and voiced by the client, it paves the way for them to pursue the hurt that underpins and is disguised by the rage. The next stage of the work centers around the many deep-seated underlying feelings that the self-righteous rage blocks them from considering. This can be and often is a lengthy and methodical process.

Unfortunately, there are scant opportunities for those who are maligned by the crippling effects of self-righteous rage to gain a deeper understanding of the condition and its relationship to racial trauma. Too often, the attention is focused on anger and anger management. If the underlying hurt and degradation that fuel the rage were a focal point instead of the "anger," it is conceivable that self-righteous rage could be parlayed into righteous rage, which is less self-destructive and is not as interpersonally and relationally detrimental. With righteous rage the strong, intense emotions are more directly channeled and are far less diffuse than they are with self-righteous rage. The former also tends to be less egocentric because the underlying nonracial, emotional, psychological, and relational injuries are not as pervasive.

Righteous rage is a conscious, deeply felt, externally expressed rage that is often driven by a moral and ethical imperative to seek justice, fairness, and equality. It is a regulated rage that is often channeled and appropriately expressed through acts of activism, protest, and resistance, all tied to a quest for social justice. It is guided by an abiding commitment and adherence to what is ethically and morally just. It is a principled rage that eschews achieving justice through means of injustice. In this sense, it is a type of rage that recognizes the importance and sanctity of relationships and the value of constructive engagement. Constructive relational engagement is always a driving force and potent organizing principle that underpins righteous rage. Righteous rage is a manifestation of rage that acknowledges and values the sacredness of humanity, the centrality of relationships, accountability, fairness, and justice. The concept of *eloquent rage* (Cooper, 2018), coined by Black feminist and Rutgers University Professor Dr. Brittany Cooper, seems to be emblematic of righteous rage. According to Cooper (2018), eloquent rage is the culmination of Black women's transformation of the anger associated with the injustices of racism and sexism into a powerful liberatory force that not only fuels their activism but propels them to *superhero status*. This type of rage is clearly and appropriately embraced by Black women and is the vehicle that propels not only their activism but their process of self-actualization as well.

Righteous rage, like other forms of rage, is all consuming. It is every bit as omnipresent as is the racial oppression that catalyzes it. Thus, those who are motivated by righteous rage are personally driven; there is never a reprieve from the fight for fairness, justice, and equality. The metaphorical on-off switch is permanently affixed in the "on" position. The potential for psychoemotional burnout and exhaustion is exceedingly high, while having quality time for relationships is often low and *scheduled* around the latest fight for justice. Fealty to the cause and the fight for racial and social justice can, and often does, take precedence over relationships, at least temporarily. While with righteous rage there is a high regard and respect for the sanctity of relationships that is not present with self-righteous rage, the two do share, however, a similar view of "you are either with me or you're against me" toward relationships. In other words, loyalty to *the cause* is of paramount importance to the formation and viability of a trusting relationship. In the vignette discussed earlier, Barbara made it known to all her Colleagues of Color, "either you are with me, or you are a white enabler." For the likes of Marsha, as well as Barbara's other Colleagues of Color, there was simply no middle ground: either you are in the fight or you are with the white power structure. While the position assumed by Barbara was based on an honorable cause (i.e., the pursuit of racial justice) and not intended to be divisive, ultimately it was precisely what it was not intended to be. While the tunnel vision associated with righteous rage is focused on "the cause" and is not nearly as self-centered as it is with self-righteous rage, the relational consequences are often similar. The demands for loyalty and high levels of commitment to the cause associated with righteous and self-righteous rage can have the unintended consequence of splintering relational bonds. The process of repairing relational ruptures precipitated by righteous rage tends to be a far easier process than those by self-righteous rage. This is largely because the relationship challenges ignited by righteous rage are seldom characterized by the type of toxic and belligerent personal attacks that are often associated with self-righteous rage. With righteous rage, there is always a high interest in and an underlying commitment to protecting the sanctity of relational connectedness, although the rippling effects of rage sometimes make this a challenging feat to accomplish successfully.

Rage, regardless of type or mode of expression, is a predictable manifestation of racial trauma. As Stoute (2021, p. 285) notes, it is a "functional and dynamic adaptative construct operating in the psyches of the oppressed." Grappling with the sophisticated entanglements of race, rage, and relationships is an extraordinarily complex interpersonal and intrapsychic dynamic that is virtually unavoidable for those with racial trauma. As with other invisible wounds of racial trauma, so little is known about the psychological underpinnings of rage, and it remains nameless, misunderstood, and ignored in spite of being the serious, life-altering condition that it is. The lack of a critical understanding about the phenomenon of rage also means that all the complex emotions and behaviors associated with it suffer from inattention and a lack of interrogation.

SUMMARY

Rage is a multifaceted, complex emotional response to the continual, intensive, long-term exposure to racial degradation, marginalization, and oppression. It is not partial to gender, class, sexual orientation, or generational issues. It is an invisible wound of racial trauma that affects all domains of one's life experiences. Despite its prevalence, the dynamics, functions, and deleterious effects of rage often escape scrutiny or critical understanding. Prisons, penitentiaries, the excessive caseloads of probation and parole officers, and the offices of guidance counselors and principals at every school level are inundated with Black and Brown people suffering from unacknowledged, unaddressed, and unregulated rage. Too often, it is simplistically misunderstood, mislabeled, and ultimately mistreated by whites as "anger issues" and its existence is vehemently denied by People of Color for fear of reprisal. Understanding and addressing rage is critical to understanding and addressing racial trauma.

CHAPTER 11

Intangible Loss and Invisible Collective Grief

All the invisible wounds that have been discussed thus far could very well be combined into the single invisible wound of *loss*. For those subjected to racial oppression and trauma, living with loss is a common and inescapable everyday experience. The exposure to loss is constant, and yet, as is the case with other invisible wounds, it is rarely overtly acknowledged and, in this case, properly mourned and grieved. The lack of recognition of experiences of loss endured by the racially oppressed exacerbates the overall condition by stripping it of its significance.

Unfortunately, the depth of the experience and its overall effects on the well-being of People of Color are frequently ignored, minimized, and dehumanized. Even the experience of loss is characterized by loss, that is, the loss of appropriate recognition and validation of its significance and legitimacy. Following the 2020 murders of George Floyd and Breonna Taylor, countless numbers of Black people were expected to carry on life as usual while they mourned, yet again, the senseless public lynching-type deaths of more innocent Black people. Though besieged with anger, rage, and grief, Black people were still expected to be perfectly emotionally regulated and show up for work, often in predominantly white spaces. They were expected to keep their feelings contained, remain emotionally present, and be prepared to advise their white colleagues and counterparts what they could do to make a difference. Unfortunately, there were very few sacred places where Black people, and especially mothers, could metabolize their grief and loss both in connection to the Floyd and Taylor murders as well as to a host of other related contemporary and historical experiences.

Loss is not unique to nor only experienced by People of Color. It is a fundamental dimension of living. The loss of loved ones, property, jobs, and a host of other valuable objects, commodities, and materials are commonplace for many of us, regardless of who we are. In one sense, to live and to experience life is to experience loss at some point. Unfortunately, in addition to experiencing these normal developmental and fact-of-life losses, many People of Color are also strapped with having to contend with a barrage of seemingly never-ending intangible losses that traverse the life cycle. Intangible loss is a formidable force in the lives of people with racial trauma because it is pervasive yet invisible, is crippling but lacks recognition, and has wide ranging effects on the well-being and daily functioning of People of Color.

DEFINING CHARACTERISTICS

It is important to delineate the critical distinctions between tangible and intangible loss. Although the two are connected, there are also some important distinctions that are noteworthy. Unlike tangible losses, intangible losses are neither physical nor quantitatively measurable. There is no visible concrete manifestation of the loss itself, as is the case with tangible loss, such as the loss of a limb. Intangible loss, for the most part, is emotional, psychological, and spiritual. Accordingly, there is no easily identifiable concrete, physical, and measurable representation of the actual loss. Thus, an intangible loss involves the denial or stripping away of that which is intrinsic to the psychoemotional well-being and daily functioning of an individual and/or group. It is likely that virtually all tangible losses involve some underlying intangible loss, although the reverse is not necessarily true. For example, the death of a parent (tangible loss) could also represent the loss of a major source of unconditional love (intangible loss). In this case there is a tangible loss that is inextricably intertwined with an intangible loss. The dynamics surrounding loss for People of Color is complicated and nuanced. On the one hand, they are confronted with the same array of losses that all other human beings must contend with, and they must also simultaneously struggle with a bevy of racially based intangible losses that are germane to being a Person of Color. Herein lies a major difference and difficulty for People of Color, whose lives are typically replete with intangible losses that may or may not be overtly connected to physical losses.

INVISIBLE WOUNDS AND LOSS

As noted earlier, each of the invisible wounds discussed in this book contains some important elements of an intangible loss that are embedded within the wound itself. Next, I will highlight the intangible losses that are embedded within each of the identified invisible wounds of racial trauma.

Internalized Devaluation

In many ways, intangible loss is the core defining experience of internalized devaluation. The intangible loss of dignity and respect constitute the hallmark of internalized devaluation. When one's dignity and respect are assaulted and ultimately stripped from the essence of one's being, one also inevitably loses one's sense of humanness. The everyday experiences of People of Color are often significantly organized by the constant pursuit of and quest to retrieve the sense of dignity, respect, and recognition of one's humanity that has been stolen, destroyed, and fiercely denied. The loss of dignity and respect is a piercing and life-shaping intangible loss. For many Black people, the Black Lives Matter movement represents a crystallization of the effort to regain what has been taken and ultimately lost (destroyed). The movement is not just a moniker to remind whites about the humanness of Black people, it also serves to assist Black People in restoring and reclaiming the dignity and respect that have been punctured over centuries due to racial oppression. The Black Lives Matter movement of the twenty-first century was preceded by the civil rights movement of the 1960s, when Black people often marched with signs and placards declaring: "I AM HUMAN," or "I AM SOMEBODY." Whether in the 1950s and '60s or in the 2020s, the loss of value attached to the lives of Black and other People of Color has profound consequences on how they are viewed by others as well as how they see the world and themselves. Loss of dignity and respect sharply influences how one sees oneself.

Assaulted Sense of Self

The intangible loss associated with an assaulted sense of self centers around the lack of clarity that one has about who one ultimately is as well as the lack of freedom to authentically express who one is, especially in white places. The intangible loss is of being free, of clarity about who one really is, and of freedom to express it. It is extremely difficult to freely interact and express oneself, particularly in white places, when there is constant pressure to adjust, remake, modify who one *really is* in order to facilitate the comfort level of whites or be accepted and/or included by them. This shifting *identity dance* is never done voluntarily nor with a sense of inner peace. There is often an underlying sense of grief and sadness associated with having to relinquish the core of oneself as a tactical maneuver. Doing the *dance* is an accommodation to whiteness, racism, and an effort to avert rejection, criticism, or harsh judgment. It is exceedingly difficult to feel free to be (who you are) when you know that doing so can cost you an opportunity, or in some cases, your life. The loss of the power and freedom to *be* is a damning intangible loss.

Voicelessness and Powerlessness

Having to be hyperalert regarding what one says, whether one should speak, and how one should speak if/when one does are all indicators of an intangible loss. As mentioned in Chapter 8, the loss is not, essentially, about one's literal voice or inability to speak, although in some instances it may be; it is, however, ultimately about the denial of individual agency and the ability to advocate on one's own behalf. Living a life walled off by oppression and subjugation does not imbue one with the freedom to be, to speak one's truth, or to act in concert with one's wishes and desires without the potential for reprisal. Once again, the loss of voice and personal advocacy stifles spontaneity and authenticity in interpersonal relationships and contributes to psychological homelessness as well as a host of other residual issues that will be discussed later in this chapter.

Psychological Homelessness

Psychological homelessness is one of the most devastating, pervasive, and challenging intangible losses. The feelings associated with it are felt intensely yet they are often difficult, nearly impossible, to acknowledge, name, or have validated. There is no vocabulary to aptly describe the experience, and like many wounds of racial trauma, it is not a recognized phenomenon. Psychological homelessness is essentially an intangible loss of a sense of belongingness. The homelessness referred to here is the lack of a metaphysical and spiritual place. For many People of Color, the loss of belonging is precipitated by living in a world that centers around and caters to white people and whiteness. The values, mores, ways of being of People of Color are often peripheralized in virtually all areas of society. The powerful, unspoken, but widely influential worldview is "the white way is the right way." For People of Color to be incorporated into the white world often means they must accommodate white ways of being. To "fit" into (white) society, it behooves one to know how to act white, talk white, be white-like in order to "belong." Even then, the sense of belonging achieved is conditional and largely based on deception, that is, the cultivation and projection of an idealized white self that is more embraceable than an authentic racialized self. While foregoing and/or suppressing the essence of one's authentic being is an extraordinarily effective adaptive response that allows People of Color to function well in white spaces, the underlying painful experiences of grief and loss associated with this process remain hidden from view. It is common for some People of Color to become mired in self-blame and to experience a loss of self-respect due to what they perceive as their shameful willingness to prostitute themselves in exchange for white acceptance. Obviously, these issues are complex and involve so much more than isolated People of Color willingly "prostituting" themselves and sacrificing the core of their being to win favor with whites. The essence of racial oppression and the hallmark of white supremacist ideology is designed to systemically engineer all aspects of a people's existence and to convince them that the madness that maligns their lives is of their own making, free will, and personal agency, a process that is critical in the nurturing of intangible loss.

Equivocating and accommodating whiteness demands living between two worlds and accepting that one will rarely ever fit fully and comfortably in either. It is committing to a life of marginalization. It means recognizing and making peace with the notion that, as a Person of Color, you will often be treated as a pseudo-American. Racially speaking, People of Color and whites live in two very different, often diametrically opposed, worlds. Whites enjoy the privilege of living in a world where they are the makers, interpreters, and enforcers of the rules and what is considered normal, American, and human, while People of Color live in a world marred by racial subjugation where they are expected to be the compliant, metaphorical rule followers even when doing so is to their detriment. People of Color must learn how to cope and live with the duality of living in two vastly different worlds, straddled across a racial divide, never feeling that they fully belong in either. Homelessness is an obvious and predictable outcome, and it is often compounded by loss and grief. The loss of home essentially means living without the comfort of knowing that you are safe, secure, and valued and that you belong.

Rage

At first glance, it probably seems preposterous to associate loss with rage, yet the two experiences are intricately intertwined. In very simplistic terms, rage is the chronic loss of affect regulation.

As previously mentioned, rage is the culmination of repeated experiences with degradation, devaluation, and dehumanization, all of which involve the loss of one's sense of value, humanness, and, ultimately, dignity and respect. The tremendous and overwhelming sense of hurt, powerlessness, and voicelessness experienced by those who feel racially targeted contributes to the formation of rage, which is an all-consuming, debilitating, uncontrollable, combustible state of unregulated/dysregulated affect. Thus, rage is fueled by loss and is the manifestation of it as well. In fact, the psychoemotional manifestations of intangible loss pervade the lives and lifecycles of many People of Color.

Vignette: Matias and Lucia Revisited

For Matias, discussed in the previous chapter, addressing issues of loss was every bit as critical to the therapeutic process as helping him to uncover his self-righteous rage and to transform it into righteous rage (which is less egocentric). Both Matias's and Lucia's lives were inundated with a flurry of intangible losses. In fact, it was Matias's threat to leave that motivated Lucia to seek therapy. Loss was a central but unacknowledged organizing principle in their lives.

Matias was riddled by the loss of a father's love that he could do nothing to earn; his light complexion always left him feeling insecure about his connections within the social justice communities that meant so much to him; and, of course, there was the perpetual loss of dignity and respect that he felt everyday as a Man of Color who also carried wounds of growing up poor. He and Lucia had also experienced the devastating loss of a pregnancy to miscarriage.

Lucia had to endure not only the loss of dignity and respect that comes with being a darker-skinned Latina but also the loss of dignity and respect that comes with being a woman. Unfortunately, her relationship rarely afforded her the space or opportunity to discuss and/or have her plight validated. This, too, constituted a major intangible loss. The therapy sessions had to be a place where the gravity of their intangible losses, both individually and collectively, and Matias's rage could be explored.

The exploration of (intangible) loss almost always starts with an exploration of the loss of dignity. The prompt for this process with Lucia was: "I want to hear about all the experiences you have had with loss." Before I could finish with my standard prompt, she began to rock back in forth in her chair, intermittently looking at Matias, and she began to cry. This is when she first began to talk about her miscarriage in therapy, and the first time ever in a substantive way. She was overcome with guilt because she recalled praying many nights "asking God to please not let it be a boy." She did not want the pain and agony of raising a Boy of Color in this world. She now fears that she was punished for being too picky. Matias responded with intense rage, saying, "You see! This is how f*^%ing white supremacy is contributing to genocide. If it ain't this, it's COVID; and if it ain't COVID, they are gunning us down in the streets like we are animals." I applauded Matias for his passion, insights, and sophisticated racial analysis, and then stated: "However, in this moment, I think it would be so helpful for you and Lucia if you could channel all that passion toward her in a loving way by letting her know what your heart is feeling toward her right now."

Vignette Analysis

Creating space to name, honor, and acknowledge the bevy of intangible losses that were entangled in Matias's and Lucia's lives was a major turning point in the therapy. While Matias needed considerable coaching and guidance in unearthing his deeper, more vulnerable feelings, he was able to do so in a way that Lucia had never experienced before. She had only experienced his rage. It was liberating for him to begin the process of discovering that he had feelings other than anger and rage. The loss of an opportunity to become a father was instrumental in helping him become more sharply attuned to the loss and grief he was experiencing by the lost opportunity to be fathered.

EMOTIONAL/PSYCHOLOGICAL MANIFESTATIONS

The emotional manifestations of intangible loss are complicated and often difficult to discern. Anger and rage, for example, are two emotional expressions that typically result from the constant and consistent exposure to intangible loss. In fact, although not intentional, expressions of anger and rage frequently obscure the underlying loss and grief associated with it. The experiences of deeply seated grief and loss are always just slightly below the surface. Given the onslaught of daily slights, dignity assaults, and other intangible losses that People of Color must endure, living with lingering feelings of grief and loss is inevitable.

The history of People of Color in the United States has been saturated with experiences of hatred, bigotry, and violence. People of Color's physical property has been consistently assaulted and destroyed by whites as have their progeny and other family members, the sacredness of their bodies, their leaders, their elders, and their cultural icons. Opportunities to live fully franchised, empowered lives worthy of dignity and respect have also been individually and systematically denied to many People of Color over multiple generations. Consequently, there is a deeply rooted, nagging, often times low-grade but persistent sense of despair that many People of Color live with, often without consciously realizing it. The despair is the culmination of experiencing generations of loss, especially intangible losses such as hope, security, safety, and one's sense of value and humanity, just to cite a few. The emotional tax of these recurring experiences and losses comprises a type of daunting and largely unacknowledged intergenerationally transmitted collective grief. The manifestation of grief is complicated because, like most intangible losses, it is invisible. Grief is universally experienced among People of Color; it is deeply felt but nameless and thus marginally understood. This kind of grief is felt poignantly in the present but is solidly rooted in the past; not just one's individual past, but one's collective past as well.

Invisible Collective Grief (ICG) refers to the generalized emotional response that a related group of people or a shared community has to a set of commonly shared losses. Whites have subjected many racially oppressed and traumatized groups to a protracted history of every type of loss imaginable, both tangible and intangible. The dehumanizing and dignity piercing experiences of enduring land stealing, persecution, the rape and murder of indigenous people, the assignment of Japanese Americans to internment camps, the Chinese Exclusion Act that legalized discrimination against Chinese people, the colonization of Latinx people, and the brutal enslavement of Africans still flow uninhibitedly through the bloodlines and veins of many People of Color as I write these words. The emotional weightiness of these indignities and assaults to the soul are transmitted intergenerationally. As my great-grandmother, the granddaughter of a slave, often reminded me during my childhood: "Kenny, you don't have to be in slavery to have slavery in you." She wanted me to know that although I had never been enslaved literally, the legacy of slavery nevertheless continues to live inside of me.

The enormity of invisible collective grief may or may not be consciously experienced by a given individual, however it is prevalent within the collective soul and consciousness of the group. Many People of Color tend not to be consciously cognizant of the underlying sense of despair and grief that permeate the entire community or to even have a language to aptly describe it. Instead, it is often understood and expressed as "fatigue," or a type of "heaviness," "sadness," or "worry." As is the case with most manifestations of despair, there is also a sense of fleeting and intermittent hopelessness that underpins it. The labeling and malignment of some segments of Communities of Color as "lazy," "shiftless," "lacking in drive and motivation" could very well be indicative of hopelessness, despair, and what it looks like when an entire community is grief-stricken because their sense of hope has been punctured. Having to confront the blatant and harsh realities of constantly being treated as a second-class citizen—or noncitizen—of living as a target under constant surveillance, and of hopelessly watching the historical and unabating murders of one's people without reprisal or accountability takes an emotional toll. The murders and/or untimely deaths of cultural icons and symbols of hope for Communities of Color—Martin Luther King, Malcom X, Nelson and Winnie Mandela, Emmet Till, Medgar Evers, Cesar Chavez, Maya Angelou, James Baldwin, Tupac Shakur, Michael Jackson, Selena Quintanilla Pérez, Kobe Bryant, Whitney Houston, just to cite a few—significantly contribute to the invisible collective grief that many People of Color live with daily. These cultural icons were largely regarded as members of the tribe who defied the odds, who successfully escaped the high walls of white supremacy and stood proudly on both the literal and metaphorical global stage. In ways that often escape conscious recognition or analysis, the deaths of these cultural icons, for many People of Color, are emotionally linked to the murders of Trayvon Martin, Tamir Rice, Breonna Taylor, Ahmaud Arbery, Sandra Bland, Eric Garner, George Floyd, Walter Scott, the ten victims of the 2022 white supremacist's shooting at the Tops Friendly Market in Buffalo, New York, and the many others, too numerous to name here. Individually and collectively, the unnamable feelings attached to these losses create a sensation of heaviness that is commonly referred to as "fatigue." Unfortunately, there is very little recognition of the underlying despair, compounded by an absence of redress for it, and thus it continues to seethe and simmer as a complex alchemy of rage and grief. Protests and public acts of civil disobedience have been a principal mechanism for offering some metaphorical *communal salve* for addressing invisible collective grief, but unfortunately, more often than not, these experiences too frequently involve the imposition of more loss on the psyches of Communities and People of Color. Living with an inundation of intangible losses rubbing up against unacknowledged invisible collective grief is quite emotionally burdensome, which helps to at least partially explain why so many People of Color complain about feeling "exhausted." Whether conceptualized as exhaustion or grief, it has a widely debilitating effect on the day-to-day interactions of most People of Color.

BEHAVIORAL/RELATIONAL/ INTERPERSONAL MANIFESTATIONS

Intangible loss, hopelessness, despair, fatigue, and invisible collective grief are toxically entangled for many People of Color. One of the many consequences of living intimately with this complex array of emotions is that many People of Color are forced to live with a heavy dose of anticipated loss and grief. Parents of Color, especially Black parents, who have recurring anxiety about their children having an untimely encounter with certain elements of law enforcement or not being treated fairly in school or some other social settings are not only grappling with intangible loss but anticipated grief as well. Anticipated grief requires the processing of strong feelings in the present based on a loss that is anticipate in the future. The combination of experiencing anticipated grief and invisible collective grief while simultaneously metabolizing intangible loss severely and significantly influences how Parents of Color parent. Many Children of Color are raised to be hyper-sensitive about who they are and where they are and to be hyper-cautious about how they behave. Too many Parents of Color are actively engaged with helping to shape and prepare their children for their futures while quietly agonizing and hoping that they won't one day, too soon, have to bury them. This is the stark reality of parenting within the context of intangible loss and anticipated and invisible collective grief. For many People of Color, and especially parents, the convergence of invisible collective grief (which transports losses from the past to the present), intangible losses (which inform the present), and anticipated grief (which is felt in the present but attributable to what might happen in the future) constitutes an emotionally overwhelming experience that affects everyday interactions and relationships.

Just as living with intangible loss breeds a sense of hypercaution for some, it can contribute to a wave of recklessness for others. Sadly, there is a segment of Children of Color, particularly adolescents, who believe in the inevitability of their untimely deaths. They understand the complexity of the conditions in which their lives are embedded. They understand all too well that they are perceived as the disrespected other, as menaces to society who must be controlled, contained, and confined. They present themselves to the outside world with bravado and invincibility, but beneath the surface they are hampered by a dauting fear, a sense of disillusionment, despair, and unmourned loss that leaves them hopeless about their futures. They witness what we all witness, that is, the ways in which society at large doesn't appear to value their lives. Beneath the surface of their bravado and feigned invincibility is an unopened container of grief. A container that blocks them from processing their sadness, losses, and grief and that leaves them only with the rawness of their unacknowledged rage. Unfortunately, what most of society perceives and responds to is their "anger," their total disregard for human decency, and their disrespectfulness. The inventory of invisible wounds they are compelled to live with remains invisible and punishment is relied upon as the treatment of choice, whether in the form of school expulsion, juvenile detention, and/or incarceration. Healing and (trauma-based) treatments are rarely considered viable methods of intervention. This orientation toward punishment is not just applied toward the treatment of Children of Color but toward People of Color across the lifecycle. Living with the invisible wounds of intangible loss and invisible collective grief affects virtually all domains of everyday life for most People of Color.

Living with the loss of dignity, respect, safety, and the overall personal freedom to *be* is an integral part of the everyday consciousness of many People of Color. Losing sight of these unfortunate markers of the impacts of living amid a pro-racist society can be emotionally, psychologically, and physically deadly. The hyperconsciousness about the prevalence of intangible losses, whether they are consciously named and recognized or not, culminates in the development of a type of hypervigilance that many People of Color live with regarding these issues. Hypervigilance is a heightened state of awareness and sensitivity to one's surroundings. In the context of racial trauma, it is difficult to be inundated with intangible losses and stripped of one's sense of dignity and respect while being subjected to constant surveillance and NOT become hypervigilant.

Being hypervigilant has a dramatic effect on People of Color's relationships with others, both within and outside of their respective racial group. Since race and racism are so prominent throughout all areas of society, it is difficult to accurately read or know whether race is an issue in any given space. Thus, it is safer to assume that race *is* an issue, even in the absence of persuasive and compelling data. Having the absolute certainty that an adverse experience, such as being denied a loan, was not racially motivated is not a comfort or privilege that many People of Color have the luxury to enjoy. The hypervigilance, and the anxiety that often accompanies it, has a profound effect on everyday interactions with everyday people.

A similar dynamic exists with the intangible loss of respect. A significant portion of the world of People of Color, including most everyday interactions, is organized by the phenomenon of respect. Most People of Color place a very high level of importance on respect. To the naïve, nonracially astute onlooker, their obsession with respect seems illogical, inexplicable, and trite. Yet, to those who live lives that have been characterized by an unending onslaught of contemporary and historical disrespect, it is a highly desirable and precious commodity; one that, both literally and figuratively, many have died for and many are willing to die for. What many whites consider to be the irrational hyperracial sensitivity of many People of Color is really an expression of the reinjury of an invisible wound.

There are very few interactions that People of Color are engaged in that are devoid of a hypervigilance about respect. Even interactions among People of Color are shaped by the interlocking dynamics of respect and disrespect. These issues are so emotionally charged because they are inextricably linked to internalized devaluation, assaulted sense of self, and piercing intangible losses. For this reason, many cross-racial relationships, regardless of context, are potentially explosive landmines. Given our racial socialization and the prominence of white supremacist ideology throughout society, it is rather "easy" and commonplace for many whites, while remaining oblivious to the assault, to say or do something that is perceived and received by People of Color as profoundly disrespectful. Because these types of experiences typically reaggravate an existing wound, the response by People of Color is usually a strong one, often laced with anger and rage. Since many whites are not only oblivious to their whiteness but to the dynamics of racial trauma as well, they are often ill-equipped to respond in ways that are constructive and facilitative. Adamantly insisting that one has been misunderstood, counter attacking and demanding respect, or highlighting the Person of Color's hyperracial sensitivity are common, predictable, and understandable replies; they are just not constructive or helpful. Unfortunately, they are often perceived as typical white fragility responses that exacerbate the racial strain in the relationship.

These exchanges are extraordinarily complicated because the actual precipitating event may be rather miniscule in scope and totally unintentional. However, it is not the size or scope of the actual issue but rather the underlying ways in which the interaction emotionally aggravates a preexisting invisible wound connected to the loss of respect and, quite possibly, invisible collective grief. The following vignette provides a powerful example of a cross-racial interaction that was usurped by a seemingly minor racial miscue.

Vignette: "What I Meant to Say . . . "

Sheila, a white clinical supervisor, mentioned in a group supervision session that "the overwhelming majority of my staff is comprised of 'colored people,' and we talk about race all the time." The People of Color in the group appeared stunned and looked at each other with expressions of disbelief, while remaining silent.

Ginny, another white supervisor, proceeded to commend Sheila for her courage and willingness to openly discuss race with her clinical team. Sheila thanked Ginny for her kind remarks and reiterated that talking about race was important to her.

Jasmine, a self-identified Woman of Color looking baffled and agitated, stated: "I'm sorry but I can't continue this conversation, I need to process the disrespect that just happened." She then turned toward Sheila and asked in a rather terse and agitated tone: "Did you just say, 'colored people' a few minutes ago?" She went on to say: "Excuse me, sis, but we ain't been called colored people since the 50s or 60s when *your* people decided to put that label on us. 'Colored people!'" she repeated sardonically. "What color am I?"

Sheila appeared initially shocked, then embarrassed and annoyed. She had heard enough. In an elevated voice she asked, "Why are you so angry? This is why we can never have conversations about race. If you had given me a little more time, I would have changed what I said, it was a mistake. I don't know where that came from, I know it is People of Color. I would have corrected myself if you hadn't been so disrespectful and rude. You attack me for no reason whatsoever and don't give me a chance to even respond, I would have corrected myself. I think you owe me and the group an apology for your angry outburst. That was totally uncalled for." The interaction continued to escalate until the supervisor intervened.

This brief vignette is a classic example of how the invisible wounds of racial trauma—most notably here, the struggle to negotiate intangible loss and the hypervigilance associated with it—can dramatically alter the course of a conversation and ultimately a relational interaction. It did not help matters that the original emotional trigger was exacerbated by Sheila's oblivion to her whiteness and her lack of knowledge regarding racialized trauma. On the surface, Sheila's (mis)use of the term "colored people" seemed rather benign when considered in isolation and out of context. However, from Jasmine's perspective and that of the other People of Color in the group, it represented so much more than a semantical miscue. For them, it triggered a trauma-induced reaction and was a painful reminder of the historical denigration of Black people over lifetimes, of the ways People of Color are often invisible to whites and yet constantly prone to being defined by them. Admittedly, Jasmine could have, ideally, addressed the infraction with greater decorum and in a manner that would have been more "acceptable" to Sheila, however the complex mixture of intangible loss, grief, and combustible rage that fueled her hypervigilance simply did not allow for that. She was in a state of emotional dysregulation that seemed to eliminate any possibility of her initiating a calmer conversation. Unfortunately, Sheila's demand for an apology and her ensuing castigation of Jasmine's alleged "rude, angry, and disrespectful" reaction only served to further aggravate an already tumultuous interaction. This vignette underscores both the pervasiveness and the complexities of the invisible wounds of racial trauma as well as the seemingly insurmountable faultline that underpins many cross-racial relationships.

SUMMARY

Intangible loss is a metaphorical connective tissue that binds together all the other invisible wounds of racial trauma. This loss is extraordinarily complex in its constitution because it is often unnamed, unacknowledged, and disguised by its entanglement with a host of other potent emotions, such as rage, grief, and hypervigilance.

Grief, both individual and collective, is a critical affective dimension of intangible loss. In many ways, grief and rage are interrelated parts of the same emotional sphere, one internally directed, the other externally focused. Both grief and rage are emotional byproducts of intangible loss and are exceedingly emotionally and psychologically draining. Unfortunately, these very complicated and overwhelming emotions are often characterized by many People of Color only as "exhaustion." While many People of Color are cognizant of the taxing physical demands of navigating racial oppression and trauma, too many underestimate and remain oblivious to the potent emotional toll associated with intangible loss and collective grief. These powerful emotions, along with all the psychological and behavioral manifestations that accompany them, are silent assassins that hamper, and in many cases destroy, the hopes, dreams, and well-being of many unsuspecting People of Color.

CHAPTER 12:

Orientation Toward Survival

The *orientation toward survival* is an invisible wound that can best be understood by analogizing it to the psychological concept of *paranoia*; except, unlike the latter, it is not rooted in delusional thinking. Instead, it represents a type of "healthy cultural paranoia" (Boyd-Franklin, 2003) based on the daily slights and persecutory behavior that many People of Color, especially those who are Black, experience and must contend with while participating in routine everyday events. It is the response to the all-too-common and painful experiences that many Black People experience such as to random, unprovoked, and life-threatening traffic stops by law enforcement or to being blocked access to one's own place of residence or, worst yet, to being murdered by law enforcement while at home. It is connected to the type of unfortunate experience that Eric Brown, a Black, licensed real estate agent, encountered back in August of 2021, in which he, along with Black clients Mr. Thorne and his son, were all handcuffed at gunpoint by the local Police in Wyoming, Michigan, as he was showing them a house that was for sale. The two Black men and a child were reported as burglars by local neighbors, which precipitated police involvement that ultimately resulted in drawn weapons with all three, including the child, being handcuffed (Lukpat & Medina, 2021). What would have very likely been a normal uneventful event for whites, was once again a memorable traumatic event not just for the three Black people involved in this daytime nightmare and their families but for most People of Color, like me, who live vicariously through every single one of these horrific and dehumanizing experiences. For many People of Color, Black People in particular, these assaults are constant, and they live resoundingly in the consciousness of those who are racially targeted, terrorized, and victimized. It is these types of predictably unpredictable events that provide the foundation for the orientation toward survival. Developing a keen understanding of how this wound operates in the lives of most People of Color is key to understanding a critical dimension of their everyday life experiences.

DEFINING CHARACTERISTICS

The orientation toward survival is both a worldview and a *metaphorical reflex.* It constitutes a kind of obsessive-compulsive, healthy cultural paranoia response to racialized stress and the experiences of being targeted. It is a survival-affiliated anxiety generated by the belief that the world is a threatening and over-reaching place for People of Color and that one's survival, whether physical, emotional, or psychological, is always potentially under siege. As a worldview, it is born out of, profoundly shaped by, and entangled with all the other invisible wounds of racial trauma. It is the byproduct of being coerced to live in a world that is inundated with racial inequality, discrimination, and assault. A world where some are compelled to live under an incessant critical and often demeaning white gaze and surveillance that could adversely affect one's life at any point, especially in ways that could be a matter of life or death. It is an approach to life that is deeply embedded in the desire to survive (Hardy, 2019). The adoption of an orientation toward survival is inevitable when one's life is besieged with actual or imagined threats, physical harm, denial of fair and equitable access to resources, and discrimination. When one's life is targeted and one must live under siege, the relevance and significance of the will and need to survive is elevated, which contributes to the formation of a *survival instinct*, or *survival reflex*. The survival reflex is similarly rooted in the same set of experiences and circumstances that give rise to the survival worldview.

Orientation toward survival and psychological homelessness are often linked. Because of the powerful forces of individual and systemic racism throughout society, there are very few places where People of Color can feel authentically safe, secure, valued, welcomed, and free from racial assault (either physically or spiritually). Even the racial socialization process of many People of Color is often laced with life lessons and cautionary tips about what is required to *make it* (survive) in the "white man's world." Racially based lessons regarding what to wear, what not to wear, what type of hair style is best, what to do with one's hands when in public, especially in stores, how to talk, how fast or slow to walk, what tone of voice is best, and when, how, where, and under what circumstances to speak are all intergenerationally transmitted strategies for survival. If the previous sentence required some effort to read it, think for a moment what it is like to have to live it! Sadly, it is only People of Color who must be systematically tutored, mentored, and prepped for how to survive in a country that claims to be "one nation under God, indivisible, with liberty and justice for all."

When the sociocultural context in which one's life is and has been embedded over generations has demanded deliberate and unrelenting attention to the matter of survival, an orientation toward survival becomes virtually instinctual for the people living it. I could fill the pages of this chapter with accounts of the steady stream of public and unprovoked attacks, unjustifiable arrests, and fatal cases of "mistaken identities" that People of Color, particularly Black people, have been subjected to, nationwide, just during the period I have been writing this book.

An integral part of living life as a Person of Color is being thoughtful and purposeful about how to survive, that is, how to cope with, withstand, and overcome daily acts of racism. Since the lives of People of Color are constantly susceptible to racial threat, harm, discrimination, and/or assault, there is very little time, and it is not prudent to take the time, to comprehensively weigh every situation on its individual merits. This is how and why the orientation toward survival reflex becomes honed and cultivated. The reflex has become refined over generations and often is activated without conscious thought. It is akin to the reflex of quickly withdrawing one's hand after touching a hot stove. No one must be told to remove their hand from a blazing hot stove. Similarly, the orientation toward survival is a reflex to counteract and overcome racial threats, harm, and discrimination.

There are several other defining characteristics of the orientation toward survival that are important to identify and highlight, for instance, it is 1) conscious and unconscious; 2) adaptive and maladaptive; and 3) exacerbated or mitigated by class and socioeconomic status.

Conscious and Unconscious

The orientation toward survival is often a simultaneously conscious and unconscious process. At the conscious level, many People of Color are acutely aware of living under a constant state of white critique, judgment, surveillance, and threat. Thus, there is a vast array of prophylactic measures that many People of Color consciously adopt to offset, contend with, and/or mitigate the impact of racial discrimination, hurt, and harm perpetrated by whites. These measures are tactical and specifically designed to enhance the probability of survival. Some of these measures have been discussed in earlier chapters of this book and include conscious tactics, such as refusing to engage in authentic conversations about race with white people, code-switching, self-policing and deliberately modulating one's tone, and exhibiting hyper-compliant, docile, nonthreatening behaviors in interactions with law enforcement and other power structures guided by white supremacist ideology. These accommodating and deferential behaviors are informed and fueled by the conscious recognition that they help to ensure survival by providing a safeguard against white backlash, domination, and assault. In this vein, many People of Color in the workplace must consistently metaphorically "turn the other cheek" when slapped in the face by an onslaught of racial microaggressions. They must do so to keep their jobs. In other words, doing so is necessary for *survival.* As my client Tamika shared during a therapy session: "I had a white coworker who deliberately kicked me after we had a very tense conversation about the news of an innocent Black woman who was 'mistakenly' killed by the police. She literally kicked me, deliberately! I have been pissed with myself ever since that moment because I really wanted to kick her ass. Yet I swallowed the shit! I said nothing. I wouldn't even go to HR because, why bother! Do you think they would believe me over a white coworker? So, I just took it, and it's been over a week now and it is still eating at me. I didn't say or do anything because I need my job. I have four kids I need to support. The funny thing, Doc, is that I would NEVER encourage my children to accept such racist and abusive behavior. Yet sometimes you have to do what you have to do." Tamika's "turning of the other cheek" was intentional and tactical. It was a conscious measure she employed to protect her job. The issue here is not whether she had a choice but rather whether she was conscious of the connection between her actions and surviving in the workplace, which she obviously was, which is the point here. This is an example of a circumstance where the orientation toward survival was a conscious process. There are, however, many instances where it occurs at a deeply unconscious level, which makes it more difficult to address.

The unconscious manifestations of the orientation toward survival are much more difficult to discern, deconstruct, and/or address. When the orientation toward survival is unconscious, it tends to be more reflex-like. The unconscious orientation toward survival may also be expressed through a wide range of behaviors that on the surface reveal very little about the connection to the phenomenon of survival. Behaviors that are typically characterized as "workaholism" or "serial job seeking" or high risk–low reward are usually driven by an unconscious orientation toward survival. The seeming "obsession" with work and working or with searching for the right job are actions that are typically driven by an underlying anxiety regarding one's sense of (in)security and capacity to survive. In each of these situations, the overt behavior obscures the underlying anxiety about survival. The behaviors in question here will be discussed in greater detail in the Behavioral/Relational/Interpersonal Manifestations section of this chapter. The conscious and unconscious dimensions of the orientation toward survival are, in some ways, loosely determinative of whether it is adaptive or maladaptive.

Adaptive and Maladaptive

There is often a razor-thin line that separates the adaptive and maladaptive manifestations of the orientation toward survival. Nevertheless, understanding and differentiating between the two is important. In one sense, the mere existence of the orientation toward survival successfully achieves the feat it is intended to accomplish, which is to center issues of survival. It facilitates the ability to develop effective coping skills and to combat adversity with agility and expediency because of the constant consciousness about survival. The preoccupation and obsession with surviving requires one to constantly be on guard. These tendencies help to strengthen emotional and physical endurance.

The orientation toward survival is the intangible resource that has, at least in part, historically enabled the descendants of enslaved Africans to transcend slavery; Indigenous and Latinx People to persevere despite centuries of barbaric attacks, cultural appropriation, and oppression; and other People of Color to stand tall with dignity and grace despite being discriminated against and treated with malice and disgrace. These incredible feats probably would not have been possible without an orientation toward survival. It has been a prominent pathway to survival for generations of People of Color. Whether channeled through a strong sense of faith, spirituality, or religion or through the vessel of hard work, these manifestations of the orientation toward survival have been and continue to be a major source of spiritual salvation. It is one of the many reasons why the Black church has historically been so central in the lives of Black People. In addition to providing access to scripture, the Black church also provided a sanctuary that promoted faith, hope, and endurance, while repairing and reinvigorating the souls of Black people to meet the demanding challenges of surviving in a world that seemed more committed to and invested in their demise than their survival.

As is the case with many issues in life, virtually anything that can be used to assist with adapting and coping can also be misused and/or abused in ways that inhibit it. This is certainly the case with the orientation toward survival. When the preoccupation with survival reaches the point where it becomes a rigid, narrowly focused fixation that is all consuming, it becomes maladaptive. The drive to survive, in this case, is often unconscious and takes priority over all other matters. The intense focus on survival morphs into a "survive by any means necessary" mentality. Thus, anything or anybody that is perceived to interfere with or pose a threat to one effectively satisfying the instinct to survive is ignored, discarded, or circumvented. This is generally true whether it is a person, place, or thing. Even significant relationships, whether with a colleague, acquaintance, or intimate partner, can easily be relegated to "nonpriority status" if they are perceived to interfere with survival. In fact, at this level of orientation toward survival, it is common for relationships to be regarded as principally transactional. The value affixed to them is predicated on the extent to which they facilitate and strengthen the orientation toward survival. Unfortunately, these motives are often strictly unconscious and therefore hamper both self-awareness and transparency in interpersonal relationships. In fact, the unconscious, narrow, and intense focus on survival at any cost, by any means necessary, is a major feature of the maladaptive manifestation of the orientation toward survival. The depth of this wound and its maladaptive features can be either expanded or contained and constricted based on the presence or absence of other sociocultural variables, especially social class. Since there is a dimension of this wound that is closely tied to class oppression and poverty, the enormity and emotional impact of it is even greater for People of Color who also happen to be economically oppressed.

Class as a Mitigating and/or Aggravating Factor

Class, like race, is also a powerful organizing principle that can either bestow an individual or group with extraordinary privileges or strip them of basic human dignities. People of Color who enjoy class privilege and the benefits that often accompany it (e.g., access to financial resources, a stable place to live, social approval, and access to food and other resources) have a "protective factor" that helps to mitigate exposure to wounds of racial trauma. Access to financial resources, education, employment, and social status can help significantly quell some anxieties about survival, at least materially speaking. However, the underlying survival concerns and anxieties associated with race and racial trauma remain, regardless of economic or social status. Class privilege can certainly lessen the intensity of the orientation toward survival, but it does not eliminate it. Unfortunately, mitigation is not elimination! The fact of the matter is that People of Color with class privilege remain hampered by their racially subjugated lives. Unlike their lower-income, resource-depleted Counterparts of Color, they do not have the burden of juggling the double jeopardy of racial and class oppression. However, unlike their white counterparts with class privilege, they also don't have the luxury to "enjoy" their class privileges free of racial slights, discrimination, marginalization, and, ultimately, worries about survival.

For People of Color who are also poor, working class, and/or chronically unemployed, in the words of poet Langston Hughes, "life ain't been no crystal stair" (Rampersad & Roessel, 1994, p. 30). They must contend with the recurring threats associated with being People of Color in a society that devalues them racially, while also facing the stark challenges of daily threats rooted in their socially stigmatized and devalued positions as poor, economically stressed human beings. They understand all too well that they live in a society that equates economic status with worth, well-being, and one's overall value—the same attributes that are also often assigned to whiteness. However, regardless of racial identity and background, the experiences with food and housing insecurities, as well as dealing with the social stigmatization of being poor or economically stressed, often contribute to an orientation toward survival for the poor that is strikingly similar to the phenomenon experienced by People of Color racially, regardless of class status. What this typically means for People of Color who are also poor or economically stressed is that the orientation toward survival is intensified, exacerbated, and complexly entangled in a web of class and racial oppression dynamics as well as the trauma that emanates from them.

The intermixing of race and class is further complicated by the fact there are first-generation American, often college-educated People of Color with considerable wealth and class privilege who were born into poverty and lived their formative years under austere financial circumstances. Often, the contemporary class status that they hold is usually not enough to offset the early wounds of class-based trauma that are often the product of poverty or living under economically stressful conditions. The ability to accurately sort out and disentangle class- and race-based trauma wounds, especially those attributable to an orientation toward survival, is exceedingly complicated. The presence of class privilege often obfuscates the underlying survival anxiety and concomitant emotional, psychological, and behavioral manifestations associated with it that are both class-based and racially based.

EMOTIONAL/PSYCHOLOGICAL MANIFESTATIONS

For the many reasons already cited throughout this and previous chapters, it is common for People of Color to live with a distressing sense of insecurity, discomfort, and anxiety about feeling safe, both emotionally and physically. This is one of many costs of being coerced to live so intimately with racial oppression. The intangible loss of safety is such an integral part of the everyday lived-experiences of People of Color that the underlying emotions attached to it often remain suppressed and removed from the view of the naked eye. As noted earlier, the orientation toward survival is both a worldview and a reflex; neither is ostensibly connected to demonstrative, overt expressions of emotions. However, beneath the surface, anxiety and fear are ever-present and palpable emotions. Anxiety and fear are exquisitely intertwined and may not be distinguishable for those who struggle with both. Anxiety is generally conceptualized as a response to an unknown threat or internal conflict, whereas fear is focused on known external danger. Steimer (2002) explained that

> Anxiety is a psychological, physiological, and behavioral state
> induced in animals and humans by a threat to well-being
> or survival, either actual or potential. It is characterized by
> increased arousal, expectancy, autonomic and neuroendocrine
> activation, and specific behavior patterns. The function of these
> changes is to facilitate coping with an adverse or unexpected
> situation. (p. 231)

Many People of Color suffer from both fear and anxiety and, given the pervasive and protracted history of racism and the assault of Black and Brown bodies, the line of demarcation between fear and anxiety becomes understandingly and significantly blurred. Existing in a constant state of uncertainty where one must be hyperalert to the prospect that one's racial background or identity can expose one to adverse circumstances and maltreatment is intensely anxiety producing. It contributes to constant questioning of oneself and others. It is crazy-making and emotionally and psychologically destabilizing to always have to wonder whether race has been a factor in an adverse decision, whether the denial of a job, promotion, loan, house, or myriad other experiences. For many People of Color, these experiences are sources of both fear and anxiety. What many whites naïvely refer to as People of Color "playing the race card" is really a byproduct and expression of the constant state of race related fear and anxiety, often triggered by behaviors perpetrated by white people, that People of Color must contend with. Since racial bias and discrimination have been such salient dimensions of life throughout history, it is risky and potentially self-harming for People of Color to not consider them a critical intervening variable in many cross-racial interactions. To do so, on the other hand, also means to live in a constant state of anxiety while scanning and searching for confirming and/or disconfirming data. Having to live with a steady stream of anxiety connected to one's survival and well-being can interfere with the ability to cope successfully with other, non-race-related life challenges. It also contributes significantly to the intensification of rage.

It is sad and unfortunate that the underlying fear and anxiety that many People of Color experience in connection with the orientation toward survival is so fundamental to living life as a Person of Color that it often escapes conscious awareness. Racially based life lessons and admonitions that are instilled during childhood, such as "You have to work twice as hard as the white person to be half as successful," are deeply engrained in the psyches of People of Color and help to feed the orientation toward survival and the anxiety that accompanies it. Both the orientation and the anxiety become "normative." It is the toll that People of Color pay when living in a racially stratified society that systematically devalues People of Color while vociferously denying it. Despite how normal and familiar it might appear, over the long haul, the toll of it all does affect the emotional, psychological, physiological, and relational well-being of many People of Color.

BEHAVIORAL/RELATIONAL/INTERPERSONAL MANIFESTATIONS

As has been previously asserted, the orientation toward survival represents a type of necessary, although not necessarily conscious, fixation or obsession. The feat of ensuring that one is being treated equitably, fairly, and humanely requires effort. It is not something that can be taken for granted, given the current state of race relationships in our society. Consequently, many People of Color, by necessity, develop *habits of survival* that are rigidified, automatic, habitual responses that are driven by survival anxiety and the orientation toward survival. Habits of survival are simultaneously functional and dysfunctional. On the one hand, adopting habits of survival is instrumental to empowering People of Color to address perceived and real threats to survival. This is the functional manifestation of it. On the other hand, the extent to which habits are rigidified, automatic, and reflexive constitutes the dysfunctional dimension, in that the response is "rigidly habitual" and thus always the same whether it is warranted or not. Since habits are simultaneously functional and dysfunctional, the task in working with People of Color is never to completely eradicate the habits but rather to enhance the functional dimensions while simultaneously eliminating or minimizing the dysfunctional aspects.

There are six habits of survival that are relatively common for People of Color, and they are: 1) the warrior habit; 2) the oppressed oppressor habit; 3) the subservient habit; 4) the feigned subservient habit; 5) the racially split habit; and 6) the hustler habit. These habits, both individually and collectively, require scrutiny and exploration when working with racial trauma. A brief descriptive profile of each follows.

The Warrior Habit

People of Color who embody the warrior habit tend to address their concerns about survival by exhibiting a perpetual willingness to "fight," to resist boldly and unashamedly, all perceived and actual threats of domination, discrimination, and injustice. That is, anything or any issue that poses a threat to their survival as racial beings automatically elicits a push back, a "fight" response. This habit is driven by an abiding commitment, passion, and relentless energy to confront all issues, individual and systemic, that pose a threat to the well-being and survival of People of Color. It embraces the view that People of Color must actively confront racial domination and marginalization at all costs and by any means necessary. This habit is fueled not only by survival anxiety and fear but by a vacillation between righteous and self-righteousness rage as well. Functionally, it provides an opportunity to activate one's voice, to create a channel for the expression of rage, and to counteract potential acts of devaluation, to cite just a few of the benefits. On the other hand, this habit can, potentially, stifle growth and strain relationships because it requires constant confrontation and engagement in "a fight" even in instances where there is no fight to be fought. Once a warrior, always a warrior! Fighting becomes a rigid and automatic reflex. It is not only the first response but the second, third, and all ensuing responses. For example, this was the major difficulty that my client Matias had, which was destroying his relationship with his longtime partner, Lucia, as well as his work relationships. The combative and contentious qualities often associated with the warrior habit can make some interpersonal relationships, especially cross-racial ones, difficult to negotiate. There is a persistent emotional intensity that fuels the warrior habit which can be taxing for close interpersonal relationships. People of Color who adopt the warrior habit usually express very little patience with and tolerance for white fragility, microaggressions, and acts of racial discrimination. In some ways, the warrior habit is in stark contrast to the *oppressed oppressor habit,* in which the intense energy is most often directed toward one's symbolic self rather than toward whites directly.

The Oppressed Oppressor Habit

The hallmark of the oppressed oppressor habit is its relationship to secondary-level oppression, whereby the victims of oppression become the vehicles of their subjugation. This habit deals with issues of survival by finding fault in the oppressed and thus blaming the victim. The oppressed oppressor is vigilant in holding other People of Color singularly responsible and accountable for their plight and the threats to their survival. Thus, the oppressed oppressor habit asserts that People of Color themselves, not whites, must do a better job of dismantling racism and creating more viable pathways for survival. This position often emanates from a deep place of racial pride and a commitment to self-determination; however, the messaging is frequently obscured by the pervasive blame-the-victim demeanor. The oppressed oppressor, often unconsciously, finds solace, safety, and a sense of security in advocating white-dominant messages and values to People of Color as a prescription for survival. Embracing whiteness and exhibiting white-like tendencies allows the oppressed oppressor to identify more closely with being white and to subsequently diminish one's underlying anxiety about surviving. The oppressed oppressor is often critical of other People of Color in ways that routinely fail to take the effects of racial oppression into consideration, which nourishes the blame-the-victim dynamic. The oppressed oppressor is as deeply concerned about the well-being and survival of People of Color as is the warrior, yet they differ substantially in terms of methodology. Whereas the modus operandi of the warrior habit is to fight and offer active resistance, the oppressed oppressor habit centers around finding fault within People of Color and demanding that they cease to participate in behaviors that reinforce stereotypes and threats to one's existence. As you might imagine, it is common for there to be active and steady tension between People of Color who exhibit these two often-conflicting habits of survival.

The oppressed oppressor habit, in its own unique way, does involve a type of fighting back that can be quite helpful to people with racial trauma. In a way, it does emphasize the significance of self-empowerment and accountability. However, it can also reinforce devaluation and exacerbate the assaulted sense of self by blaming the victims of oppression while making allowances for those who oppress. This habit also contributes to the calcification of the psychological homelessness of those possessing the habit. The relationship sphere of the oppressed oppressor is often characterized by high levels of tension, within-group discord, and a sense of isolation and alienation. Belongingness is often elusive because this habit relegates those who exhibit it to the status of being a *stranger in one's own tribe*. Moreover, their safety, security, and sense of survival among whites is conditional and based on their adherence to the ways of the oppressed oppressor habit. Thus, it is common to feel trapped between two worlds and to never completely belong to either. Both the warrior and oppressed oppressor habits may be, and often are, explosive and generate a considerable degree of emotional intensity. These qualities are unique to these specific habits and are not necessarily characteristic of habits of survival in general. In fact, the subservient and feigned subservient habits are notable exceptions.

The Subservient Habit

Submission, acquiescence, and exhibiting an accommodative-style behavior and demeanor are central components of the subservient habit. There is a noticeable absence of rabble rousing, emotionally escalating behaviors and overt intense emotional expressions in the subservient habit. In fact, this habit requires and is predicated on hypercompliance and possessing an adroit ability to metaphorically "fly beneath the radar." Internally, there is an unconscious acceptance of white superiority, a belief in the inherent futility of fighting back, and an underlying fear of the threat that is inevitably posed to one's survival by fighting back. Offering little to no resistance is regarded as a primary tool for ensuring one's survival. During a couples therapy session, Kathleen, a middle-aged African American woman, expressed the sentiments of the subservient habit best in reference to her husband Jerome and his behavior at work during a heated exchange. She said, "I tell Jerome all the all-time that it ain't his concern about how other Blacks are treated on the job. There will always be racism. The white man will always be on top. We are not going to change white folks because everything plays to their advantage. His job is to keep his head down, mouth shut, and do as the man tells him do. Like I was raised to believe, you catch more flies with honey than shit! Why waste time and energy burning out to change something that is the way it is intended to be. I learned to just do as I am told; it is the best way to get what you want and to survive."

As Kathleen's comments and mindset reveal, there is a degree of acceptance and acquiescence to the prevailing racial order. Unlike someone with the warrior habit, she sees very little utility in pushing back against what she perceives (and perhaps experiences) as "the way things were intended to be." The subservient habit is often strongly and positively reinforced by many whites, especially those who find it so much easier to "talk to and be with," hire, and promote People of Color who adopt this habit of survival. Hence, People of Color adopting this habit are often extrinsically rewarded by whites, especially in white spaces such as the workplace. They are considered "safe" and euphemistically referred to and thought of as "good team players," "lacking a chip on their shoulder," "pleasant to be around," and "not prone to playing the race card." They are heralded as and rewarded for being a "great coworker" or "just another member of the team, without all the racial drama." The warm embrace by whites helps to abate the underlying survival anxiety experienced by People of Color who exhibit the subservient habit. Unfortunately, the relationship that "the subservient" has to subservience is akin to that of "the warrior" to fighting. Whereas the warrior fights even when there is no fight to be had, the subservient is universally subservient, even when there is no material or existential gain from doing so. The act of responding with subservience becomes rigid and automatic. There is an element of the subservient habit that requires selflessness.

The subservient habit, often unbeknownst to those for whom it is an integral part of their approach to managing survival anxiety, requires a great deal of emotional suppression. It demands that one not see what ones sees, not fully honor and/or metabolize the enormity of feelings that one inevitably feels. Hence, there is a steady undercurrent of despair, low-grade sadness, and hopelessness. As I reflected on and repeated the words of my client, Kathleen, I felt a sadness embedded in her acceptance that "things are the way they were intended to be." The fact that she didn't see the necessity or utility of fighting did not mean that she was emotionally unaffected by the realities of her world. Thus, beneath the widespread acceptance by whites and the abatement of race related survival anxiety, there is a profound "tears of a clown" phenomenon that exists for so many People of Color who adopt the subservient habit. Thus, beneath the public persona of happiness and coping, there also exists an undercurrent of sadness, grief, despair, and rage that is often masked or expressed by somatic concerns, by reliance on substances, or by a host of other seemingly unrelated manifestations. Unlike with the other habits discussed thus far, the rage is usually more internally focused. Unfortunately, internalized rage does not garner the same attention as its externalized counterpart and is, therefore, much harder to detect. The presence of these underlying feelings often makes it difficult for those who rely on the subservient habit to be fully and authentically emotionally present and accessible in intimate relationships.

Feigned Subservience Habit

On a surface level, the feigned subservient habit can often be mistaken and misinterpreted as the subservient habit or a mutation of it. At first glance, many of the same salient behavioral features that define the subservient habit, such as exhibiting hypercompliant, accommodative, and acquiescent behaviors, are noticeably present with the feigned subservient habit. However, there is a major difference between the two habits that has to do with the root of the subservient behavior. The subservient habit is based on internalized devaluation, the (unconscious) acceptance of white superiority, and an authentic absence of the desire to fight or resist. It is rooted in and emanates from secondary-level oppression. For the feigned subservient habit, the display of subservient behaviors is intentionally tactical and performative. While the behaviors are certainly tied to and motivated by survival anxiety, the actual act of subservience is precisely that, an act. It is feigned behavior that is designed to create the illusion that one is a hypercompliant, acquiescent member of "the team," who can be expected to ingratiate themself to whites. The overt expression of subservience is a sophisticated ploy, an often well-thought-out tactic designed with a particular outcome in mind: survival.

Within most Communities of Color, there is a commonly understood unspoken code of conduct and behavior that many People of Color must adhere to in order to survive in a white dominated world. Paramount among these behaviors is appearing hypercompliant, racially neutral, nonemotional—especially about racial issues—and remaining docile and noncombative. The feigned subservient habit is fueled by an understanding of these perceived, white-prescribed behavioral dictates and the mastery of performing them. These behaviors, when performed by the feigned subservient, are not done from a place of authentic internalized feelings of inferiority but as a tactical means to an end. It enables the feigned subservient to coexist with whites in a way that is nonthreatening, nonconfrontational, nonconflictual, and harmonious, at least on the surface. As such, underlying survival-related fears and anxieties are somewhat allayed. While the performance helps to diminish survival related anxiety, it does not negate other complex psychoemotional consequences, such as the energy required to constantly suppress authentic feelings and beliefs as well as the rage often rooted in the indignity of having to do so. The feigned subservient is a type of warrior in disguise. The main difference is that the fight deployed is a subversive one that fails to generate the type of overt tension, animosity, or push back that the warrior habit routinely generates.

Interpersonal relationships of those with the feigned subservient habit are infinitely more challenging than one would expect. One the one hand, the feigned subservience habit projects an image of an easygoing, agreeable, noncombative person. On the other hand, this image is a façade that often obscures one's authentic underlying thoughts, feelings, and beliefs. The modus operandi of one invoking the feigned subservient habit is becoming an expert at scanning "the field" and skillfully and convincingly responding and/or presenting oneself in a manner that delivers the desired outcome and ensures survival. This habit requires those who exhibit it to be "chameleon-like" and able to adjust to virtually any situation in whatever way it requires. It is difficult to exhibit, perhaps even possess, a core self when one believes that *who one is* must be adapted to fit the circumstances at hand to feel safe and achieve a sense of belonging. Herein lies another significant way in which the subservient and feigned subservient differ: the subservient have a core self that is consistently presented, regardless of the circumstances. The feigned subservient, on the other hand, present as subservient but will also adapt as dictated by the circumstances. While this conditional dynamic is designed to curb survival anxiety, it ultimately and unwittingly exacerbates it by constituting a disruptive force in most interpersonal relationships. For example, over time, there are always questions about the trustworthiness or potential caginess of the feigned subservient. In traditional psychological parlance (where descriptive analyses of the effects of racial trauma and oppression are woefully negligent), the feigned subservient habit would typically be linked to terms such as manipulative, passive-aggressive, and/or sociopathic. Unfortunately, these terms are quite misguided and misleading. They, unfortunately, locate the etiological factors within the individual's psyche, with little recognition of the powerful, racially based sociocultural forces that play such a significant role in their evolution. This tendency to misinterpret origin exists for all the habits of survival. The racially split habit, at first glance, could be easily confused with and misidentified as a feigned subservient habit.

The Racially Split Habit

The racially split habit, though often confused with the feigned subservient habit, is a distinctive habit with discrete features. Like the feigned subservient habit, it is context driven in that it is activated by the physical presence and expectations of white people. However, unlike the feigned subservient habit, the racially split habit has broad sweeping implications for the totality of one's being and is much more expansive than simply "pretending to be subservient." It involves a process of racial splitting that bifurcates the self into an authentic racial self (who one genuinely perceives oneself to be racially) and a white institutional self (who one believes one must be to survive).

For many People of Color, survival, whether in the workplace or in society at large, requires constant effort, consciousness, and some degree of personal compromise. The racially split habit enables the Person of Color to hold onto their integrity and racial identity, particularly while in the presence of their racial tribe or in racially evolved places. It affords one the freedom to be one's authentic racial self in every sense of the word, that is, how one walks, talks, breathes, shake hands, and interacts with others, to cite a few mundane examples. The same self, however, must become subordinate to or be placed in abeyance when in the presence of white people or in predominantly white spaces. It is the *white institutional self* that must be prominently on display in white spaces and among white people. This version of the self operates and behaves within the parameters of the implicit code of conduct that many whites expect—"nice, respectable, articulate, professional"—People of Color to adhere to as a precondition for being "a good fit" or belonging. The racially split habit does not necessary require subservience (at least not explicitly), an overt denial of one's racial identity, or prohibitions against having discussions about race. However, it does dictate how and to what extent these issues may be addressed.

The racially split habit, in some contexts, is commonly referred to as "code-switching," a term that speaks only partially to the full anatomy of the concept that is being discussed here. Code-switching originated as a linguistic term used to refer to a process of alternating between languages. The racially split habit certainly involves alternating one's speech between two language systems; however, its scope is broader: It permeates the totality of one's being. It includes not just the cadence, diction, or vernacular of one's speech, which can be an integral component of the splitting process, but also what one eats, how one moves, whether one chooses to share or not to share, how one dresses, and a host of other behaviors. Even the way many People of Color greet each other or shake hands can differ quite noticeably from how they do so with whites. Thus, the racially split habit routinely involves more than what is typically ascribed to code-switching, in the traditional sense.

The racially split habit helps those who employ it to survive in two vastly different worlds, one white and one that is in *live and living color*. It requires a delicate juggling act that becomes a well-honed reflex for many People of Color. It paves the way for many People of Color to move seamlessly between the "white world" and the world of People of Color. The vacillation between worlds, and the required adjustments to how one appears racially in each, is so commonplace for many People of Color that the process requires very little conscious thought, as is the case with any other type of reflex. For example, it is intuitively understood by many People of Color that when in the presence of other People of Color, it is essential for the authentic racial self to be present and actively engaged. There is virtually no circumstance where the presence of one's white institutional self would be needed, appreciated, welcomed, or warmly embraced in spaces dominated by People of Color. Similarly, there are very few white spaces, situations, or circumstances where People of Color can feel free to be their authentic racial selves without having to defer to their institutional white selves to ensure their acceptance, safety, and survival. The relentless "dance" that is required to live between two worlds in the interest of survival is one that many People of Color do exceedingly well, which doesn't mean it is free of life-altering consequences. It takes a toll on the energy and spirit of People of Color as well as on their relationships with friends, colleagues, and loved ones. It is emotionally and psychologically exhausting because it requires both hyperalertness and hyperresponsiveness to one's surroundings. The racially split habit requires People of Color to delicately and expertly walk the tightrope that connects the worlds of whites and People of Color. Whether real or imagined, there is often an underlying and lingering sense that one must constantly display credentials to "prove" that one "belongs" in the white world when interacting with whites or that one is Black, Brown, Asian enough to be included in spaces and community with other People of Color. There are consequences associated with failing to strike the appropriate balance between the two worlds. There are also often consequences for People of Color who refuse to engage in racial splitting. Phrases such as: "Malcom's attire was a little too ethnic to comply with our standards of professionalism" or "He was a brilliant employee, but his dreadlocks were not a good look or fit for what we are trying to achieve here" are coded expressions that highlight a failure to prove that one is white enough to belong. Similarly, comments referring to a Person of Color as an Oreo, banana, coconut, Uncle Tom, or sell-out, etc. all speak to the same phenomenon: that the required balance between the racially split worlds of a Person of Color has been breached. Oreo, banana, and coconut are all disparaging terms often used by People of Color in reference to other People of Color who are perceived to be too white on the inside. These are some of the relational consequences that occur when the line of distinction between the authentic racial self and the institutional white self becomes too blurred. The blurring of boundaries is also a critical dynamic that underpins the hustler habit, although in this case it is a boundary between "living and surviving" and "hustling," as it is often referred to colloquially.

The Hustler Habit

Those who reflect the hustler habit are often guilty of establishing very porous and diffuse boundaries between *hustling* and all other aspects of living. Hustling, as it is used here, refers to channeling boundless energy and drive into working and work-related activities that often mask underlying anxiety about survival. Hence, the act of working, or hustling, is as much a reflex as it is a voluntary activity. In fact, it is often perceived as a powerful, and in many cases the only, potential antidote to most racially based threats to survival. It is perceived as a critical lifeline to survival, and anything that compromises it is perceived as threatening to one's survival. The hustler habit consists of an obsessive-compulsive-like relationship with working/hustling that is driven by survival anxiety and an orientation toward survival.

As a habit of survival, the term "hustler" is used neither pejoratively nor to imply illicit, unethical, or criminal activity, although the hustler habit could conceivably involve any and/or all of these behaviors in rare cases. "Hustler" is used to capture the endless drive, emotional attachment, and relentless and boundless time, effort, and energy that are devoted to a unique approach to work that is complexly entangled with survival. In a sense, "hustling" qualitatively and experientially involves so much more than simply "working." It has a certain life and death quality to it that is often expressed with considerable narrowly focused intensity and attention. It means working hard and demonstrating a drive to perform tasks and take on responsibilities that others may be reticent or unwilling to do. For many People of Color—especially those who are immigrants, documented and undocumented, or those who have also had to endure class oppression in conjunction with racial oppression—the hustler habit is a predictable response to these hurdles. As noted earlier, hard work and hustling are often perceived as the only viable pathway to survival. Consequently, due to the perceived inextricable connection between work and survival, hustling takes precedence over virtually all other matters. This mindset is simultaneously a service and a disservice to those who approach life and living with the hustler habit.

On the one hand, the unparalleled drive, focus, and energy that fuels this habit helps to manage and regulate underlying fears about survival. There is also some measure of success and accomplishment that one enjoys as a result of one's "labor," both literally and figuratively speaking. "Success and accomplishment," in whatever way it is ultimately and subjectively measured, constitute mediating factors. In other words, they help to allay fear and anxiety about survival. Unfortunately, the joy and calming effects of these experiences are often short-lived and supplanted by the underlying fear and anxiety that they may not be enough, and perhaps more effort may be required. It is this view that (re)activates and reenergizes the driving force to work harder and to intensify hustling. The words of my client Roberto, an engineer, best summed up this phenomenon: "I am a lot like Aladdin, the Disney character, who went from 'zero to hero,' but you can't get caught up in believing that you can relax because you have it made. In this world, as a dark-skinned Latino man, you can never let your guard down. You have to keep fighting the good fight because you can go as quickly from hero to zero as you do the other way around. So, my mantra is, I will NEVER be outworked, and no employer can ever claim to overpay me because that is how I was raised to survive in the white man's world. They might outsmart me, but they will never outwork me!"

There are several noteworthy points to be extracted from Roberto's brief disclosure. The first is his perception that he lives in a world that is bifurcated by race. Thus, he refers to "this world" (presumably the world he lives in) and "the white man's world." Secondly, even though he is a successful engineer, there is a level of insecurity he feels about his continued success and, ultimately, his survival. Finally, his reference to his employer being unable to ever claim that he is "overpaid" speaks powerfully to his resolve to do more than what is customarily prescribed, not necessarily because he wants to, but because he believes that his survival depends on it and he wants to avoid the demotion from "hero to zero." This is the essence of the hustler habit. It is not only a lifeline to survival, it also produces peak performances and provides a platform for success. It is, in large part, what has made it possible for so many People of Color to survive and achieve against daunting odds. The drive to survive provides the energy and force field that fuels the hustle, that is, the countless hours of back-breaking hard labor without a complaint, the performance of menial tasks for meager wages, the working as an official or unofficial street vendor, or the 12-hour days devoted to work in an office suite. For Roberto, and others like him, hustling means remaining unshakably resolute about not being outworked. Regardless of the task and the effort, the motivating force is the same: survival. Unfortunately, and as might be expected, there is a downside to the all-consuming energy and focus that the hustler habit requires.

The underlying drive, restlessness, and anxiety that underpin the hustler habit can have deleterious effects on the formation and maintenance of meaningful intimate relationships of all types. The anxiety about survival and the intense focus on hustling as a mechanism for achieving make taking time off, relaxing, or devoting attention to other important life issues a constant challenge. After all, taking time off or relaxing often translates into abandoning opportunities to invest in one's efforts to survive. Thus, issues, activities, and events that are not deemed vital to survival are often minimized, marginalized, or dismissed. Since the boundaries between work and other aspects of life are often severely blurred, it is common for the energy connected to work to interfere with personal relationships and, in some cases, even compete with them. Relationships that are entangled with work are usually the most viable, often because they are fused with the hustle and pose no immediate threat. Finding balance and defining appropriate boundaries in one's relationship is an incessant challenge for one who adopts the hustler habit. Unfortunately, relationships are too often viewed and valued based on whether they are an asset or a liability to one's efforts to navigate survival. This dynamic might serve an immediate need at a given moment, however, over time it exacerbates other co-occurring invisible wounds, such as psychological homelessness and intangible loss, to cite a few.

All habits of survival share a common foundation, regardless of how the actual habit is manifested. As has been stated repeatedly throughout this chapter, survival and the efforts to secure it are critical motivating factors. Habits are rigidified responses that remain fixed regardless of the circumstances. In some instances, it is possible to possess more than one habit or to have some features of one habit intermixed with another. Even in the rare instances where this occurs, it is habitual and not the result of a conscious, volitional decision.

In working with habits of survival, the clinical goal is always to address the orientation toward survival by transforming habits of survival into strategies of survival, which requires making a more conscious and volitional response based on circumstances in place of rigidified internal reflexes. To facilitate this process, it is often incumbent upon the therapist to name and introduce the client to the entire range of habits. Once this is achieved, the therapist must gradually and methodically guide the therapeutic process toward assisting the client to adopt new habits and to develop the ability to be more intentional about when and under what circumstances they might be employed. This is a key step toward transforming habits of survival to strategies of survival. This process will be discussed in detail in Section III.

SUMMARY

The orientation toward survival is a worldview and an emotional, psychological, and behavioral reaction to a persistent belief that one's survival is threatened. It is a direct consequence of racial oppression and the numerous ways in which the well-being of

People of Color has been systematically and historically attacked, assaulted, and in some cases annihilated by whites. The orientation toward survival is the culmination of centuries of imposed collective generational suffering, which has contributed to a collective generational survival reflex. Thus, as has been highlighted throughout this chapter, the anxiety that many People of Color experience regarding the imminent threat to their survival is not relegated to the physical self, although that is a relevant concern as well. The threat to survival is much more encompassing and can occur in the workplace and school and while driving, walking, or engaged in virtually any societal event or activity where one's authentic racial self is unguardedly on display. In this regard, the orientation toward survival can become a bit of an obsession, especially since it is perceived as being critical to one's survival and ultimately one's life. It is not just a recurring thought, but a rigidified reflexive impulse as well.

The rigidified reflexive reaction contributes to the formation of habits of survival, which are automatic responses that are relied upon to help alleviate survival anxiety attributable to racial oppression and trauma. Habits are simultaneously functional and dysfunctional and may manifest in a variety of ways.

There are six principal habits that are routinely associated with the wounds of racial trauma: warrior; oppressed-oppressor; feigned subservient; subservient; racially-split; and hustler. Each has distinctive attributes, and it is possible for a person to exhibit elements of more than one habit. The intersectionality of race with other sociocultural factors, such as social class, can either mitigate or exacerbate the orientation toward survival as well as the habits of survival. Nevertheless, both the orientation toward survival and the reliance on habits of survival serve a viable role in the everyday lives of People of Color; however, the rigid reflexive responses and patternicity tend to interfere with daily life. Since habits of survival serve a viable and functional purpose, the therapeutic goal should never be to eliminate them, but instead to transform them into strategies of survival, which are conscious and volitional. This process will be discussed in greater detail in Section III.

SECTION III:

ADDRESSING THE INVISIBLE WOUNDS OF RACIAL TRAUMA

CHAPTER 13

Strategies and Techniques

Providing racially sensitive, trauma-informed therapy is not based on a discrete model of therapy; instead, it is best conceived as a meta framework for working with People of Color who are experiencing racial trauma. It requires the racially informed, racially sensitive therapist to position themself to make an impact. Many of the prescribed steps toward "positioning" oneself to have an impact have been discussed throughout Chapters 11 and 12. The therapeutic principles discussed in Chapter 5 help to form and inform a set of clinical strategies and techniques that are critical for the therapist to consider when working with Clients of Color who are wrestling with the invisible wounds of racial trauma. These strategies can be useful adjuncts to augment the work that many therapists may currently be doing.

The strategies contained in this chapter are designed to address some of the unique clinical challenges that are embedded in conducting intensive racially sensitive, trauma-informed work. The Validation-Challenge-Request (VCR) approach is used to provide the foundation for taking the initial rudimentary steps for counteracting internalized devaluation, for overcoming an assaulted sense of self, and for actualizing self-love while planting the seeds for restorative work. In fact, VCR is a key strategy for positioning the therapist to work effectively with all the invisible wounds of trauma.

THE VALIDATE-CHALLENGE-REQUEST MODEL (VCR)

The VCR approach (Hardy, 2017) is both a worldview and technique. The worldview dimension of it dictates the overall effectiveness of the technique. It is rooted in the belief that good and bad are contained in the same shell and that there is something potentially redeemable and worthy contained in even the most egregious and outlandish behavior. It asserts that we tend to see what we look for, thus the seeking of pathology, for example, renders the finding of the same. Sometimes a shift in what we ultimately look for can substantially alter what we see (Hardy, 2017, p. 47).

In this regard, the VCR technique is a strength-based approach that is predicated on the development of the relational muscles, especially the *complexity* one, that were introduced and discussed in Chapter 5. If the worldview of the therapist is one that is based on dualistic, dichotomous thinking with firm lines of demarcation between "good and bad" for example, then "seeing" the entanglement of good and bad, love and hate, etc. will be a challenging task. Alternatively, when the therapist demonstrates an appreciation for and an ability to see "the good embedded in the bad" and vice versa, it paves the way for the beginning of important restorative work to begin. Through the adoption of the VCR as a worldview, the therapist can, for example, with greater visual acuity see the lovability embedded in a client who may deem oneself unlovable and void of self-love. It is this worldview that propels the therapist to endlessly search for that which may be shown but not seen, and to see beyond that which is not shown.

The technique dimension of the VCR centers around what the therapist does and how it is done. It involves using the Validate-Challenge-Request approach to engage in race related conversations that draw heavily from the six relational muscles described in Chapter 4. There are four guiding principles associated with the VCR approach that the therapist must keep in mind: 1) The act of validation must always precede challenges, confrontations, or expressions of criticism. 2) It is the client, *not* the therapist, who decides when one has been adequately validated. 3) When providing feedback to a client, it is imperative that the therapist use the word "and," instead of the great eraser "but," when transitioning from a validating message to one that is designed to challenge, correct, or criticize. 4) It is the interplay between validation, challenge, and request that drives its effectiveness.

The Act of Validation

Validation refers to the process of identifying and naming the unique gifts, traits, and/or redeemable qualities that are often buried under and within the piles of negative valuations that a client may have internalized, possess about themselves, or typically present to the outside world. Each positive quality can be considered a *badge of ability* that is often hidden from a client's view and thus is extremely difficult for them to see, recognize, and/ or embrace. Because the badge of ability is hidden, it is difficult for others to see as well. It is important to note here that "validation" is *not* to be confused with "acknowledgment," "expressions of gratitude," or "agreement." Validation is also *not* the same as the concept of "reframing," although there are some common features. Both validation and reframing involve looking at a current situation from a different perspective. However, validation also relies on the therapist's ability to see the hidden gifts and redeemable parts of a client's life and behavior that are unseen and unacknowledged and therefore often underappreciated. Validation is emotional, psychological, and behavioral "gem excavation" work. This is the facet of the VCR approach that has restorative capabilities. Through authentic expressions of validation, the therapist can extract personal attributes from the web of negative valuations that have an overwhelming and debilitating effect on the client's functioning. The validation process is solely focused on spotlighting the client's hidden, unseen, and unacknowledged gifts, attributes, and redeemable qualities which can provide a foundation for counteracting devaluation, restoring a whole sense of self, and promoting self-love. It is important for the therapist to refrain from any action that may be construed as a challenge, criticism, castigation, or condemnation at this stage of the therapeutic process. Walking this tight rope is necessary for all therapists and particularly imperative for white therapists, given the long history of devaluation that many People of Color have suffered at the hands of white people. Depending on the gravity of a client's level of devaluation and self-contempt, it may be necessary for the therapist to spend several sessions devoted primarily, if not exclusively, to validation and thereby remain invested in gradually and methodically restoring the client's sense of self and increasing their capacity for self-love.

Expressing acts of validation must be initiated by the therapist and must always precede challenging, confronting, or criticism of a client, regardless of the issue. This principle is closely related to the second, which asserts that it is the client, not the therapist, who decides when the act of validation has been adequate.

The Timing and Duration of Validation

There is no hard, standard, quantifiable rule regarding how long the therapist should express validation devoid of challenges or other similar messages, whether a mild critique or full-frontal confrontation. Since the depth of devaluation that Clients of Color experience vary quite significantly, depending on their circumstances, the therapist must be highly attuned to the process and to each client's wounds. Devoting close attention to these issues can help provide the therapist with a guide for determining how long acts of validation are indicated. When the therapist moves too rapidly from validation to a challenge, it undermines the authenticity of the former. If the therapist is properly attuned with the client, it becomes relatively easy to discern when it may be appropriate to move the process from validation to challenge. The pacing of this process is dictated by the client, and it requires the therapist to be able to hold intensity and resist the urge to move too quickly from validating to challenging.

Often there are some subtle markers that signal when the client is ready and open to have the process transition from validation to challenge. Some of these indicators are: a) There is a shift in the depth of the therapeutic conversation, evidenced by the client sharing more intimate and substantive information; b) There is an increased openness and receptivity to receiving feedback from the therapist; c) The client begins to adopt some of therapist's language, phrases, characterizations, and/or conceptualizations; d) The client demonstrates an embracement and integration of the redeemable quality, hidden gift, or unique personal attribute(s) encapsulated within the validation. Once these markers are evident, it is generally safe for the therapist to broaden the therapeutic conversation and process to include a challenge.

When the transition from validation to challenge has been executed prematurely, it is important that the therapist respond to the misstep by returning to expressing validation, which should be routinely relied upon to recalibrate any therapeutic setbacks.

The "challenge" component of the VCR approach is a critical part of the process and helps to reinforce the validation messages by acknowledging and addressing what is not working well for the client. In other words, the challenge is often a component of the very attribute that has been the focal point of validation. It is imperative that the execution of challenges be done with impeccable timing and grace. Under no circumstance, should a therapist challenge a client before the client has been properly and adequately validated. In many instances, the wounds of internalized devaluation, assaulted sense of self, and rage make it nearly impossible for clients to receive challenges prior to the restorative work that validation affords. In fact, for many clients, receiving validation may be difficult because it is incongruous with the dominant and recurring messages of devaluation that they are accustomed to receiving. Nevertheless, the challenge component of the VCR approach is integral to the process of change. To oversimply, the *validation* messages are designed to highlight *what's working*, the *challenge* messages acknowledge *what is broken or not working*, and the *request* messages are to solicit the client's input and support, to draw the client to cosign a plan for moving forward that builds on what's working and eradicates or minimizes what is not working. The V, C, and R are highly interrelated, and the effective execution of the VCR approach must emphasize and reinforce this delicate relationship. To do so requires the therapist to demonstrate the relational thinking principle (discussed in Chapter 5) by embracing a both/and perspective and eradicating the use of either/or and "yes, but" language.

Embracing Both/And

The effective transition from V to C to R is a critical and delicate dimension of the therapeutic process. When not executed properly and skillfully, it can be a major deterrent and threat to the therapeutic process. When the transition is clunky and clumsy or lacking in authenticity and congruency, it can appear quite condescending to a client, especially those who enter the process with suspicion, guardedness, and worries about trust. Again, it is crucial for the therapist to embrace VCR as a worldview in order to effectively execute the strategy dimension of the approach. A significant part of the worldview involves thinking relationally and having well developed complexity muscles (see Chapter 4). These therapeutic attributes enable the therapist to effortlessly *see* the interlocking of "good" *and* "bad," "strength" *and* "weakness," or how a behavior can be simultaneously functional *and* dysfunctional. When transitioning from validation to challenge, it is important for the therapist to honor and highlight the interrelatedness between the validation and challenge by embracing both/and while vigorously avoiding the use of "but" and *either/or* framing of the experience. Hence, it becomes possible for the therapist to extol a client's rage, especially as a major liberating force of passion and personal empowerment that should neither be shunned nor denied, and to challenge the client about the ways in which their rage is also a tremendous source of self-destruction. The use of the word "and" is not just a matter of semantical significance but of deeply philosophical and psychological significance as well. It positions the client to embrace their rage and cultivate a healthier relationship with it and to more clearly identify the parts of it that are self-inhibiting and potentially injurious to their relational network. For this reason, the final step of the

VCR approach, "request," is every bit as critical as the previous two steps.

The Integration and Synergistic Interplay of V-C-R

The effective use of the VCR approach requires the therapist to utilize each step of the process, even though the timing that is devoted to each may vary substantially. The efficacy of the approach is greatly diminished if any one of the three steps is avoided or poorly executed. The "validation" is needed because of its restorative capabilities. The "challenge" often helps to further fortify the restorative work by positioning the client to do reparative work, that is, attending to self-defeating messages and practices and replacing those with different ways of being, which are often contained in the "request." The request is an invitation to consider a change and a solicitation for cooperation. Whether the client responds affirmatively or negatively, the work and mission of the therapist is the same: to execute the VCR approach.

The following vignette offers a closer look at the application of the VCR.

Vignette: "Blue Black"

Claudia is a thirty-four-year-old Puerto Rican woman who entered therapy, as she reported, "to gain control of my out-of-control life." She was recently fired from her job as a clinical social worker for lack of professionalism, for insubordination, and for violating her company's dress code policy. She dismissed the legitimacy of the termination of her employment by attributing it to a series of "racist bullshit that white people get away with on a daily basis." She said that she is "sick and tired of everybody trying to control my life, wanting to make me who they think I should be." In addition to her woes at work, Claudia reported that her personal life was in shambles as well. While she has had an active dating life, she has yet to find a partner who wants the same thing she does. She stated that her relationships always feel empty and superficial. She further lamented: "I never feel that I am good enough. I feel like everyone I have ever dated wanted me to be someone I am not and that who I am is not good enough."

Born to Puerto Rican parents, Claudia is the middle child among three daughters who spent their formative years in Puerto Rico before moving to New York as young adults. Claudia reports that she is the darkest member of her family and that her younger sister, Alexa, passes as white. Claudia has vivid and painful memories of being referred to as "Negrita" by her parents, which was regarded as a term of endearment in her family, but one that she never interpreted endearingly. Among her extended family and friends, she was often described as Blue Black, that is, so dark that her Blackness seemed blue. In school she was often called "Blue" by her classmates of all races. Her most poignant memories from school are laced with feelings of humiliation, isolation, shame, scorn, and self-rejection. She recalls that during her childhood and adolescence, she actively prayed and implored God to make her white; she remembers harboring considerable anger toward her parents for making her dark and envying her much lighter and white-passing sister. During her late adolescent and collegiate years, she began bleaching her skin—on numerous occasions, at the request of an intimate partner. According to her last therapist, Claudia has had ongoing struggles with low self-esteem, intimacy issues, and maintaining stable relationships.

Here is an excerpt of our dialogue from one of our early therapy sessions in which I used the VCR approach:

KVH: Claudia, I have noticed and really appreciated how incredibly honest, insightful, and self-aware you have been in our sessions. Your ability and willingness to name and confront such deeply shameful and potentially embarrassing things about yourself are refreshing to witness.

C: Thank you! I guess that is just who I am, and I never thought about being any of the things you mentioned.

KVH: It makes sense to me that you probably wouldn't notice it because it is a gift of sorts, and the beauty and gift of a gift is that you can have it and not know you have it. Although sometimes I think it can serve us well to at least know what gifts we might possess.

C: I guess. I never really thought about having a gift. My life feels shitty, and all I know is that most people in my life don't look at me and see anything positive, let alone a gift.

KVH: Once again, I think it is commendable that are you are so honest and willing to be so transparent with how you are seeing and feeling about your life. I work with some who would find it difficult to allow themselves to embrace, and especially share so openly, such painful parts of themselves. Yes, I agree it is incredibly hard to block out others' negativity, including the way they see us, even when what they see has so little to do with who we really are, but may be more reflective of what we have internalized.

C: Can you say more about that, I think you lost me.

KVH: I think as POC, and Black people in particular, there are so MANY negative messages out there that ultimately shape how we see ourselves. It is difficult to not be affected by the messages . . . like you being called

"Blue" or "Blue Black." At some point, we begin to organize our lives as if those messages are real and then consciously and unconsciously seek confirmation.

C: [Deep sigh] It is so unfair, and it hurts. [she begins to tear up]

KVH: Have you always been this open, honest, and congruent with yourself about yourself?

C: I guess; I don't really know . . . . It is not something that I have ever thought about.

KVH: I think being Black and being the recipient of so many negative messages make it hard for us as people to love ourselves and sometimes even each other. I still cringe and regret the amount of time I spent early in life not loving myself as a Black Person. It taught me that it is important to talk about self-love in spaces like this.

C: Honestly Ken, it is not something that I have ever thought about in quite the way you just framed it. I guess I just know that I am dark, and being dark is not a good thing in our society. Your family lets you know, the people you love and date let you know it. I know for sure my life would be happier and less stressful if I could have traded places with either of my sisters. They don't have to deal with the "Oh I like you, but you are too dark" bullshit or all the unflattering nicknames, jokes, that are used to refer to you. Most times I laugh it off to play it down, but the truth is, it hurts.

KVH: So living in the skin you are in has made life tough for you. I think it is one of the many painful ways that whiteness affects our lives. I know this stuff is hard to talk about and sometimes even harder to admit, yet I am so impressed that you are so honest, insightful, and willing to lean into it without safeguards.

C: I am still thinking about your comment about self-love. I guess I have never spent a lot of time thinking about this. My first thought is, of course I love myself, but maybe I don't know.

KVH: There is a part of me that believes you are too insightful, self-aware, and honest with yourself about yourself to not know. You don't really know?

C: Well, as a child I used to think that I could scrub the darkness off my skin, then later I started bleaching my skin when I learned that Michael Jackson used to do the same thing. I never associated this with not loving myself, I just didn't want to be dark. I have lost more than one partner over this. Everyone tries to be discrete, but it is easy to pick up on the shame and embarrassment. You are okay to have sex with behind closed doors, but being out in public together in an intimate way is strictly taboo.

KVH: I can hear the hurt and anguish in your voice and see it on your face. I remain impressed with your willingness to speak so candidly and say it as you see and experience it. Despite how painful it all is, you don't run away from it. This is not always an easy thing to do, especially early on in this process. How would you describe your relationship with your dark skin, being Black, and not feeling good enough?

C: I don't know, Ken. I guess it depends on the day and what else is going on in my life.

Claudia entered therapy with a dominant view of herself as worthless, largely due to a barrage of negative, devaluing messages that she had received all her life and that had become deeply internalized. While her pursuit of therapy was precipitated by a work-related setback, it was clear from the start of our work together that her struggles extended well beyond the workplace and were deeply rooted in racial trauma. Much of my engagement with her was intentionally buttressed by acts of validation—my way of doing the initial groundwork to counteract devaluation and to begin the very long and delicate process of repairing her assaulted sense of self. I gently infused the notion of self-love into the therapeutic process because of my belief that this love is punctured when devaluation and an assaulted sense of self is an integral part of one's being. It was gently introduced, without fanfare, because it was intended to be the planting of a seed. My efforts to validate Claudia centered around highlighting, extolling, and celebrating her willingness to be so incredibly honest with herself and with me. I wanted to convey to her that I could *see* her insightfulness, honesty, and the courage she exhibited in her willingness to share and give voice to her shame. This is the part of the work that is potentially restorative and must be promoted as early as possible. It is often necessary to consistently repeat the validation because it often too risky for those suffering from devaluation to open themself up to receive affirming and validating messages, even when they are desired. If all one has ever been told is what they are not, it is hard, scary, and much too vulnerable for them to open up to entertain what they are, might be, or could potentially become.

There was a point in the session where Claudia stated, "I am still thinking about your comment about self-love. I guess I have never spent a lot of time thinking about this. My first thought is, of course I love myself, but maybe I don't know." I responded by saying: "There is a part of me that believes you are too insightful, self-aware, and honest with yourself about yourself to not know. You don't really know?" This was the only place in the session where I transitioned from validation to challenge. It was a very mild challenge and was carefully executed by first restating "the attribute," that is, her *insightfulness, self-awareness,* and *honesty with herself about herself,* followed by the question: "You don't really know?" My question was a challenge that she seemed able to embrace, largely, I believe, because she felt validated prior to being challenged. At this juncture of the work, it would have been premature to make a request, which came much later in the therapeutic process. The bulk of my work with Claudia over the initial several sessions was focused on validation.

The VCR approach is an important tool and worldview for governing and guiding racially focused trauma-informed work. Its effectiveness is greatly enhanced when it is organically integrated into how a therapist works with all clients rather than making it an isolated, disconnected strategy that one uses only with selected clients. It is also important for the therapist to use the VCR approach throughout the therapeutic relationship as well as in conjunction with the usage of other strategies and techniques. The use of racial storytelling as a therapeutic technique is a strategy that relies heavily on the therapist's effective use of the VCR approach, especially since so many of these stories can involve shame.

RACIAL STORYTELLING AS A THERAPEUTIC STRATEGY AND TECHNIQUE

Racial storytelling is a semistructured process whereby clients are asked to tell their unique racial story verbally, in writing, or by some combination of the two. This therapeutic tool is used, partly, to honor and integrate the power of storytelling and oral history that have been such a rich tradition for many People of Color. One of the many purposes of the storytelling is to give voice to the varied circumstances that shape the racial life experiences of the client. It is important to create a space for clients to tell not only the racially based stories from their own experience but those that have been passed down intergenerationally as well.

Racial storytelling is akin to the family history collection process. It can be conducted at a predetermined stage of therapy, with a defined start and end point, or it may be extended across the process of therapy. In any event, it is the therapist's responsibility to stitch together the racial stories that emerge, the presenting problem, the wounds of racial trauma, the family of origin issues, and the goals of therapy. Given the delicacy and vulnerability that this process typically entails, it is extremely important for the therapist to use the VCR approach intimately and extensively.

Racial storytelling paves a way for Clients of Color to challenge and potentially overcome voicelessness and shame as well as to recognize and address sources of collective grief. It can be a powerful tool for addressing and overcoming threads of psychological homelessness by reminding clients how they are connected to others by aspects of their shared stories. Clients are encouraged to reach out to others (e.g., family members, friends of the family, and others) to collect, corroborate, and/or confirm data and to acquire missing parts of their story. As noted in Chapter 5, racial trauma work is relational work.

To initiate and execute the racial storytelling process, the therapist invites the client to think about themself and their life and assemble what they remember and can learn about them into three distinctive yet highly interrelated stories: 1) stories of suffering; 2) stories of struggles; and 3) stories of survival. The therapist also encourages the client to use culturally/racially sanctioned artifacts to help embellish, augment, and/or support the telling of their stories. Expanding the boundaries of therapy to encompass, for instance, the sharing of personal photos, pictures, and other artwork, music, poetry, race-related historical artifacts, is a critical component of the racial storytelling process.

During the introduction and execution of the racial storytelling process, it is important for the therapist to provide a very brief overview of the parameters of the three types of stories without being overly descriptive or prescriptive. There is considerable overlap and interrelatedness between and among the stories, which adds to the depth and complexity of the process. Thus, too much detail offered by the therapist can potentially stifle the client's imagination and creativity while also inadvertently imposing restrictive and unnecessary boundaries on the process.

Stories of Suffering

Most clients typically commence the process by discussing their stories of suffering, although they could conceivably start with any of the three, since they are highly entangled with each other. Stories of suffering are designed to center around the emotional pain, hardships, setbacks, and obstacles that one and one's family have suffered because of racial trauma and oppression. These stories afford clients the opportunity to explore and share how the core of their racially based suffering may also be complexly entangled with other manifestations of oppression, such as class, gender, and sexual orientation as well as contentious and complicated family-of-origin dynamics. Stories of suffering are most comprehensive and revelatory when they are examined through a relational and intergenerational lens. Doing so allows the client to begin exploring connections between their past and their present and to their relatives, extended kin, and ancestors. Stories of suffering can crystalize the development of the preliminary steps necessary for counteracting psychological homelessness. Untold and unacknowledged stories of suffering can fracture, even destroy, bonds of connection; however, when told, acknowledged, and witnessed with dignity, grace, and humility, they can also help mend, heal, and promote emotional and relational connectedness. Although seldom consciously acknowledged, virtually all stories of suffering are de facto accompanied by stories of struggle, which also must be honored and explored.

Stories of Struggle

Stories of struggle are born out of experiences of suffering. In many ways, the act of struggling is a byproduct of suffering. Thus, *struggle* is both a noun and a verb, that is, both a condition and an action. Stories of struggle are essentially about the actions that one has been compelled to take or failed to take in relationship to suffering. Stories of struggle highlight the efforts, actions or inactions, and activism that were taken to overcome suffering and, hopefully, to ensure survival. These stories may provide some preliminary insights into which habits of survival a client uses, why, and how they developed.

Stories of struggle often involve acts of acquiescence, whereby the overwhelming nature and depths of suffering are too forceful to fight or overcome. In this case, the stories of struggle are embedded in one's efforts to "struggle" with living with overwhelming and debilitating conditions. Whether the stories of struggle are deeply entrenched in activism, apathy, or acquiescence, the telling of the story is vital to addressing racial trauma. Even stories of struggle that are defined by acquiescence and are typically perceived as "giving up" or "giving in" can contain or produce an underlying, hidden strength that may serve as a pathway to personal transformation, especially if the therapist is using the VCR approach appropriately. Regardless of the content or anatomy of the stories, having the opportunity to tell their own story, in their own words uninterruptedly, free from threat, punishment, or reprisal is robustly potent and massively transformative for clients with racial trauma.

It is through the telling of stories of struggle that both client and therapist can begin to shine a different light on behaviors that are often simplistically perceived as immoral, criminal, "sociopathic," and/or socially undesirable. The type of criminal and socially unacceptable behaviors that are often highly visible components in communities of People of Color with racial trauma who live in poor neighborhoods are often rooted in stories of struggle and an orientation toward survival. While many of these behaviors are, understandably and admittedly, abhorrent and void of justification, they do often contain an underlying explanation. Stories of struggle often highlight the scarcity of options available to the traumatized and oppressed. In addition to the underlying pain and despair connected to these stories, they also often contain threads of hope, creativity, ingenuity, patience, tolerance, and tenacity, which are all attributes that can be instrumental to survival. These are the traits that can be delicately and methodically unearthed by the VCR approach. It is important for the therapist to make sure that clients are granted ample opportunities to share their stories of struggle. Failure to do so can significantly slow down the process of therapy and/or prevent the therapist from developing a comprehensive understanding of the client's inner world. The stories of struggle are intricately connected to both stories and habits of survival. After all, living with racial trauma and oppression creates an unrelenting driving force to incessantly search for survival pathways.

Stories of Survival

Stories of survival are essentially stories of perseverance, endurance, and, in one sense, overcoming the formidable obstacles and barriers imposed by living along the margins of society. They assist client and therapist alike in understanding the psychoemotional journey from suffering to survival. They provide the client with an opportunity to explore and consider how all three stories are exquisitely entangled and how, for example, one's ability to survive may be very strongly predicated on the ability to shamelessly embrace one's suffering. It many ways, it is the embracing of suffering and the ensuing struggles that enables one to grasp the depths of one's *greatness,* that is, the fortitude to transcend adversity and persevere. Stories of survival often contain particles of hope and perseverance that can be quite psychoemotionally liberating for clients; however, the therapist must be able to see, excavate, and validate these hidden gems. These are the building blocks that the therapist can use to help the client begin the process of transforming *habits* of survival to *strategies* of survival.

Habits of survival, as described in Chapter 12, are rigidified, simultaneously functional and dysfunctional, reflex-like responses to the orientation toward survival trauma wound. The habits of survival are an integral part of a client's story of survival, and yet one may not be conscious of its presence or impact. Through the telling and processing of the client's story of survival, it becomes possible for the therapist to extract, deconstruct, and analyze a client's habit of survival. This process is critical to the process of change because it enables the therapist to help the client transform the habit of survival—a rigid, reflexive response—to a strategy of survival, one where the client can consciously exercise more volition and choice over how they navigate efforts to survive. This transformation, and the growth process involved in it, frees the client to "choose" from a broader range of survival strategies rather than rigidly relying on one that may or may not be suitable for the circumstances at hand. It also provides the client with a greater sense of agency to consciously discard (self)destructive, harmful, or dysfunctional dimensions of the habit. During this important phase of the therapeutic process, the therapist takes a very active role in highlighting how the stories of suffering, struggle, and survival are inextricably intertwined with the habits of survival and vice versa. Strategies of survival, which may be comprised of extractions from all three stories as well as from the habits of survival, are conscious, volitional tactics that a client can employ to address underlying anxieties about survival without the self-destructive elements contained in habits of survival.

Shawn Corey "Jay-Z" Carter, Becalis Marlenis (Cardi B) Almánzar, and Curtis (50 Cent) Jackson are merely three examples of a host of very successful, well respected, wealthy entrepreneurs whose early lives were mired in poverty and were profoundly shaped by racial and/or class oppression. Carter and Jackson are both former drug dealers who relied on a hustler habit to survive and ultimately to escape the walls of oppression. Almánzar, a former stripper born into poverty, was the target of both gender and racial oppression growing up in the Bronx, New York. Almánzar, Carter, and Jackson channeled their racially based degradation and rage into rap music, and ultimately, all three performers transformed their respective habits of survival to strategies of survival. In each of these cases, and in numerous other less famous and celebrated examples of this phenomenon, variations of the skillset that helped them formulate the hustler habit allowed them to escape the restraining and debilitating conditions they were born into as children to become the thriving, successful, savvy businesspeople and politically engaged social justice advocates (especially in the cases of Carter and Almánzar) that they are today. Their hustler "habit" of survival has now been reconfigured and transformed into a "strategy" of survival. It is worth noting here that the examples of Carter, Almánzar, and Jackson were used because they are famous public figures who exemplify the transformation from a habit to a strategy of survival. There are, obviously, myriad other more pedestrian examples of this same process that do not involve questionable social behavior or wealth, fame, and fortune. In fact, the life experiences of many therapists, particularly Therapists of Color, have involved the transformation of habits of survival into strategies of survival.

The therapeutic value and power of incorporating racial storytelling into the clinical process as a means of addressing the invisible wounds of racial trauma is multifold. It helps clients to engage in "voice lessons," which are critical to overcoming voicelessness. Methodically tracking the progression from "suffering to survival" and creating space for critical self-reflection can be a massively empowering and restorative experience for clients. It also provides the client with a context for doing all the foundational work that is necessary for transforming dysfunctional and self-defeating habits into functional and growth-enhancing strategies of survival. Often newly developed and/or discovered strategies of survival can also serve as major arteries for rechanneling rage. As noted earlier, there is no one uniform way in which racial storytelling can or should be integrated into the therapeutic process. It can be implemented as a free-standing process, or it can be intermixed with other tools, such as the racial genogram, which is very similar in scope and function.

THE RACIAL GENOGRAM

The racial genogram is a derivative and adaptation of the cultural genogram (Hardy & Laszloffy, 2017) as both a training and a therapeutic tool. The racial genogram and its predecessor, the cultural genogram, use the same format and structure as the standard family of origin genogram (McGoldrick & Gerson, 1985) that is widely used in clinical practice. While the standard family genogram is typically a three-generational diagram that principally focuses on family-of-origin issues, the cultural genogram follows the same format and structure but is heavily skewed toward the examination of culture as a broad, multidimensional concept (Hardy & Laszloffy, 2017). The racial genogram is a spinoff of the cultural genogram and is narrowly focused on the issue of race and racial dynamics. Like its predecessors, the racial genogram attends to the centrality of family dynamics; however, it does so specifically through the prism of race and racial trauma.

Regardless of the type of genogram being deployed, it is usually a good idea for the therapist to provide specific instructions to the client regarding how to construct a genogram and to offer a template that includes a legend explaining the salient symbols associated with the diagram. It is also important for the therapist to highlight the following additional instructions relative to constructing a racial genogram:

1. Ask the client to use a unique color to represent each racial identity depicted in their three-generation genogram. Thus, if a client's family was racially homogenous, they would use only one color. On the other hand, if there are individuals from different racial backgrounds in any of the three generations, a different color should be used for each racial identity. The actual colors selected and to which race they are affixed is completely arbitrary and should be left entirely to the discretion of the client. However, once a particular color has been assigned to a specific racial identity or group, that particular color must be

used only for the racial identity/group to which it was originally assigned. Biracial and multiracial family members should be depicted using multiple colors that reflect the colors of both parents. In these cases, one individual could be represented by several different colors. For example, the shape for a child of a "blue" parent and a "red" parent would contain both a blue section and a red section.

2. Encourage the client to consider and identify all racially based *pride* and *shame* issues that are organizing principles within the family. Pride issues are those racially based traits, behaviors, qualities, and other factors that are positively connoted and provide a source of pleasure, fulfillment, or satisfaction for an individual or family. Shame issues, on the other hand, are those racially based traits, behaviors, qualities, and other factors that are repudiated, disavowed, or deemed unacceptable and unsatisfactory. For example, in the family of my client, Claudia, discussed earlier, possession of a light-skinned complexion was considered an issue of beauty and pride, while her dark skin was often ridiculed and considered less attractive. Encourage the client to choose one symbol to denote pride issues as well as one for shame issues. The selection of the pride and shame symbols and to whom they are affixed is left entirely to the discretion of the client, based on their family's unique story. For example, my client, Claudia, used a halo to denote how light skin was viewed in her family. Thus, all members of her family who enjoyed the pride and privilege of having light skin had a halo symbol next to their names on her racial genogram. In contrast, Claudia's circle on the genogram had the symbol of a skull head, as did other members of her family, to denote that their darker skin was considered a shame issue.

3. Encourage the client to identify how a range of racially based physical characteristics, such as hair, eyes, complexion, lips, physique, etc., are regarded within the family.

4. Encourage the client to consider, graphically depict, and discuss, if appropriate, the family's experiences with immigration and any implications associated with race.

5. Encourage the client to identify all family-sanctioned and/or -perpetrated *implicit messages* that were expressed about race within the family.

6. Encourage the client to identify all family-sanctioned and/or -perpetrated *explicit messages* about race that were expressed in the family.

7. Encourage the client to identify and discuss any race related taboos connected to the family.

8. Encourage the client to explore within-group race-related conflicts and to hypothesize about the source(s) of the conflict.

9. Encourage the client to explore how race-related differences were typically handled within the family.

10. Encourage the client to consider, analyze, and/or hypothesize about what the overall three-generational impact of race has been on the family as well as themselves (from the client's unique perspective).

There is considerable overlap between and among the aforementioned *Racial Genogram Reflection Questions* that clients are asked to use as a supplemental working framework to assist with the construction of the racial genogram. The overlap is intentional and designed to compensate for potential gaps in memory and how these issues can be forgotten or deeply buried as a coping mechanism.

The racial genogram can either complement the racial storytelling process or, with a few added features, can be used in lieu of it altogether. Regardless of how it is used, the overall goal is the same. It is a powerful tool designed to facilitate a client's exploration of their racial self, background, and intrafamilial racialized experiences, while also providing additional information that might shed light on the formation and maintenance of the invisible wounds of trauma. When properly executed and explored within the context of therapy, it allows the client to see that which has been visible but not seeable and to begin the important process of developing a more integrated racial sense of self.

A major component of the racial genogram process involves the naming and claiming of racially based shame. This is largely precipitated by the focus on pride and shame issues and the deep underlying pain, humiliation, and devaluation that is often connected to these issues. This is one of several reasons why it is imperative for the therapist to fully commit to creating a safe, consistent holding space for the client while also liberally and effectively using the VCR approach throughout the entire therapeutic process. The act of validation is crucial; it is the glue that holds all the frayed pieces together while the work unfolds. While the emotionally focused dimension of the work guides the process, it is also important for the therapist to simultaneously begin to gently "plant seeds" for some minor cognitive restructuring; that is, providing clients with new and alternative ways to understand and perceive old phenomena differently. The therapeutic use of *petite lectures* is an effective vehicle for sowing the seeds for cognitive restructuring.

PETITE LECTURES

Petite lectures are miniaturized, didactically oriented, psychoeducational axioms designed to invite clients to begin thinking differently about themselves, the issues they struggle with, and a host of other related issues. Petite lectures can also be quite instrumental in helping to frame the process of therapy, in working around defensiveness, and in providing a pathway for integrating principles of relational ethics and racial and social justice into clinical practice. They are metaphorical fortune cookies, in that they are designed to offer the client relatively brief, simple messages they can bring to mind outside the therapy room to help them navigate everyday life. They are metaphorical "lectures" and do not consist of any form of therapeutic pontification. Thus, they are not *lectures* in the purest sense of the term; instead, they are intended to be microeducational nuggets that are designed to motivate a client to begin to think differently, even if the emotions connected to old thoughts don't change immediately. They are most effectively executed when they are clear, concise, thought provoking, and frequently referenced. They can be delivered in a variety of formats, including verbally, in writing, or using audio recordings. Regardless of the format used for delivery, ideally they should reflect the therapist's core beliefs about trauma, relationships, hurt, and healing and be tailored to the client's needs. They can be created by the therapist, formulated from extracts from poetry, literature, or other creative sources, or a combination of all of these.

The following is a collection of petite lectures that I have created to guide my racially based trauma-informed work:

PETITE LECTURE: THE SHAME OF SHAME—SILENCE AND SECRECY

There is no emotion more powerful than shame. It is shameful to acknowledge that you have shame. Where there is shame, there will also be silence and secrecy. You can never fully exercise your voice or be all that you wish to be as long as you are held hostage by shame, silence, and secrecy.

This lecture is often used to motivate clients to "see" the powerful effects of shame and devaluation and their potential to stifle growth and progress. It makes explicit the connections between shame, devaluation, and voicelessness and provides the client with another way to look shame and to think about the consequences of failing to name and claim one's shame, and it illustrates how easy it is to be emotionally, psychologically, and behaviorally paralyzed by shame.

PETITE LECTURE: RUNNING UP THE DOWN ESCALATOR—MOTIONS WITHOUT MOVEMENT

You have been running up the down escalator for much of your life; you can see the top but can never quite get there, although you are trying. You can't get there because you are confusing *making motions* with *making movement*. They are not the same! You have worked hard, and I think it's time for you to make movement.

This petite lecture is designed to invite the client to think differently about why certain efforts they have been made have not produced the type of results they may have been striving to achieve. It acknowledges the efforts being expended to affect change and highlights the ways the approach one is taking is not working, likely because it is not the approach that is needed. The hope is to create a powerful and persistent—whenever an escalator is encountered or used—reminder of the client's unique circumstance.

PETITE LECTURE: ANGER VERSUS RAGE

Anger and rage are not the same emotions. R(age) is anger that has aged. It is a strong emotion that usually exists over a long time, maybe even generations. Rage is what you have when something has happened to you. As a Person of Color, there is a lot that has happened to you, and thus rage is inevitable. To deny your rage is to deny your history and all that has happened to you. Rage deserves to be expressed, and it needs a channel to be expressed through so it can be heard and be a force of reckoning.

This petite lecture is used to accomplish several purposes: 1) to help clients recognize and embrace that rage is a response to trauma, and thus distinguished from anger, which has been weaponized by whites and used as a tool to silence People of Color; 2) to invite and encourage clients to think about the intergenerational and historical nature of rage and to conceptualize it not as something to be shunned or ashamed of but rather as a source of inner power; and 3) to indicate that rage must be embraced and channeled and that, when this occurs, it is and will be a force to be reckoned with.

PETITE LECTURE: RACIAL SUFFERING— STRUGGLE AND SURVIVAL

Unfortunately, as People of Color, we have been born into a struggle where some degree of suffering is inevitable. It was someone's plan that we wouldn't be here today, and yet here we are. We are resilient. We have suffered but we have also survived lynching, acts of brutality in its most heinous forms, discrimination, murder, rape, and assaults to our souls, and here we are defying the odds. One cannot reach the true depths of one's potential and one's greatness without embracing one's suffering.

The purpose of this petite lecture is to assist the client in embracing the notion that the pain and suffering that one has endured can have a deeper purpose if one is open to exploring this potential. It also invites the client to apply strategies of survival that may be embedded within their experiences of suffering and struggle. Finally, this lecture, like most of the others, is designed to foster and promote a deeper sense of hope.

PETITE LECTURE: UNMUTE YOUR MICROPHONE

The rules of racism have taught us that silence is golden but have neglected to tell us silence is actually "golden handcuffs." Voiceless people are a powerless people. We are taught to remain silent to survive physically, but in silence, our souls are assassinated. The "choice" we are given is between the survival of our physical self or of our soul. We can neither truly survive nor thrive when our metaphorical microphones are on mute, when our volume is turned off. If we want to survive, we must unmute our microphones and increase our volume!

Here, the goal is to promote the importance of using one's voice and to highlight the value of challenging and making a concerted effort to overcome voicelessness. This lecture is designed to disrupt the message of survival that often teaches People of Color to keep their heads down and their mouths shut to thwart being perceived as too angry, race-obsessed, or noncooperative. These messages and the ensuing behaviors they give birth to are deleterious to the overall well-being of People of Color and they reinforce the wounds of racial trauma. The focus of this lecture is to challenge the essence of these lethal internalized messages.

PETITE LECTURE: WHAT YOUR EARS NEED TO HEAR

> The power to speak, to tell one's own story in one's own words, is the ultimate expression of personal power. The purpose of speaking one's truth is not to convince others or to seek agreement or to be understood. The power and purpose of speaking is for YOUR mouth to say those things that YOUR ears need to hear for the liberation of YOUR soul.

This lecture is designed to challenge and/or replace deeply internalized messages connected to devaluation, an assaulted sense of self, and the alleged futility of exercising one's voice, which is essentially one's personal power and sense of agency. The message embedded in this lecture is to emphasize that the *act of speaking* is an act of self-advocacy, selfcare, and self-empowerment and is *not* about whether someone else endorses, invites, or welcomes it. The client is reminded that the act of speaking is an act of activism and that it involves so much more than simply speaking!

PETITE LECTURE: RACIAL EUPHEMISMS AND RACE ERASING PHRASES

> Race-erasing phrases such as "somebody who looks like me," "other people," "the dominant group," or "people of other ethnicities or groups" are all are parts of the language of the racially oppressed. They are racial euphemisms designed to erase race or avoid saying "white," "Black," or other race identifying descriptions. You will know when you are walking

toward personal and internal liberation when you can say "white people" out loud and name race clearly, specifically, and nonreactively.

The tenacles of secondary-level oppression and racial trauma are so deeply integrated into the everyday experiences People of Color that they can be operative without conscious awareness. This petite lecture is designed to expose one of the many ways how People of Color speak is deeply rooted in the soils of racial oppression. The tendency to discuss race, and especially whiteness, without overtly naming it is a clear response to trauma. The history of punishment and the fear of being punished for speaking too overtly about race are etched in the psyches and behaviors of so many People of Color. While this behavior is understandably adaptive, it is equally assaultive to one's well-being. This lecture is designed to make the implicit explicit and to motivate clients to be more intentional about taking the risk to name race explicitly. Once again, there is a liberatory power embedded in the process of naming.

PETITE LECTURE: SPEAK UP, STAND UP

It is hard to stand up when you don't speak up. It is hard to speak up when you are not standing up. You must speak even when you are convinced no one is listening or wishes to hear what you have to say. You must speak up to stand up, and you must stand up so you can speak up!

The purpose of this lecture is very similar in scope and function to the other lectures that center on speaking and challenging voicelessness.

PETITE LECTURE: TEARS

We only cry when we have something to cry for and about. For People of Color, there is lots to cry about. Our tears honor the spirits of our loved ones, including ancestors and all the intangible losses that shape our lives: the loss of dignity; the loss of being seen and valued; the loss of freedom to be; and a host of other losses. We must let our tears run free to honor, to remember, to never forget, but most importantly, to heal.

PETITE LECTURE: LIVING IN RAGE, LIVING ENRAGED, AND OUTRAGE

Living under the reigns of white supremacy means that People of Color must live in a state of rage and ultimately become enraged. One cannot live "in rage" without being or becoming enraged. There can be no enragement without outrage. Rage kills! You cannot survive or thrive without developing a healthy relationship with your rage. Enragement must be transformed to outrage and outrage must be guided, directed, and channeled.

The purposes of this lecture are: 1) to normalize rage as a predictable byproduct of living under racially oppressive conditions; 2) to reinforce the notion that rage can be simultaneously functional and dysfunctional, depending on how it is used/expressed; and 3) to emphasize that guided, directed, and channeled rage can be an infinite source of personal power, healing, and transformation.

PETITE LECTURE: CRYING AND THE CLEANSING OF THE SOUL

> Crying is a necessary act for cleansing the soul. It is the way we let go of and expunge all the hurt, pain, and growth-inhibiting energy that needs to be released for the heart and soul to thrive.

I often ask Men of Color how often they cry and when was the last time they cried; and the answers were always astonishing. Internalized message of maleness, masculinity, homophobia, and the mandate to be strong contribute to a set of conditions that make it difficult for many men to cry and/or acknowledge that they do. The purpose of this lecture is to encourage men, and all other clients for whom crying is a taboo, to consider the ways in which suppressed emotional expression negatively affects their heart, their soul, and their ability to be emotionally present in relationships.

Petite lectures can be a powerful therapeutic tool for addressing the invisible wounds of racial trauma, especially when they are formulated with specific wounds in mind. As noted earlier, it is helpful when the therapist can repeat, reference, and/or reintroduce the lecture(s) often, especially in seamlessly integrated ways throughout the therapeutic process. However, before reinforcing any lecture, it is important that the therapist ascertain whether the lecture resonates with the client.

SUMMARY

Working effectively with and addressing the invisible wounds of clients with racial trauma often requires the therapist to embrace therapeutic strategies and techniques that extend beyond those typically affiliated with traditional psychotherapy approaches. The Validate, Challenge, Request (VCR) approach; racial storytelling; racial genogram; and petite lectures are strategies and techniques specifically designed to address the invisible wounds of racial trauma and the racially based therapeutic needs of Clients of Color. Embedded within each of these strategies are elements that are specifically designed to achieve the following therapeutic goals:

1. Counteract devaluation
2. Promote self-love and repair the assaulted sense of self
3. Promote relational connectedness and counteract psychological homelessness
4. Transform habits of survival into strategies of survival
5. Transform voicelessness into voice activation
6. Acknowledge and rehumanize loss
7. Address, normalize, and promote the rechanneling of rage

CHAPTER 14

Stages of Treatment

Conducting intensive, racially sensitive, trauma-informed therapy requires the therapist to provide a zone of safety where Clients of Color can be reflective about their race related pain and have a place to metabolize it. Secure, sacred places to deeply explore the invisible wounds of racial trauma are virtually nonexistent for many People of Color. Much of the pain associated with the "thousand cuts" inflicted by the "normal" everyday acts of racial oppression that many People of Color sustain is just beneath the surface. The type of therapeutic work desired and needed to heal this pain cannot be easily packaged into rigidly structured eight-to-ten-session treatment protocols. In contrast, the healing process requires careful pacing that allows the client adequate time to think, reflect, explore, and breathe as well as to sort through the complexities of race. While there is no uniform or prescribed structure nor any particular evidenced-based treatment protocol that therapists must strictly adhere to, there are several critical stages of the therapeutic process that are important to consider and address. These stages are informed by practice-based evidence and, as such, are not connected to a specific model of therapy nor a specific theoretical orientation. Instead, they are critical stages of the therapeutic process that can be integrated into a therapist's preferred model of therapy, provided they are executed in a racially sensitive, thoughtful, and comprehensive way.

The following stages are critical components of providing racially sensitive, trauma-informed therapy (Hardy, 2013):

1. Affirmation and acknowledgment
2. Creating space for race
3. Exploration of the presenting problem and connections to race
4. Expanding the scope of the racial inquiry
5. Naming
6. Exploration of communal healing
7. Addressing invisible wounds
8. Witnessing

Step 1: Affirmation and Acknowledgment—During this critical stage of the process, it is imperative that the therapist, while serving as the "broker of permission," convey by words and actions the understanding and affirmation that race is a substantive, worthwhile, and legitimate issue to consider within and outside of therapy. The effective implementation of this step is driven as much by the attitude and overall demeanor of the therapist as it is by specific actions the therapist might take. Assuming that the therapist is guided by the therapeutic principles discussed in Chapter 5 and has been diligent in conducting their own racially based self-of-the-therapist work, the skillset needed to effectively negotiate this step should be an integral part of one's clinical toolkit. Acknowledgment and affirmation pave the way for conversations about race to unfold and to be approached directly. In addition to conveying acceptance of the premise that race is a significant organizing principle, the therapist, again as broker of permission, must also assume a proactive role in establishing the foundation for step two of the process: creating space for race.

Step 2: Creating Space for Race—This step is best facilitated by centering conversations about race throughout the process of therapy. This is achieved when conversations about race are treated with genuine interest, depth, and a sense of curiosity. This means that the therapist is actively engaged in an authentic, inquisitive, and a proactive way rather than cautiously clinging to the periphery of the therapeutic process as a passive, tepid, disengaged observer. Creating space refers to specific actions the therapist takes to convey, both implicitly and explicitly, to the client that this is a space where conversations about race can be had in an honest and open way. It is not, however, predicated on the therapist remaining silent and disengaged or working hard to not take up too much space or staying out of the way of the client. When space has been created for race, it is far easier for racially based conversations to occur organically throughout the process of therapy. Developing this important space dispels the notion that there must be a designated or predetermined time, place, or set of circumstances established for conversations about race to occur. It frees both the therapist and the client to work seamlessly with race as an integral dimension of the therapeutic conversation. In particular, it grants the therapist space to explore issues of race at any stage of the therapeutic process, including, and especially, during the early stages of therapy, while exploring the anatomy of the presenting problem.

Step 3: Exploration of the Presenting Problem and Connections to Race—Since Clients of Color rarely enter therapy specifically identifying racial trauma as an area of concern, the eyes of the therapist must be trained to see the invisible wounds associated with it. The wounds of racial trauma are frequently intermixed with other stresses that a client may be experiencing. During this step of the process, it is important for the therapist to conduct a comprehensive exploration of the presenting problem while also paying close attention to race. This part of the process should culminate with the therapist having formulated a good developing understanding of: a) the presenting problem; b) the invisible wounds of racial trauma; c) who is connected to both the problem and possible solutions; d) solutions that the client has tried; and e) other sociocultural or familial factors that may be connected to both the problem and to potential solutions. During this important exploration, data collection, and assessment process, the racial genogram and/or the racial storytelling strategies may be extraordinarily useful. For either of these strategies to be effective, Steps 1 and 2 must have been successfully executed. If space has not been created for race or if the client is at all dubious about whether the issue of race is one that the therapist considers valuable, the efficacy of the racial genogram and racial storytelling will be significantly impeded.

Step 4: Expanding the Scope of the Racial Inquiry—Once the therapist has a sense that the racially based therapeutic conversations are occurring fluently, fluidly, and somewhat organically, the next important step is to expand the scope of the inquiry. While there are multiple ways that the therapist might achieve this endeavor, requesting that the client either conduct a racial genogram or engage in the process of racial storytelling are two effective strategies for accomplishing this feat. Since both experiences require having extensive conversations about potentially delicate racial issues, the timing regarding when a client is asked to do either is an important matter to consider. As the therapist continues to explore the presenting problem and gain more information about it, the racial genogram and the racial storytelling processes can be rich sources of information. The intersections of the invisible wounds of racial trauma, family and community of origin issues, and the influences of other potential sociocultural forces can all be thoroughly examined during this process. With the therapist's guidance and support, each strategy facilitates the client's ability to develop new insights and to critically consider a host of underlying issues that may have heretofore been ignored, denied, or overlooked.

There are no firm rules or best practices regarding how either strategy must be used throughout the therapeutic process. The two strategies may be used in conjunction with each other or independently. The racial genogram may be conducted within therapy, over multiple sessions, or it may be assigned to and be completed by the client as homework that will be viewed and discussed during a future therapy session. Racial storytelling can be executed as an oral history or it may be recorded, videotaped, or communicated through various art forms. Given the amount of work that clients are expected to devote to these tasks, it is crucial that the therapist allocate ample time to review the fruits of their labor and guide the client through an intensive introspective process. Whether conducting a racial genogram, engaging in racial storytelling, or both, it is of the utmost importance that the therapist encourage the client to consider including members of their relational network in these processes. Doing so can be one of a series of efforts to promote and solidify relational connectedness and provide a foundation for addressing psychological homelessness. Even if family members or other relevant parties are not included in the process at this, or any other, stage of the therapeutic process, it is important for the therapist to remain open to the possibility of including others and being a strong advocate for it. The therapist must convey the resolute message to the client that the involvement and/or inclusion of others in the therapeutic process is more likely a matter of "when" rather than "if." The adamance of this philosophical position is rooted in the belief that intensive, racially sensitive work is relationally focused, thus communal approaches are heavily drawn upon. Despite the strength of this strongly held philosophical conviction, the client is the final arbiter of who, if anyone, is invited to participate in the process.

Step 5: Naming—At this stage of the therapeutic process, the therapist should have an increased understanding of the client's suffering and a growing number of clinical hypotheses. It is critical to the therapeutic process, and the client's growth and development, that all the nameless phenomena associated with race and racial trauma begin to be named. Thus, it is important for the therapist to spearhead the *process of naming*. It is through this process that the therapist and client can begin to forge, and rely on, a common language, which will pave the way for more intensive and comprehensive work.

The process of naming also enables the client to have their "craziness"—that is, their internal second guessing, acts of self-deprecation, and feelings of being an imposter—acknowledged and dismantled by having it all externally named and validated. Invisible wounds (individually and collectively), habits of survival, shame, and racial oppression are but a few examples of phenomena that warrant naming. As naming is incorporated into the therapeutic process, it helps create a shared language, common understanding, and a new way of thinking, being, and seeing one's world. The use of petite lectures can be helpful in facilitating these shifts. The petite lectures can facilitate a client's ability to engage in a type of cognitive restructuring process that enables them to perceive a set of issues from a different perspective. The effectiveness of using petite lectures as a therapeutic strategy is greatly reliant on the naming process, as is true for other clinical strategies and techniques as well. When naming is introduced and executed is also quite consequential to the process of therapy and to clinical outcomes. For example, it is generally more beneficial to the client and to the therapeutic process when the naming step follows, rather than precedes, the exploration of the presenting problem and conducting a racial genogram or engaging in racial storytelling. When the naming process is introduced too soon, it tends to place the client in the position of searching for experiences to align with what has been named rather than the beneficial naming of what has been experienced. This cautionary note is intended as a general guideline, not a mandate. There might be a host of circumstances that would necessitate the opposite of what is suggested here.

At first glance, it might appear mundane to devote designated time and attention to the naming process as an integral part of therapy, however, it is crucial because it acknowledges, validates, and reifies the racially based suffering of People of Color and the hidden effects of racialized trauma. Naming is essential not only for addressing the wounds of racial trauma but also for creating a context for healing them. Part of the context of healing for many People of Color resides in having access to formal and/or informal communal healing structures and processes. Whether informal structures—such as barber shops, beauty salons, churches, temples, mosques, and synagogues—or somewhat mental-health-focused structures—such as retreats, racial affinity groups, movement groups, and healing circles—these experiences provide endless opportunities for people with racial trauma to speak, to be heard and seen, and to feel consensually validated. The naming process provides language that facilitates a client's ability to participate in communal healing processes. Once this is in place, it is necessary and critical for the therapist to take the next step.

Step 6: Exploring and Integrating Communal Healing Practices—It is important that intensive racially focused trauma-informed therapy not become too siloed. The naming step must be expansive enough to acknowledge, explore, and name communal healers and/or healing practices that have been or may be a resource and source of strength for the client. In some cases, this process may involve identifying and acknowledging the ruptures that may have taken place between the client and a communal healing resource that has been lost. This was the case with my client Anaya, a queer South Asian woman who became increasingly disenchanted, disillusioned with, and disconnected from the gurdwara (i.e., Sikh shrine) that she and her family had always attended due to the rampant homophobia she experienced there. The opportunities for communal healing that the gurdwara had once offered her were no longer existent now that she was cut off from her house of worship. Thus, her experience was further exacerbated by the increasing sense of alienation she experienced living in a Christian society as a spiritually uprooted, queer, Sikh, Woman of Color who is neither Black nor white in a world that often treats race and gender as rigid binaries. Without an intentional exploration of the communal healing practices, the psychological homelessness that she was experiencing as a queer, Sikh, Woman of Color would have very likely remained tangential or unacknowledged and ultimately unexplored in therapy.

Once the therapist has a comprehensive understanding of the communal healers and/or practices that are central to a client's life, it will be easier to incorporate dimensions of this work into the process of therapy and approaches to healing. Soliciting petite lectures from religious, spiritual, and community healers on behalf of a client can be a powerful intervention in and of itself. Therapists should proactively support a client's participation in ancillary groups—whether therapy, affinity, movement or meditative—and healing circles, which can be effective healing-inducing and trauma-reducing adjuncts to traditional psychotherapy.

The exploration, identification, and integration of communal healing resources can help bolster the therapist's skill and confidence in effectively executing Step 7.

Step 7: Addressing the Invisible Wounds of Racial Trauma—In one sense the entire therapeutic process involves addressing the invisible wounds of racial trauma. Once again, it is worth noting that there is no clearly defined timetable for when or how long this process should occur. There is no specific number of sessions nor timeframe. Each of the aforementioned steps offers micro-opportunities to address the invisible wounds of trauma and to contribute to the process of healing. The salience of this seventh step is to remind therapists that, while there are certainly elements of healing that are naturally embedded in the therapeutic process, it is also imperative to be intentional and laser focused about addressing invisible wounds. It is imperative that the therapist understands that, regardless of what the therapeutic process involves or how it is structured, therapy must pointedly address the wounds of racial trauma by establishing a healing environment wherein clients can accomplish the following clinical tasks: 1) externalize devaluation; 2) reconstitute the self and enhance self-love; 3) overcome voicelessness; 4) address psychological homelessness by repairing and restoring relational connectedness; 5) rechannel rage; 6) address loss and collective grief; and 7) convert habits of survival to strategies of survival.

Step 8: Witnessing—This process refers to the act of inviting and including members of the client's relational network into the therapeutic process to bear witness to the changes that have been made and to serve as a resource to help fortify the client. The people who are invited to witness play a vital role in helping to create a healing community for the client that can relied upon both during and after therapeutic treatment.

SUMMARY

There are eight critical steps of the treatment protocol recommended for therapists committed to providing racially sensitive, trauma-informed therapy. The steps are discussed in a linear fashion in this chapter but do not necessarily require rigid adherence to this particular order. Most of the steps, with the exception of Steps 1 through 3, are interchangeable based on the principle of equifinality and, theoretically, can be followed in any order, depending on the circumstances and the needs of the client. These steps provide a general framework for the process of therapy and the treatment of the invisible wounds of racial trauma. It is conceivable, although unlikely, that a client may not suffer from any of these wounds; some clients may experience all or some of these wounds with varying levels of intensity and urgency. All the critical, intervening variables should guide the course of therapy and inform what the therapist attends to, when, and how.

CHAPTER 15

The Process of Therapy

The main therapeutic goal of providing racially sensitive, trauma-informed therapy is to address the invisible wounds of racial trauma in a comprehensive and methodical way. This means that the therapist must focus on the following: dismantling and externalizing internalized devaluation, attending to the assaulted sense of self by promoting a reconstituted self; overcoming voicelessness; rechanneling rage, promoting relational connectedness; addressing intangible loss and collective grief, and converting habits of survival to strategies of survival. This work is not a linear process and must be deeply and seamlessly integrated throughout the therapeutic process.

DISMANTLING AND EXTERNALIZING DEVALUATION

Since internalized devaluation is a common, deeply rooted wound for so many People of Color, every phase of the therapeutic process should involve actions that breakdown, disaggregate, and counteract the multitude of aspects of devaluation that encumber the heart, psyche, and soul of People of Color. The effective use of the VCR approach is a critical tool for counteracting devaluation. In fact, upon initial contact with a Client of Color, it is important for the therapist to be fervently committed to finding the traces of a redeemable quality or the unseen badge of ability or gift that lies buried beneath the layers of devaluation. Since many People of Color are accustomed to and anticipate that all aspects of their lives will be regarded pejoratively, providing a steady flow of authentic validation is curative and transformative.

As is the case with thoroughly addressing all invisible wounds, the process is time consuming, and the therapist must be consistent, persistent, patient, and methodical in their approach. Usually, there are no quick fixes, nor are there dynamics that require a one-and-done intervention. Thus, for the client who has lived a life of perpetual devaluation and has deeply internalized it, effectively addressing this wound can be a challenging clinical endeavor. To be effective, the therapist must guide the client carefully and methodically through the following process: a) identify strains of internalized devaluation; b) name and explain; c) seek acknowledgment and affirmation; d) externalize; and e) counteract.

Identifying Internalized Devaluation

As odd as it may seem, the very first step involved in dismantling and externalizing the stronghold of internalized devaluation is to be able to see and identify the intricacies of it. While internalized devaluation is a pervasive and debilitating condition for many People of Color, the lack of language for and recognition of it often makes it difficult for them to see. For many People of Color, devaluation is acknowledged, discussed, and processed in terms of "respect" and "disrespect," which are the critical organizing principles associated with it. The need and the demand for respect, as well as the strong allergic reaction to being "disrespected," are seldom processed as "devaluation," which is a much deeper, more insidious and injurious psychological phenomenon. Hence it is common for People of Color to have a very strong reaction to certain situations or circumstances without having a clear sense of the origin (devaluation) of the strong underlying affect attached to the experience. The following vignette is a poignant example of internalized devaluation that could benefit from further inquiry.

Vignette: Chicken?

The Tri-State Midland Behavioral Health Center (TMBHC) is a large midwestern service provider to a broadly diverse clientele population and who is the employer of a diverse workforce. The CEO and Board of Directors of TMBHC, as it is often referred to, has been committed to transforming the organization from a predominantly White organization to one that espouses and practices racial equity and inclusion. As such, the organization has been actively engaged in a multiyear process of examining all aspects of its operation to eradicate systemic and institutional racism. The white CEO and predominantly white executive leadership team have been challenged by the task they have taken on, but they remain committed to the process. They sought my assistance as an external consultant following a huge racial conflict in response to a Black History Month celebration. One of the less substantive, perhaps even symbolic-only, changes that the organization made was to celebrate different cultural groups throughout the year. To commemorate Black History Month, the onsite cafeteria served soul food, which consisted of baked macaroni and cheese, collard greens, corn bread, and fried chicken. The menu instantly provoked the ire and scathing criticism of many Black/African American staff. Bobby, a senior vice president and the only Black member of the executive leadership team, was so irate he could hardly formulate a complete sentence. He stated, incredulously and emphatically, to his white counterparts: "*CHICKEN?* WE ARE SERVING *CHICKEN* TO HONOR BLACK HISTORY MONTH?" He went on to lament: "Whose racist, stereotypic, poor idea of a commemoration was this? Chicken? I am insulted beyond words!" The entire issue was embarrassing, perplexing, and divisive for the staff and the leadership. There were several Black staff who genuinely appreciated the recognition and several who were in staunch opposition and felt offended. The leadership was perplexed by what they considered to be a good and noble intention that had gone sideways.

After conducting several sessions with the Black staff, including those who had different reactions to the soul food incident, the role that devaluation played in the reactions became increasingly clear. The meetings were very painful and emotionally intense. They started with fierce accusations regarding who was authentically Black and who was a "white wannabe." It was abundantly clear how present white people were in the minds and psyches of those in attendance of the exclusively Black/African American meeting—not a single white person was physically present. Virtually none of the participants was aware of the ways in which internalized devaluation was pitting them against each other or fueled the shame and repudiation they felt about the serving of soul food, a cuisine that they all acknowledged they not only consumed but grew up eating as well. After several intense back and forth interactions between Bobby and me, Bobby was eventually able to acknowledge that his strong objections to serving soul food, especially fried chicken, in the company cafeteria was deeply rooted in the scathing ridicule and hurtful jokes he had had to contend with much of his life that centered around Black People devouring fried chicken and watermelon (Black, 2018). He continued to point out that when he imagined Black people eating soul food in the cafeteria, they would appear to be "spectacle-like," like animals being amusingly observed in a zoo by critical and judgmental white onlookers. Several other Black participants recalled the "fried chicken" comments made by white golfer Fuzzy Zoeller about Tiger Woods after the latter won the PGA Masters Tournament in 1997. Zoeller commented: "He's doing quite well, pretty impressive. That little boy is driving well and he's putting well. He's doing everything it takes to win. So, you know what you guys do when he gets in here? You pat him on the back and say congratulations and enjoy it and tell him not to serve fried chicken next year. Got it." Zoeller then smiled, snapped his fingers, and walked away before turning and adding, "or collard greens or whatever the hell they serve" (Norris, 2020, para. 9).

It is extremely difficult for Bobby and many others like him, who have historically been terrorized by white surveillance and harsh racial critiques, to embrace any aspect of their life that has been strongly criticized, ridiculed, and rejected by white people. An integral part of my work with the group centered around externalizing devaluation and enhancing their understanding and appreciation for how it was creating a wedge in the relationships among staff. I asked the group to consider and discuss the origins of soul food and the ingenuity and creativity of "our people" who were able to create an internationally recognized cuisine out of the scraps discarded by white slave owners. I then asked each of them to consider what was interfering with their ability to regard this *story of survival* with a strong sense of ancestral pride and instead made it evoke shame and embarrassment. Finally, I ask them to take a moment to reflect on how far we have come as a people to have the scraps from the slave master's house served in the cafeteria of a major company like TMBHC to honor not just all of them but those who came before them as well. Bobby, with tears slowly crawling down his cheeks, was speechless as he warmly embraced me while whispering that he could not thank me enough for the heartfelt and liberating conversation.

As this vignette demonstrates, it is possible for one to surrender to internalized devaluation and not know it. Therefore, the first step of the externalization process often involves the therapist assisting the client in identifying the threads of devaluation, especially those that may not be readily apparent. Once they are identified, the therapist must then devote time to the next critical step of the process: naming and explaining.

Naming and Explaining

Naming involves attaching the term *devaluation* to a behavior so that it can be easily identified and concretized by all parties. It also involves naming the myriad underlying emotions often associated with devaluation, such as shame, humiliation, and rage. Once devaluation and all its component parts have been named, it is often necessary for the therapist to offer some insights about the anatomy of the condition. In other words, it is important for the therapist to address issues such as why/how it is devaluation, what the hidden dimensions and associated subtleties are, and how it stifles one's development, relationships, etc. This is the explaining dimension of the process. These may seem like mundane conversations to have with a client, however, so often, many of the dimensions of devaluation are far removed from the client's consciousness. Since naming and explaining can be a very emotionally taxing experience, appropriate pacing of the session and the therapist's active monitoring of the client's reactions and underlying emotions are critical during this step of the process.

Acknowledgment and Affirmation

Once the naming and explaining step has been successfully executed, it is generally wise and prudent for the therapist to seek confirmation from the client that the notions that have been shared about the anatomy of devaluation resonate with the client's developing understanding. If they don't, this may indicate that more time is needed to comprehensively explore the intricacies of internalized devaluation. If, on the other hand, the client affirms the assertions and hypotheses, this signals that it is time for the therapist to commence the final steps of the externalization process.

Externalization

The major focus of this part of the process involves the client developing a keen understanding that many of the behaviors associated with internalized devaluation—whether self-doubt, feeling like an imposter or less than, or battling feelings of worthlessness—are shaped by external forces. The client begins to develop an awareness that "I am because of what has happened to me, not because of what is wrong with me." The externalization process draws heavily on the racial storytelling and racial genogram disclosures to reconnect the frayed parts of a client's life in a way that facilitates the externalization process. The petite lectures and stories of survival can provide very valuable concrete information to help with externalizing devaluation. My group sessions with the Black/African American staff at TMBHC demonstrated a small example of what the externalization process can look like in a nontherapy, nonclinical context. The principles, strategies, and techniques that were employed in the Black/African American affinity group meeting would be identical to those that a therapist might utilize in therapy. Once a client has made progress with the externalizing process, developing the skills to counteract devaluation is the next and final step to effectively address devaluation.

Counteracting Devaluation

Whereas the externalization of internalized devaluation involves expunging it from the core of one's being, the process of *counteracting* refers to metaphorically creating an impenetrable wall that thwarts the (re)internalization process. It is created by developing a type of metaphorical antibody that enhances one's ability to intercept and thus protect oneself from future racially toxic, demeaning, devaluing messages. This process is achieved by the therapist's widespread and liberal use of the VCR approach, by helping clients identify and embrace their badges of ability (Rubin, 1976), and by doing intensive ongoing work designed to address the assaulted sense of self. There is a self-defeating, symbiotic relationship between devaluation and an assaulted sense of self. It is internalized devaluation that ultimately contributes to the assault of oneself, and once this occurs, the self is much more susceptible to the wound of internalized devaluation. Thus, reconstitution of the self is critical to counteracting devaluation and to repairing the assaulted sense of self.

RECONSTITUTING THE SELF

Reconstituting the self is a crucial step toward addressing the invisible wounds of racial trauma. It involves the twin processes of self-deconstruction, that is, developing a keen awareness of how savagely one's sense of self has been assaulted, and reconstitution, the process of by which the self is rehabilitated, repaired, and reconstituted. The development of self-love as a racial being is a fundamental component and goal of self-reconstitution work. hooks (2001, p. xxii) astutely asserts that "the denigration of love in the black experience, across classes, has become the breeding ground for nihilism, for despair, for ongoing terroristic violence and predatory opportunism. It has taken from many black people the positive agency needed if we are to collectively self-actualize and be self-determining. Many of the material gains generated by militant anti-racist struggle have had little positive impact on the psyches and souls of black folks, for the revolution from within that is the foundation on which we build self-love and love for others has not taken place."

Sadly, countless numbers of People of Color spend an entire lifetime trying to regain what has been violently stripped from them as a result of living in a pro-racist society. The shameful shunning of one's physical characteristics that fail to meet the white standard—whether the width of one's nose, the texture of one's hair, or the shape of one's eyes—and the doubts one has about one's belongingness, intelligence, what one eats, wears, etc. all contribute to an assaulted sense of self. Developing a healthy and whole sense of self cannot be attained if/when these toxic self-incarcerating messages reside within the hearts, psyches, and souls of People of Color.

This phase of the therapeutic process calls for the client to engage in an even deeper state of self-introspection, self-interrogation, and self-reflection than is typically considered customary. The therapist, extracting important information from the racial storytelling and/or racial genogram exercises as well other clinical data, must be probing, curious, and validating while avoiding any therapeutic positioning or posturing that might be construed as rejecting or judgmental. This process often evokes a great deal of shame and embarrassment for some clients. Thus, how the therapist responds while witnessing such a difficult and delicate process is of paramount importance and can either encourage clients to go deeper or deter them from doing so.

From the earliest stages of child development, People of Color are inundated with white supremacist, demeaning, and negative valuations of what it means be a Person of Color in a racially oppressive society. The opportunities to explore the depths of one's authentic racial self, without white influence, white characterizations, and white critiques are rare. Some People of Color successfully combat and overcome these self-defeating and self-annihilating messages through intensive self-focused work; however, for many others, the self-harm can persist for a lifetime. The major introspective and self-exploratory work associated with the self-reconstitution stage centers around the premise: "You cannot *love* yourself if you don't *know* yourself; and you can't *know* yourself if/when you can't *be* yourself; and you can't *be* yourself if you have never had the opportunity to deeply *explore* yourself." This premise serves as a framework for guiding the process of therapy during this phase by crystalizing the major components of self-reconstitution work. Formulating it into a petite lecture is often a good way of ensuring that the sentiment has some resonance with the client. It also gives the therapist a quasi blueprint for pursuing self-reconstitution work. It makes clear that the pathway to self-reconstitution and self-love begins with self-exploration, knowledge of self, and ultimately making peace with *being* oneself. Since People of Color spend an inordinate amount of time either trying to disprove what white people believe they are, code-switching, or hiding critical pieces of who they are in order to survive, the process of authentically getting to know oneself racially is not an easy task. Racially sensitive, trauma-informed therapy should be a process and, ideally, a metaphorical place where such critical work can be done in a way that is honorable, respectful, and dignity-affirming.

Ideally, the exploration of self is a comprehensive process by which one not only explores one's racial self but also one's other dimensions that may also be stifled by sociocultural oppression (e.g., gender identity, sexual orientation, class, etc.). It also involves inviting clients to imagine who, how, and what they might have been if racial (and other forms of) oppression had not robbed them of the right to truly and authentically *be*. The point of clinical inquiry and therapeutic pursuit evolves around the interconnected processes of exploring, getting acquainted with, being, and discovering love of self. Carefully and methodically guiding a client through this process is vital to repairing an assaulted sense of self. Once again, this is a place where openness to embracing communal practices can be extraordinarily helpful to the therapeutic process. Inviting participants from the client's relational network to provide insights, testimonials, and affirmations can help deepen the focus of the work as well as help fortify it. As always, the purpose of including members of the client's relational network is to help create and solidify a healing community and to offer a safeguard against psychological homelessness.

There is also a deeply experiential aspect of self-reconstitution work that is important for therapists to promote. The As-If technique is a strategy that the therapist can use to help facilitate the client's participation in a dimension of the work that requires *doing and being* in addition to the more internal psychologically focused introspection work that is also crucial. The As-If technique is a semistructured exercise in which the client is asked to respond to several different circumstances "as if" they were totally and completely free of the restraints that the shackles of racial oppression has placed on them. The circumstances to be proposed by the therapist must be designed with considerable forethought as well as a keen knowledge of the client to ensure that the timing, pace, and difficulty of the assignment are appropriate. This task often requires clients to stretch beyond their comfort zone and to risk vulnerability. Thus, it is important for the therapist to thoughtfully propose circumstances that systematically range from the least difficult to most difficult to process. The following are examples of As-If processes a client could be invited to perform:

1. Between now and our next session, please write down or record five accommodations or self-sacrifices you make in your personal life, professional life, or both to appease or make white people comfortable.
2. In the follow-up session, the client would be asked to conduct their life for one day as if the accommodations were no longer necessary.
3. During our session next week, can you commit to speaking, behaving, and showing up physically *as if* you were free from the shackles of racial oppression?
4. Can you designate one day next week as a day to act *as if* you are free of racial oppression at work in your interactions with white coworkers?
5. Can you designate one day next week as a day you will act *as if* you are free of racial oppression at work in your interactions with Coworkers of Color?
6. Can you act *as if* you were free of racial oppression regarding your choice/style of dress or some other aspect of your physical appearance that you would negotiate differently if you were free?

Based on a therapist's knowledge of a client, the As-If tasks can be much more targeted and specific than these examples. The overall objective of the exercise is to encourage and support the client's efforts to take small steps to reconstitute the self in a supportive, nurturing, and gently challenging environment. The emergence of a reconstituted self also requires that the client address the wound of learned voicelessnessa, which contributes significantly to an assaulted sense of self.

OVERCOMING VOICELESSNESS

In many respects, the As-If exercise is as much about developing and/or regaining one's voice as it is about reconstituting the self, especially since the phenomenon of "voice" involves so much more than speaking. Reconstituting the self and overcoming voicelessness are highly interconnected, and healing from and repairing one de facto requires the same for the other. When one is free to be, one also enjoys a sense of personal agency and the ability to speak and/or advocate for oneself. Thus, addressing voicelessness is essential to counteracting devaluation, to reconstituting the self, and to healing from the wounds of racial trauma. Overcoming voicelessness requires intensive work centered around the client receiving metaphorical *voiceless*-ons.

The concept of "voice lessons" refers to the process by which a client is encouraged and taught to develop, strengthen, and/ or refine their voice. The lessons are designed to help the client cultivate, nurture, and access the internal resources required to stand up and speak up in the interest of self-advocacy. Voice lessons are an integral part of working clinically with voicelessness. There are some aspects of the lessons that are quite rudimentary and didactically oriented, while others require more emotionally intensive work. Encouraging clients to routinely use I-messages and to develop some mastery of the Voice Wheel are two basic and fundamental voice lessons that a therapist can employ to build a foundation for addressing voicelessness.

For decades, the importance of using I-messages has been widely cited in the communication and psychotherapy literature (Satir, 1988). In this context, the use of I-messages is crucial because it locates and elevates the voice of the client as a preliminary step toward overcoming voicelessness. When using I-messages, the voice of the client, and in this case the voiceless, is no longer hidden within vague and passive references to "some people," "others," or other generalities. The use of I-messages invites the client to own their words, position, and personal agency. Consequently, the matters that at first glance appear to be rather simple are often found to be very challenging for many clients who have spent significant portions of their lives struggling with voicelessness. What on the surface appears to be a mundane, semantical matter is actually one of considerable substance, as it relates to overcoming voicelessness.

In addition to emphasizing the importance of using I-messages, the therapist must also encourage the client to practice and use the Voice Wheel as another helpful preliminary step for developing one's voice. The Voice Wheel is a simple mental template that can help the client structure their thinking and help them execute their voice. It is important to reemphasize here that voicelessness is not a matter of choice; it is a trauma-based response. Hence, when one's standard way of being has been mired in voicelessness, not knowing exactly what to say nor how or when can impede one's developing efforts to cultivate and execute one's voice. Under these circumstances, it is easier to default to the familiar position of voicelessness, which is a trauma reflex. The Voice Wheel provides the client with a preexisting template that can be used to help activate their voice. The Voice Wheel consists of the following prompts: "I think . . . "; "I feel . . . "; "I wish . . . "; "I want . . . "

The client can arbitrarily use any one of the four prompts for voice activation and then complete the wheel. For example, a client could respond to a racial slight that they typically might remain silent about by stating: "I feel offended by the comment . . . " or "I think of that term as racially insensitive," or "I want to respond to something you said, and I feel uncomfortable doing so." As indicated in each of these short examples, the design and structure of the Voice Wheel requires the client to use I-messages and to express thoughts, feelings, needs, and desires. Each of these, individually and in totality, helps to activate one's voice as well as to solidify personal agency and responsibility.

Once the initial groundwork has been established, the therapist must build on it by gradually delving into the more challenging and substantial aspects of voice lessons. For example, the therapist must intentionally increase both the intensity and intimacy of the process. Developing a voice is not a simple matter. It requires overcoming voicelessness, which is a process that, as previously noted, can be quite challenging for many Clients of Color. After all, despite the massive deleterious effects voicelessness has on the souls and well-being of People of Color, it does afford numerous secondary benefits. For instance, remaining silenced allows for some sense of (pseudo)safety, a perceived ability to survive, and help with effectively managing stress. Thus, the process of overcoming voicelessness is often very anxiety-producing and fear-inducing. While the shift from voicelessness to voice, along with the sense of personal empowerment that often accompanies it, is highly desired, it is also terrifying for many clients. Some portion of the fear and anxiety is rooted in historical precedence and the fact that People of Color have a protracted history of being brutally punished, in the best of circumstances, and murdered, in the worst of circumstances, for acting *as if* they were free by exercising their voices. Hence, voicelessness for many People of Color is a visceral, intergenerationally transmitted, trauma-coping reaction. Attempts to guide Clients of Color away from the lethal effects of voicelessness is akin to taking away what is perceived to be a protective factor against white aggression and punishment. Consequently, this phase of the therapeutic process is among the most emotionally intense and challenging. Also, beneath the surface of voicelessness are deep feelings of despair, helplessness, and rage, emotions that are likely to emerge during this phase of the process. This aspect of the work involves so much more than simply learning effective communication skills. Since elements of voicelessness are largely visceral and reflexive, developing a voice and overcoming voicelessness must also involve voice lessons that attend to the deep underlying emotional experiences that often remain hidden, from even the clients themselves.

The therapist must be adept at highlighting the myriad

ways in which voicelessness manifests throughout a client's life and behaviors. The deeper the gravity of one's wound of voicelessness, the more sophisticated the strategies for concealing, justifying, or detoxifying it. This means that the therapist must also be exceedingly mindful about how the wound is expressed throughout the process of therapy. Unfinished statements, partially disclosed thoughts, the use of racial euphemisms, the extensive use of phrases such as "I am not sure," "I have to think more about that," or "I don't know" are often markers of voicelessness. They permit the client to "verbally" participate in the therapeutic process but do very little to overcome voicelessness. They often reveal the inner turmoil and conflict of being hopelessly trapped between the tension of "speaking" and remaining "silenced." Obviously, this isn't always the case with these expressions; however, it is prudent for the therapist to hypothesize about the potential connection between the client's reliance on their usage and their voicelessness.

The use of petite lectures focused on speaking, silence, and voicelessness, such as those referenced in Chapter 13, can be a very effective therapeutic tool for helping the client to overcome voicelessness. The potential for cognitive restructuring that petite lectures offer is valuable for this phase of the work, especially for the dimension of voicelessness that is analogous to a visceral reflex. The incorporation of racially and culturally based therapeutic aids can also be a valuable component of voice lessons and the therapeutic work focused on overcoming voicelessness. Acknowledging, elevating, and incorporating the voices of racial/cultural icons who write, speak, or deliver sermons about various aspects of voicelessness and, more importantly, who embody what it looks like to have a voice can be inspirational, healing, and transformative when used throughout the process of therapy.

Overcoming voicelessness, like all other invisible wounds,

involves ongoing, intensive, comprehensive work. The progress associated with it is often slow, and setbacks are a predictable part of the process. In fact, it is common, during the early stages of voice work, for a client to assertively exercise their voice one day, and experience total regression the next. The transformation from voicelessness to voice can be exhilarating and liberating one day, and be threatening and stifled by fear, anxiety, and self-protection the next. An integral part of voice lessons and the work of the therapist is to make sure that the client is aware of these predictable and normative developmental shifts. Otherwise, the self-doubt of the client will be parlayed into that which is familiar, that is, a return to a chronic state of voicelessness. Overcoming voicelessness has far-reaching implications for healing racial trauma. Not only is it essential for promoting self-advocacy, it is also a potent antidote for thwarting hopelessness and helplessness as well as for recalibrating rage. Possessing the skill, willingness, and ability to exercise one's voice on one's behalf is key to the liberation of one's soul and is an important step toward overcoming voicelessness. When one's voice is consistently and systematically blocked, the regulation of rage becomes difficult and must be acknowledged and rechanneled to thwart self-destruction.

RECHANNELING RAGE

The wounds of voicelessness and rage are inextricably tied together, and as the therapist attempts to address one, the need to attend to the other is invariably highlighted. When one's voice is routinely silenced, as in the case with voicelessness, an emotional silencing occurs as well, particularly in those triggered by marginalization and injustice. As the therapist works intensively with a client to overcome their voicelessness, addressing their rage with the same degree of intentionality and vigor also becomes necessary.

The racially sensitive, trauma-informed therapist must be prepared to work intensively with the strong affect often associated with rage and must have a keen understanding of the ways in which rage is distinguishable from anger. As a client begins to develop a voice and to simultaneously connect to the affect that voicelessness has kept contained and suppressed, the actual process of therapy can become quite emotionally laden and flooded with expressions of strong affect. It is critical that the therapist not respond with fear, anxiety, or emotional reactivity. The therapist must avoid discouraging the expression of the strong affect and prematurely prescribing how it should best be expressed. To do so, would inevitably quiet the rage but it would also unfortunately and inadvertently silence the client as well, thus unwittingly reinforcing voicelessness. This is but one small example of the extraordinary clinical complexities and dilemmas that are central to working with rage.

When the therapist understands and embraces the notion that rage is a byproduct of trauma and oppression and is therefore not to be confused with anger, which is a much more immediate and episodic emotion, it is also understood that "anger management" protocols are not viable treatment options for racial trauma. The understanding of rage as a trauma-based phenomenon also effectively dispels the racially based stereotype that rage is an innate trait for People of Color, especially Black people. In fact, it helps to underscore the notion that those who are systemically oppressed and traumatized will often have trouble with emotional regulation, which includes rage. To heal racial trauma, the therapist must work with rage skillfully and effectively.

Effectively addressing rage in therapy is a delicate process in which the therapist must meticulously attend to five interrelated steps. The clinical steps for addressing rage consist of 1) identifying rage; 2) defining and naming rage; 3) validating rage; 4) exploring and assessing the intricacies of rage; and 5) developing strategies for rechanneling rage. These important steps for addressing rage are not intended to eradicate it, which is essentially impossible to do before the conditions responsible for aggravating it are eliminated. The steps are designed to help the client regulate and rechannel rage. Since so little is known about rage as a clinical phenomenon and there is no clinical nomenclature to describe it, *identifying* then *defining and naming* rage must be the first tasks performed by the therapist.

Identifying Rage

Identifying rage is the first critical step the therapist must execute in working effectively with rage. While this seems like a simple endeavor, it is slightly more difficult than it may seem. First, the therapist must gain an understanding of how and to what "object" the client's rage is typically targeted, since it may be directed toward oneself (internalized) or toward others (externalized). Determining how the rage is expressed is the next important assessment for the therapist to make. Internalized rage can be manifest as suppression, which is a conscious process, or repression which is unconscious. Righteous and self-righteous rage are both typically associated with externalization.

Of course, the manifestation of externalized rage that features a demonstrative emotional outburst—accompanied by yelling, fist pounding, and a host of other aggressive behaviors and antics—is relatively easy to identify. However, there are a vast array of other rage expressions that are much harder to detect. To work effectively with rage, the therapist must be able to identify, with impeccable clarity and accuracy, the entire range of emotional expressions that exist on the rage spectrum. These must be not only identified but named as well. It is the therapist's conversance with the anatomy of rage and the language associated with it that helps to inform and sharpen the interventions that will be used throughout the course of treatment. Whether rage is internalized or externalized, clinically manifested as quiet rage (a seething understated expression), self-righteous rage (destructively entitled, self-absorbed) or righteous rage (channeled through social activism), the therapist's ability to conduct a differential diagnosis and to proceed accordingly is highly germane to the overall efficacy of the treatment. Rage, regardless of type, severity, where it is directed, and if and how it is expressed, must be defined and named.

Defining and Naming Rage

The process of defining and naming rage is pivotal to addressing and treating it. As previously noted, anger is often conflated with rage, and regardless of how it is labeled, it has been weaponized by whites and used as a negative, racially stereotypical trope. Many People of Color, especially Blacks, are quickly and easily offended when referred to as "angry" because of the associated racial stereotype. Given these societal realities, it is important for the therapist not only to name rage during the early stages of the process but to operationally define it as a trauma-based response that is separate from and will be distinguished from anger. Sometimes this process requires more than one cursory conversation or gesture by the therapist. It is crucial for the therapist to convey to the client the racial normativity of rage and that rage is a predictable human response to a set of unpredictable, inhumane, and abnormal circumstances. The use of petite lectures can also be very effective in reinforcing and crystalizing this message. While it might appear mundane, it is important that the therapist point out any time the client inadvertently uses the terms *anger* and *rage* interchangeably. It is often necessary for therapists to consistently remind Clients of Color that *rage* is what you have when something has happened to you and that living with racism contributes a great deal to how People of Color navigate and respond to the world around them. In other words, rage is an intense psychoemotional response to oppressive and traumatic social circumstances; it is not a racially based genetic condition. The therapist must not only embolden the client's use of the term *rage* but also actively promote the authentic embracement of it. This is crucial preliminary work that provides a foundation for the more intensive work that will ensue. The therapist, through the process of validating the phenomenon of rage as a traumatic response, makes it easier for the client to explore it.

Validating Rage

The therapist's validation of a client's rage is neither an expression of agreement nor an endorsement. Instead, it is an affirmation of and a testimonial to the therapist's ability to see beyond the overt expressions of outrage, fury, and hurt expressed by a client, their ability to see that which is redeemable and not seen by others. The therapist's validation of rage often helps create a sacred holding space for the client, wherein the vulnerability that often lingers just beneath the surfaces of rage can be both expressed and witnessed.

The VCR approach is often a very effective tool for responding effectively to rage. On the one hand, it enables the therapist to authentically hold the client's experiences with and expressions of rage without condition, yet it also invites the client to consider (at the appropriate time) the harmful aspects of it, followed by suggestions for how it might be better regulated without suppression and without the elements of self-destructiveness. Validation is, figuratively speaking, an effective *relationship lubricant.* It facilitates emotional and relational connectedness by preventing stuckness, stagnation, or escalation. Thus, when rage is appropriately validated, the client tends to feel metaphorically held by the therapist, which often culminates in a strengthening of the therapeutic relationship, which makes conducting a more in-depth analysis of rage facile.

Exploring and Assessing Rage

Rage is a complex, multidimensional emotion that is frequently feared and often misunderstood, even by those who are besieged by it. Consequently, a major task associated with working effectively with rage involves exploring and understanding the vast array of other emotions and experiences intermixed with it.

Rage has many faces and therefore a range of expressions associated with it. Working effectively with rage requires the therapist to have a thorough understanding of the nuances of it and the ability to thoroughly assess how the intricacies of it are embedded throughout the life experiences of a client. As previously noted, rage can be either internalized or externalized, which can dictate how it is expressed. There are aspects of internalized rage that resemble despair, despondency, and depression. When internalized, the hypervigilance that is often associated with some expressions of rage is directed toward the self, often expressed in the form of self-loathing and/or a range of self-punitive behaviors. The therapist must be able to see and treat what very much appear to be the symptoms of depression or sadness as manifestations of internalized rage. The therapist's ability to work with strong emotions and to operate from a relational perspective make it possible to treat both conditions rather than conceptualizing the symptoms as an either/or issue.

With externalized rage, the sense of hurt, disillusionment, and despair that often underpins the constant outbursts of anger, hostility, and belligerence is often difficult to acknowledge and validate, yet it is incumbent upon the therapist to do so with skill, grace, and tenacity. When appropriate time is devoted to the exploration and assessment of the nuances of rage, the therapist will be more effective in helping the client to both recalibrate and rechannel rage, which are always the goals of rage work. It is exceedingly difficult to rechannel that which is not completely understood or adequately assessed. The therapist's success in helping a client to develop a detail-level view of the dynamics of rage and to understand how they might be affected by it is the linchpin to both rechanneling rage and healing a major wound of racial trauma.

Executing Rechanneling Strategies

To reiterate a point that warrants repeating, rage is simultaneously functional and dysfunctional. It is a powerful source of psychic energy that can motivate, energize, and mobilize. Unfortunately, it can also be a major source of energy depletion; it can be an emotional barrier and a cataclysmic force of self-destruction. Simply stated, the goal of rechanneling rage is to build up and maximize its functional dimensions while simultaneously minimizing or eliminating the destructive-self-destructive cycle associated with the dysfunctional manifestations of it. While this is easy to state, it is infinitely more difficult to accomplish. Rage tends to become dysfunctional when it becomes polarized and subject to psychological splitting. When this occurs, one's expression (and experience) of rage becomes rigidified; it is unaffected by circumstances or any other intervening variable. In other words, the way rage is experienced, processed, and expressed remains the same regardless of the situation or circumstance. The process of rechanneling rage requires replacing negative, self-destructive, self-defeating patterns of expression with more situationally fluid, constructive mechanisms. The work that the therapist conducts during the previous exploration and assessment phase is extraordinarily valuable during this stage of the therapeutic process. There are several critical tasks that are vital to successfully rechanneling rage. To thoroughly and effectively execute the tasks associated with this step, the therapist must focus intensively on working with both internalized and externalized rage.

Internalized rage is often directed toward oneself, which is safer than expressing it overtly. Thus, in the case of internalized rage, the therapist must first skillfully and sensitively address the complex underlying array of emotional issues that may block the client's ability to express their thoughts and feelings genuinely and openly. The therapist must also work closely with the client to develop the skills, intestinal fortitude, and external resources necessary to begin to externalize rage. The success of this work, of course, also depends on the relative success the therapist has had in assisting the client to externalize devaluation and to begin the process of repairing the client's assaulted sense of self. When working with internalized rage, developing strategies for externalizing is the precursor to rechanneling. In other words, internalized rage must be channeled to externalized rage before it can ultimately be constructively rechanneled. For many clients, this can be a very challenging, frightening, time-consuming process that requires the racially sensitive, trauma-informed therapist to be patient, nurturing, and validating. While transitioning from internalized to rechanneled externalized rage is a daunting task for clients, working with externalized rage is a more challenging undertaking for most therapists. The fact that externalizers tend to externalize makes confronting this manifestation of rage a clinical tightrope to walk.

The clinical expression of externalized rage is, as one might imagine, the total antithesis of its internalized counterpart. The constant expression of high-octane anger, fury, and strong affect is palpable in and outside of therapy. The functional dimension of externalized rage is that it is discharged; voicelessness is not an issue, although regulation is; and it is a much-needed form of activism and resistance. The dysfunctional dimension of externalized rage is that it is a one gear vehicle for which moderation and regulation are nonexistent. The most devastating feature of externalized rage is that those who rely on it seem to lack an ability to look inward, to self-evaluate, or to engage in critical self-examination or self-interrogation. This is where the clear line of demarcation exists between internalized and externalized rage. With internalized rage, there is a basic inability to consider outside forces, thus virtually everything is evaluated internally. With external rage, the sole focus is always external to the self.

Prior to attempting to rechannel rage, it is imperative that the therapist first engage the client in a process that authentically affirms and validates rage and also paves a pathway for self-reflection and self-interrogation. The therapist must be able to respectfully *thread the therapeutic needle* of helping the client to understand that while they are *not* responsible for the plethora of rage inducing situations that exist in society, they can and do have some agency regarding how they respond. The plea and tasks are not to eradicate rage but instead to be intentional about cultivating a relationship with it. This task must be accomplished before the rechanneling process can be enacted. Once this step has been embraced by the client, the therapist can assist the client in being more strategic and discretionary regarding the use of their rage. The rechanneling process also enables and empowers the client to develop and consider other means and modes of expressing their rage, which enhances its efficacy. With informed guidance from the therapist, the client may extract additional strategies for expressing rage from their stories of suffering, struggles, and survival. The goal is to assist the client in holding on to their rage while letting go of the self-defeating, self-destructive methods of expression that have become rigidified and for which there is compelling data to suggest that they are neither helpful nor healthy.

One of the greatest clinical challenges in working with all forms of externalized rage is the client's tendency to reflexively externalize, that is, to look at and possibly blame others rather than to self-reflect. It is commonplace for the therapist to quickly become the target of a client's externalized rage. Despite whatever discomfort this might cause, it is critically important for the therapist to stay engaged, to validate, and to respectfully but firmly encourage the client to participate in a deeper level of self-reflection and interrogation. Once again, the use of the VCR approach enables the therapist to authentically validate the client's feelings and to express their own respective position with truth and integrity. It also makes it possible for the therapist, despite the intensity of the moment, to make genuine requests of the client that are ensconced in intimacy, sensitivity, and vulnerability.

Self-righteous rage is the most challenging, volatile, and explosive form of externalized rage. Clinically, it is analogous to attempting to handle live frayed electrical wires while standing in a pool of water. The clinical engagement with self-righteous rage is challenging because it requires the therapist to work intimately and extensively with the deep pain that is beneath the rage while also being on the receiving end of a panoply of angry, defensive, and blaming attacks. Understandably, the process of rechanneling rage is impossible before the therapist and client successfully disentangle all sources of rage and treat them as the separate but interconnected phenomena that they are. Racially based self-righteous rage is fueled by racial injustice; however, it is often complexly and unconsciously (at times) compounded by exposure to other painful experiences with domination and marginalization. When rage from multiple forces of marginalization, unfairness, and injustice converges, it contributes to and creates a form of undifferentiated complex rage that inevitably culminates in a sense of (destructive) entitlement. The dominant worldview of clients struggling with self-righteous rage is that life is unfair, inequitable, and that one only gets what one fights for, and merely fighting for what one believes one deserves is tantamount to being entitled to it. There is a very thin line between self-righteousness, self-indulgence, and self-destructiveness—all prominent features of destructive entitlement. The clinical management of self-righteous rage is challenging for most therapists and is particularly so for those who have not engaged in intensive, racially focused self-of-the-therapist work.

When the sources of rage are not differentiated, it is difficult to engage in the rechanneling process. Moreover, rage is often expressed in random and diffuse ways, which makes it appear purposeless, self-serving, and spurious. Sorting out the sources of rage and attempting to offer some opportunities for healing must be accomplished before rechanneling can be successful. These accomplishments allow the work to be more targeted and specific to the actual source or precipitating event(s). The following brief vignette of a former client, Deirdre, offers a textbook example of a person maligned by self-righteous rage.

Vignette: The Many Sources of Rage

Deirdre was born in a small impoverished rural town in Alabama that was punishing and unforgiving of her as a Black person with dark skin and thick, coarse hair. She was viciously teased throughout her childhood and adolescence, often referred to as "grease monkey." She remains haunted by the seemingly endless barrage of poignant and painful memories of racial slights that she experienced throughout her formative years. Unfortunately, her home life failed to provide her with the respite she often desperately needed from the public scorn, criticism, and rejection she often experienced. She was the oldest of three girls born to parents who, as children, had never received love and nurturance themselves and were therefore significantly impaired in their ability to provide these to their offspring. Deirdre's mother was functionally available but emotionally disengaged and often scathingly critical of Deirdre throughout much of her life. She has no memories of ever being physically held by her mother or told, "I love you." On the other hand, she has countless memories of being spanked, hit, and corporally punished. Her relationship with her father, who routinely and openly had extramarital affairs with numerous other women in the same community, was a major source of anger, hurt, and embarrassment. She despised her father not only for his endless dalliances that blatantly disrespected both his wife and his children but also for his tacit acceptance of his younger brother molesting her when she was thirteen. Neither parent ever overtly acknowledged the rape nor comforted her nor confronted the perpetrator. Deirdre's relationship with her mother was complicated. She openly admits that she loved her mother, felt grateful to her for "giving all that she knew how to," and, on good days, felt tremendous compassion for her for having such a hard life and probably never ever experiencing the true meaning of love in her life. She credits her mother for being a hard worker and for financially supporting her through college. She stated repetitively that without her mother's support, she would not be the college-educated professional Black woman that she became. Yet, on the other hand, she lived with a sense of choking guilt, knowing that the job her mother relied on to survive financially had cost her much more than whatever below-minimum-wage money she earned. Deirdre reported that she knew, but never disclosed, that her mother had been raped by her employer, the husband of the white couple for whom she worked as a domestic worker for over 20 years. All these experiences nurtured a complex emotional bond she had with her mother; although not one without many blemishes. Deirdre also felt intense anger toward her mother, which was rooted in what she described as her mother's "passivity and helpless surrender to victimization." She blames her mother for allowing Jake, her husband and Deirdre's father, to ruin both of their lives. She faults her mother for not fighting back, standing up, and, most of all, not protecting her while she was a vulnerable child. Deirdre said that she considered her mother's behavior to be regrettable, unforgivable, and most importantly, unforgettable and unresolvable. From Deirdre's perspective, her relationship with her mother "is what it is" and cannot be repaired. She often said, "She is my mom, and I guess I love her because she is my mom, but we will never truly have a real mother–daughter relationship. When she dies, I can't imagine shedding a single tear because in a sense, my mother died a very long time ago and my father is not even worth the breath it requires to say his name."

Even this abridged version of Deirdre's background is typical of those struggling with self-righteous rage. As is often the case, there is no single source of degradation, loss, and despair, and thus there is no single source of rage. As one whose formative developmental years were maligned and marginalized due to growing up poor, Black, queer, female, sexually assaulted, emotionally neglected, and essentially powerless, the existence of deeply seated rage was predictable, inevitable, and should be understandable. Despite the critical connection that all these factors have to Deirdre's rage, she most often expresses it in relationship to race, since race is a recurring daily trigger for her as a Black woman. She finds it difficult, both personally and professionally, to overcome the daily grind, burden, and weightiness of walking though the world as a member of what she considers to be a racially targeted group.

In her professional work as a law professor, she is a fearless and tireless advocate for the marginalized. Unfortunately, her advocacy invariably disintegrates and becomes quickly overshadowed by a kind of belligerent, confrontational, and accusatory style of interacting with others that is off-putting and counterproductive. Consequently, many of her colleagues, and even some students, often characterize her as self-absorbed, polarizing, angry, and quick to play the race card. It is likely that there have been times when these claims have been unwarranted and times when they were probably justified in one sense or another. Unfortunately, even under circumstances where aspects of Deirdre's behavior have been definitively questionable and culpable, she demonstrates an absolute inability and unwillingness to assume any degree of personal responsibility, often belligerently citing racial bias or racism as the culprit. This is one of the many behavioral manifestations of living a life that has been overwhelmed and severely compromised by layers of sociocultural trauma and oppression exacerbated by a toxic and degrading family of origin experience. The common and unifying themes produced by her life circumstances are that the world is unjust, unfair, unequal, and deprived of everything except deprivation itself. She believes that she deserves what she deserves, regardless of how it is obtained. The world is perceived and acted upon in accordance with what she perceives as fair or unfair. It is the confluence of these experiences and perspectives that formulates the foundation for self-righteousness and (destructive) entitlement.

Neither this experience nor the emotional-psychological-behavioral profile is unique to Deirdre. Thus, it is not only her story, rather it is the story of anyone whose life has been inundated with traumatic experiences that have been converted to self-righteous rage. It is virtually impossible to help the likes of Deirdre develop a healthier, less destructive relationship with their rage without first devoting a substantial amount of time to sorting out and sorting through the varied sources of the rage and then helping the client begin a process of healing the enmeshment of past/present hurts. This type of therapeutic process requires time, intensive relationally based emotionally focused work, and the integration of and reliance on communal healing strategies. Once the client has a greater understanding of their rage and its sources and has the opportunity to address it and all its attendant issues in a sacred validating and healing environment, the process of rechanneling rage becomes easier. The goal of rechanneling is to help clients manage rage instead of allowing it to manage them. Since there is always a dimension of rage that is functional, the goal of therapy at this juncture is to assist the client with transforming self-righteous rage to righteous rage.

Righteous rage is dynamically rooted in the same soil as is self-righteous rage. That is, both are the result of extensive exposure to painful experiences with devaluation, marginalization, and degradation. The major distinctions, however, are that righteous rage tends to be less self- and individually-focused, it has a clearly delineated channel, and it is a bit more regulated than self-righteous rage, although rage, in and of itself, is a state of dysregulation. With righteous rage, unlike with its self-righteous counterpart, there is a premium placed on the significance of staying in the relationship with others. While a relentless commitment to and push for justice and fairness underpins righteous rage, the energy and driving force that fuels it emanates from a broader ethical–moral imperative, not solely from a place of personal woundedness and trauma. In other words, there is a spiritual component inextricably connected to the channeling process. Whereas "regulation" is one of the core issues on which to focus when working with self-righteous rage, "moderation" must be a focal point of clinical work with righteous-rage.

The rechanneling of rage is a liberating experience, especially for the soul. It is also emotionally cathartic, empowering, personally generative, and has the potential to serve the common good. Despite the personal benefits extracted from the channeling process, it can also inadvertently promote and support a type of narrow focus and self-absorption that can lead to relational isolation. The "cause" that is the target of one's (re)channeled rage can become one's principal and only cause. Such as, for example, the case of the civil rights activist who is tirelessly committed to "the cause" and yet has little time, interest, or energy for anyone or anything else, family and loved ones included. Fighting for the cause takes on a life of its own and can constitute the nucleus of one's universe. This is the potential dysfunctional component of righteous rage, and because it is not overtly harmful or discomforting to self or others, it can more easily fly under the radar than self-righteous rage, which makes almost everyone uncomfortable.

In many instances, righteous rage is properly channeled and expressed constructively. Hence, the core of rage-related clinical work must be directed toward assisting the client in finding balance in their life, especially in terms of relational connectedness. While righteous rage is properly channeled, the focused drive, energy, and attention that this requires can unwittingly exacerbate other trauma wounds, such as psychological homelessness, the orientation toward survival, and loss. Relentless and laser focused attention devoted to "the cause" can breed a sense of isolation and disconnection from, as well as a seemingly justifiable and benign neglect of, significant relational attachments and other responsibilities. It is important for the therapist to assist the client, firmly and consistently, in stitching these allegedly disparate dimensions of their life together.

Even clients for whom rage has been appropriately channeled (or rechanneled) may nevertheless lack a sophisticated understanding of rage and all its effects on everyday life and relationships. Through the natural course of therapy, the client can learn and develop new strategies for channeling rage. Developing the skills and capacity to engage in emotionally intensive relational repair work can be a powerful vehicle for rechanneling rage—directing and redirecting emotional energy back toward the source of one's hurt, pain, and rage but in ways that do not compromise one's personal and relational integrity. This process requires the therapist to be willing to conduct relationally based work with multiple participants present in the process. For example, in working with Deirdre, including her estranged mother and other family members was very important and integral to her healing process. Similarly, the therapist must also be well versed with and amenable to encouraging clients to explore a host of nontraditional psychotherapeutic tools as vehicles for rechanneling rage. Various forms of writing, performing arts, sports, and spoken word are all examples of nontraditional ancillary strategies that a client can use as socially sanctioned conduits for rage or as complements to the existing measures that they have previously found to be effective.

As the rechanneling process begins to create a viable pathway for the client to appropriately release rage, it simultaneously opens space for the exploration of other salient emotions that are often entangled with rage, such as loss. As noted in Chapter 11, loss is a powerful, pervasive, underlying emotion for many People of Color, and it is connected to all the invisible wounds of racial trauma, whether named or not. Loss, whether associated with the denial of dignity, respect, one's voice, or emotional–relational connectedness with a desired object, routinely nourishes and feeds rage. And, as Deirdre's case illustrates, painful experiences with loss are not relegated to race alone and can be a disruptive force in other areas of one's life as well. As the therapist sorts out the sources of rage and explores effective avenues for rechanneling it, they must simultaneously devote focus to disentangling loss from rage. Acknowledging and addressing loss, particularly loss that is complexly interspersed with rage, is critical to the therapeutic process of healing racial trauma.

ADDRESSING LOSS AND COLLECTIVE GRIEF

The transition from a state of volatile rage to a deep sense of painful despair and somberness can be rapid. In many ways, rage is a scab that shields the yet unhealed pain of loss beneath it. When the metaphorical rage scab is removed through the rechanneling process, it creates the opportunity for the client to explore and begin to metabolize the range of unacknowledged intangible losses and grief that have been either completely ignored or truncated by expressions of unchanneled internalized rage. For Deirdre and many others like her, the vehemence of her rage blocked all possible arteries for experiencing and expressing grief. When one has been perpetually devalued and disrespected and one's sense of self similarly assaulted, rage is infinitely more accessible and "useful" than grief. The former allows for some mobilization of energy, while the latter often leads to numbness, inertia, and psychoemotional immobility. Clinically, it was important that I, Deirdre's therapist, acknowledge and validate the legitimacy and utility of her rage, while also encouraging her to explore the deep losses buried beneath it. This was not an either/or proposition but one that required her to embrace the psychoaffective entanglement of both her rage and her grief.

As is often the case with many People of Color, Deirdre was overwhelmed by not only the tangible and intangible losses of her life but those that have been intergenerationally transmitted to her as a Black woman born and raised in the rural segregated South. The losses, both tangible and intangible, of her forebearers are passed on through the generations and are, essentially, her losses. The losses of dignity, respect, safety, and humanity have been passed on. She frequently wondered how to make sense of and to heal from the sexual abuse and rape that ravaged generations of women in her family. Although it was never overtly addressed, it was widely understood as an indisputable truth. The shame, humiliation, and deep sense of grief never allowed it to be overtly acknowledged. Perhaps, this is why Deirdre often tearfully and rhetorically asked throughout our therapy sessions, "I wonder how many times my grandmother, great-grandmother, and great-great-grandmother were raped by white men during slavery and Jim Crow? How many were raped by men they knew or in some cases even thought they could trust?" These reflections made it even harder for her to understand what could have driven her Uncle Johnny to sexually violate her and why there was such a "low pulse" response by her parents. She wondered if it garnered so little reaction because it is so prevalent and because the lives of women, particularly Black women, are considered so worthless that it doesn't matter. The loss of worth and dignity was palpable for her. Prior to the emergence of these themes in our work,

Deirdre had never allowed herself to consciously reflect on these issues, although she admittedly had strong feelings about them and often struggled with horrific nightmares. Both the individual and the collective grief were like having a noose around her neck. Admittedly, her many struggles with loss were not all neatly and visibly connected to race, but race played a very prominent role, often in ways that were not easy to discern.

Acknowledging and addressing loss require that the therapist name it, for a variety of reasons. First, when one's everyday life is inundated with loss, as is usually true for those with chronic racial trauma, that loss is regarded as a fundamental of life and essentially becomes "normal." Unfortunately, the underlying emotions associated with loss also become common shocks that are so frequent in occurrence that they too become "normal" or are easily suppressed, denied, or expressed as rage. The lack of recognition of underlying grief is not a mitigation. Even if there is no (overt) acknowledgment or embracement of loss, the body knows it, houses it, and responds to it. This is one of many reasons why it is so critical for the therapist to explicitly name loss. It is also crucial for the therapist to name loss because so many of the experiences of loss that are the most devastating are those that are intangible; that is, not necessarily visible or overtly measurable. When loss is not named clinically, the client is denied a precious opportunity to undress and address the pervasiveness of the intangible losses that underpin their rage and, most importantly, their pain. For example, Deirdre had a very clear and acute understanding of the embarrassment, humiliation, and shame she felt as a result of being called "grease monkey" in elementary and middle school and not being invited to her high school prom because she was considered too dark and unattractive. Understandably, she still, many years later, has lots of anger about the maltreatment and the impotency of those in power to protect her. However, what she had not spent very much time considering was the bevy of intangible losses ignited by and associated with those experiences. She had never seriously processed the losses of hope, innocence, security, or dignity that were directly connected to her school experiences as well as to her family of origin. As a result of those experiences, she lost a sense of spontaneity, inner trust, and freedom that manifested in her continuously second guessing her actions, whether she belonged, and when she would be exiled or criticized again. While her rage often generated intense attention from others, she nor those in her relational orbit spent any time attending to the deeply seated pain, agony, despair, and hopelessness she traveled with throughout her daily life. Because these losses were principally intangible and unacknowledged, Deirdre never had the opportunity to mourn them or the host of non-race-related losses that were also powerful organizing principles in her life.

In addition to naming loss, it is also important for the therapist to create opportunities for the expression of unacknowledged grief and mourning. In exploring unacknowledged grief, the therapist must cast a broad net and be expansive in their approach. Thus, racially based grief work must be examined contemporaneously as well as historically. The murder of George Floyd in 2020, the uptick in brutal attacks on innocent Asian Americans on U.S. streets, the starvation and senseless deaths of many Latinx children at the U.S.–Mexico border, and countless other similar experiences are sources of tremendous despair and hopelessness for many People of Color that are rarely acknowledged or treated. All too often, the focus both within and outside of therapy is primarily on how angry these people are and rarely on how hurt and aggrieved they are. The deeply felt but rarely acknowledged or articulated grief is complex in that it is very much connected to current losses but also to those that have been collected and passed down over generations. Their grief is entangled with the grief and losses experienced by their extended family and their ancestors. The therapist must be willing to address contemporary grief as well as that which is historically based.

The therapist's focus on racially based grief must be intentional and intense emotionally focused work. Some of the rudimentary aspects of this work may involve having the client generate a list of feeling words that range from sadness to depression to help facilitate naming and describing their emotional experience. This task is vitally important to the many clients who are overwhelmed with unacknowledged grief and who often don't have the words to describe their experience because it has never before been acknowledged. The tactics used to achieve this goal may range from asking the client to generate a list of terms, adding to it continually as their experience shifts, to the therapist providing a list for the client. Regardless of the methodology employed, the goal is the same, which is to help the client attach feeling (words) to experiences of loss so that the process of mourning, and ultimately healing, can begin to take place. Understanding, acknowledging, naming, and connecting underlying feelings to intangible losses paves the way for mourning. It is difficult to mourn that which has not been acknowledged. Pushing painful experiences aside, ignoring or denying them, or sublimating grief into rage are neither heathy, helpful, nor sustainable strategies for dealing with loss. The therapist must use therapy as a sacred place to help the client mourn current and past losses. Unfortunately, there is no one golden, universal, fail-safe strategy for facilitating this process, and what is needed can vary from client to client and from therapist to therapist. Yet, promoting a healthy process for mourning unacknowledged racial loss often involves the interrelated processes of naming, claiming, and proclaiming. One could argue that the funeral, as a death and mourning ritual, involves the same process. For instance, the bereaved acknowledges (names) the loss of a loved one, claims their relationship to the deceased, and the funeral is an official public announcement (proclamation), usually with others bearing witness. Helping clients mourn loss involves the same three-step process. The first step, *naming*, is ultimately about acknowledging or intellectually embracing an experience, which in this case is the loss. *Claiming* is the next step and refers to the client's willingness and ability to internalize and emotionally accept the loss. The final step, *proclaiming*, centers around the public display or acknowledgment of the loss, which is integral to the mourning process.

The therapist's ability to effectively expand the therapeutic process to address loss, grief, and mourning is critical to healing the invisible wounds of racial trauma. It is the willingness and ability of the therapist to uplift, legitimize, and microscopically focus on the intricacies of loss, particularly those that are intangible, that pave the way to addressing other, more sophisticated and unnamed manifestations of loss, such as the loss of home and sense of belongingness that so many People of Color experience due to variety of circumstances. The loss or lack of a spiritual existential home (i.e., psychological homelessness) is a common and deeply painful experience for many People of Color. There are two defining characteristics that psychological homelessness shares with the other wounds of trauma: 1) It is largely nameless and invisible, while the effects of it are not; and 2) loss is a major associated feature. To fully address the condition clinically requires the therapist to address both issues thoroughly, thoughtfully, and systematically.

ADDRESSING PSYCHOLOGICAL HOMELESSNESS

The unnamed condition of psychological homelessness requires those who are burdened with it to live in a world that feels largely void of safety, security, and a sense of belonging and rootedness. It is a life of disconnection that often leaves the soul in a state of unrest. There is a perpetual sense of yearning for an unattainable, elusive, hard to define "something else." In many ways, psychological homelessness is the painful culmination of being relegated to the status of "other" or "outsider." It may demand a baffling and anxiety provoking vacillation between two or more worlds, never enjoying the comfort or privilege of feeling as if one truly belongs. It is the immigrant-citizen, for example, who is *too* foreign to ever be fully accepted as a citizen and will always have to hear and feel pressured to answer the dreaded question "Where are you from?" followed by, "No, where are you REALLY from?" The very same immigrant-citizen is also *too* American to ever be fully trusted and embraced unconditionally in their culture of origin. While this is generally true for most immigrants, in tends to be more poignant for those who are People of Color, who lack the privilege of being able to physically "blend in." The inability to blend in is even more pronounced if the Person of Color speaks with what is considered an accent—of any type. It is a condition that creates hell in the lives of Indigenous, Latinx, Black, and mixed-race people who are too light or white to be fully embraced as an authentic Person of Color and too dark or not white enough to ever be fully embraced by whites. The consequence is living always in a state of confusion, emotional vacillation, searching, and nomadism. It is difficult to live as psychologically homeless without feeling despair, disconnection, alienation, and a deep sense of loss. Having always to prove oneself and to prove that one "really belongs" are lifelong chores for many People of Color, chores that are often as fruitless as they are endless. This burden of proof pervades all sectors of one's life, including the workplace and especially in predominantly white spaces, where the intricacies and significance of race tend to be denied or minimized whenever it is convenient.

Because psychological homelessness is commonly unnamed and rarely addressed clinically or otherwise in a comprehensive and thoughtful way, Clients of Color often blame or question themselves for not fitting in or belonging. Self-reflective, self-indicting questions such as "Why I am not Asian/Latinx/Black, etc., enough to fit in or to be fully embraced by my people?" or "Am I *really* too white, as I am accused of being?" are commonplace. Psychological homelessness has extensive implications for how People of Color live and function in their daily lives. Hence, it is a salient clinical issue that a therapist can ill-afford to ignore.

Following the same course as with other unnamed invisible wounds, the first important step for the therapist in addressing psychological homelessness is to name it. There is a tremendous emotional burden that can be lifted simply by introducing and naming the condition for clients. There is something that is immediately liberating about having it named. It facilitates the client's development of a keen understanding of it in a way that allows for emotional release and freedom from the burden of self-blame. Naming also enables the client to finally connect their experiences with the puzzling emotions that they have been feeling.

While extremely important and necessary for healing, the naming process is not a panacea, and so much more is usually required of the therapeutic process. There is a mutual parasitic-type relationship that exists between psychological homelessness and an assaulted sense of self. The two wounds contribute to and feed off one another. Thus, it is unusual to suffer one condition and not the other. As the therapist works intensively with the client to promote self-love and a reconstituted self, the naming process significantly boosts efforts to establish and/or reestablish belongingness and a sense of home. Furthermore, as the client begins to restore or build a stronger sense of "home" or "relational connectedness," it helps to fortify the reconstituted self. Once psychological homelessness has been named and explored, the therapist can gently shift the clinical focus to working with the client around self-exploration and self-acceptance, the next step of the treatment process: claiming.

The main thrust of the claiming process is to assist the client in embracing all parts of who they are (and aren't), pride/shame issues, aspects of their sociocultural privilege and subjugation, and a host of other related issues. This phase of the treatment requires a tremendous amount of and commitment to self-examination, self-interrogation, and self-reflection. Racial storytelling can be an effective and valuable mechanism for highlighting, exposing, and extracting information that could be of great therapeutic value for this phase of the process. The therapist's firm embrace of and adherence to a relational *both/and* perspective is essential to the effective execution of this segment of the treatment process. After all, the therapist's fidelity to this worldview makes it possible for them to encourage the client to entertain the possibility that they don't have to buy into the trap of being Asian *or* American; Latinx *or* white; privileged *or* subjugated. Entrapment in the push-pull of the "or" is always a hallmark of and precursor to psychological homelessness. This entrapment is a frequent and common issue that is rarely defined as a presenting problem despite its pervasive effects on the life of a client. Enam, a former client of mine, is merely one of a host of clients whose struggles in life were saturated with psychological homelessness. Enam is a very light complexioned, almost white-appearing, Pakistani immigrant who spent much of her adolescence and early adulthood battling psychological homelessness while trapped in the duality of the "or." She never felt comfortable publicly acknowledging that she was from Pakistan because it never felt safe. In the rare instances she did, she had to contend with denigrating and accusatory comments about terrorism. She learned to remain mute about her country of origin, quietly and publicly disowning it. She strongly identified with People of Color in the United States, perceiving herself as a Person of Color. Her peer group, as well as those she dated during her courtship years, were all People of Color. Although she phenotypically appeared white, in the presence of whites she was often reminded that she was "other"—a dangerous other, in fact. Among People of Color, with whom she felt a strong emotional bond, she was also treated as other, a near-white or semiwhite person—often treated with suspicion and mistrust. Consequently, she not only felt estranged from her native Pakistan, which felt like home but not home, but also dislodged and rootless in the United States, despite having lived in this country most of her life. She felt not white enough and too Pakistani/Muslim among whites, and too white and not Brown enough when in the presence of her Friends and Colleagues of Color. This is the essence of psychological homelessness, and it is not unique to Enam or to immigrants. The following vignette about Maya, a current client, reflects a similar dilemma that also was calcified by the tyranny of the "or."

Vignette: Betrayed by Complexion

Maya is a 42-year-old blonde-haired, blue-eyed, Indigenous, female member of the Powhatan Renape Nation, who lived on the Rankokus Reservation in New Jersey until her early thirties. In many ways, her daily struggles typify those of clients who enter therapy with underlying symptoms of psychological homelessness. She often reported feeling inexplicably despondent and repeatedly stated: "I don't know where I belong, where I fit. I left the reservation because I needed a different life. Now I am thinking that was a mistake and I should go back." She works as a social worker in a medium-size urban city and has constantly contentious relationships with most of her coworkers, whom she often feels misunderstood by. She acknowledges that she has a great deal of historically based, deeply seated anger toward white people, especially as a collective. She detests what she describes as their blind sense of entitlement, their insatiable colonialist thirst, and their reckless cultural appropriation. Unfortunately, her relationships with her Colleagues of Color are not much better. She describes them as "clique-ish," petty, and at times just as racist as her white colleagues. Her anger toward her Colleagues of Color is in some ways more intense and unforgiving than that toward whites. She sees and defines herself as a Person of Color. She states that, "in my bones, I know I am Native. I am not white, and by today's language, I am a Woman of Color. Unfortunately, I don't feel like I can ever say this even though it is what I know and what I feel. My so-called sisters are always there to remind me that I am not one of them and it hurts like hell. Yet, white people remind me daily that they see me as a 'less than' Indian."

Maya's story and dilemma, like Enam's, are all too familiar. She, like so many others, is forced to live with a powerful schism between what she intuitively knows and feels internally and how she appears to the external world. She is and feels "Native," a reality that is obscured, perhaps even negated, by her phenotype. Maya could not start the process of healing and overcoming her bouts with psychological homelessness until she could begin to embrace the wholeness of herself; this includes the parts that she warmly welcomes and the parts that she repudiates. Until she could begin to accept the tension and dichotomy within herself, she could never be accountable to or in relationships with other People of Color who did not enjoy the privilege or presumption of being or passing for white. Accordingly, she could never share with them the tremendous pain and sense of isolation that she was living with until she had admitted it to herself. She would not be able to authentically admit to her Colleagues of Color that the anger she often expressed toward them left hidden her desperate yearning to be authentically connected to and in sisterhood with them. Maya not only had to embrace all these complex painful and vulnerable emotions and experiences, she also had to stake claims to the shameful parts of her that had white skin as well. As one might imagine, the exploration of this process triggered a tsunami of loss, grief, rage, and moments of debilitating shame. Ultimately, she began to think of her white skin as a gift, not necessarily one to flaunt with pride, privilege, and prestige, but one carrying a historical marker from her ancestors to remind her of their ancestorial stories of suffering and survival. She began to realize that the white skin that showed up so glaringly on the outside had a much deeper, darker story of despotism attached to it internally. She was much more able to see pride and power in the fact that the human suffering imposed on her land and her people could not destroy or weaken her soul or spirit as a proud member of the Powhatan Renape Nation. It was claiming these parts of herself and her story that catalyzed the process of (re)negotiating relationships differently and starting her journey *home.*

Once the wholeness of oneself has been explored, interrogated, and embraced, there appears to be something inherent in the process that is often deshaming and empowering. The client establishes an inner clarity, confidence, and peace about who they are, which begins to change how they interact with others. Rather than constantly feeling the urge and the need to twist, shape, and reconfigure who one must pretend to be to fit in with a given group, the client has a newly established solid (reconstituted) sense of self, which frees the client to show up as their authentic self, regardless of the individual or group with whom they are interacting. For the likes of Maya, this meant interacting with other People of Color and feeling the freedom, confidence, and clarity to self-identify as a Person of Color, albeit one that does so with white skin privilege. She is much more able to convey understanding and empathy rather than anger, resentment, rejection, and overall defensiveness when she is reminded of her white part. She can constructively engage with other People of Color, acknowledging that it is their various respective hues and need for within-group racial loyalty that provides proof of their shared history of being victims of white dominance, aggression, and oppression. Another major element of this work requires the client to not only have a conscious awareness of their relationship to whites and whiteness but also to be able to discuss it openly and with a sense of clarity, regardless of context or audience. This is possible only if/when one is clear and resolute about who one is racially.

Since this phase of the work is very much dedicated to promoting and establishing relational connectedness, it is imperative for the therapist to involve other participants, whether family members, friends, cultural healers, etc., in and throughout the therapeutic process. While important throughout the entire process of therapy, the focus on relationally based, interpersonal work is extremely important at this juncture because it helps to fortify and reinforce the individual internal work that the client has done. It also gives the client a live portrait of how some relationships might have to shift to accommodate the individual personal changes that they have made.

Addressing and overcoming psychological homelessness play a significant role in healing racial trauma, creating opportunities for the client to address contemporary and intergenerational loss, collective grief, and mourning. This process also opens the door to self-embracement and self-love and potentially to rechanneling rage and restoring community and a sense of belongingness. In other words, it helps those who are psychologically homeless and have been racially traumatized to find an existential home. There is a powerful connection between psychological homelessness, safety and belongingness, and survival anxiety. The absence of a psychoemotional space where one feels safe and a sense of belongingness can contribute to high levels of anxiety, uncertainty, and insecurity about survival. Therefore, as the therapist explores psychological homelessness and its intricate connections to the other invisible wounds of racial trauma, considerable attention must also be devoted to how all these experiences are entangled with survival anxiety or the orientation toward survival. Racially sensitive, trauma-informed therapy must address survival anxiety, that is, the orientation toward survival and the habits of survival, in a sustained and comprehensive manner.

ADDRESSING SURVIVAL ANXIETY: TRANSFORMING HABITS OF SURVIVAL TO STRATEGIES

As described in Chapter 12, the orientation toward survival condition and state of mind is largely unconscious and is driven by race-related anxiety connected to survival in the broadest sense of the term—physically, psychologically, and existentially. It is a direct reaction to racial oppression and the multitudinous ways in which People of Color feel targeted and surveilled by most of white society. The preoccupation with survival propels many People of Color to develop trauma-based *habits of survival*, which are rigidified, reflex-like responses that are simultaneously functional and dysfunctional. Like any other habit, the orientation toward survival and habits of survival are routinized practices that are very difficult to relinquish. On the positive side, habits offer some momentary relief and abatement of survival related anxiety; however, on the other hand, they often inhibit personal growth, grossly distort decision-making processes, and affect what and how priorities are established. For example, the hustler and warrior habits both prioritize the hustle and the fight, respectively, over personal relationships. While these actions are referred to here as *priorities*, they are in fact reflexes, in that they are not necessarily the result of a conscious decision-making process. Instead, they represent impulses.

Clinically, working with and addressing the orientation toward survival must be executed by conducting a thorough and methodical assessment of the client's habits of survival. This process is most effective when it commences with the therapist devoting ample time to identifying the habit (or habits) of survival that the client defaults to, while also assessing how the habit may be connected to and reinforced by other wounds of oppression. The therapist might consider, for example, how righteous rage and the warrior habit are often fiercely interlocked and reinforce each other or might explore the central role that voicelessness plays in the subservient habit. It is also important for the therapist to be mindful that habits are not only intricately linked with other wounds of trauma but may also be fused with each other as well. Thus, it is conceivable that a client could display characteristics of two habits that are rigidly integrated but that do not retain their pure forms.

In addition to identifying the client's habit(s), the therapist must also have a keen understanding of how the functional and dysfunctional dimensions of it operate within the client's life and their network of relationships. A major element of this stage of the process also involves naming the habit. Maybe just one of the habits described in Chapter 12 is named, or maybe a combination of several different habits, or it could be those that are specifically codified and labeled by the therapist. The methodical and meticulous deconstruction of the habit(s) comprises the next important step in the treatment process.

In the deconstruction process, the therapist highlights the

functional aspects of the habits and also the specific ways in which the habits are harmful to the client and their relational network. This assessment is often made possible by the therapist's drawing heavily on the client's *stories of struggle* and *stories of survival*, acquiring feedback from family members and others participating in the process, and in vivo clinical observations. This process is very difficult and extremely time consuming. The therapeutic goal is never to completely eradicate a habit of survival but rather to a) eliminate the self-destructive component(s) while strengthening the functional aspects of it; b) transform rigidly reflexive automatic *habits* to *strategies of survival*, which are more volitional and targeted; and c) assist the client in developing new strategies that can be consciously and intentionally chosen and applied to suit a given situation.

The VCR approach can be a very useful tool for conducting the deconstruction process. In fact, it is of paramount importance that the therapist solidly validate the components of the habit that are growth producing, facilitative, and functional as an initial step. This part of the process must be well established, and it requires total buy-in from the client before the nonfunctional components of the habit can become a useful focal point. Since habits are connected to anxieties about survival, clients tend to hold onto them as a matter of life-or-death, which underscores the importance of the therapist's timing and tact when addressing these issues. Once the functional aspects of the habit have been appropriately celebrated, honored, and validated, it is important that the therapist spend time exploring, deconstructing, and naming the self-defeating, nonfunctional dimensions of the habit and how these dimensions are connected to other emotional–psychological–behavioral misalignments in the client's life. Following these important steps, the therapist is in a much more empowered position to promote the adoption of other habits that can be converted to strategies. The use of petite lectures at this stage of the process can be very effective in helping expose the client to additional habits and new potential strategies.

By expanding the range of habits the client has access to, the therapist is de facto assisting the client to grasp the notion that the use of and reliance on a habit can be volitional and strategic rather than reflexive and self-destructive. When behavior becomes volitional and strategic and directed consciously toward specific circumstances, it effectively becomes a *strategy of survival* and is no longer a habit. Addressing and ameliorating other racial trauma wounds can also help the client develop new strategies for addressing survival anxiety. Once again, it is worth noting that the efficacy of this work is tremendously enhanced when it is relationally based and, when appropriate, delicately integrated with communal healing practices that are racial-trauma focused.

SUMMARY

Healing the invisible wounds of racial trauma requires, at a minimum, the therapist to focus the therapy competently and comprehensively around addressing the intersections of internalized devaluation, assaulted sense of self, voicelessness, rage, loss, psychological homelessness, and an orientation toward survival. All these wounds share three salient features, which constitute a common denominator: 1) they are invisible to both the oppressed and oppressor; and 2) there is no common language to describe them; and 3) they are quite debilitating and warrant acute attention. Consequently, a central strategy for addressing each of these wounds individually and collectively involves the process of naming. This important dimension of the clinical process is foundational, in that it helps to reify the wounds and it provides the client with what may very well be their first experience of having the wounds validated and treated with dignity and respect. It is difficult to treat and heal from that which is neither named nor recognized. Whether rage, loss, or anxiety about one's survival, the process of naming is crucial.

For illustrative purposes, the healing and therapeutic process has been described quite lineally throughout this chapter. The dynamic, circular, and fluid dimensions of the work have been difficult to adequately capture in text. In real time, these wounds are complexly fused, often reinforcing each other, and may not be easy to isolate. They may be experienced with varying levels of intensity in any given client, oftentimes varying even within the same family or across generations. The therapist may not have the clinical luxury to neatly sort through the wounds in quite the same manner they have been described here. Since it is rare for Clients of Color to seek therapy for the unnamed, nonclinically diagnosable "problem" of racial trauma, it may often be that the therapist is confronted with attempting to address a nameless condition with an intense mix of emotional features with strongly felt but unexpressed racial undertones. Thus, identifying and naming the invisible wounds of racial trauma are central to the process of treating and healing the wounds of racial trauma. It is reasonable to assume that these wounds will persist as long as racial oppression exists, and oppression shows little signs of ending in this lifetime. Thus, while the conditions that produce the wounds and the wounds themselves persist, the invisibility of them and the lack of attention they garner throughout the therapeutic process do not have to remain, nor should they. Hence, understanding, addressing, and establishing the groundwork for healing racial trauma must become a fundamental focus of the therapeutic process and all therapy with Clients of Color.

EPILOGUE:

Final Thoughts and Reflections

I have approached this important piece of work from the vantage point of a therapist who also happens to be Black. As a clinician, it should go without saying, I believe in the process of therapy as a powerful tool for promoting healing. I often think of healing as an intimate and intense process that requires finding, touching, and bringing permanent soothing to the soft and tender places where it hurts or to places that have been hurt at some point. I have an abiding faith and belief in the process of therapy and in those of us who are the trusted stewards and purveyors of this sacred act.

This book lays out a quasi blueprint for using the process of therapy as a mechanism for addressing racialized trauma and the suffering that People of Color experience because of it. This book highlights the racial trauma of People of Color in a way that has been woefully absent in our field and throughout society. As a therapist, I have a sense of optimism that the information contained herein will make a difference in the lives of People of Color. And yet the nontherapist part of me—the part that existed long before I became a clinician, the part of me that has been significantly impacted by being a Black person, born and raised in the United States of America—is doubtful. As a Black person, I am keenly aware that what has been "prescribed" here by the therapist in me, regardless of how thorough and comprehensive it might be, is, in and of itself, still not enough. Healing the pain of racial trauma is important, and it is simply not enough. Systemic measures that routinely expose and subject People of Color to racially based pain and suffering must also be addressed. Therapy alone is not enough; it will fall short despite my abiding belief and confidence in its tremendous healing potential. So much more is needed. There is an urgent and dire need for our society to heal as well.

The "more" that is needed is social transformation. Broad, sweeping, radical, societal change is needed to stop the metaphorical hemorrhaging that underpins the suffering of People of Color that then necessitates a healing process. Therapeutic healing alone will not bring forth transformation, however transformation does possess the power and potential to promote permanent healing. It is through transformation, not therapy alone, that the racial context in this society will begin to shift. Transformation demands that we change the landscape, and doing so will bring about societal healing. This process must start with a three-step racially inspired societal healing process that focuses on (1) acknowledgment, (2) apology, and (3) action (targeted directly).

If white society could set aside its current fears, anxieties, and commitment to old ways of *thinking and being* to authentically operate within a society-wide framework of racial acknowledgment, apology, and action, we just might be able to transform and transcend our protracted history of severely strained cross-racial relationships. *Acknowledgment* not denial, *apology* not dismissiveness, and *action* not passivity will pave the way for forgiveness, reconciliation, and transformation. It would drastically and forever shift the racial landscape and the complex race relationships that have historically maligned human beings if whites would authentically undertake such a robust society-healing, reparative, and transformative initiative on behalf of a commitment to racial equity. The 2008 apology for slavery offered by the United States House of Representatives was an important first symbolic step (Lewis, 2016). However, more substantive and sustainable efforts are needed if we are ever to peacefully and equitably coexist as a healthy, functional, multiracial society. We need to follow the steps that other countries (e.g., Australia and South Africa) have taken and create a National Day of Acknowledgment, create a National Day of Remembrance, organize and conduct truth and reconciliation panels to be held throughout the country, and adopt and implement a strategy for reparations. The 2020 U.S. government stimulus checks that were issued during the COVID-19 pandemic demonstrated how political leaders can craft and implement strategies to identify and deposit funds into the hands and bank accounts of those who are deserving of funds. The same determination, will, resolve, and comprehensive strategies could be employed to implement a reparations initiative. These types of initiatives would allow the whole country to begin its healing and transformation process by finally cleansing both its hands and its soul of the centuries of Indigenous, Black, Asian, and Latinx blood that can neither be hidden nor denied.

Both the therapist and the Black man in me agree that full and complete healing from racial trauma can truly become a reality only when our society and our nation can heal from the racial malignancy that has occupied its mind, body, and soul for centuries. The bigger issue and much larger question is: Do we, as a Nation with lofty ideals that espouse freedom, justice, and equality for all, have the will and moral fortitude to address and offer redress for past atrocities and modern-day racial transgressions and human suffering? I certainly hope so.

BIBLIOGRAPHY

American Psychiatric Association. (2013). *Diagnostic and statistical manual of mental disorders* (5th ed.). American Psychiatric Publishing.

Anderson, C. (2016). *White rage: The unspoken truth of our racial divide.* Bloomsbury.

Angelou, M. [@DrMayaAngelou]. (n.d.). *I've learned that people will forget what you said, people will forget what you did, but people will never forget* [Twitter profile]. Twitter. Retrieved May 15, 2022, from https://twitter.com/drmayaangelou/status/1036327789488734208?lang=en

Angelou, M. (n.d.). Retrieved May 15, 2022, from https://www.goalcast.com/maya-angelou-quotes-to-inspire-your-life/

Black, W. R. (2018). How watermelons became Black: Emancipation and the origins of a racist trope. *Journal of the Civil War Era, 8*(1), 64–86. https://www.jstor.org/stable/26381503

Boszormenyi-Nagy, I., & Spark, G. M. (2013). *Invisible loyalties.* Routledge.

Boyd-Franklin, N. (2003). *Black families in therapy: Understanding the African American experience* (2nd ed.). The Guilford Press.

Centers for Disease Control and Prevention. (2021). *Working together to reduce Black maternal mortality.* https://www.cdc.gov/healthequity/features/maternal-mortality/index.html

Coates, T. (2015). *Between the world and me.* Spiegel & Grau.

Cooper, B. (2018). *Eloquent rage: A Black feminist discovers her superpower.* Picador.

DeGruy Leary, J. (2005). *Post traumatic slave syndrome.* Uptone Press.

Dobner, J. (2013). *Mormon church explains defunct ban on blacks in priesthood.* SALT LAKE CITY (Reuters) https://www.reuters.com/article/us-usa-mormons-race/mormon-church-explains-defunct-ban-on-blacks-in-priesthood-idUSBRE9BA03I20131211

DuBois, W. E. B. (1903). *The souls of black folk.* A. C. McClurg & Co.

Dunbar, P. L. (1895). *Majors and minors*. Hadley & Hadley, Printers and Binders.

Fanon, F. (1967). *Black skin, white masks* (C. L. Markmann, Trans.). Grove Press. (Original work published 1952)

Freire, P. (2005). *Pedagogy of the oppressed* (M. B. Ramos, Trans.). Continuum. (Original work published 1970)

Freud, A. (1937). *The ego and the mechanisms of defense* (C. Baines, Trans.). Karnac Books, Ltd. (Original work published 1936)

Hardy, K. V. (2007). Untangling intangible loss in the lives of traumatized children and adolescents. In L. A. Vargas & S. L. Bloom (Eds.), *Loss, hurt and hope: The complex issues of bereavement and trauma in children* (pp. 50–63). Cambridge Scholars Publishing.

Hardy, K. V. (2008). On becoming a GEMM therapist: Work harder, be smarter, and *never* discuss race. In M. McGoldrick & K. V. Hardy (Eds.), *Re-visioning family therapy: Race, culture, and gender in clinical practice* (2nd ed., pp. 461–468). The Guilford Press.

Hardy, K. V. (2013). Healing the hidden wounds of racial trauma. *Reclaiming Children and Youth, 22*(1), 24–28.

Hardy, K. V. (2016). Anti-racist approaches for shaping theoretical and practice paradigms. In A. J. Carten, A. B. Siskind, & M. Pender Greene (Eds.), *Strategies for deconstructing racism in the health and human services* (pp. 125–139). Oxford University Press.

Hardy, K. V. (2017). The validate, challenge, and request approach: A practical tool for facilitating difficult dialogues. In K. V. Hardy & T. Bobes (Eds.), *Promoting cultural sensitivity in supervision: A manual for practitioners* (pp. 47–54). Routledge.

Hardy, K. V. (2018). The self of the therapist in epistemological context: A multicultural relational perspective. *Journal of Family Psychotherapy, 29*(1), 17–29. https://doi.org/10.1080/08975353.2018.1416211

Hardy, K. V. (2019). The sociocultural trauma of poverty: Theoretical and clinical considerations for working with poor families. In M. McGoldrick & K. V. Hardy (Eds.), *Re-visioning family therapy: Addressing diversity in clinical practice* (3rd ed., pp. 57–72). The Guilford Press.

Hardy, K. V. (Ed.). (2022). *The enduring, invisible, and ubiquitous centrality of whiteness*. W.W. Norton & Company.

Hardy, K. V. & Laszloffy, T. A. (1995). *Therapy with African Americans and the phenomenon of rage*. In Session: Psychotherapy in Practice (Vol. 1, No. 4, pp. 57–70). John Wiley & Sons.

Hardy, K. V., & Laszloffy, T. A. (2017). The cultural genogram: Key to training culturally competent family therapists. In K. V. Hardy & T. Bobes (Eds.), *Promoting cultural sensitivity in supervision: A manual for practitioners* (pp. 61–74). Routledge.

hooks, b. (2001). *Salvation: Black people and love*. Harper Perennial.

Justich, K. (2021, February 24). *UCLA gymnast Nia Dennis opens up about being a young Black athlete: "I was always told that I didn't have the look."* Yahoo Life. https://www.yahoo.com/video/ucla-gymnast-nia-dennis-young-black-athlete-213606633.html

Lampen, C. (2021, September 1). *What we know about the killing of Elijah McClain.* The Cut. https://www.thecut.com/2021/09/the-killing-of-elijah-mcclain-everything-we-know.html

Lewis, D. (2016, May 27). Five times the United States officially apologized. *Smithsonian Magazine.* https://www.smithsonianmag.com/smart-news/five-times-united-states-officially-apologized-180959254/

Lukpat, A., & Medina, E. (2021, August 8). Black real estate agent and clients handcuffed at house viewing. *The Seattle Times.* https://www.seattletimes.com/nation-world/black-real-estate-agent-and-clients-handcuffed-at-michigan-house-viewing/

Macionis, J. J. (2016). *Society: The basics* (14th ed.). Pearson.

McGoldrick, M. (2019). Homelessness and the spiritual meaning of home. In M. McGoldrick & K. V. Hardy (Eds.), *Re-visioning family therapy: Addressing diversity in clinical practice* (3rd ed., pp. 93–107). The Guilford Press.

McGoldrick, M., & Gerson, R. (1985). *Genograms in family assessment.* W.W. Norton & Company.

Menakem, R. (2017). *My grandmother's hands: Racialized trauma and the pathway to mending our hearts and bodies.* Central Recovery Press.

Norris, L. (2020, November 10). *A look back on Fuzzy Zoeller's incredibly racist comments about Tiger Woods at the 1997 Masters.* Sportscasting. https://www.sportscasting.com/a-look-back-on-fuzzy-zoellers-incredibly-racist-comments-about-tiger-woods-at-the-1997-masters/

Obama, M. (2018). *Becoming.* Crown.

Raheim, S. (2019). The power of song to promote healing, hope, and justice: Lessons from the African American experience. In M. McGoldrick & K. V. Hardy (Eds.), *Re-visioning family therapy: Addressing diversity in clinical practice* (3rd ed., pp. 449–463). The Guilford Press.

Rampersad, A. & Roessel, D. (Eds.). (1994). *The collected poems of Langston Hughes.* Alfred A. Knopf, Inc.

Richeson, J. A. (2020, September). Americans are determined to believe in Black progress. *The Atlantic.* https://www.theatlantic.com/magazine/archive/2020/09/the-mythology-of-racial-progress/614173/

Rubin, L. B. (1976). *Worlds of pain: Life in the working-class family.* Basic Books.

Russell, S. (2018, September 13). Names have power: The United States of Indigenous names. *Indian Country Today.* https://indiancountrytoday.com/archive/names-have-power-the-united-states-of-indigenous-names

Satir, V. (1988). *The new peoplemaking* (2nd ed.). Science & Behavior Books, Inc.

Steimer, T. (2002). The biology of fear- and anxiety-related behaviors. *Dialogues in Neuroscience, 4*(3), 231–249. https://doi.org/10.31887/DCNS.2002.4.3/tsteimer

Stoute, B. J. (2021). Black rage: The psychic adaptation to the trauma of oppression. *Journal of the American Psychoanalytic Association, 69*(2), 259–290. https://doi.org/10.1177/00030651211014207

Tangney, J. P., & Dearing, R. L. (2002). *Shame and guilt.* The Guilford Press.

US Department of Health and Human Services. (2021). *Profile: Black/African Americans.* https://minorityhealth.hhs.gov/omh/browse.aspx?lvl=3&lvlid=61

van der Kolk, B. A. (2014). *The body keeps the score: Brain, mind, and body in the healing of trauma.* Penguin Books.

VandenBos, G. R. (Editor in Chief). (2007) *APA dictionary of psychology.* Washington, DC: American Psychological.

Watts-Jones, T. D. (2010). Location of self: Opening the door to dialogue on intersectionality in the therapy process. *Family Process, 49*(3), 405–420. https://doi.org/10.1111/j.1545-5300.2010.01330.x

Zimmerman, M. J., & Bradley, B. (2019). Intrinsic vs. extrinsic value. In E. N. Zalta (ed.), *Stanford Encyclopedia of Philosophy* (Spring Edition). The Metaphysics Research Lab, Department of Philosophy, Stanford University.

INDEX

ABOUT THE AUTHOR

Dr. Kenneth V. Hardy is a clinical and organizational consultant at the Eikenberg Institute for Relationships in New York, NY, where he also serves as director and conducts a yearlong Race and Racial Equity Mentorship Residency for clinicians and other allied professionals interested in enhancing their racial competency skills. Additionally, he provides *Racially Focused Trauma Informed* training, executive coaching, and consultation to a diverse network of individuals and organizations throughout the United States and abroad. He is a former professor of family therapy at both Drexel University in Philadelphia, and Syracuse University in New York, and has served as the director of children, families, and trauma at the Ackerman Institute for the Family in New York City. He is the author of *The Enduring, Invisible, and Ubiquitous Centrality of Whiteness, Culturally Sensitive Supervision: Diverse Perspectives and Practical Applications, Promoting Culturally Sensitive Supervision: A Manual for Practitioners, Revisioning Family Therapy: Race, Class, and Gender,* and *Teens Who Hurt: Clinical Strategies for Breaking the Cycle of Youth Violence.* Dr. Hardy is a frequent conference speaker and has also appeared on ABC's 20/20, Dateline NBC, PBS, and the Oprah Winfrey Show. He maintains a practice in New York City.